The Russian Economy

The Russian Economy: From Lenin to Putin

Steven Rosefielde

Blackwell
Publishing

BLACKWELL PUBLISHING
350 Main Street, Malden, MA 02148-5020, USA
9600 Garsington Road, Oxford OX4 2DQ, UK
550 Swanston Street, Carlton, Victoria 3053, Australia

First published 2007 by Blackwell Publishing Ltd

1 2007

Library of Congress Cataloging-in-Publication Data

Rosefielde, Steven.
The Russian economy : from Lenin to Putin / Steven Rosefielde.
p. cm.
Includes bibliographical references and index.
ISBN-13: 978-1-4051-1337-3 (hardcover : alk. paper)
ISBN-10: 1-4051-1337-5 (hardcover : alk. paper) 1. Russia (Federation)—Economic condition—1991– 2. Soviet Union—Economic conditions—History. I. Title.
HC340.12.R663 2007
330.947—dc22

2006030594

A catalogue record for this title is available from the British Library.

Set in 10/12pt Times
by Graphicraft Limited, Hong Kong
Printed and bound in Great Britain
by TJ International Ltd, Padstow, Cornwall

The publisher's policy is to use permanent paper from mills that operate a sustainable forestry policy, and which has been manufactured from pulp processed using acid-free and elementary chlorine-free practices. Furthermore, the publisher ensures that the text paper and cover board used have met acceptable environmental accreditation standards.

For further information on
Blackwell Publishing, visit our website:
www.blackwellpublishing.com

Contents

Figures

Tables

Preface

Now that the cold war is a faded memory, and capitalism appears to have triumphed over communism, why should academics devote time to Russian economics? Shouldn't Russian economics be swept into the dustbin of history? Wasn't the great Soviet experiment just an intoxicated moment, an evolutionary dead end that proved there is no alternative to democratic free enterprise?

Some may protest that communism isn't dead; that the Soviet Union's demise only demonstrates the inadequacy of the Bolshevik path, not the inferiority of other socialisms. The objection could be valid but still leaves Russian economics dangling. If the Russian economic system before and after Communist rule were indistinguishable from democratic free enterprise, then there is little to be learned for students of contemporary international economic affairs by devoting courses to Russia. David Engerman, however, recently reminded us that economists knew Russia was "exceptional" before Lenin, and now are beginning to appreciate that nothing fundamental has changed as cold war ideology fades into oblivion.[1] We are in the process of recovering our objectivity. The Russian economic system is worthy of academic study today because it served its rulers' needs for five hundred years without ever embracing democracy and free enterprise. Czars, commissars, and now presidents have found ways to develop, modernize, grow, and improve living standards with managed markets, plans, and mixed arrangements. They have sometimes succeeded in narrowing the gap between the East and the West, but even when the gap was widening, the system survived and stands as a challenge to the claims of globalism.

This text follows Engerman's injunction to recover the past in order to better appraise Russia's and the world's future. It identifies the cultural patterns that made Kremlin markets and plans unique, something more than the generic concept of what Gregory Grossman calls the "command economy," and explains their costs and benefits.[2] The command economy on closer examination was just one chapter in a haphazard experiment to construct an economy which criminalized private property, business, and entrepreneurship in part or whole. This will be demonstrated by giving equal attention to other Soviet epochs spanning War Communism, the New Economic Policy (NEP), Reform Communism, and Gorbachev's Market Communism 1987–91. Along the way the text makes plain the causes of Soviet communist failure and sheds light on reform possibilities within the Bolshevik paradigm. It casts doubts on the presumptions of contemporary globalism, and reveals Russia's post-Communist course behind the facade of statistical distortion and deceptive rhetoric. Students will be schooled in the fundamentals without cold war and socialist baggage, allowing them to understand how the Russian economy works, while gaining insight into how easily socialist ideals and concepts can be co-opted. And they will also acquire a deeper appreciation of what Bolshevism was, as distinct from what it claimed to be.

The benchmarks used to appraise Russian performance throughout are Bergsonian social welfare and Pareto efficiency. They provide a bridge between cultural particulars and neoclassical economic theory, enabling students to discern why the inner workings of rival systems matter, without being lost in a haze of macro-performance indicators and normative relativism.

Acknowledgments

My greatest intellectual debt is to Abram Bergson who pioneered modern neoclassical welfare economic theory, consistently using it as a tool for adjusting Soviet national income statistics and interpreting performance in an epoch when partisanship often clouded judgment.

Understanding Soviet and Russian behavior turned out to be far more complex than Bergson and most Sovietologists imagined. A myriad of scholars and other professionals guided me through the labyrinth. Some of the most helpful were Alexander Gerschenkron, Alec Nove, William T. Lee, Ralph William Pfouts, Emil Ershov, Yuri Yaremenko, George Kleiner, Valery Makarov, Vitaly Shlykov, Jan Rylander, William Van Cleave, Stefan Hedlund, and Quinn Mills. To them, all the innumerable others, my tireless secretary Nancy Kocher, Ling Wang my graduate assistant, and my family, I offer sincere gratitude.

Acronyms

ASUP	Automatic System of Management and Planning
CIA	American Central Intelligence Agency
CIS	Commonwealth of Independent States (former Soviet Republics)
CPSU	Communist Party of the Soviet Union (KPSS)
CEM	Council of Economic Ministers
EU	European Union
GARF	State Archive of the Russian Federation
GDP	gross domestic product
Genshtab	Soviet Armed Forces General Staff
GEU	Chief Economic Administration
glavk	Main Sub-ministerial Department
Gosarbitrazh	State Arbitration Agency
Gosbank	State Bank
Goskomstat	State Statistics Committee
Goskomtsen	State Price Committee
Gosplan	State Planning Agency
Gossnabsbyt'	State Committee for Material-Technical Supply (wholesale procurement and distribution agency)
Gosstandart	State Standards Committee
Gosstroi	State Construction Agency
GosTekhnika	State Committee for New Technology
GPPF	Grand Production Possibilities Frontier
GRU	Main Intelligence Administration of the General Staff of the Russian Armed Forces
Gulag	State Concentration Camp System
GUPF	Grand Utilities Possibilities Frontier
ILO	International Labor Organization

IMF	International Monetary Fund
KGB	State Security Committee (secret police)
khrozraschyot	economic cost accounting (self-financing state enterprises)
kolkhoz	collective farm
LM-IS	Liquidity Money-Investment Savings
MEI	Marginal Efficiency of Investment
METI	Ministry of Economics Trade and Industry (Japan)
MFT	Ministry of Foreign Trade
MTS	Machine Tractor Station
NEP	New Economic Policy
nepmen	private businessmen without property ownership right
NKVD	People's Commissariat of Internal Affairs (Secret Police)
NMP	net material product
OECD	Organization for Economic Cooperation and Development
OPK	Defense Industrial Complex (alternative name for VPK)
PAB	The Pareto–Arrow–Bergson economic welfare standard which combines consumer sovereignty in the private sector, popular sovereignty in the public sector, with efficient, socially approved, income transfers
piatiletki	five-year plan
PFF	Production Feasibility Frontier
Politburo	Political Bureau (Highest State Political Body)
PPF	Production Possibilities Frontier
prodrazvertska	product requisitioning (without compensation)
Promplan	Industrial planning agency
RDT&E	Research Development Testing and Evaluation
Sovkhoz	state farm
STO	Labor and Defense Council
Tekhpromfinplan	enterprise technical, industrial, financial plan
TsSU	Central Statistical Administration (predecessor of Goskomstat)
Tsugprom	Central Industrial Directorate of VSNKh
UPF	Utilities Possibilities Frontier
USSR	Union of Soviet Socialist Republics
VPK	Military Industrial Complex
VSNKh	Supreme Economic Council
WTO	World Trade Organization

Part I

Foundations

Soviet communism was a beacon of hope during the twentieth century for billions of people who saw it as a path to utopia, but it was a god that failed. There were two reasons. First, the system, even in its purest form, proved to be intrinsically inferior. Second, elements of traditional Russian political culture, which we shall call Muscovy, further impaired the system's operation. Communism could have done better in a different cultural setting, but even under the best circumstances was unlikely to provide the social welfare benefits promised.

Part I illuminates these points by acquainting readers with key aspects of Russia's Muscovite culture and by elaborating a benchmark called the Pareto–Arrow–Bergson standard that illuminates how Muscovy and Soviet planning departed from the social welfare ideal.

1

Muscovy and the West

Summary

The Russian economic system is worth studying because it differs drastically from Western democratic free enterprise and utopian ideals like optimal socialist planning. The roots of today's post-Communist economy can be traced to the fifteenth century when Muscovy asserted its hegemony over Russia's rival principalities, allowing the Kremlin to impose a patrimonial, rent granting, autocratic, serf-slave system, where even the aristocracy was denied inalienable property and civil rights. Subjugation has since been the cardinal feature of Russia's Muscovite economic system, including the Communist interlude. It has permitted Kremlin rulers to live in open or discretely concealed imperial splendor amid a sea of destitution.

Russia's autocrats, in response to Western economic and military competition, sought to square the circle by espousing Western ideals and adopting market principles. During the nineteenth century forced labor was gradually abandoned in agriculture and industry and rudimentary representative institutions introduced. The results, however, were disappointing because Muscovite privileges undermined the effectiveness of private enterprise and token self-governance. Martial values, bureaucracy, secret police meddling, and stultifying corruption further impaired competitiveness.

Experience showed that Russia could not achieve western standards of efficiency without ridding itself of the rule of men. The Kremlin still refuses to believe it. Russia's leaders remain hopeful that they can find a way to reap the benefits of individual empowerment while curtailing economic liberty. The dissolution of the USSR has changed many things, but not this delusion.

Until the Kremlin repudiates Muscovy, the past will be a better guide to Russia's future than the promise of westernization.

In Russia, the most radical changes, despite appearances, actually reinforce the traditions of the society they are meant to change.

Geoffrey Hosking 2001

Russia Peculiar, Not Universal

Russia has long been an enigma. For more than two hundred years scholars acknowledged that Russia was out of step with the West because, as Alexander Gerschenkron put it, Muscovy missed humanism, the reformation, the renaissance, and enlightenment but most remained hopeful. Before 1917 they were convinced that Russia was destined to embrace democratic free enterprise, even though it was a semi-feudal patrimonialist, rent-granting autocracy with a fledgling state-managed industrial market. When Lenin criminalized business, entrepreneurship, and private property, westernizers admitted their miscalculation, only to predict communism couldn't last. Wrong again. Stalin rapidly industrialized the Soviet Union and the Kremlin became a superpower during the cold war. Scholars had to accept that central planning worked, but foresaw a period of liberalizing reform that would bring about convergence between the East and the West. The reforms materialized, but the systems continued to diverge. And when the Soviet Union imploded, economic liberals once again heralded the inevitability of "transition." Perhaps someday they will be right. Whatever the outcome, a millennium of experience suggests that if westernization is ever achieved it won't be quick, or easy.

The problem doesn't lie with democratic free enterprise or optimal planning. The performance potential of both is better than anything Russia has ever mustered. It inheres in the Muscovite culture dominating the operation of markets, plans, and mixed economic mechanisms. Much of the debate about the merit of markets and plans which raged during the cold war was misguided. The models devised were too abstruse and ignored Muscovy's peculiarities, causing Sovietologists to overestimate postwar Soviet economic performance and post-Soviet transitologists to misappraise contemporary prospects.

There is little to be gained by revisiting the post-Czarist experience with failed frameworks. Russia needs to be understood in terms of the Muscovite motives that govern it, evaluated with neoclassical norms highlighting the divergence between the real and the ideal. Sovietological frameworks weren't flawed by logical lapses in western micro and macroeconomic theories. The problem lay in supposing that Russian economic behavior was somehow governed by western principles of social rationality (see chapter 2).

Muscovy

Russia's autocrats from Ivan the Great, Grand Prince of Muscovy onward relied on "servitors" to manage economic affairs on imperial properties and their own estates. Czars were implicit owners of all they surveyed. They granted servitors use of their properties, and in later years revokable ownership rights in return for tax collection and service. They acted as rent-grantors and recipients as rent-seekers without the protection of the western rule of law. Servitors oversaw and staffed a vast bureaucracy which administered the economy, extracting taxes and income from a servile peasantry. They seldom considered the possibility that free labor might be more productive than coercion, or pondered the benefits of private ownerships and competitive scientific management. The system was divided between a small minority of "haves" and an oppressed majority of "have nots." It could have been organized along totalitarian lines, but wasn't. Czars didn't bother to micro-manage and servitors didn't profit maximize. They didn't compete or pay competitive wages. Each layer in the productive hierarchy merely coerced, extracted rent, and exploited those beneath them with only inadvertent regard for economic efficiency.

A federal scheme might have been tried with independent princes empowered by inalienable property and civil rights, administering their domains, and voluntarily revenue sharing with the center. But Russia's rulers preferred a different arrangement based on the principle of patrimonialism. Under this system everything in the Czar's domain belonged to him, but could be granted to loyal servitors on a probationary basis. Entitlements and civil rights were treated symmetrically. Servitors consequently were weaker than their western counterparts because they lacked an independent power base buttressed by inalienable property, entitlements, and the rule of law. Rebellious factions and coalitions emerged from time to time, and some succeeded, but dynastic continuity was usually preserved by playing off weak rivals against each other. The game was profitable for autocrats. Czars maintained large national armies, guarded their regimes with secret police, and indulged in "la dolce vita," oblivious to the country's economic potential and welfare. They didn't profit-maximize, straitjacketed market forces, and suppressed consumer sovereignty. Their rent-granting authoritarianism was inefficient, oppressive, cruel and unjust, but it allowed the nobility to flourish, while the peasantry withered.[1]

The West

Muscovite autocracy is diametrically opposed to what Samuel Huntington has called the "idea of the west," predicated on individualism, private property, the rights of man, and rule of law.[2] The modern version of the "idea" which has evolved over thousands of years places the actualization of everyman's human potential at the top of society's agenda. The good economy is bottom up, not top down. It is founded on a Lockean social contract obligating citizens to acknowledge each other's basic rights, and committing everyone to abide by the rule of negotiated contracting, administered by an impartial judiciary. Adam Smith was the first to show that if people rationally utility maximize in a fair play economy the wealth of nations will be optimal, even though each person narrowly pursues his or her own interest. Self-seeking and social welfare are reconciled through free competition under the rule of law. Supply in this conception is responsive to demand, making the system consumer sovereign. Individual preferences rule, rather than those of special interests. Democracy extends the principle to the public sector. Kenneth Arrow has shown that although democracy is less efficient than private profit-seeking in making supply responsive to household demand, it is the best mechanism for providing public goods. The ideal society from the west's perspective therefore is democratic free enterprise (including west European social democracy as a special case) which provides equal opportunity and energizes people to maximize national welfare (see chapter 2).

Mutual exclusivity

Muscovy and the West are mutually exclusive. Muscovite economic systems, whether feudal Czarist, planned Communist, or market post-Communist cannot be western. The concept of westernized Muscovy is an oxymoron because autocracy and economic predation cannot coexist with Arrow representative democracy (see glossary [democracy]) and consumer sovereignty. Denying people equal opportunity to actualize their human potential precludes democratic free enterprise.

Transition

Mutual exclusivity neither prevents Muscovy from borrowing some features of westernization, nor excludes transition. Kremlin rulers can tolerate limited individual autonomy and could have a change of heart. But until they surrender most of their political and economic power, autocracy will always trump liberalization.

Socialism

Socialism is a branch of the idea of the West. It is an affirmation of Paretian self-actualization with an enhanced Lockean social contract stressing the importance of humanism, communitarianism, altruism, egalitarianism, and social justice. Some schools like European social democracy try to achieve these goals by placing minimal restrictions on democratic free enterprise. Advocates of Langean market socialism do the same, but require the criminalization of private business, entrepreneurship, and property as well as state administrated auctions assuring competitive pricing. Still others see benevolent planning as the best strategy for attaining Paretian socialist ends with greed-proof means. The will of the enlightened people is indispensable to all precluding demagoguery. Espousing socialist principles however doesn't assure their implementation. Lenin and his successors were masters of co-option. They persuaded many that the means (planning) guaranteed the ends (socialism), claiming that this made the Soviet Union good and the West bad without any proof of benevolence. In doing so, the Kremlin succeeded in reversing polarities. Instead of the idea of the West being self-evidently superior to Muscovy, "communism" was portrayed as transparently better than "capitalism." Seeing through this sleight of hand is essential for understanding Russia's past and future. Muscovy and the West are mutually exclusive because autocratic and democratic sovereignty share no common ground. This was true before 1917 and nothing fundamental has happened since to change matters.

Epochs

However, post-Czarist Muscovy wasn't static. It tried to modernize and create a superior third way in a series of haphazard experiments. There were six main epochs, all carefully scrutinized in this volume: War Communism, NEP (New Economic Policy), Command Communism, Reform Communism, Market Communism, and post-Communism (see glossary). War Communism, sometimes described as a period of elemental chaos, was Lenin's first attempt to construct a marketless economy based on requisitioning and rationing. When this failed, a mixed strategy (NEP) was adopted featuring market leasing and state industrial administration, followed soon thereafter by Stalin's recriminalization of markets and reinstatement of requisitioning and rationing, this time enhanced by five-year planning (Command Communism). Despite public proclamations of unprecedented success, the Kremlin knew better. After Stalin died his successors embarked on a treadmill of fruitless incentive, planning, and administrative reforms to enhance the system's efficiency (Reform Communism), leading to Gorbachev's reintroduction of Market Communism and the Soviet Union's sudden death. Boris Yeltsin and Vladimir Putin renounced Communism and expanded Gorbachev's markets after the fall (post-Communism), but didn't steer Russia to democratic free enterprise. Instead of transitioning, they used the post-Communist moment as an opportunity to muddle back to pre-Bolshevik market Muscovy.

Russia's Choice

During the cold war many scholars denied that the gulf dividing Russia from the West was unbridgeable even though the Soviets criminalized business, entrepreneurship and private property. They demonstrated the formal mathematical equivalency of perfect planning and perfect competition and showed how planners could simulate best Western management practice. The approach shed valuable light on the comparative possibilities of planned and market systems, private and public ownership, and competing social priorities, but downplayed the predatory attributes of Muscovite autocracy. In doing so some specialists missed the big picture. Russia's leaders weren't philosopher kings and had no intention of constructing a humane and equitable economic system. Good outcomes were never in the cards, whatever the theoretical potential, and this as much as anything explains the Soviet Union's eventual demise. Post-communist prospects aren't materially better. Putin continues to believe that he can have it all, Muscovite autocracy and Western efficiency. But he is wrong. Russia can westernize or remain autocratic, but it cannot do both.

Review

Soviet leaders believed that Communism was universal and ineluctable. It necessarily would develop out of the West's Enlightenment and become its capstone. There was no room in Marxist ideology for Muscovite communism. There was only one true communism, based on Enlightenment principles, epitomized today by the Pareto–Arrow–Bergson standard. The story of Russian economics from Lenin to Putin is the Bolshevik search for true communism, the scientific assessment of its merits, and the discovery that Soviet communism wasn't the "end of history." This outcome was accidental. Russia was, and remains, different from the West because of its Muscovite culture.

Questions

1. What are the core economic principles of the "idea of the West?"
2. What are the core economic principles of the Russian Muscovite model?
3. Why are free individual utility seeking (including private property, entrepreneurship, and business), equal opportunity, competition, the Lockean social contract, and the rule of law important for social welfare?
4. How does alienable property and civil rights enhance autocratic power, and degrade individual utility seeking?
5. Can Pareto optimality be achieved if the few dominate the many? Explain.
6. What is satisficing? Can an economic system which satisfices be Pareto micro-efficient? Explain.
7. Growth depends on scientific and technological progress, and entrepreneurship. Is the "idea of the West" compatible with optimal growth? Can the Muscovite model be as growth efficient as democratic free enterprise? Explain.
8. If the Muscovite model is micro- and macroeconomically sub-optimal, why have Russia's leaders clung to it? Explain.
9. Are there any grounds for believing that Muscovite rulers could subjugate people without discouraging their initiative, and impairing competitive efficiency? Why do many imagine that Russia can have the benefits of democratic free enterprise while remaining autocratic? Explain.
10. If the Muscovite model and democratic free enterprise are mutually exclusive, does this preclude transition? Explain.

2

Economic Fundamentals

Summary

The analysis and interpretation of Soviet and post-Soviet economic performance is clouded by partisan claims. Abram Bergson, Paul Samuelson, and Kenneth Arrow devised a welfare theoretic model based on the earlier work of Vilfredo Pareto capable of dispelling this micro- and macroeconomic fog, called the Pareto–Arrow–Bergson (PAB) method, or the Pareto standard for short. It is compatible with Huntington's idea of the West and will be applied as the guiding light throughout the text. The essentials are as follows:

- Economics is the science of rational utility seeking. Under ideal conditions it can be shown that individuals and societies are able to maximize their welfare. An individual living in isolation can do so by devising sets of demand and supply programs; choosing the best joint solution (equilibrium), taking account of pleasure (consumption), pain (work), and the opportunity costs of leisure. In an economy with two or more participants, potential expands disproportionally due to widened consumption possibilities, specialization, and efficiencies of scale.
- Welfare maximization in the multi-participant case isn't unique. Optima can be defined in two senses. The most familiar is Pareto optimality, where each and every individual maximizes his or her utility through voluntary, negotiated exchange, with public goods democratically determined. Work, production, and distribution are "consumer sovereign." "Ruler's sovereignty" is the other possibility. Instead of individuals being the ultimate arbiter of welfare, authorities impose their preferences on others' demand and supply programs, acting paternalistically or for their own advantage. And regardless of whether

outcomes are consumer or ruler sovereign, everyone is free to appraise merit from his or her perspective.

- Both social welfare optima can be achieved with perfect markets, perfect planning or some perfect mixture. Market participants and planners craft demand and supply programs, identify the ideals, and realize them differently. Individuals devise programs, negotiate transactions, and achieve equilibrium through automatic Walrasian price (inventory adjustment) and Marshallian supply (profit maximizing) processes. Planners compile demand and supply programs for others, equilibrating them with commands, oversight, controls, and incentives. They can replicate the Pareto outcome or optimize ruler's preferences.
- The law of demand, the law of supply, and the law of demand and supply equilibration in the Paretian case all depend solely on price, and income, given the rule of contract law. They may apply in Pareto efficient planned economies, but are altered in real economies by state controls, incentives, coercion and command.
- Private ownership is a tool for individual utility maximizing. It is essential for Paretian, but not ruler sovereign outcomes.
- Market and planned economies may yield identical results, in which case they adhere to the same universal micro- and macroeconomic laws. But this won't typically be the case, even under ideal conditions.
- Neither market, nor planned economies are perfect. Both microeconomically and macroeconomically malfunction in their own unique ways. Comparative performance depends on their respective efficiency. Systems can be judged on efficiency, or subjective merit. There is no indisputable best. Nonetheless, the complexities of "ruler's sovereignty" and the Soviet experience suggest that non-Paretian systems are inferior, and the PAB standard pinpoints all its shortcomings.

I cannot forecast to you the action of Russia. It is a riddle wrapped in a mystery inside an enigma.

Winston Churchill, BBC broadcast, October 1939

Pareto–Arrow–Bergson (PAB) standard

Studying Muscovite economy can be disconcerting. Students are confronted with contradictory claims about performance and significance. Nikolai Bukharin and Evgeny Preobrazhensky, amid the catastrophe of War Communism, somehow managed to conclude that the Bolsheviks had reached the first stage of communism, and Soviet leaders thereafter from NEP to perestroika never ceased extolling the superiority of Soviet socialism. By contrast Lord Lionel Robbins, Ludwig von Mises, and Friedrich von Hayek all argued forcefully that Bolshevik central planning was humbug. Positivists assume that the dispute can be settled by the competitive test. But the statistics have always been suspect (Lenin insisted that statistics were a weapon of class war), and even if Muscovy underperformed on some metrics it could always be claimed that it was still superior because it was fairer, and more just. Yes, democratic free enterprise served consumers better, but the Soviet Union delivered full employment, price stability, steady growth, egalitarianism, a social safety net, and socialist humanism.

How can this fog be dispelled?

Some rules are self-evident. Apples must be compared with apples, and oranges with oranges. Statistics must be standardized, and their reliability assessed. Likewise, ideals must be compared with ideals (perfect competition with perfect planning), and realities with realities (imperfect Western with imperfect Eastern performance). The Muscovite experience in all its manifestations, micro, macro, and composite, can also be appraised with ideals, as long as the norm is explicit.

Arguably, the neoclassical Pareto–Arrow–Bergson (PAB) standard serves these purposes best.[1] It isn't unique, but is compatible with Samuel Huntington's idea of the West embodying the micro- and macroeconomic principles of democratic free enterprise and the welfare state. Each name represents a key element of the concept. Pareto stands for the principle of individual utility seeking (consumer sovereignty); Arrow for popular sovereignty over public goods, and Bergson for the welfare theory that provides a roadmap for analyzing all Pareto–Arrow states achievable with lump sum transfers. The essentials are elaborated below, but boil down to a theoretically integrated set of norms for assessing Muscovite performance from the standpoint of democratic free enterprise, or EU social democracy. They allow us to appraise how the Soviet Union and Russia deviate from the micro economic efficiency of the West, as well as evaluating comparative macro characteristics including unemployment, inflation, income distribution, social justice, and growth. And they make us the judge of Muscovy's merit insofar as we feel that ethical principles transcend democratic utility seeking.

Students desiring a more thorough grounding in the nuances of PAB should consult the author's comparative systems text.

Essentials

Economics is the science of rational utility seeking; a sub-branch both of production engineering and psychology which assumes that utility seekers can judge what is good for them, discern comparative worth, and select consistently (transitivity principle). Decisions are economic if they do, and non-economic if they don't.[2] This means that much of what is conventionally called economics in inefficient systems isn't. Factor allocation, production, finance, and distribution are merely processes, not economic activities, unless they are governed by rational choice.

Pareto micro-optimality

Utility optimizing doesn't place an undue burden on decision-makers. Individuals don't have to know exactly how much they prefer one good to another (cardinality). They only have to distinguish better from worse (ordinality), methodically searching their opportunity sets and maximizing, given incomes and price constraints. If their search is efficient and complete, the result is Pareto ideal (Vilfredo Pareto, 1848–1923) because no one can enhance his utility through voluntary exchange without another losing. An economy that permits every individual to completely utility maximize is Pareto optimal.

Inefficiency

No economy is Pareto optimal. People don't always display good judgment in their roles as workers, supervisors, managers, civil servants, leaders, and consumers. They may be lazy, ignorant, incompetent, and rash. They may collude in restraint of trade, and their economic liberty may be circumscribed by bad laws, rules, and mis-governance. These lapses may afflict any economy, but are apt to be especially severe in systems that criminalize private property, business and entrepreneurship, and substitute authoritarian public programs.

Satisficing

Also, individuals sometimes act as if they believe that the best is the enemy of the good. They are satisfied with what they get and have no interest in finding something better, even if transaction costs are zero. Contenting oneself in this way is called satisficing. It is prevalent in repressive societies that thwart personal advancement. Theory suggests that Pareto efficient, or systems close to it should outperform satisficing rivals like the Soviet Union.

Mechanisms

Paretian efficiency is achieved in market economies through the invisible hand, that is, the Marshallian quantity adjustment mechanism (profit-seeking), the Walrasian price adjustment mechanism (inventory clearing), and the Keynesian adjustment mechanism (macroeconomic regulation of multiplier effects). These micro-processes theoretically can be simulated in planned economies and the Soviets discovered that they could bypass Keynes, achieving full employment, price stability, and growth with a combination of incentives and controls, without ever coming close to attaining Pareto optimality.

The Marshallian adjustment mechanism is illustrated in the production space (figure 2.1), which contains a downward sloping demand curve (bid price determined by diminishing marginal utility), and an upward sloping supply curve (offer price determined by increasing marginal costs). If this market is initially in disequilibrium at point q_{E*}, the demand will exceed the supply price, which means that profit maximizing is incomplete because marginal revenue exceeds marginal cost. The Marshallian rule requires that the firm increase production continuously as long as the demand exceeds the supply price until the market clears at point E. Should the manager overshoot E, the supply will exceed the demand price, causing the firm to run a loss, which can only be eliminated by returning to point E, which is stable in both directions. But if tastes shift, causing the demand curve to drop (D′), a new disequilibrium will arise, which in turn will be automatically rectified by the Marshallian quantity adjustment mechanism at the new equilibrium E*.

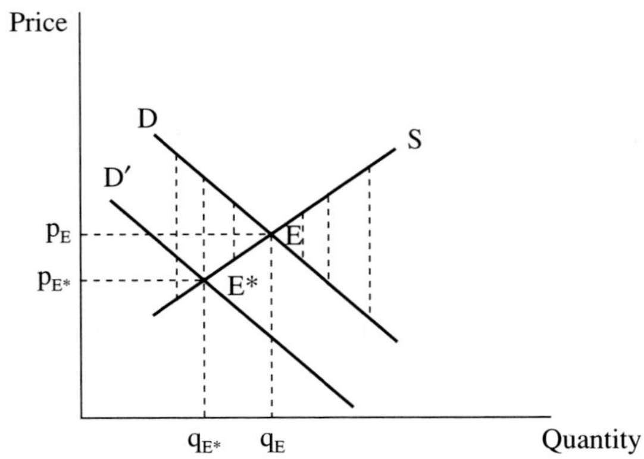

Figure 2.1 Marshallian production adjustment

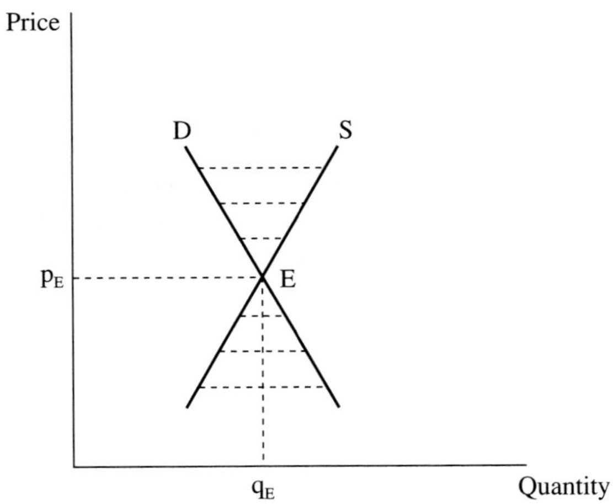

Figure 2.2 Walrasian price adjustment

The Walrasian price adjustment mechanism is depicted in the retail space (figure 2.2), which contains a downward-sloping demand curve (bid price determined by diminishing marginal utility) and an upward-sloping supply curve (offer price determined by the cost of holding inventories). If this market is initially in disequilibrium above the market clearing point E, the retail establishment will be in an excess supply disequilibrium, where the supply held, exceeds customers willingness to pay. Faced with a glut, the proprietor holds a "sale," that is, cuts price, and continues to do so until inventories held are exactly equal to those the public demands. Should the proprietor overshoot the market, cutting prices too drastically, demand will immediately exceed supply, propelling the price back to the stable equilibrium at E.

The joint action of these automatic quantity and price adjustment mechanisms is called the law of demand and supply equilibration, which together with the laws of demand and supply illustrated in the demand and supply curves must apply in any Pareto-efficient economy. They are the essence of Adam Smith's invisible hand, applying in competitive markets but not in economies that criminalize private ownership, business, and entrepreneurship.

Sovereignty

Consumers are said to be sovereign when their demands govern supply. This includes private and democratically determined public goods within the limits illuminated by Arrow. The concept is congruent with Pareto optimality. But since no system is Pareto efficient, none is completely consumer sovereign. There is a broad spectrum of alternative possibilities. The most common is planners' or systems directors' sovereignty where ruler's preferences reign. This may be good or bad depending on outcomes, but in any case raises the issue of whose norms should be supreme, those of authorities or the people?

Welfare

Pareto optimality is attractive because it dispenses with the need to make complicated judgments. Analysts merely assume that individuals know best. If their utility is maximized, then the outcome is ideal. However, suppose that everyone were a devil except you. The Pareto result from the majority's point of view would be best, but from your virtuous perspective it would be satanic. Clearly Pareto optimality isn't infallible. Abram Bergson was the first to show that this relativity can be quantified and evaluated with "social welfare functions" given prescribed norms. Judgments aren't unique and contain cardinal aspects, but do provide benchmarks for rational debate. Social welfare functions have a further advantage. They can adjust welfare scores based on value added for the harm caused by waste, terror, mass homicides, forced labor, militarism, and imperialism.

Paretian geometry

Pareto principles can serve as benchmarks for assessing the performance of the Soviet economy during various phases of its development with the aid of four familiar diagrams.

Factor supply and allocation are connected with production in the Edgeworth–Bowley box displayed in figure 2.3. The coordinate axes forming the sides of the box indicate voluntary equilibrium supplies of capital (k) and labor (l). The sides end where the derived utility in consumption of each factor is just equal to the foregone value of leisure. The box's interior contains all possible allocations of labor and capital in the production of the two goods (q_1) and (q_2) shown at the lower and upper intersection of coordinate axes (their origins). The space also contains two nested, convex, radial sets of isoquants, one for each of the goods. The further any isoquant lies from its respective origin, the higher the output level designated by the isoquant superscripts.

If an economy is in a state of total utility-maximizing equilibrium, there must be one corresponding point inside the Edgeworth–Bowley box. This point represents the utility optimizing supply assortment and the maximum volumes consistent with it. If they didn't, the utility maximizing process would be incomplete. The condition can be geometrically expressed as an isoquant double tangency (point E) because production at other points along either isoquant would mean that more of q_1 or q_2 could be generated without lowering the output of the other.

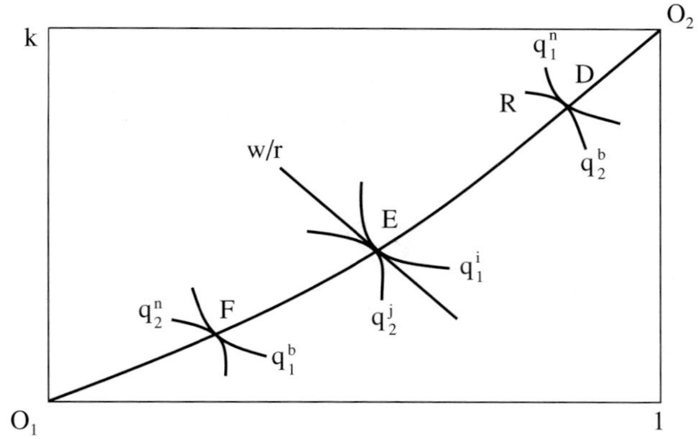

Figure 2.3 Pareto factor-production space

It is also possible to imagine a set of Pareto equilibria for alternative counterfactual configurations of factor and product demand. These entail minor adjustments of the sides of the Edgeworth–Bowley box (not shown), and correspond with other isoquant double tangencies. The set of all efficient factor supply, input allocation, and production points, actual or counterfactual is called the contract curve, and represents a menu of actual and potential Pareto optimal outputs (GDPs). The locus is useful because it allows us to visualize the characteristics of inferior economies. Any point other than E along the contract curve like D or F, generated for example by the Soviet Union, is inferior because the goods supplied don't maximize consumer utility. The outputs at D and F could be efficiently produced, if the actual pattern of demand were different, but it isn't. And of course, if the Soviet economy operated at point R, off the contract curve, it would be even more inferior because factor misallocation means that planners could have done better by sliding down the isoquant to point D. All counterfactual outcomes on the contract curve are classified as technically efficient because even though consumers disprefer them, they could be counterfactually ideal. All other points in the Edgeworth–Bowley box are technically and economically inefficient because they fail to maximize utility and minimize systemwide cost. E is the only true Pareto equilibrium.

These principles are depicted in an alternative way in the production space (figure 2.4). The coordinate axes represent outputs q_1 and q_2 instead of the factors k and l, which have been suppressed. The space inside the coordinate axes contains the equilibrium production point E, and all counterfactual Pareto equilibria like D and F forming the contract curve in figure 2.3. This locus remapped in the production space is called the production possibility frontier (PPF), and like its Edgeworth–Bowley box twin serves as a Paretian supply ideal for two products jointly. As before, point E and only point E is a true Paretian equilibrium. Other points on the PPF are technically, but not economically efficient, and all points off the frontier are inefficient, although it can be said that points along the ray from the origin through E other than E, are right assortments in the wrong volumes.

The merit of Soviet economic performance is easily evaluated with this conceptual apparatus. Insofar as planners failed to ascertain and act upon individual consumer

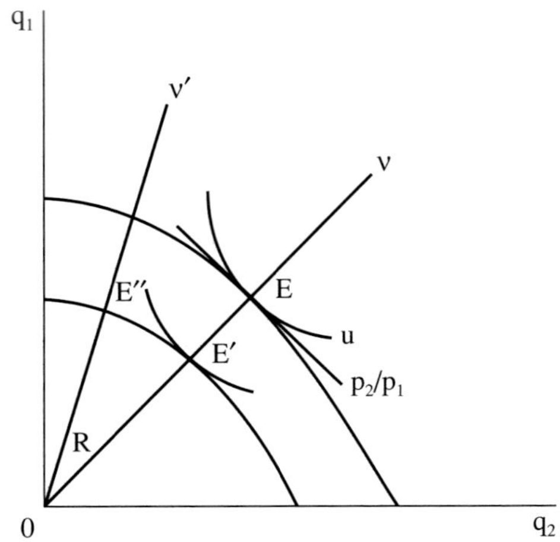

Figure 2.4 Pareto production possibilities

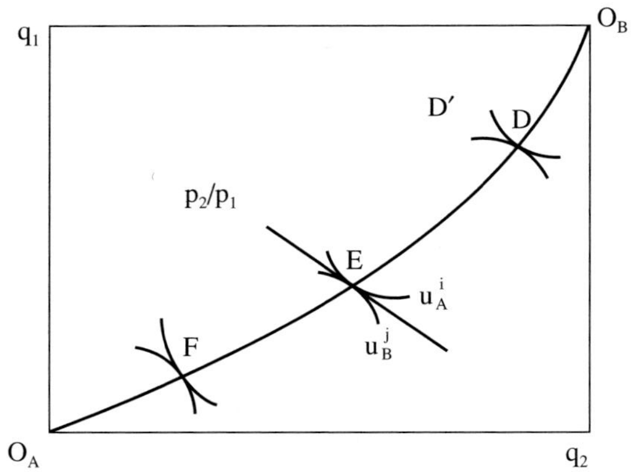

Figure 2.5 Pareto retail distribution

preferences, the USSR could not have operated at the Pareto ideal point E. Nor could it have been technically efficient with respect to counterfactual individual demand for the same reason and because planning deficiencies prevented factors from being allocated efficiently to alternative use. The Soviet Union necessarily operated below (E′ or E″), on a planning constrained production feasibility frontier (PFF), due to the intrinsic deficiencies of administrative command planning, but could have operated above it if workers were compelled to work enough extra hours.

Distributional merit can also be illustrated geometrically with reference to the Pareto standard. The Edgeworth–Bowley box employed for this purpose and displayed in figure 2.5 takes the equilibrium outputs q_1 and q_2 and arrays them sequentially along the coordinate axes. The end points represent the total amount of each good produced at E in figure 2.4 available for distribution between individuals A and B in a two participant economy. Points on the box's interior represent feasible distributions of the goods between the parties, who are guided by their convex, nested indifference curves (iso-utility) radiating from the lower and upper origins.

If an economy is in a state of total utility maximizing equilibrium, there must be one corresponding point inside the Edgeworth–Bowley distribution space. This point represents the utility-optimizing retail allocation of the Pareto ideal output supply because otherwise the utility maximizing process would be incomplete. The condition is expressed geometrically as an indifference curve double tangency (point E) because distribution at any other point along either iso-utility curve would mean that one participant could attain greater utility without reducing the other's utility, given the equilibrium income distribution.

Point E is the only Pareto efficient distribution in the Edgeworth Bowley box, but if tastes were different, including the voluntary supply of labor then purchasing power would be redistributed, generating a locus of counterfactual Pareto ideal distributions, represented by the contract curve in figure 2.5. Just as in the production case, contract curve points other than E can be viewed as technically efficient in the sense that the distribution would be ideal, if purchasing power were allocated in some alternative Pareto efficient way. Points off the contract curve however are always technically and economically inefficient because better outcomes are possible for one participant without reducing the utility of the other, given the prevailing income distribution.

The distributional inefficiency of the Soviet retail sector is easily visualized with the aid of figure 2.5. Consumption could not occur at E, or any other point on the contract curve because the underlying supply produced in figure 2.4 lies on a production feasibility frontier. And, if this objection is waved by redefining the distributional contract curve in terms of the actual Soviet production point, retail distribution could only be (restrictively) economically efficient if participant incomes were determined by respective labor value added. Since wages were arbitrarily set by the state price committee (Goskomtsen), it follows that the Soviet retail distribution was always economically inefficient. And, as will be shown, the situation was far worse because retail supplies were rationed making it impossible for distribution to occur on either the Pareto or restrictive contract curve.

The Pareto standard is also helpful in evaluating the utility possibilities of diverse economic systems. This is accomplished by mapping the Pareto ideal retail distribution point E in figure 2.5 into utilities in the utilities space shown in figure 2.6. The coordinate axes array ordinal iso-utilities in increasing order from the origin, and points within the space identify the iso-utility level attained by each participant consuming his or her respective share of the retail distribution. The Pareto optimal utilities are those at point E, and can be complemented with a set of counterfactual utility optima derived from other points on the retail distribution contact curve. This set called the utility possibilities frontier (UPF) can also be derived for some purposes by redistributing the Pareto ideal supplies between the participants.

Either way, it should be obvious that Soviet ordinal utility states are inferior to the Pareto ideal in every instance because the USSR underproduced (taking leisure into account as a good), produced dispreferred items with inferior characteristics, failed to optimally distributed supplies in the retail sector, and could not have efficiently redistributed them with the tools of administrative command planning.

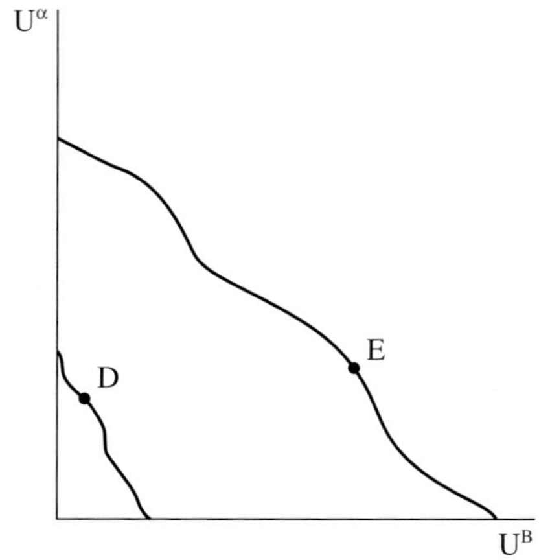

Figure 2.6 Pareto utility possibilities

Instead of generating Pareto ideal utility at E, the Soviet system only allowed its citizens to achieve the iso-utilities shown at D.

Macroeconomics

Pareto efficiency isn't limited to the present. Individuals routinely "trade with the future" (Irving Fisher).[3] They can borrow, invest, and repay out of their future streams of income, or accelerate consumption accepting lower living standards later. Profit maximizing enterprises face similar choices involving capital widening, research, development, technological progress, diffusion and ultimately the optimal rate of economic growth (what Robert Solow calls the "golden age growth rate").[4] Just as in the static case, it can be shown that if rational individual utility seeking is complete, every participant will not only maximize his/her utility in the present, but at every instant thereafter. Growth isn't an end in itself. Faster isn't better, if society's time profile of consumption is inferior, and/or the characteristics and assortments of goods in rapidly growing economies are undesirable. In appraising dynamic merit what counts is human welfare, not oblique indicators of progress, a critical insight fundamental to the PAB standard. Figure 2.4 can be used to illustrate the concept. Growth can be depicted as an outward shift of the production possibility frontier (not shown). If the location of the Soviet growth point is above or below the ideal, or on the wrong ray from the origin, then it is inferior in exactly the same sense as the static analysis.

The same principle applies to the assessment of employment, inflation, and income distribution. These phenomena should not be evaluated mechanically. They must be defined in terms of optimal individual choice, measured consistently, and only then employed to judge comparative merit. The Soviet economy could overemploy or underemploy factors of production, visualized as altering the dimension of the Edgeworth–Bowley box in figure 2.3. Income distribution can be appraised by reference to point E in figure 2.5.

And it should also be born in mind that the attainment of Keynesian goals, full employment, price stability, equitable income distribution, and optimal growth East and West may come at a substantial price.[5] As LM–IS analysis demonstrates, unemployment may be eradicated with monetary, fiscal or some policy combination. Each Keynesian adjustment alternative affects the configuration of nano supply and demand generating different Pareto optima. The same principle holds for non-Keynesian Soviet disequilibrium adjustments. PAB theory requires us to sweat the details, to ascertain whether nominal indicators of success are really camouflaging profound social welfare failure. For example, many workers during the Yeltsin era were kept on the employment rolls even though plants were idle. The official unemployment rate was only 2 percent, much better than in America, while the real figure was approximately 25 percent. Once this is appreciated, it becomes obvious why Muscovite macroeconomic self-congratulation and Western applause was often misplaced. As previously observed, despite the Soviet Union's comprehensive shortcomings from the Paretian vantage point, partisan judges could still award the laurel to Muscovy on exotic ethical grounds, but it is also true that whatever the East did, there existed a superior Pareto alternative.

Production potential

Sovietologists, especially American disciples of Bergson, including the Central Intelligence Agency broadly adhere to the PAB standard in appraising the experience of the former USSR. Many following Bergson moreover have gone even further contending that Soviet statistics can be adjusted sufficiently to permit comparisons that are compatible with some Pareto principles. Specifically, Bergson has claimed that Soviet production satisfied the "production potential standard," which if true would mean that there was no need to mentally discount comparative size (US/USSR GDP) and comparative GDP growth statistics because ruble prices didn't measure marginal rates of product transformation (technical efficiency, given planners' preferences). The USSR's GDP, he argued, was meaningful in the restricted sense that assortments were responsive to fiat opportunity costs, and could be adjusted to reflect Pareto rates of transformation "on average" at counterfactual, constrained points like R in figure 2.4. If one blinked, it might almost be possible to suppose that adjusted factor cost valued GDP was akin to technically efficient production on a Pareto production possibility frontier, at some point other than the economic equilibrium E.

In trying to grasp the realities which caused the Soviet Union to crumble, it is important to avoid being beguiled by this esoterica. Soviet managers were plan constrained. Even if they desired to transform products at fiat, or Bergsonian adjusted factor cost, plan constraints precluded them from doing so. Moreover, supply inefficiencies under administrative command planning were ubiquitous and chaotic. Observed output could not have corresponded to counterfactual points on a Paretian possibilities frontier, or even a frontier governed by planners' nano-preferences. Soviet supply accordingly was technically inefficient. Production didn't occur on a Paretian feasibility frontier, and marginal rates of transformation cannot be inferred from adjusted factor cost prices, which in any case were unknown to Soviet managers. Points like R in figure 2.4 aren't determined by Pareto indifference curves, and neither official fiat prices, nor Bergson's adjusted factor cost version tells us anything about supply or demand side meanings.[5] The four Pareto diagrams developed above and applied throughout the text clarify the ways in which actual Soviet behavior departed from the neoclassical ideal, and if properly interpreted alert us to the futility of administrative command planning. Systems directors knew that R was inferior, but couldn't simulate the price information required to assess inefficiency costs, or direct production to the Pareto optimum at point E. The GDP statistics generated by the system were opaque. Although, they sometimes gave the appearance of success, the reality was usually grim.

Review

The Pareto–Arrow–Bergson standard, encompassing all economically efficient states of democratic free enterprise, and EU social democracy provides a theoretically consistent micro-macroeconomic framework for analyzing and appraising Muscovy. It can penetrate and dispel the partisan fog that often has obfuscated the Soviet experience by exposing the extent to which factor allocation, production, and distribution were non-economic. Paretian rational choice played a restricted role in productive governance, and planning was more about power than communist social welfare.

Abram Bergson and the Central Intelligence Agency claimed that it could do even more; that PAB provided a basis for statistically correcting the distortions of Soviet fiat prices permitting direct comparisons of East–West production potential. This claim is false and superfluous.[6] PAB doesn't need adornment. Its principles are sufficient to unravel "the riddle wrapped in a mystery inside an enigma."

Questions

1 Why are we able to use the Pareto benchmark for assessing the performance of competitive and controlled economies?
2 What is the *law of demand*? What are the four factors required for its efficient operation?
3 Why do utility and demand curves have the same slope?
4 Why is utility maximized by choosing the product assortment where the budget constraint is tangent to one's highest indifference curve?
5 Why may outcomes be detrimental if individuals don't choose rationally because they are swayed by passion or pressured by others into purchasing things they dis-prefer?
6 What is the *law of supply*?
7 If the law of demand boils down to the assertion that people can and will ascertain which consumption programs are best for them, what does this suggest about their corresponding supply programs?
8 Why must firms produce to the point where their budget line is tangent to their highest isoquant for supply to be efficient?

9 Why is profit or dividend maximizing essential for efficient supply? Illustrate your response.
10 Demand and supply are both specified as functions of price, ruling out other extraneous influences like government commands. Is this specification essential for achieving Pareto outcomes? Explain.
11 What is the *law of supply and demand equilibration*?
12 Consumption and supply programs are computed subject to price and income assumptions. The actions of participants however affect these initial assumptions. Why does this imply that supply and demand schedules will adjust slightly during the negotiating process?
13 What is the Walrasian excess demand price adjustment mechanism? In which markets does it best apply?
14 What is the Marshallian excess price quantity adjustment mechanism? How is it related to profit maximizing?
15 How should the interplay of Walrasian and Marshallian mechanisms be sequenced?
16 How do the terms of the implicit social contract underlying the law of supply and demand equilibration affect the merit of economic outcomes?
17 Under what conditions can economies with large state sectors and strong communitarian obligations still be classified as Pareto optimal?
18 Is government ever compatible with Pareto optimality? (*Hint*: discuss Bergson's concept of Pareto class social welfare functions.)
19 Why is "transparency" an essential ingredient of democratic Paretian economies?
20 Macroeconomics deals with aggregate economic growth, employment, inflation, income distribution, and social justice. Are these concepts independent of Pareto optimality theory, or integral aspects? Explain.
21 Illustrate GDP growth for a two goods economy in figure 2.4. Are points other than the Pareto equilibrium E* on the growth production possibility frontier, counterfactually technically efficient in the same sense as counterparts on the pre-growth frontier? Explain.
22 Are points beneath the growth PPF, and off the economically efficient assortment ray inferior? Is Muscovy likely to perform at E*? What does this tell us about the merit of Muscovite growth?
23 The Soviet labor force participation rate, influenced by anti-parasite laws compelling people to work, typically was 10 percent higher than America's, and the Kremlin after 1929 always claimed zero unemployment. Does this really mean that there was no transitory unemployment (Soviet census data indicate 5 percent transitory unemployment)? Is Soviet forced labor a plus or negative from the PAB perspective?
24 The Soviets claimed to have eradicated inflation through state price fixing. In fact, there was always some open inflation, repressed inflation, and hidden inflation. From a PAB perspective, should this dubious accomplishment weigh heavily in Muscovy's favor, taking into consideration that price fixing precluded supply being responsive to consumer demand? Elaborate.
25 The Soviets claimed to have an egalitarian distribution of income. Indeed, wage dispersion was low. But goods were allocated by rationing instead of Walrasian pricing (including wages). Could the real distribution of income, judged from the results of rationing, actually have been extremely egalitarian with the party elite super rich, and everyone else poor? Explain.

26 The Soviets claimed that the provision of free education, housing, transportation, and medicine made communism socially just. But were these services substandard, and who actually had access to high-quality services?

27 The Soviet disequilibrium control system was wired to facilitate resource mobilization; that is overemployment and overcapacity utilization. The West relies on Keynesian fiscal and monetary policy to achieve Pareto-compatible full employment, price stability, growth, and socially just public programs. What are the pros and cons of each approach? Which, in your view, is better?

Part II

Soviet Communism: Lenin and Stalin

When the Bolsheviks seized power in 1917, despite a half century of Marxist preparation, Lenin didn't have a blueprint for constructing socialism. There were abstract principles, but no operational plan. Trial and error consequently was the order of the day, even though this was obscured by a smokescreen of confident rhetoric.

The Soviets experimented with three distinct forms of socialism (1917–53): crude requisitioning and rationing (War Communism), leasing markets (NEP), and planned requisitioning and rationing (Command Communism). These phases are often treated as a progression from naïve to scientific command planning, with a brief market-based interlude that failed. The characterization has some merit but it is essential to grasp the Muscovite thread connecting them to understand what was right and wrong about the Lenin–Stalin episode, and to grasp why Russia's post-Communist economy has gone awry. The chapters which follow elaborate the theory and practice of War Communism, NEP, and Command Communism, and evaluate the statistical record.

3

War Communism: 1917–1921

Summary

John Reed called November 7, 1917, "the day that shook the world." The Bolshevik putsch indeed was an epochal event, but what did it mean? Was it a "revolution" or a regime change from autocracy to a proletarian dictatorship? The answer lies not in the romantic programs of Vladimir Lenin, Nikolai Bukharin, and Evgeny Preobrazhensky, but in whose demand governed the supply of collective and household goods. Was the proletariat (all productive citizens) economically sovereign, or the party-state?

Careful analysis of the Bolsheviks' initial attempt at building a socialist society (1917–21) during the period known as "War Communism"* reveals that the party-state, not the people, were placed in command continuing the Czarist pattern. Although, the nationalization of the means of production formally transferred ownership from the Muscovite autocracy, nobles, and emergent capitalists to the Russian people, the state diverted these assets to itself, claiming to serve as custodian until the battle against the people's enemies was won and the state withered into oblivion. The Bolsheviks in their capacity as custodian established themselves as a monopsonist employer instead of delegating that responsibility directly to worker self-managers. Lenin appointed "communist commissars" to oversee the economy, who assigned deputies to run factories, institutions, infrastructure, and distribution on a command basis. Market activity of any kind was criminalized, even for agents acting on the state's behalf, with the principles of "natural economy" and "physical systems management" substituted instead. State authorities compelled everyone to work, dictating conditions and terms of employment. They commandeered and rationed supplies including grain tax in kind (*prodrazverstka*), repressing the people's economic freedom and consumer sovereignty. Since Lenin's appointees had no professional economic experience, the economy virtually collapsed. Russia suffered a population deficit of 19.7 million from 1918 to 1923. Some of these were civil war combatant deaths, but most were the consequence of Lenin's rash and dictatorial policies. The Bolshevik regime change was a mock revolution, which set the pattern for the shape of things to come: NEP, Command Communism, Reform Communism, Market Communism, and post-Communist Market Muscovy.

*The Bolshevik coup d'etat was considered illegal and resisted by supporters of the Czar and other groups, touching off a civil war, compounded by foreign intervention from 1917 to 1921. The term War Communism emphasizes this contested sovereignty and the extraordinary nature of the times.

November 7: Revolution or Regime Change?

November 7, 1917, is a date deeply engraved in history. It marks the overthrow of Russian Czarist rule and its replacement by Bolshevik power. No one contests the regime change. But why is it important and what did it really signify? Was it a great fracture, cleanly separating the past from the future, or a continuation in a mock revolutionary guise? The answer depends on how the event is conceptualized. If pre-November 7th Russia is perceived as an autocracy and the Soviet epoch as a "proletocracy" brought about by a mass popular uprising, then the break is absolute. The "proletariat" once subordinated to the Czar and market becomes master, dispossessing the crown, nobility, capitalists, and the bourgeoisie, ruling justly in the broad social interest. There are no points of continuity. The event was revolutionary, like the American revolution where democracy displaced autocracy.

But if the criterion is Muscovite authoritarian control, perceptions flip. There is no break, only splinters. Russia is an authoritarian society throughout (first autocracy, then a communist dictatorship), with a privileged stratum of "servitors" (vassals obliged to serve the crown) who exploit the people for the supreme ruler and themselves, while masquerading as benefactors. Authoritarian politics is in command, this time with a new ruling clique, cadre and, ideology. Autocracy rather than free enterprise or perfect socialist planning determines production, consumption, and inegalitarian distribution.

Which interpretation is correct? Was there a "revolution" or a regime change with a socialist mask? The answer depends on the facts. If the Bolsheviks constructed a democratic, proletarian sovereign society (not a dictatorship in the name of the proletariat), which reflected the will of all the people, not just a stratum, then November 7 constitutes an authentic popular disrupture; the revolutionary triumph of socialism over autocracy. Alternatively, if Lenin created a Muscovite dictatorship over the proletariat (and peasants), then Bolshevism was mostly the continuation of Czardom with new costumes, rulers, cadre, and more encompassing institutions of administration and control.

Great Fracture

There are no grounds for doubting that Czarist Russia was an autocracy, even though some fledgling democratic institutions did emerge after the upheavals of 1905.[1] Caesar ruled the state, and the imperial household possessed much of the nation's assets. The aristocracy owned the lion's share of the remaining property, with individual peasant farms accounting for only a tiny portion of national wealth. Peasant agriculture after emancipation in 1861 was communal, and only began to privatize with the P. A. Stolypin reforms (1906–11).[2] More than 80 percent of the population was agrarian.[3] Industrial and merchant capitalists existed together with artisans (*kustars*) and various professionals, nonetheless Russia was essentially pre-enlightened, because supply wasn't competitively responsive to the majority's preferences. The system, especially the agrarian component, was mostly a natural economy managed by physical assignment as distinct from a consumer sovereign market system.

Verification of the "great fracture" hypothesis therefore seems only to require proof that after coming to power on a wave of popular discontent, Bolshevism was politically and economically consumer sovereign; that popular demand governed the supply of public and private goods. But matters are more complex because Lenin and others have argued that capitalism and therefore to some degree consumer sovereignty ruled supply before November 7. Bolshevism from this perspective replaced capitalism, not autocracy, and consequently the change in the scope of economic sovereignty wasn't as drastic as it might seem.

The litmus test here is whether Russia underwent a cultural revolution, switching from individualistic to socially compassionate values. It is easily demonstrated that the regime change didn't satisfy this criterion. To start, pre-Bolshevik Russia wasn't a western democratic free enterprise system. There were few businessmen in Czarist Russia in a modern sense. Peasants sold their surplus crops in local and regional markets, and the nobility exported grain, but agricultural production was mostly communal (*mir* and *obshchina*). Productive activity and consumption were organized according to custom, not the dictate of profit maximizing agrarian entrepreneurs.[4] Private urban economic activity adhered more closely to the Western pattern, but its share of GDP was small. Most industrial enterprises were owned by the nobility, or foreigners with privileged access to Muscovite state contracts,[5] and the non-aristocratic, native entrepreneurial community was politically impotent against the power of the Czar, state and nobility. Thus while Czarist Russia had a private business sector, which carried out most of its transactions through the market, economic sovereignty resided with the Czar, nobles, and state bureaucracy, operating in a pre-modern, rent-granting mode, not with the capitalist "class," or individuals freely maximizing their utility under the rule of law.

An analogy with the Newar–Hindu economy of Bhaktapur Nepal in 1971 is instructive. This town located near Kathmandu is largely self-sufficient. The community of 40,000 inhabitants is divided into 320 thars (social units), based primarily on patrilineal relationships and occupations. Everyone is more or less born into a productive role, and kept in his or her place through a caste system which regulates what is produced, how work is performed, and goods distributed. Individuals have limited discretion, but are permitted to maximize their utility in production and consumption including market participation within this constraint. Their actions are mostly governed by the requirements of caste, and vedic and tantric ritual rather than the rule of contract law. Although, in a formal sense, the economy might appear capitalist, or even Paretian, production and consumption are a communitarian ceremony, more a social ballet than "a for-profit," individualistic exercise in personal betterment. It is pre-modern and only obliquely connected with Enlightenment economic principles.[6]

The Czarist economy was similarly antique. It had a Muscovite autocratic-feudal system with an embryonic free enterprise component, where economic liberty was constrained in myriad ways. The Czar's and his nobles' existence, like their Brahman counterparts in Bhaktapur, were governed predominantly by Muscovite ceremony rather than the logic of "homo-economicus." The rent-seeking aristocracy played its assigned tasks collecting taxes, serving as bureaucrats, overseeing the national defense, and participating in court ceremony. The peasantry was enmeshed in communal webs, which extended to seasonal workers employed in the cities. Only a few were able to operate freely under the rule of law like their textbook brethren.[7]

And as in Bhaktapur, property rights mainly had pre-modern meanings. In the Newar city most households owned their homes, land, and businesses, but the uses of these assets were controlled by the community. Although the distribution of Czarist property rights was more concentrated, with the autocrat claiming ultimate ownership of everything including peasant land, despite granting alienable titles to the nobility, the effect was much the same.[8] Property in both domains provided only tenuous support for individual profit and utility maximizing. It signified possession, but not the right of equitable use under the rule of law. People and groups competed and intrigued to acquire the benefits of proprietary administration, but their behavior in a larger perspective was governed less by Pareto than the web of pre-modern relationships.

This illuminates an important aspect of the November 7 regime change. The Soviets tirelessly asserted that the nationalization of the means of production made their power seizure revolutionary because it was tantamount to the establishment of proletocracy. But the reality behind the rhetoric was less radical. Asset claims were merely transferred from the Czarist to the Soviet state and overseen by new types of rent-seeking administrators who were more interventionist in their micro-management, but otherwise the continuities dominated the changes. Masters relied on dictate rather than market competition. Evidence supporting a great fracture therefore must be sought in the connection of workers' and citizens' demand with the supply of goods for collective and household consumption. Did the new Soviet economic mechanism assure that consumer preferences were sovereign, or did the communist dictatorship prevent democratic control over public goods, and consumer command over supplies for individual use? The Bolsheviks insisted that they gave the people what they wanted, and protected them from exploitation (as had the Czar), but did the arrangements they put in place really allow this? This question would become a recurring theme immediately after November 7 during War Communism, and throughout the NEP, Command Communist, Reform Communist, Market Communist, and post-Communist eras.

War Communism

The first economic regime devised by Lenin from November 7, 1917 to March 1921 was War Communism, a term that emphasizes the chaos of the time. The Bolshevik putsch didn't go unopposed. Factions loyal to the Czar resisted Soviet power, precipitating a civil war, complicated by Russia's on-going war with Germany and subsequent interventions by the British, French, Americans, and Japanese. This was an unfavorable environment for calmly constructing a socialist utopia. Battling "enemies" and consolidating authority took precedence over "due process," leading many scholars to conclude that the initial Bolshevik model was more an exercise in crisis management than a rational design for a proletarian future.

Perhaps, but old Bolshevik luminaries like Lenin, Nikolai Bukharin, Evgeny Preobrazhensky and Leon Trotsky all took their schemes seriously, believing for a while at least that they reflected ideal communist principles and for this reason the period can also be conceived as "Utopian Bolshevism." The core concepts were "natural economy" and "physical systems management," the notion that factor allocation, production, distribution, and consumption could all be orchestrated in "natural" terms, that is, physical units of measure, without regard for prices and values. Lenin suggested that this could be best accomplished by treating the economy as a post office, where comrades would email orders to a central coordinator who would forward them to the appropriate warehouses, or manufacturers for processing, and shipping. "Accounting and control-these are the chief things necessary, for the organizing and correct functioning of the first phase of Communist society. All citizens are here transformed into hired employees of the state "syndicate" (trade union). All that is required is that they should work equally, should regularly do their share of work, and should receive equal pay."[9]

His intent is clear. The new order presupposes that workers and peasants possess all the requisite economic skills for running expropriated economic institutions and will do so willingly working for the state according to their ability in return for equal pay (or still more idealistically receiving only what they need). The "dictatorship of the proletariat" helps the workers organize productive activities and represses capitalists so that the state can wither, ushering in direct proletarian democracy. The Bolsheviks' rhetorical goals therefore are "revolutionary." They aspire to empower all productive citizens by granting them some job choice and influence over the supply of collective and household consumer goods, subject only to obligations to work according to their ability, accepting egalitaritarian compensation and job assignments in society's interest.

Bukharin and Preobrazhensky go one step further advocating a moneyless economy and claiming that this had already been achieved thanks to the post-November 7 hyperinflation which made the ruble worthless. Following Marx, they argue for egalitarian physical rationing, simplifying Lenin's own scheme. No need to bother with "pay." Consumers under their plan wouldn't have to provide their credit card numbers to "postal" officials. They would receive everything they wished gratis within the limits of their egalitarian allotment.[10]

Leon Trotsky, the commander of the Red Army was scornful of this utopianism, advocating the creation of a Red Labor Army instead that would dragoon everyone into military economic service as the best form of socialist employment, both during and after the Civil War. The proposal was inconsistent with Marx's humanist vision of a proletarian society that eliminated conflict, and empowered everyone to freely actualize his or her potential, but was compatible with Lenin's actions.

While Lenin talked about revolutionary empowerment, his deeds belied his words. Nationalization of the means of production was portrayed in Lenin tract *State and Revolution* as a vehicle for transferring Czarist and capitalist assets directly to the toiling masses, but in practice he treated the transfer as an installment plan where the state acted as the people's custodian until class conflict was eradicated, and the state withered into oblivion. The industrial enterprises, transport and communications network, governmental institutions, banks, insurance companies, land and resources in the interim became state properties, managed as monopolies by state appointees, operating under the supervision of communist commissars. Instead of fostering worker self-management, which he viewed as non-Marxist anarcho-syndicalism, Lenin imposed stringent state-party control over the means of production. As in Trotsky's scheme discipline and obligation took precedence over worker empowerment and self-management.[11]

The state's "right" to act as sole source employer was buttressed by criminalizing business. On the morrow of the putsch, Lenin not only nationalized the means of production, but outlawed private hired labor, entrepreneurship, production, commerce, finance, investment, and international trade. These prohibitions were nominally aimed at would-be capitalists, but they applied equally to any state employee including managers and workers councils who might desire to act at variance with government edicts. No one was permitted to start new businesses, hire, borrow and lend, produce, market, distribute, or invest state assets without explicit permission from Bolshevik authorities. Anything not authorized was forbidden including consumption, sale, and leasing of personal items (like apartments and homes), and barter. Peasants under this regime could produce for their own consumption, but couldn't sell or barter their goods without the state's consent. The perfect freedom promised by Leninism in this way immediately degenerated into straitjacket authoritarianism, destined to become even more extreme under Stalin. There was no possibility of consumer sovereignty under these arrangements. Job choice was restricted, and conditions and terms of employment were non-negotiable. People consumed what they could, with forced substitution the rule. And of course, since democracy was deferred until the state fully withered, the would-be electorate had no control over the production and provision of public goods. The rule of men so conspicuous in Muscovite Russia persisted unabated, with even less recourse to the rule of law than during the latter days of Czarist times.

The principle of rent-granting command reigned supreme. Lenin himself stood at the apex of this new autocracy. His "servitors" called "communist commissars," operating under the aegis of the Council of People's Commissars (Lenin's economic cabinet) and the VSNKh (Supreme Council of the National Economy) set up December 15, 1917, were empowered by him to act as commanders overseeing various political and economic portfolios. Just as the Czar's bureaucratic agents, they weren't given detailed assignments, but received broad mandates instead to get the job done using whatever means necessary. During War Communism this meant "*prodraverstka*," forced requisitioning of foodstuffs, with or without compensation, and physical distribution to intermediate input use, or final consumption. The same principle applied broadly as well to other goods, and encompassed dragooning hapless souls in the Trotsky's Red Labor Army, or otherwise compelling state employees to work on terms they often considered unacceptable.

The plight of ordinary Russians was dire. It bore no discernible relationship to the revolutionary images and slogans of the avant-garde, the utopias of Kazimir Malevich and Vladimir Tatlin.[12] Not only were they more dependent than ever on authoritarian caprice, but Bolshevik commissars were managerially incompetent, and Lenin criminalized the kind of individual utility seeking that could have saved commissars from themselves. Although, Bolshevik supporters blamed all woes on the "enemies of the people" (*vragy naroda*), the catastrophe which ensued was mostly of Lenin's own making. Industrial output during War Communism fell 69 percent, according to official statistics, and agrarian output plummeted 40 percent, causing widespread famine.[13] As a consequence the population plunged 19.7 million below demographic expectation (1918–23) (population deficit including unrealized births).[14] Since the Russians surrendered to Germany at Brest Litovsk on March 3, 1918, few of these casualties are ascribable to World War I, but civil war combat deaths were an important contributory factor. Presumably, the situation would have been even worse had Russia been a modern society. As in Newar, communalism and other traditional support mechanisms provided some shelter from Lenin's rash experiment in natural economy. Nonetheless, the tragedy stands. Given the opportunity to achieve democratic socialism, Lenin opted instead for authoritarian "continuity," preferring a mock revolution to popular empowerment.[15]

Analytics of War Communism

The behavioral properties and potential of the War Communist economy can be depicted geometrically using the Pareto–Arrow–Bergson (PAB) standard elaborated in chapter 2 and illustrated in figures 2.3–2.6. Starting with the factor space (Edgeworth–Bowley input-production box), imagine an ideal Pareto peacetime version of communist physical systems management, where factor characteristics (e.g. labor skills and capital engineering specifications), input supplies, and technologies ideally reflect working class and peasant sovereign preferences, given strict egalitarianism in income and personal wealth.

The real supply of factors will be substantially smaller than the ideal because capital capacity was under-utilized during War Communism, and the stock itself was shrinking due to war, poor maintenance and repair, and the absence of new investment. Land similarly was inadequately maintained, and former capitalist managers were denied equal opportunity. A large portion of the industrial labor force returned to the countryside, and new arrivals in agrarian communes weren't permitted to put their skills to best use. As a consequence of all these forces, the dimensions of the Edgeworth–Bowley box, both the capital and labor vectors, were much smaller than ideal. (Capital and labor with inferior characteristics are normalized into fewer units of ideal capital at the optimal marginal rate of transformation.)

Production in the Edgeworth–Bowley box occurs when factors are inserted into enterprise production functions (isoquants) for either or both goods arrayed on the southwest and northeast origins (q_1 and q_2). The production functions for these activities are depicted as nested sets of isoquants radiating from each origin. Output levels are indicated by the superscripts. Larger numbers indicate higher production. The superscripts displayed in figure 3.1 are all lower than War Communist ideal (figure 2.3) because existing technologies, capital, and labor weren't put to best use. Skilled workers and former capitalist managers often were driven into farming, and VSNKh supervisors didn't harness production potentials. Likewise, capital depreciated and obsolesced at

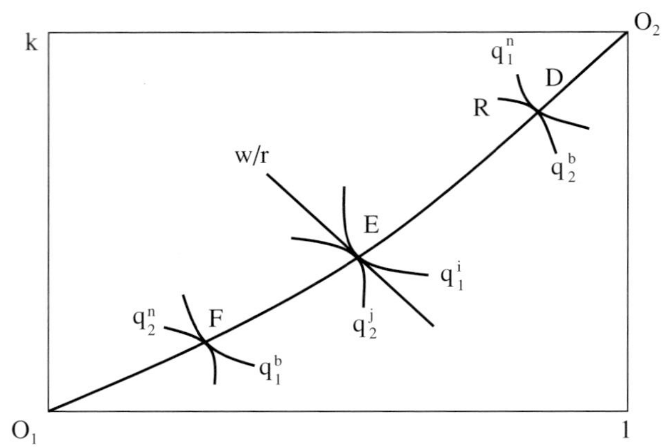

Figure 3.1 War Communist factor-production space

abnormally rapid rates. Consequently, output and total productivity for any combination of outputs along the contract curve throughout War Communist was far below potential.

Moreover, efficiency was further degraded because production didn't occur at point E, the double tangency on the ideal physical systems management contract curve where demand and supply are equilibrated (figure 2.3), or the actual contract curve (figure 3.1) because Marshallian quantity and Walrasian price adjustment mechanisms were criminalized.[16] The assortment of goods and services produced at point F, D, or R were dis-preferred and marginal technical rates of factor substitution weren't uniform. This meant in the latter case that output in one activity could always have been increased by reallocating factors along one of the isoquants without diminishing the production of the other good.

We know these inefficiencies were real and significant because the Soviet Union didn't devise an operational planning mechanism until 1928; authority over production was jointly vested in VSNKh administrators and red directors (see glossary) who were prohibited from maximizing profits, a sine qua non of the Marshallian quantity adjustment mechanism; and the Walrasian price adjustment mechanism only operated de facto in segments of the agrarian sector. Moreover, moral hazard created by state ownership and the absence of the rule of law, severely impaired whatever Walrasian processes were operative.

The same phenomenon can be visualized alternatively with the aid of the production possibility frontier (PPF) (the contract curve for ideal War Communist regime) and a corresponding production feasibility frontier (PFF) derived from the actual War Communist contract curve. These frontiers depicted in figure 3.2 make it easy to see that the War Communist economy wasn't minimally technically inefficient at point E′. Nor was it minimally economically and technically inefficient at point E″. It was more severely under-productive at point R, generating a GDP far below War Communist potential because it lacked effective Marshallian and Walrasian adjustment mechanisms or surrogate perfect planning. (The set of all points R in figure 3.1 may or may not define a continuous feasibility frontier, insertable into figure 3.2.)

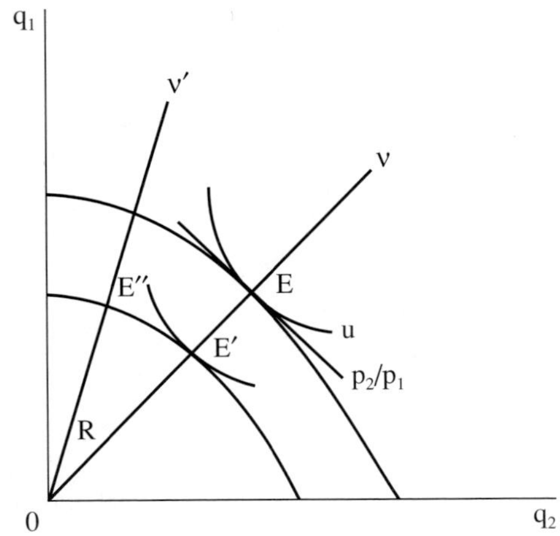

Figure 3.2 War Communist production possibilities

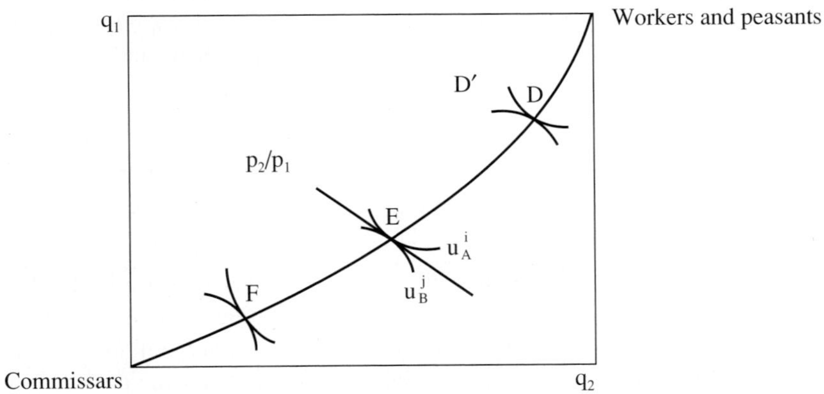

Figure 3.3 War Communist distribution

The state monopoly on banking and finance further aggravated matters. As Irving Fisher demonstrated long ago, finance is a powerful device for mobilizing illiquid assets. Capital which might otherwise lie idle, can be transferred to good use if entrepreneurs are able to borrow loanable funds, but they weren't.

These supply side woes were compounded by distributional inefficiencies. While the Bolsheviks doubtlessly carried egalitarian rationing too far under War Communism, moral hazard and adverse selection enabled VSNKh insiders to acquire large unearned incomes. This distortion is illustrated by point D′ in figure 3.3, which shows administrative insiders not only received an inordinately large share of GDP, but the distribution itself was inefficient. Workers and peasants could have been made better off without diminishing the utility of the privileged on the War Communist contract distribution curve.

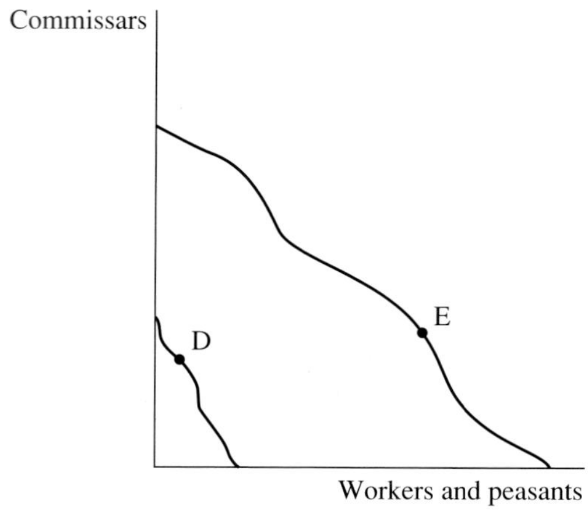

Figure 3.4 War Communist utility possibilities

Finally, the utility possibilities and feasibilities frontiers displayed in figure 3.4 reveal that while the extreme inefficiencies of War Communism lowered social welfare from the market socialist ideal at E, to point D, the powerful and corrupt didn't fare badly.

Review

War Communism was both a pragmatic attempt to secure power after the Bolshevik coup d'etat, and an effort to characterize the regime's actions in idealistic terms. Its guiding principle was forced requisitioning and rationing, implemented the Muscovite way by empowering state agents to coerce the unwilling. This entailed criminalizing private property, business, and entrepreneurship, all potential sources of resistance to requisitioning and rationing. The approach, absent effective planning, was doomed to failure and had catastrophic economic consequences. Lenin belatedly conceded the truth, tactically abandoning planless physical systems management in 1921.

Systems Profile

Main features of the War Communist economic system

- *Culture*: Muscovite authoritarian/anti-authoritarian, with a proletarian bent. Anti-authoritarianism is a mix of passivity (withdrawal into agrarian communalism) and opportunism evoked by state oppression.

- *Motivation*: Iron-fisted party-state domination and great power building (partially with the assistance of foreign cells and sympathetic socialist parties abroad), unmitigated by socialist humanist concerns.
- *Mechanism*: Natural resources, land and the entire industrial and administrative means of production including housing, gold, and other valuables were state owned and controlled. (Although peasants acted as if the land were theirs, and didn't pay explicit ground rent to the state.) State administration over households was comprehensive. The state physically managed the economy without markets and was prone to moral hazard. Industrial finance and banking were state monopolies. The industrial sector, and derivatively the national economy was administered by VSNKh, the supreme economic council. Managers called "red directors" were appointed by the state, but lacked formal functional autonomy. Administration and production were lumped together. Most non-agrarian laborers were state employees. The state set wages, and workers were powerless whenever the state chose to disregard trade unions and worker councils. The rule of men prevailed. There was no planning. The USSR was a one-party state, which had sovereignty over the provision of public goods.
- *Institutions*: State ownership of means of production, land, and natural resources (but peasants were convinced that the land was theirs regardless of state nationalization); agrarian communes (*mir* and *obshchina*). There were some private farms on state lands. VSNKh (Supreme Economic Council), STO (Labor and Defense Council), government monopolies (including foreign trade), cooperatives, captive trade unions, and worker councils were key elements of the state industrial control apparatus.

Main inefficiencies

- *Law of demand*: State commandeering, requisitioning, forced substitution, monopsony demand for labor, privileged access to goods and services.
- *Law of supply*: Worker supply curves were weak functions of wages because of high urban industrial unemployment. Agrarian communalism made private farming a weak function of rates of return. Industrial production was unresponsive to price and profit incentives. Absence of rule of law created endemic moral hazard, and corruption.
- *Law of equilibration*: Intra-state unplanned sector (VSNKh) requisitioning and rationing was an ad hoc process. Moral hazard and adverse selection were severe problems due to the absence of the rule of contract law. Walrasian labor market equilibration had little impact on communal farming, and virtually none in state industrial employment where unions and worker councils negotiating for workers were subordinate to the state and communist party. Keynesian macro equilibration was impaired by absence of a link between household consumption and investment (no multiplier effect). Also, there were no competitive money or loanable funds markets. The state was a monopolist in investment and finance.

Tactics of War Communist economic management

Topic	*Problem*	*State response*
State ownership	Circumscribes individual utility-seeking	Enforced with stern repression
Criminalization of business	Depression	Commandeering, dragooning, requisitioning and rationing
Agrarian communes	Pre-modern, inefficient	*prodrazverstka* (oppressive grain taxation); internal mutual support, but external trade including barter banned unless expressly state approved
Unemployment	Wasted potential	None. No macro regulatory policy
Development	Pre-modern economy and culture	Assessed problem from the prism of class struggle, instead of fostering a deeper Muscovite cultural transformation

Systemic structure	*Share of GDP*	*Productivity*	*Coercion*
Markets (black)	10	Low	High
State	20	Low	High
Communal agriculture	70	Low	Moderate

Systemic characteristics	*Degree/intensity*
State macro-regulation	None
State micro-regulation	
pro-competitive	None
welfare/security	Low
Public works programs	Low
Criminal dis-services, rent-seeking/embezzlement	Moderate

Causes of macroeconomic disequilibrium	
Sticky wages and benefits	High
Sticky prices	High
Investment avoidance	High
Capital flight	High
Misinvestment	Not applicable
Liquidity preference	Low
Insecure agrarian rights	Extremely high
State property rights	Extremely high
Foreign capital flows	Not applicable
State corruption	High
Macro-policy mismanagement	Extremely high
Class conflict	Extremely high

Main performance indicators

Per capita GDP (Bergson) (US = 100)	7–15
Maddison	14–28
Per capita GDP growth 1917–21 (table 3.1/Eason, table 11.9/p. 72) (percent per annum)	−18
Unemployment	15+
Retirement support burden	None
Non-working mothers and wives	Low

Direction of reforms

Comprehensive physical management systems founded on administration, requisitioning, and rationing.

Questions

1 Lenin nationalized land, resources, the means of production, housing, gold, and other assets. Were any of these actions unprecedented? Explain.
2 The War Communist state became the sole non-agrarian employer. Had the state ever been a principal employer before November 17, 1917?
3 Business was criminalized and goods rationed to the population on a comparatively egalitarian basis? Were there precedents for these actions? Explain.
4 The Bolsheviks allowed agrarian communes and individual farmers to treat the land as theirs, including buying and selling it for agrarian use. Did this arrangement mimic that of the Czars? Could Bolshevik crop and property taxes be construed as implicit rents paid to the state landlord? Explain.
5 List the economic "liberties" denied Russian farmers and explain how they impaired individual utility maximizing.
6 Who was the economic sovereign in the household goods sector, consumers or the state? Explain.
7 Who was the economic sovereign in the public goods sector, the electorate or the state?
8 What were Lenin's concepts of the ideal War Communist economy?
9 How did his modeling affect product characteristics, production, distribution, and income distribution?
10 How did Lenin's requisition-rationing theory differ from practice? What were the costs and benefits of his policies?
11 Compare Nikolai Bukharin's and Evgeny Preobrazhensky's War Communist concepts with reality. Was their theory a valuable guide for effective policy-making?

12 Compare Leonid Trotsky's theory of optimal proletarian labor mobilization with reality. Was his theory a useful guide for socialist humanist policy-making?
13 What is "consumer choice"? Did the Russian people have it? Was it circumscribed under Lenin's models?
14 What is moral hazard? Why was it especially grave in War Communist Russia?
15 What is adverse selection? How did it affect the behavior of "red commissars" and other VSNKh officials?
16 How could the War Communist industrial sector have been transformed to full socialist physical systems management?
17 What steps were taken in this direction?
18 How could the War Communist agrarian sector have been transformed to full socialist physical systems management?
19 What steps were being taken in this direction?
20 What would have been the benefits of full socialist physical systems management? Distinguish between feasible and ideal central planning.
21 How would full socialist physical systems management have differed from market free enterprise?
22 Why is moral hazard and adverse selection more troublesome for socialist physical systems management than free enterprise?
23 Did the Bolsheviks employ neo-classical Pareto-efficiency theory to analyze whether free enterprise or physical systems management was best for Russia?
24 What are the four basic aspects of Muscovite culture shaping Russian economic behavior?
25 How did these cultural influences manifest themselves under War Communism?
26 Did these influences maintain or intensify pre-modern arrangements and behavior?
27 Did these influences help or hinder the development of a socialist physically managed system? Explain.
28 Did Muscovite culture subvert the Bolsheviks' socialist intent?
29 What is the evidence that War Communism was economically successful?
30 What is the evidence that War Communism jeopardized Soviet power?
31 Are official War Communist economic statistics plausible from the standpoint of Pareto efficiency theory and Russia's pre-modern legacy?
32 Was Lenin's abandonment of War Communism necessary? Explain.
33 Was Lenin's policy of War Communism necessary?
34 Was War Communism socialist? If so, why?

4

NEP: 1921–1929

Summary

Lenin's "state post office" scheme for building a communist economy proved to be catastrophic. The more the civil war and foreign intervention receded, the worse Russia's hyper-depression became. The Kronstadt Rebellion led by the sailors of the Baltic Fleet March 2, 1921, inspired by Shlyapnikov's Workers Opposition program for direct, democratic workers' control seems to have persuaded Lenin to change course. In the late winter–early spring of 1921 he opted for a slow-motion tactical retreat, called the New Economic Policy (NEP), which retained state ownership of the industrial, commercial, and agrarian means of production and VSNKh's control over much of the economy, but decriminalized small business. Although the Soviets declared that small business had been denationalized this was misleading. Lenin merely permitted state enterprises to sell products to private middle men. These "nepmen" leased state facilities and operated on a for-profit basis. They were permitted to manage small enterprises hiring no more than 20 workers and sell directly to households, farmers, and the state sector. "Red directors" often chose to wear two hats, working for the state and separately on private account. Agrarians likewise were permitted to behave as nepmen, and additionally viewed the land as theirs despite Soviet decrees to the contrary. Looked at in perspective, these concessions were modest. The state continued to assert its ownership claims and direct control over an expanding state sector, but delegated some productive, distributive, and consumption decisions to the "Bolshevik market." Lenin and his successors also inaugurated a haphazard effort to liberalize and rationalize state economic governance. They created planning institutions, experimented with industrial organization and material incentives, encouraged private farming (on state land), and permitted negotiated intra-state transactions. The upshot of these disparate efforts was the creation of a dual potential, post-War Communist economic mechanism, capable of evolving into varieties of market socialism like the Lange model, a European social democracy on one hand or to a planned version of physical systems management on the other.

The NEP experience (1921–9) is best conceived as a tug of war between these tendencies, guided more by Marxist exegesis and political intrigue than objective analysis. The evidence suggests that NEP stimulated a modest economic recovery, and that further gains could have been expected from market Bolshevism, but its potential and comparative merit are obscured by the deficiencies of statistics. If government data are accepted, a return to War Communism empowered by planning should have been unthinkable, but they cannot be trusted. Contrary to the Kremlin's buoyant claims, the Russian economy appears to have been primitivized rather than modernized during NEP, even though there were some technological advances in industry. Traditional communal agriculture expanded instead of contracting and the efficiency of NEP leasing was lower than the Czar's version of private enterprise. The net effect of NEP was one step forward from War Communism and two steps backward toward a Bolshevized pre-modern economy.

New Economic Policy

On May 17, 1921, the Bolsheviks decriminalized small business and entrepreneurship. The action mislabeled "denationalization, heralded the emergence of a new, market tolerant, Bolshevized model set in motion by the abolition of *prodrazverstka* (confiscatory grain taxation) two months earlier.[1] This abrupt volte-face called the "New Economic Policy" spanned the years 1921–9. During the Soviet era it was treated as an interlude between Lenin's first attempt to construct a natural economy and Joseph Stalin's command system; an epiphenomenon providing insight into Stalin's meteoric

Market versus Planning

PAB theory establishes the existence of a class of Pareto ideal states and even allows for the possibility of philosopher king sovereignty. But it doesn't prove that there are mechanisms for achieving an optimum. During the twentieth century two schools claimed that their mechanisms could do the job best; one championing markets, the other "scientific" planning. The East–West rivalry was often conceived in these terms, with the Soviet Union cast as the exemplar of "socialist" planning and "capitalist" America the market paragon. It is useful to keep this dichotomy in mind when assessing the evolutionary development of the Soviet Union from Lenin's War Communism through its various phases to Gorbachev's Market Communism.

rise, his disenchantment with markets, and his rationale for forced industrialization during the 1930s. These themes remain important, but in the wake of later Soviet and post-Soviet developments, it is also instructive to analyze the 1920s as a partial reversion to Czarist pre-modern arrangements, and as a harbinger of subsequent Market Communist and Market Muscovite experiments under Gorbachev, Yeltsin, and Putin, rather than as a failed experiment in building free enterprise, or European social democracy.

Decriminalization of Small Business and State Leasing

As during the War Communist period, rhetoric didn't always correspond with actions. The revocation of the decree nationalizing small business, the centerpiece of NEP, for this reason is widely misunderstood. The word "revoke" implies de-nationalizing previously expropriated firms, and restoring them to their rightful owners. But this wasn't how the Soviets construed it. Of the tens of thousands of enterprises confiscated prior to May 17, 1921, only 76 were returned to their former proprietors by the presidium of VSNKh. Provincial authorities restored some others, but de-nationalization never really happened. Citizens, including former owners beginning July 7, 1921, were only authorized to lease facilities from the state, resuming old businesses, or starting new ones on the proviso that they hired no more than 20 employees.[2] These small-scale artisans, wholesalers, merchants, contractors, and professional lessees served clients in the state, cooperative, business, and household sectors, agreeing to pay fixed rents, taxes, contracting costs, and bearing business risk in return for the right to profit-seek. They can be likened to commercial tenants in contemporary shopping malls, who own their businesses, but not the buildings, land, and equipment rented from the landlord, with two important qualifications. First, the state both in its capacity as landlord and supplier was an administrative, not a business undertaking, and therefore had neither a legal, nor a competitive motive to maximize gains from leasing. Second, leaseholds were more a privilege than a right, largely unprotected by the rule of law. The Bolsheviks had already demonstrated a willingness to abrogate property rights and criminalize business in 1917, which not only meant that leases could be terminated without compensation, but more subtly that commercial undertakings couldn't be easily bought or sold since the state wasn't under any obligation to accept substitute tenants, or honor its supply contracts. New owners could be denied access to the old lessee's facilities and state suppliers. Private enterprise accordingly was precarious. Entrepreneurial expectations had to be very low. Businessmen and women could earn net income from current operations, but couldn't enrich themselves because hiring restrictions precluded significant expansion, and the expected present discounted market value of their restrictive business leaseholds was negligible. Lessee prospects were inferior not only to the competitive ideal, but to prior Czarist practice, and did little to assure a full economic recovery.

This feeble gesture was Lenin's only formal proprietary concession to "capitalism." The vast majority of heavy industrial and other enterprises employing more than 20 employees remained fully state owned, and controlled. Their facilities could not be leased, and new large-scale private entrepreneurial ventures remained illegal. Likewise, neither land nor natural resources were de-nationalized except for some restricted agrarian use. The state didn't control most agrarian production, as it did heavy industrial activity, but farms weren't operated on a for-profit basis either. Ninety percent of all farming was carried out under traditional communal supervision, including periodic repartitioning of household plots.[3] Here too, economic activity was less, not more "capitalistic" than on November 7, 1917, and agrarian productivity was notably lower (although official statistics for the mid-1920s indicate otherwise).

Market Bolshevism

The traditional characterization of NEP as resurgent capitalism obviously is unjustified. Private ownership of the means of production without private owners, and capitalism without capitalists are oxymorons. Both the New Economic Policy and the old War Communism were proletarian dictatorships based on state ownership and industrial control, not capitalist, differing only with respect to the design of the control system.

Requisitioning and rationing had been the watchwords under War Communism. Commissars supervised, commanded, and commandeered, granting as little discretion as they could to subordinates. NEP reflected a radically new attitude. Administration and supervision were preserved, but lower-ranking officials and an army of lessees were given broad autonomy, including limited authority to sell state goods to consumers at negotiated prices. They were permitted to utility seek in "market" like ways that were previously proscribed. Independent NEP wholesalers and retail merchants known collectively as nepmen obviously were market makers, serving as bridges connecting state producers with consumers. Artisans likewise manufactured for competitive sale. But more subtly, and provocatively from the left's perspective, entities within the administrative structure were encouraged to respond to market forces. Enterprise directors and administrators could choose lessees and negotiate leasing terms, creating serious moral hazards. Opportunistic state appointees could be bribed, or earn extra income by wearing two hats, leasing lucrative businesses to themselves while continuing to serve as state representatives. And they could leverage these opportunities by modifying output in state firms they controlled to further their private interests. Thus, while state ownership and control were formally enthroned, the empowerment of subordinates raised the threat of co-option, the possibility that the market, including the peasantry rather than the dictatorship of the proletariat could become sovereign within the Soviet shell (a precursor to the second economy problem under Command and Reform Communism), restoring inegalitarianism and what it considered economic injustice (see glossary entry on second economy).

This specter was a source of consternation for those who believed that it would primarily benefit insiders and outsiders seeking to exploit the working class. All attempts by Lenin and other NEP advocates to promote discretionary choice making, and hence the market accordingly were construed as "capitalist" regardless of their professed intent. Social democracy (democratic socialism with private property business and entrepreneurship) as the left perceived it was a delusion. There was only one true socialism based on comprehensive physical systems management. Everything else was capitalism.

Accountability

Lenin was sympathetic to these concerns, as were most members of the Politburo, but believed that small concessions could pay huge dividends, while the pernicious aspects of individual utility maximizing could be contained if state officials acted more responsibly and were properly incentivized. Administrators, he felt were largely unaccountable in the War Communist control system because it was difficult to assess cost-effectiveness. Their operations couldn't be put to a market test, allowing administrators to claim that they did their best regardless of costs or consequences. To mitigate abuse Lenin decreed that branches of VSNKh, the Supreme Economic Council heading the administrative economic control system would have to purchase their supplies instead of commandeering them, or receiving materials gratis through the War Communist rationing network. This new accountability mirrored his prior decision in March 1921 to replace the confiscation of peasant grain (*prodrazverstka*) with negotiated purchase.

But the Bolsheviks hadn't thought the problem through. The principle of financial self-sufficiency was initially applied to entire *glavks* (industrial subdepartments of the administrative apparatus) and trusts formed in 1921–2 (agglomerations of large enterprises), which were a hodgepodge of operational and bureaucratic entities. Their response was excessive. They dumped current production, inventories, and assets, and laid off employees to raise funds for inputs, including administrative salaries, setting off alarm bells on the left. The spectacle of widespread unemployment in the state sector coupled with deteriorating terms of trade with the countryside was taken as proof that no good could come from giving markets any quarter. The government therefore promptly reversed itself, chiding VSNKh for dumping, after which the terms of trade moved against the peasants raising the specter of urban food shortages, evoking confused fears about a new "scissors crises."[4]

Scissors Crisis

Under War Communism industrial production fell more steeply than agriculture, causing industrial and agricultural prices to diverge. The peak disparity occurred in 1923, and then reversed. The scissors image was concocted by plotting terms of trade in alternate denominators, so that one series rose, and the other fell reciprocally. The episode has no intrinsic economic importance, but was used by Stalin as a boogyman to partly justify forced collectivization by claiming that markets discouraged peasant grain marketings. The term "scissors crisis" was coined by Leon Trotsky.

We will have more to say about this later. But the larger point from the perspective of accountability and incentives is that these initial setbacks gradually prodded specialists to realize that self-sufficiency was only applicable to entities capable of covering costs out of the proceeds of sales, and all other administrative activities would have to be financed out of tax revenues. Consequently, state enterprises (*predpriyatie*), functionally analogous to for-profit western enterprises, began to emerge in 1927 as future, independent juridical units, headed by "red directors" (state appointed managers), within the VSNKh control regime, operating on the basis of *khozraschyot* (the principle of financial self-sufficiency).[5] This legalism didn't mean that Soviet firms automatically were transformed into profit-seeking state enterprises, but it did create the potential. The choice was the Soviets. They could instruct "red directors" to confine their activities strictly within the VSNKh rationing network, acquiring and transferring materials (goods) at fixed state prices in which case *khozraschyot* was mostly an administrative formality, or they could permit them to participate in the leasing market for their own advantage. This second option was tantamount to adopting Lange-type market socialism,[6] complete with its virtues and defects. On the positive side, state enterprise "self-interest" maximizing was more consumer sovereign friendly than War Communism. But it was also subject to distortion, adverse selection, and moral hazard because red directors weren't authorized to profit maximize, being guided instead by other assignments or quantitative incentives, and were tempted to wear two hats, one red, the other closet-capitalist white.

Langean Market Socialism

Academic interest in the economics of socialism was intense during the 1930s. Critics like Lord Lionel Robbins, Ludwig von Mises, and Friedrich von Hayek, focusing on the Command Communist model argued essentially that directive central planning was monkey business because systems directors could not compute Pareto equilibrium prices. Oscar Lange attempted to counter their criticism by showing how a state price board could auction goods and services to the public, forming prices that would guide state managers to replicate the Marshallian quantity adjustment process of profit maximizing Western firms. The demonstration was sound as far as it went, but brushed fatal flaws under the rug. These defects were largely disregarded in the later literature, allowing Lange's model to hold pride of place in the pantheon of market socialist schemes that retained the Bolshevik's criminalization of private property, business, and entrepreneurship. Interest in the model, like Soviet "scientific planning" has gone the way of the dodo. Egalitarian dividend maximizing, labor-owned and managed economies (the Yugoslav ideal) constitute a third way. But they too have little contemporary appeal.

There is no evidence that the Bolsheviks fully appreciated the nuances. They were groping in the dark, rediscovering aspects of Paretian optimization applicable to a natural, state sovereign economy, while remaining opposed to consumer sovereignty and popular rule. Lange's model of market socialism wouldn't be devised for another seven years, and *khozraschyot* state enterprises for the most part produced according to VSNKh assignment, responding to arbitrary optimands and private NEP opportunities rather than Langean consumer utility maximizing rules.[7] Nonetheless, the Soviets were stumbling toward a better mouse trap, and by the end of the 1920s had placed themselves in a position to construct a well functioning market socialist system mixing state and private ownership, had Stalin so desired, a model that could have been a halfway house between Brezhnev's Reform Communism and contemporary EU social democracy.

Planning

The breathing room provided by state leasing was also used by the Bolsheviks for another important purpose. As odd as it might seem, Lenin never found time during War Communism to construct a scientific physical management mechanism. He expropriated, commandeered, and installed an emergency rationing system, but neglected to establish institutes for the development of effective planning technologies, or a central planning agency to perform the necessary calculations. VSNKh consequently was a powerful administrative and executive apparatus with no formal analytic capabilities. It operated on impulse instead of intellect.

This lacuna was rectified on February 22, 1921, when Gosplan (the State Planning Agency), under the auspices of the STO (the Council of Labor and Defense), was established to "work out a single general state economic plan and methods and means of implementing it."[8] Other planning bodies like Promplan (Industrial Planning Agency) attached to the Chief Economic Administration (GEU), tasked to assist Tsugprom (the Central Industrial Directorate of VSNKh) were established by various organizations in the early 1920s, and journals like *Voprosy ekonomiki* (*Questions of Economics*), and *Planovoe khoziaistvo* (*Planned Economy*) were inaugurated to support these undertakings. Progress was slow. Planning, understood as surveying supply possibilities and choosing optimal programs, was employed more as a guideline than as a basis for command throughout NEP. Nonetheless, by the time Stalin was in a position to choose between a mixed market socialist ideal (or more realistically its Muscovite twin) and administrative command planning, the technologies and statistical support were in place to resume War Communism on a sounder foundation.

Dead Hand of the Past

This meant that whichever option was picked, technical improvements assured that Russian economic performance in the 1930s should have been better than under War Communism. State leasing combined with state enterprise profit maximizing and VSNKh regulation should have lead ultimately to a mixed market socialist consumer sovereign regime for household goods, and perhaps to representative democracy; that is, to an authentic socialist "revolution." Administrative command planning by contrast would have retained the dictatorship over the proletariat, but provided more goods for defense and the collective larder, distributed equally, or on whatever incentive basis Stalin preferred.

But these prospects should not obscure the fact that Russia's NEP economy and evolutionary trajectory were pre-modern in their reliance on ad hoc rent granting, rent-seeking administrative methods, agrarian communal regulation, insider networking, and the authoritarian rule of men. Although performance could be improved, all options remained far removed from the idea of the West. Individual economic, political, and civil rights were circumscribed, and consumer sovereignty marred by Lenin's contempt for the rule of law. Russia during the 1920s may have been moving in better directions, but its progress was still impeded not only by Bolshevik dogma, but by the partial criminalization of private property, business, and entrepreneurship and the dead hand of its Muscovite past.[9]

The Passion according to St. Joseph

Few have examined NEP with a dry eye. Instead of approaching socialist construction with an appreciation of Russia's Muscovite legacy, and a dispassionate assessment of its technical options, Bolsheviks and other observers have preferred to cast the challenges of recovery, modernization, and development as a passion story pitting the forces of economic liberalism against the promise of command planning. Lenin throughout is the seer, whose acolytes seek to fathom his policy twists and turns, and divine his intentions from a Marxist perspective after his death caused by a cerebral hemorrhage on January 21, 1924. Their job isn't to scientifically evaluate the positive and normative potential of contending strategies and policies, given prevailing institutions and rules, but to assess how to avert the snares of capitalism by undeviatingly following the correct Leninist line. As with all such exegetical approaches, this mission was portrayed as a contest between misguided sectarians, ultimately resolved by the heroic intervention of Lenin's true heir, Joseph Vissarionovich Djugashvili (Stalin).

The "passion" attributes Bolshevik economic woes to the "class struggle," which could have been overcome in only two ways: peacefully transforming everyone into productive workers, or violently "liquidating" capitalists as a "class." The first path begins with Lenin's "worker–peasant" alliance, and builds on it by transforming communal farmers into state lessees, collectivized agrarian industrial workers, private farmers, and some laborers into socialist entrepreneurs. The second, rescinds leasing and nascent private farming, forcibly collectivizes, and substitutes a natural economic planned, physically managed order.

Scripture can be cited for both doctrines. On one hand, Lenin clearly supported commodity exchange after March 1921, but on the other, NEP was often described as tactical maneuver, pending a renewed effort at building a comprehensive state production and rationing mechanism. In a series of articles and books, subsequently labeled the "The Great Debate,"[10] Nikolai Bukharin championed the cause of state leasing and some private individual peasant farming. He contended that it would strengthen the worker peasant alliance, promote stability, and allow Russia to gradually evolve into a market socialist system on a "peasant nag." To drive home the point, he exhorted the peasants to "enrich themselves" and warned his opponents that a more confrontational strategy could rekindle the "scissors" crisis and risk civil discord.[11]

Evgeny Preobrazhensky and Leon Trotsky staked out the counter-position. They didn't explicitly advocate "liquidating" the peasants or wealthy farmers (kulaks) as a class, but insisted that they would have to be heavily taxed to finance proletarian industrialization. These elements were declared to be the only available sources for "primitive socialist capital accumulation," and the peasants couldn't be spared because industry in the Soviet Union was on the verge of collapse. Preobrazhensky warned that due to more than a decade of neglect, the Russian capital stock had become obsolete and was in an acute state of physical decay. Unless the peasantry was pressed to finance rapid re-capitalization, the Soviet capital stock would crumble, putting Bolshevik power in jeopardy.[12] This scare talk created a sense of urgency. As the left characterized it, the Bolsheviks' choice was socialism, now or never.

Chto delat? (What should be done?) The technical cases for both scenarios were feeble at best, but this was irrelevant. It didn't matter whether agriculture had a comparative cost advantage as Lev M. Shanin asserted,[13] or growth should be maximized in accordance with G. A. Feldman's model.[14] The right question from the Marxist standpoint was "What would Lenin have wanted his disciples to do?" And here the answer turned partly on a political assessment of the regime's vulnerability, but more importantly on partisan intrigue. Stalin proved to be the master of backstage alliance building and consequently it was his exegesis that carried the day in installments. First, he attacked Trotsky and Preobrazhensky for conspiring to subvert the worker–peasant alliance, but soon attacked Bukharin for mis-appraising the peasant threat, before finally resolving the ostensible contradiction by forcibly imposing Lenin's scheme for the collectivized industrialization of agriculture on the peasantry. The correct Leninist path in this way was revealed to be herding the peasantry into collective farms where they could be compelled to finance the Soviet Union's primitive socialist accumulation[15] and be forcibly repressed if they resisted.[16] The facts were neither here nor there.[17] Numbers could always be concocted. What counted in the final analysis was Stalin's despotic temperament and his ability to package his totalitarianism as Leninist orthodoxy.

Collectivization

Soviet literature portrayed Stalin's decision to forcibly collectivize agriculture as a sine qua non of socialist development because it allowed Command Communism to feed urban workers while they manufactured equipment that would soon supercharge agrarian productivity. Preobrazhensky earlier called this "primitive socialist accumulation." James Millar subsequently found that this sequencing was incorrect; that the surplus ran the other way because more resources were transferred to agriculture than to industry. The matter can be variously interpreted. The important point to grasp however isn't the direction of net transfer, but the larger fact that collectivization was an economic disaster, not a success because it despotically repressed agrarian economic liberty and better results could have been achieved in both sectors with more sensible policies. The destruction of private farming was unjustified.

NEP in the Crooked Mirror of Dogma and Fraudulent Statistics

How did Lenin's NEP state leasing and industrial management rationalization strategies fare? If Stalin is to be believed, the positive effects of state leasing as Lenin had foreseen were transient. Leasing initially promoted recovery but soon became an

Table 4.1 Soviet economic performance: 1917–1928 (1917 = 100)

	1928
Net material product	170
New capital formation	120
Industry	180
producers goods	190
consumers goods	180
Freight	140
rail freight	150

Source: *Narodnoe khoziaistvo za 60 let, iubileinyi statisticheskii ezhegodnik, Statistika*, Moscow, 1977, pp. 9, 12, 167

Table 4.2 Soviet socialist economic activities (shares)

	1924	*1928*	*1929*
Capital, excluding herds	58.9	65.7	—
National income	25.0	44.0	61.0
Industry	76.3	82.4	—
Gross agricultural output	1.5	3.3	—
Retail trade	47.5	76.4	86.5

Sources: *Narodnoe khoziaistvo za 60 let, iubileinyi statisticheskii ezhegodnik*, Statistika, Moscow, 1977, p. 9. Alec Nove, *An Economic History of the U.S.S.R.*, Pelican, Baltimore, 1972, pp. 136–7. The figures for 1929 are taken from Nove

obstacle to industrial modernization. Ceteris paribus, one might expect the statistical record to show a brisk recovery, followed by pronounced industrial growth retardation due to leasing, under-investment, and a rapidly obsolescing capital stock. Alternatively, if NEP had primitivized the economy by strengthening the *mir* and *obshchina* and degraded industrial profit seeking compared with the Czarist norm, then it should not have fully recovered to superior prewar levels, nor grown swiftly thereafter.

Does the record corroborate Stalin or Adam Smith? It contradicts both. Table 4.1 assembles key evidence. The data indicate that national income (Marxist net material product) and industrial output advanced remarkably (1917–28). NMP grew at a 4.9 and industry a 5.5 percent compound annual rate. Since recovery purportedly was achieved by 1926 from the depths of the War Communist hyper-depression, NMP and industry catapulted ahead (1926–8) at compound annual rates of 30.3 and 34.2 percent. Clearly there is no post-recovery slowdown to justify forced collectivization and reversion to pre-modern communal arrangements ostensibly increased productivity growth.

The official record does not provide any indication that class enemies were gathering strength, or the state sector receding. The data in table 4.2 demonstrate that the socialist (state) component of all activities was increasing everywhere. By 1929, the socialist sphere accounted for 66 percent of the capital stock, 61 percent of national income, and more than 80 percent of industrial output and retail trade. The nepmen menace was nowhere in sight.

Table 4.3 Class composition of Soviet labor (millions)

	1913	*1924*	*1928*
Workers and employees	17.0	14.8	17.6
Collective farmers	—	1.3	2.9
Bourgeoisie, landowners, traders, kulaks	16.3	8.5	4.6

Source: *Narodnoe khoziaistvo za 60 let, iubileinyi statisticheskii ezhegodnik*, Statistika, Moscow, 1977, p. 8

This impression is corroborated in table 4.3 by the decline of the capitalist class, (bourgeoisie, landowners, traders, and kulaks) which shrank 72 percent (1913–28) and the increasing numbers of workers, employees, and collective farmers. Bolshevik power was secure from all perspectives and Stalin had the luxury of gradually shepherding NEP in the direction he desired. His decision to attack the peasantry rather than fine tune NEP thus appears rash and despotic.[18]

But there is another possibility. Perhaps the economy hadn't recovered and was sputtering. Perhaps the growth statistics were fraudulent. Agriculture reattained the 1913 level by the mid-1920s according to official statistics. But perhaps it really hadn't, as would be expected from the confiscation of landlord estates, repartition of leaseholds to the poor peasants, and hostility toward kulaks. Superior performance moreover was ideologically suspect, suggesting lower average agrarian productivity, reduced domestic crop marketings, and diminished grain exports.[19] Urban reality was similarly inconsistent with the industrial growth statistics. Despite the sharp decline in the working class during War Communism, unemployment was 1.46 million in 1924, or 17 percent of the labor force and remained stubbornly high thereafter.[20] As Preobrazhensky ceasely insisted net investment was negative and the capital stock was diminishing. How then could industrial production have skyrocketed (1926–28) in excess of 30 percent per annum? What could have accounted for the surge in factor productivity? Nothing! This conundrum proved to be symptomatic, not unique. During the 1980s official Soviet statistics reported rapid growth, while Gorbachev insisted that the economy was stagnant.

As with Stalin's later statistics, the most likely explanation is that the data were bogus. NEP is best conceived as an intensification of pre-modern communal arrangements in agriculture and a muddled effort to find some kind of workable surrogate for Czarist market enterprise in industry and commerce with "red and white" hatted managerial appointees replacing their privileged aristocratic predecessors in state industrial contracting (rent-granting/rent-seeking).

The real NEP problematic wasn't just to design a socialist economic system that could work, but to break decisively with the Muscovite legacy of rule of men, ambiguous and dysfunctional proprietary privileges, insider favoritism, and authoritarianism that shackled Russia to its pre-modern past. From an enlightenment perspective, the best ideologically feasible course would have been to pursue mixed market socialism, continuously expanding economic liberty as far as popular egalitarian sentiment allowed. But Stalin was a product of the very culture he sought to change and succumbed to its despotic impulse.

The Analytics of NEP

The behavioral properties and potential of NEP economy can be illustrated geometrically with the tools elaborated in chapter 2, figures 2.3–2.6. Starting with the factor space (Edgeworth–Bowley input-production box), imagine an ideal version of state leasing socialism where factor characteristics (e.g. labor skills, and capital engineering specifications), input supplies, and technologies reflect consumer sovereign preferences, given optimal, state imposed income and wealth distributions. The real supply of factors will be substantially smaller than the ideal because capital capacity was under-utilized during NEP, and the stock itself was shrinking according to Preobrazhensky. Land similarly was inadequately maintained and former capitalist managers were denied equal opportunity. A large portion of the industrial labor force returned to the countryside and new arrivals in agrarian communes weren't permitted to put their skills to best use. As a consequence of all these forces the dimensions of the Edgeworth–Bowley box, both the capital and labor vectors were much larger than under War Communism, but smaller than ideal. (Capital and labor with inferior characteristics are normalized into fewer units of ideal capital at the optimal marginal rate of transformation.)

Production in the ideal (figure 2.3), and real Edgeworth–Bowley (figure 4.1), boxes occurs when factors are inserted into enterprise production functions (isoquants) for either or both goods arrayed on the southwest and northeast origins (q_1 and q_2). The production functions for these activities are depicted as nested sets of isoquants radiating from each origin. Output levels are indicated by the superscripts. Larger numbers indicate higher production. The superscripts displayed in figure 4.1 were all lower than ideal because existing technologies, capital and labor weren't put to best use. Skilled workers and former capitalist managers often were driven into farming and VSNKh supervisors didn't harness production potentials. Likewise, viewing NEP as a whole, technology wasn't optimally modernized and again according to Preobrazhensky was permitted to depreciate and obsolesce. Consequently, output and total productivity for any combination of outputs along the actual NEP "market Bolshevik" contract curve were far below potential, although better than they had been under War Communism.

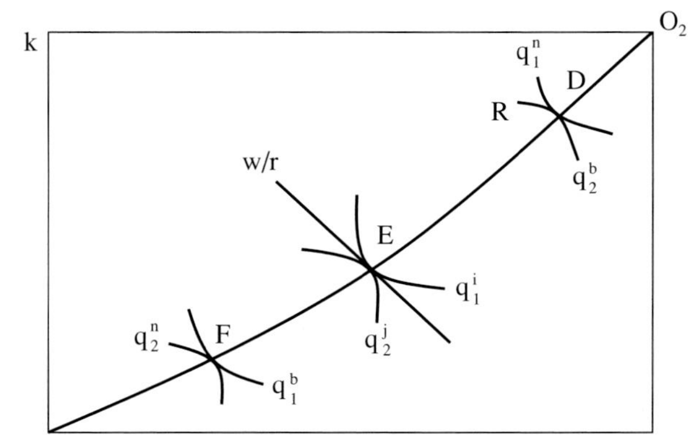

Figure 4.1 NEP factor-production space

Moreover, efficiency was further degraded because production didn't occur at point E, the ideal double tangency on the real NEP contract curve because Marshallian quantity, and Walrasian price adjustment mechanisms were constrained by arbitrary state regulations, and often malfunctioned. The assortment of goods and services produced at point F, D, or R were suboptimal, and marginal technical rates of factor substitution weren't uniform. The latter condition meant that output in one activity could always have been increased by reallocating factors along one of the isoquants, without diminishing the production of the other good.

We know these inefficiencies were real and significant because the Soviet Union didn't devise an operation planning mechanism until 1928; authority over production was jointly vested in VSNKh administrators and red directors who for the most part were prohibited from maximizing profits, indispensable for the effective operation of the Marshallian quantity adjustment mechanism; and the Walrasian price adjustment mechanism only functioned in segments of the agrarian sector, selected state-to-state exchanges, and for leaseholds. Moreover, moral hazard created by state ownership, and the absence of the rule of law, together with market power severely impaired whatever Marshallian and Walrasian processes were operative.

The same phenomenon can be visualized alternatively with the aid of the production possibilities frontier (the contract curve for ideal NEP market Bolshevism), and a corresponding production feasibilities frontier derived from the actual NEP contract curve. These frontiers depicted in figure 4.2 make it easy to see that the NEP economy wasn't just minimally economically and technically inefficient at point E″. It was severely under-productive generating a GDP at point N far below ideal NEP potential and feasibilities because it lacked effective Marshallian and Walrasian adjustment mechanisms. (The set of all points N in figure 4.1 may or may not define a continuously sub-feasibility frontier, insertable into figure 4.2.) The state monopoly of banking and finance further aggravated matters. Entrepreneurs were unable to borrow loanable funds.

These supply side woes were compounded by distributional inefficiencies. While Lenin doubtlessly carried egalitarian rationing too far under War Communism,

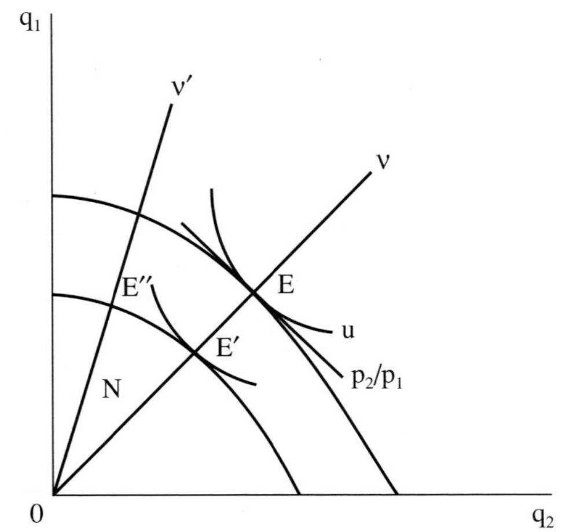

Figure 4.2 NEP production possibilities

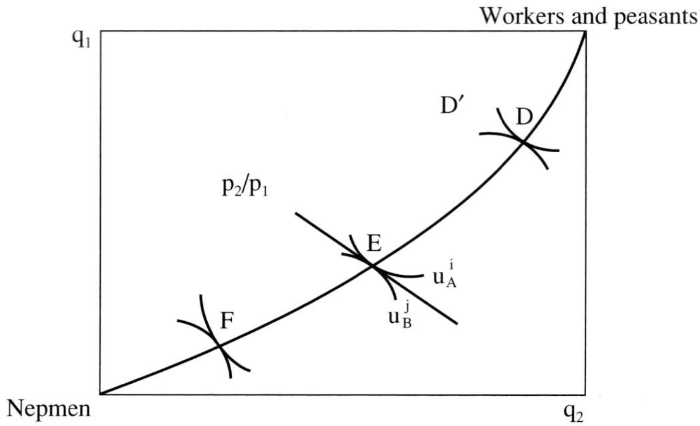

Figure 4.3 NEP distribution

widening inequality thereafter didn't make NEP efficient because moral hazard, adverse selection, and market power enabled VSNKh insiders and some nepmen to acquire large unearned incomes that would have been eliminated in an ideal, competitive market Bolshevik regime. This distortion is illustrated by point D′ in figure 4.3, which shows that nepmen and administrative insiders not only received an inordinately large share of NEP GDP, but the distribution itself was inefficient. Workers and peasants could have been made better off without diminishing the utility of the privileged on the NEP contract distribution curve.

Finally, the utility possibilities and feasibilities frontiers displayed in figure 4.4 reveal that while the extreme inefficiencies of NEP lowered social welfare from the market socialist ideal at E, to point D, the powerful and corrupt prospered.

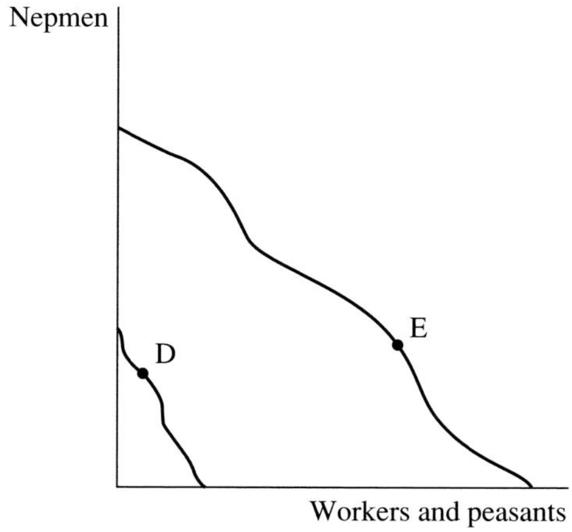

Figure 4.4 NEP utility possibilities

Review

Lenin's New Economic Policy was a tactical retreat from requisitioning and rationing that sought to enlist "controlled" market forces for the sake of economic recovery. Private property for the most part remained criminalized, but state agents, commercial entrepreneurs, and peasants were permitted to profit seek. This risked capitalist "infection" from a Marxist point of view, and more subtly, the greater menace of Market Muscovy, akin to the post-Communist experience under Boris Yeltsin. Statistics showed that the benefits seemed worth the risks, but many, including Stalin, ultimately concluded that NEP was ideologically and pragmatically undesirable, regardless of the numbers. The episode ended symbolically with forced collectivization, but more importantly, was scuttled by the recriminalization of business and entrepreneurship.

Systems Profile

Main features of the NEP economic system

- *Culture*: Muscovite authoritarian/anti-authoritarian, with a proletarian reformist bent. Anti-authoritarianism is a mix of passivity (withdrawal into agrarian communalism) and opportunism (insider and outsider moral hazard created by state leasing, and politburo intrigue).
- *Motivation*: "Velvet" societal domination, and great power building (partially through the vehicle of the Third International workers movement, founded March 4, 1919), with some attraction to market socialism.
- *Mechanism*: Natural resources, land and the entire industrial and administrative means of production were state owned and controlled. (Although peasants acted as if the land were theirs, and didn't pay explicit ground rent to the state.) Agrarian communal, and some cooperative, and farm capital were privately held. State leasing was the pillar of private small-scale commerce, industry, and professional activity, with a maximum of 20 hired employees, who together with state transactors, peasants, and households constituted the NEP market. The state regulated and controlled the market with multiple instruments. Since the lion's share of the capital stock was owned and controlled by the state, the market was authoritarian Bolshevik in character, not capitalist. NEP markets were preferential, imperfectly competitive, and prone to moral hazard. Industrial finance and banking were state monopolies. The industrial sector, and derivatively the national economy, was administered by VSNKh, the Supreme Economic Council. Managers called "red directors" were appointed by the state, and only gradually acquired functional autonomy. Administration and production were lumped together, until enterprises slowly were put on a self-financing (*khozraschyot*) basis. Most non-agrarian laborers were state employees or leaseholders. The state set most wages, and workers became increasingly powerless as trade unions and worker councils were subordinated to

state authority. Planning gained momentum throughout NEP. Initially it was employed as a guideline, but became more coercive over time. The rule of men predominated, and leaseholders weren't protected by the rule of law. The USSR was a one-party state, which had sovereignty over the provision of public goods.

- *Institutions*: NEP featured state ownership of means of production, land, and natural resources (but peasants were convinced that the land was theirs regardless of state nationalization); agrarian communes (*mir* and *obshchina*), state business leasing in industry, commerce, distribution, and professions. There were some private farms on state lands. Other important institutions included VSNKh (Supreme Economic Council), STO (Labor and Defense Council), cooperatives, captive trade unions and worker councils, state business and foreign trade monopolies, and the Politburo.

Main inefficiencies

- *Law of demand*: State commandeering, requisitioning, forced substitution, monopoly demand for labor, privileged access to goods and services.
- *Law of supply*: Worker supply curves were weak functions of wages because of high urban industrial unemployment. Adverse selection was widespread in the supply of leasehold seekers. Agrarian communalism made private farming a weak function of rates of return. Industrial production was weakly responsive to price and profit incentives. Absence of rule of law created endemic moral hazard, and corruption.
- *Law of equilibration*: Intra-state unplanned VSNKh requisitioning and rationing was an ad hoc process until 1928. First five-year plan commences in 1928. Material balance approach adopted to match plan supplies with plan uses. This was a non-price negotiated, administrative method. The NEP market with state, leaseholder, peasant, and household participation used both Marshallian and Walrasian adjustment mechanisms, combining aspects of "consumer choice and "weak" consumer sovereignty, subject to state regulation as in the Lange model. Moral hazard and adverse selection were severe problems due to the absence of the rule of contract law. Walrasian labor market equilibration had some force in the leasehold sector, but little impact on communal farming, and virtually none in state industrial employment where unions and worker councils negotiating for workers were subordinate to the state and communist party. Keynesian macro equilibration was impaired by absence of a link between household consumption and investment (no multiplier effect) and excessive risk faced by would-be leasehold investors. Also, there were no competitive money or loanable funds markets. The state was a monopolist in investment and finance.

Tactics of NEP economic management

Topic	*Problem*	*State response*
State ownership	Circumscribes individual utility-seeking	State leasing and contracting
NEP leasing	Moral hazard, adverse selection, inegalitarianism, private power over state sector	Strengthen accountability with *khozraschyot*, increased oversight
Agrarian farming, communes	Pre-modern, inefficient	Encourage independent or collective farms
Capital obsolescence, shrinking stock	Diminished productivity and growth	Increase transfer of agrarian surplus, expand capital goods production
Scissors crisis	Reduces export revenue for purchase of foreign technology	Improve terms of trade for agriculture, later increased coercive effectiveness
Unemployment	Wasted potential	None. No macro-regulatory policy
Development	Pre-modern economy and culture	Assessed problem from the prism of class struggle, instead of fostering a deeper Muscovite cultural transformation

Systemic structure	*Share of GDP*	*Productivity*	*Coercion*
Markets			
Perfect markets	0	–	–
Inefficient markets	10	Low	Low
Collusive markets	10	Low	High
State	50	Low	High
Obligation			
Communal agriculture	30	Low	Moderate

Systemic characteristics	*Degree/intensity*
State macro-regulation	None
State micro-regulation	
Pro-competitive	None
Welfare/security	Low
industrial	Moderate
nepmen/peasants	None
Public works programs	Low
Criminal dis-services, rent-seeking/embezzlement	Moderate

Causes of macroeconomic disequilibrium	
Sticky wages and benefits	Moderate
Sticky prices	Moderate
Investment avoidance	Extremely high
Capital flight	None
Misinvestment	High
Liquidity preference	Negligible
Insecure private property rights	Extremely high
State property rights	Extremely high
Foreign capital flows	None
Fear of criminality	Low
Business repression	Very high
Labor subjugation	High
Judicial risk	Extremely high
State corruption	High
Macro-policy mismanagement	Very high
Class conflict	Very high

Main performance indicators

Per capita GDP (Bergson) (US = 100)	15–30
Maddison	12–23
Per capita GDP growth 1917–29 (table 3.1/Eason table 11.9/p. 72)	–3 to 4
Unemployment	15+
Retirement support burden	None
Nonworking mothers and wives	Low

Direction of reforms

Tug of war between expansion of socialist markets and reversion to pure physical systems management (commandeering, planning and rationing).

Questions

1 Lenin revoked the nationalization of small industrial enterprise in 1921. Were expropriated properties returned to their owners?
2 Could individuals buy these properties from the state?
3 Was de-nationalization a misnomer?
4 The Bolsheviks nationalized land and resources, but allowed agrarian communes and individual farmers to treat the land as theirs, including buying and selling it

for agrarian use. Did this arrangement mimic that of the Czars? Could Bolshevik crop and property taxes be construed as implicit rents paid to the state landlord? Explain.

5 What were state industrial and commercial leaseholds?

6 Were the private business rights conferred by leasing fully comparable to those in the West? Why not?

7 Nepmen (private business "owners") and state "red directors" had fewer economic rights and privileges than their Western cousins. List the economic "liberties" denied Russian businessmen and explain how they impaired individual utility maximizing.

8 How did circumscribed opportunities affect product characteristics, production, distribution, and income distribution?

9 What is "consumer choice"? Did the Russian people have it? Was it restricted?

10 What is "consumer sovereignty"? Did Russia have it? Was it constrained?

11 Who was economically sovereign in NEP Russia?

12 What is moral hazard? Why was it especially grave in NEP Russia?

13 What is adverse selection? How did it affect the behavior of "red directors" and other VSNKh officials?

14 What is Langean market socialism? Is the NEP model consistent with it? Explain.

15 How could the NEP industrial sector have been transformed to full market socialism?

16 What steps were being taken in this direction?

17 How could the NEP agrarian sector have been transformed to full market socialism?

18 What steps were being taken in this direction?

19 What would have been the benefits of full market socialism?

20 How would full market socialism have differed from full market free enterprise?

21 Why is moral hazard and adverse selection more troublesome for full market socialism than free enterprise?

22 Did the Bolsheviks employ neo-classical Pareto efficiency theory to analyze whether market socialism, free enterprise, or physical systems management was best for Russia?

23 What Marxist principles were applied to evaluate systems options?

24 Were these principles more a matter of exegetic authority than scientific analysis of concrete alternatives?

25 Why did the Bolsheviks construct their assessments in terms of left-wing and right-wing deviations? Was this scientific?

26 What are the four basic aspects of Muscovite culture shaping Russian economic behavior?

27 How did these cultural influences manifest themselves under NEP?

28 Did these influences maintain or intensify pre-modern arrangements and behavior?

29 Did these influences help or hinder the development of market socialism? Explain.

30 Did these influences help or hinder the construction of a pure physical management system? Explain.

31 Did Muscovite culture subvert the Bolsheviks' socialist intent?

32 What is the evidence that NEP was economically successful?

33 What is the evidence that NEP jeopardized Soviet power?

34 Are official NEP economic statistics plausible from the standpoint of Pareto efficiency theory and Russia's pre-modern legacy?
35 Was Stalin's abandonment of market socialism necessary? Explain.
36 What was Stalin's rationale for forced collectivization? Was it valid?
37 Was Stalin's forced collectivization necessary?
38 Was NEP socialist? Given the introduction of differentiated wages and salaries and nepmen's profits and capital gains, what other than state ownership made NEP socialist?

5

Command Communism: 1929–1953

Summary

Supporters of Command Communism maintain that while the west was ravaged by the Great Depression, the Soviet Union was enjoying overfull employment, price stability, rapid industrialization, modernization, brisk growth, a flourishing proletarian culture, and economic justice without neglecting national security. These triumphs are ascribed to five-year command planning and agrarian collectivization. Whatever may have transpired later, it is argued, does not diminish Stalin's accomplishments. The devil must be given his due.

Stalin's pride and the font of Soviet industrial achievement (1929–53) was "*piatiletki*" (five-year planning), broadly construed as a natural economic assignment formulating mechanism, an administrative and implementery process, as well as an incentive and disciplinary regime, all of which supplanted NEP market leasing, while retaining state ownership. *Piatiletki* are best conceived as the confluence of a top-down aspirational extrapolation process and bottom-up procedures relying heavily on red director expertise, incentivized initiative, and inter enterprise contracting. The bottom-up procedures provided the center with draft "*tekhpromfinplany*" (technical industrial, financial draft plans) designed to maximize output and red director bonuses, which were reconciled with centrally drafted control figures and aggregated by supervisiory officials up the command chain, including Gosplan (the State Planning Agency) and Stalin. A considerable amount of information was lost by the time Stalin had his say, but the structure was restored down the command chain when assignments were disaggregated.

Approved *tekhpromfin* macro-plans diverged significantly from initial drafts. Stalin demanded more output and provided fewer resources, but this wasn't crucial because whatever the formal assignments, red directors were incentivized and required to maximize output on a prioritized basis, satisfying the military industrial complex first, then heavy industrial and other state entities on a contractual basis, with households left as residual claimants. Red directors were overseen by ministerial superiors, party officials, and the secret police. Although moral hazard was an omnipresent problem, resources were mobilized and overfully employed. Priorities were honored and the proletariat scraped by, all more or less as Stalin desired.

The Soviet economy under these circumstances was able to grow, industrialize, and develop by skimping on current consumption, prioritizing capital goods production, increasing capital-output ratios (capital widening), improving technology, transferring technology from abroad, enhancing know-how, shifting peasants to industrial occupations, and upgrading education. Although, household demand was largely disregarded, quality poor, prices non-negotiable and resources couldn't be competitively allocated to best use; mobilization was sufficient to assure the macroeconomic basics: overfull employment, price stability, and economic growth during the initial phase of Soviet industrialization. But the model wasn't sustainable. Central planning proved to be a weak mechanism for innovation, technological development, transfer and diffusion. Once the limits of overfull employment, harsh labor discipline, labor reallocation from agriculture to industry, population growth, and educational improvement had been reached, and diminishing returns to capital widening set in, output growth was bound to be inferior, and negligible after adjustment for qualitative shortcomings. *Piatiletki* in the long run were both macro- and microeconomically deficient.

New archival information blurs this characterization. Planning has proven to be more ad hoc and top down, closer to monkey business than a process of rational control, casting doubt on the level and pattern of reported performance and causation.

This reality contrasts starkly with Stalin's contention that agrarian collectivization and *piatiletki*, were the touchstones of unparalleled communist prosperity. Collectivization was a calamity, and *piatiletki* were merely guidelines for requisitioning, rationing, and muddling through.

The best laid plans "mice an' men Gang aft agley. An' lea' e us nought but grief an' pain, For promis'd joy!"

Robert Burns, "To A Mouse, On Turning Up Her Nest With the Plough," November 1775

Piatiletki

Joseph Stalin ruled Russia for a quarter century. His reign was a tale of two surrealities: contrasting images of miraculous communist economic development and wrenching despotism. The truth is difficult to extract, and best approached by focusing on neoclassical fundamentals, before turning to Marxist historical narratives.

Piatiletki (five-year plans) are the Soviet Union's seminal contribution to economic science. They epitomize what many have argued was the world's first viable socialist economic model, utilizing modern statistical, computational, and analytic methods in lieu of markets or primitive requisition and rationing. The earliest human records suggest that homo sapiens as rational utility seekers always have had the capacity to anticipate, evaluate, and prepare for alternative futures. They were able to implement plans independently, or through persuasion and coercion where success required the participation of others. Five-year planning wasn't revolutionary in any of these senses. Its novelty lay in the belief that the natural economy could be rationally and comprehensively programmed without market assistance. Where it previously had been thought that value driven markets were the surest path to prosperity, Stalin claimed that five-year planning consigned free enterprise to the dustpan of history with supply-side methods responsive to what Abram Bergson has called "systems directors'" preferences. Bolsheviks insisted that five-year planning was better than free enterprise both in practice and theory. Pareto social welfare optima in their view were warped by capitalist commercialism. The goods people craved weren't what they needed and often were detrimental to their well-being. Planners by contrast, knew precisely what products were required to maximize communist welfare, and how best to produce them, generating superior welfare optima. Five-year planning wasn't just feasible, it was the key to building communism, and this it was claimed together with rationalized industrial administration and *tekhpromfinplanning* explained why Command Communism succeeded where War communism failed.

Piatiletki ideally were constructed bottom up from proposed enterprise "*tekhpromfinplany*" (technical, industrial, and financial plans), drafted by red directors, and other pertinent production data from all sectors reported to Goskomstat (the State Statistical Agency), synthesized and adjusted by ministries, glavks, and Gosplan.[1] Red directors under VSNKh and later the Council of Economic Ministers in this conceptualization were obliged to prepare preliminary production plans early for the following year based on prior achieved levels, and any new tasks assigned to them. This entailed a complete elaboration of new plant and equipment needs, variable input requirements, support from the state bank to finance wages, proposed production targets, and delivery schedules. These documents provided by more than thirty thousand industrial enterprises[2] ran hundreds of pages.[3] After a sequence of consultations and negotiations with superior administrators, guided by aspirational control figures independently formulated above, composites were prepared and dispatched to Gosplan for further aggregation, reconciliation and balancing (material balancing matched estimated input supplies with designated uses). Preliminary annual plans were then compiled, reviewed by Stalin, adjusted (material re-balanced), approved, dis-aggregated and transformed into legally binding *tekhpromfinplan* assignments for implementation during the next plan year. The aggregate annual plan prepared in this way served as the basis for constructing five-year plans for each quinquennium. Central planners taking the most recent aggregate plan as their benchmark, extrapolated requirements for subsequent years based on prior plan accomplishments, and new tasks imposed by the political leadership.

These mechanics were sound. A planning pyramid couldn't be built from the top down alone because Gosplan as the capstone wasn't sufficiently acquainted with enterprise micro-assortment and production capabilities. Soviet firms produced twenty-five million distinct goods with a wide array of engineering technologies. Gosplan even in

Material Balancing

Soviet central planners under Command Communism and Reform Communism continuously compiled and updated thousands of resource inventories and accounting balances ("material balances") showing how input supplies should be distributed. Central and *tekhpromfinplans* were obsolete from the moment they were approved because nothing ever went according to expectation, making material balances an indispensable, if nonetheless ad hoc, tool of physical systems management. Although, input–output analysis, linear programming and aggregate production functions were employed centrally in the construction of annual and five-year plans, material balances in the popular literature often were conflated with planning in its entirety.

the most favorable circumstances would have been overwhelmed if it tried to centrally acquire, store, and process this information. The architects of *piatiletki* therefore by default allowed red directors to grapple with much of the detail by aggregating the subcategories of inputs and outputs into standardized sets typically consisting of six labor grades, fifteen types of material inputs, and thirty composite goods, after using the full information set to compute their *tekhpromfinplans* for further processing by ministries and *glavks*. The quality of *piatiletki* depended critically on this micro-optimization because it was supposed to reflect the production potential and optimal assortments of multi-product firms, magnified by a large factor. Each product category listed in the *tekhpromfinplan* subsumed hundreds or even thousands of sub-products (e.g. types of fasteners, or candy).[4] If the micro-assortments red directors intended to produce didn't correspond with the needs of intermediate input users, the real production potential of the system might be far below the capabilities indicated by the planned composites.

The risk that *piatiletki* might be radically disconnected from micro-production and assortment potentials increased as draft *tekhpromfinplans* were modified and aggregated up the chain of command into a set of short menus for Stalin's deliberation. Administrative supervisors, political authorities, and Gosplan itself were empowered to arbitrarily pare composite input supply requests and increase output directives or resolve paper imbalances among *tekhpromfinplans*. Although Gosplan was supposed to prepare one plan for each of the 25 million goods produced, based on 7,000 material balances, accompanied by 750,000 distributional balances (accounts matching estimated output supplies with their designated wholesale distribution) guiding the wholesale network (Gossnabsbyt'), this number was compressed to only 150-odd composites easily understood by policy-makers like fuels, construction materials, metals, machinery, chemicals, forest products, light industrial goods, and food, but detached from the underlying micro-potentials.[5]

The leadership so informed had no difficulty instructing Gosplan to modify assortments or sectoral growth extrapolated from the preceding period, adjusted for variations in research and development outlays or new capital formation. It didn't matter if red directors and their *glavk* supervisors formed a family circle (*krugovaya poruka*) and colluded in understating enterprise potential to soften assignments. If Stalin decided that red directors and planners were too timid, he would command them to try harder, regardless of prior achieved levels, leaving Gosplan to tidy up the paper imbalances. Eugene Zaleski reports that Stalin's plans were seldom fulfilled (the mean deviation above and below plan was often more than 50 percent), suggesting that even the widely discussed tendency for red directors to underutilize capacities in order to avoid "ratched" assignments were of little avail against Stalin's high aspirations.[6] Once approved and rebalanced, the aggregate plan was then sent back down the chain of command to the ministries (roughly five composite plans per ministry), where they were disaggregated by *glavk*, and then further decomposed according to agreements reached by *glavk* administrators and red directors at the initial phase of the *tekhpromfinplanning* process.

Red directors therefore knew from experience that the directives they received in the form of approved, legally binding *tekhpromfin* micro-plans were unfulfillable either as composites, or products. Their task wasn't to do what couldn't be done, but to choose among a variety of default strategies ranging from fulfilling one or more sub-plans to falsifying results in a host of ways, within limits imposed by Gosplan's input supply authorizations. The latter was particularly important. Priority inputs couldn't be ordered from wholesale suppliers in Gossnab (the state material technical supply system), or funds released from Gosbank (the state bank) without *tekhpromfinplan* approval. Planning in this sense was critical. Red directors couldn't play or pay without it. Authorization wasn't a guarantee that enterprise managers would receive the supplies needed, but it was an indispensable step in the right direction, especially when integrated with inter-enterprise contracting. Red directors during the Stalin years were permitted, and often required to enter into input acquisition and output supply contracts with their principal sources and buyers.[7] Automobile firms provide an instructive example. Chassis, motors, wheels, tires, and other components normally were manufactured offsite and transported to a central location for assembly. Acquiring the right components just in time was essential for automotive assemblers. These needs were accommodated by bilaterally negotiated contracts ideally built into the draft *tekhpromfinplans*. Contracts weren't sacrosanct, but insofar as Gosplan's modified, approved *tekhpromfinplan* "composites" allowed contractors to honor their commitments, enterprises were able to obtain the inputs essential for manufacturing goods state buyers needed. Households were prohibited from contracting. They had to take what they could get. Low priority producers in the consumers goods sectors weren't much better off. Whenever political authorities and Gosplan cut their approved *tekhpromfinplan* supply requests, they were compelled to violate contracts in turn. But enterprises higher on the priority ladder faired better, with military industrial enterprises doing best.

The contracting components of the planning system had the further advantage of providing a semblance of quality control for priority establishments which could refuse to accept defective inputs, and even sue for damages in Soviet court. Inter-enterprise contracting in these ways was the core, and ballast of Soviet physical systems management.

Central planning thus was a two level system of control, a point sometimes missed by those who take the imagery of centralized command literally. Most component production and supply, including all the micro-details were plan-negotiated at the periphery at fixed state prices, except in the case of special order goods (one of a kind items), where transactors had some discretion over prices. The center (Stalin and Gosplan) for its part controlled aspects of contracting through party, VPK (military industrial complex), KGB (secret police) and judicial allocational priorities, and affected non-contractual operations by revising and balancing aggregate input supply and demand, which in turn governed micro input authorizations and approved *tekhpromfinplan* assignments.

This functional division meant that the center's micro-demands insofar as they were explicitly formulated were haphazardly supervised by the party, VPK, KGB, and courts. Stalin was able to dictate the macrostructure of production, and the dimensions of Gulag (the state concentration camp production subsystem), but the micro-production of consumer and other "non-essentials" was often left to red directors' discretion by default. The state was technically incapable of instructing them, or design bureaus responsible for product characteristics how to satisfy consumer demand best, while household preferences were simply disregarded. Customized consumer supply was illegal, and red directors were neither penalized if their goods went unsold, nor rewarded if households clamored for them.

The sum and substance of these complex arrangements was that while Stalin's economy was centrally macro-planned and commanded, the scope of the state's rational choice and micro-direction was limited. State agents at the periphery suppressed outside private activity and followed centrally imposed rules, but weren't nano-directed by the Kremlin. Stalin's planning architecture was conducive to, and facilitated a dual economy where the micro demand of privileged entities like the VPK and heavy industry were rational choice empowered, and those of ordinary people disregarded. In a perverse way, this partitioning was sensible, given Stalin's rejection of both socialist (NEP leasing), and capitalist markets. If suppliers were forbidden to profit maximize subject to household preferences, then the best the state could do was to make red directors responsive to important government purchasers like the Ministry of Defense, forming the foundation for what Vitaly Shlykov calls "structural militarization."

Structural Militarization

Josef Stalin created a military industrial complex (VPK) under Command Communism that became a vast empire unto itself capable of successfully lobbying the Kremlin for ever greater resources beyond any sums justified by the external threat. The VPK succeeded in this regard because Stalin shared its goals, and continued to succeed thereafter under Reform Communism for similar reasons. Even during the Yeltsin years, when weapons production fell 90 percent, VPK domains remained undiminished, ready to resume excessive arms production as indicated in Putin's military modernization plan. Vitaly Shlykov calls this systems embedded Muscovite predilection for bloated defense activities "structural militarization," a concept that dovetails with the characterization of Muscovite regimes as authoritarian martial police states.

Official descriptions of Soviet central planning hid this pragmatic dualism because Stalin wanted physical systems management to be perceived as scientifically fostering

Industry purchasing ⇒ ⇓ Industry producing	X_1 X_2 X_n	X_f X_g	X_{f*}
	Quadrant I intermediate input processing $\sum_{j=1}^{n} a_{ij} X_j$	Quadrant II final demand and gross output	
$X_p = X_f$ $X_o = X_i$	Quadrant III payments to Primary inputs Gross outlays		Quadrant IV transfers

X represents the value of an activity. The subscripts designate:
j = the jth intermediate sectoral production activity
i = the ith intermediate sectoral purchaser
f = the final purchaser of the specified sectoral output
g = the gross value of the intermediate and final deliveries
p = input payments by the jth purchasing sector
o = gross outlay by the jth producing sector

Figure 5.1 Schematic representation of transactions table of a static open input–output model

proletarian prosperity and peace, not catering to the VPK and heavy industry at the people's expense. Many Western specialists knew better, but this knowledge usually was overshadowed by a focus on the mathematical and programming aspects of the process, especially its centralized component. Material balances, input–output analysis, linear programming, and optimal incentives were treated as techniques which enabled "systems directors" to rationally control macro outcomes. Their preferences were said to be sovereign in this sense, implying that Stalin's choices governed the main contours, even though other principles determined the particulars.

The input–output table displayed in figure 5.1, developed by Wassily Leontief from pioneering research undertaken during the Czarist period by Vladimir Dmitriev illuminates the rational choice facilitating possibilities of centralized computation.[8] The matrix depicts demand and supply relationships throughout the economy, divided into four quadrants. Final demand is arrayed in quadrant II, expressed as deliveries of goods and services to households directly (X_f) and indirectly via government programs (X_g). X_f and X_g are vectors of products produced in sector X_i, which by assumption were rationally selected by Stalin and hence reflect his demand.

Table 5.1 The 1966 Soviet AFC I–O flow table

Row / *Column*	*1* *AGRIC*	*2* *FUELS*	*3* *METAL*	*4* *SM+E*	*5* *Oth M+E*	*6* *CONNAT*	*7* *CHEM*	*8* *FOOD*
1 – AGRIC	17,707990.	994.	2012.	1350.	180.	202440.	35950.	32045421.
2 – FUELS	1354525.	5721210.	2276687.	973989.	665093.	1559152.	1198363.	701172.
3 – METALS	50849.	101213.	8453005.	5453272.	2538476.	2286044.	602485.	237828.
4 – M+E	1431600.	293635.	471096.	2203997.	1382959.	542434.	123429.	204797.
5 – Oth M+E	133680.	88803.	147785.	2076302.	1509977.	162479.	56019.	69192.
6 – CONNAT	554857.	350128.	186926.	1069528.	463411.	6016634.	509163.	601930.
7 – CHEMICAL	1170613.	250451.	345476.	1575417.	356732.	701355.	4472269.	180529.
8 – FOOD	821828.	20828.	43176.	101146.	29809.	114664.	500364.	1953547.
9 – LGHT–IND	893302.	119970.	493281.	604977.	162091.	742440.	619246.	701866.
10 – CONST	0	0	0	0	0	0	0	0
11 – TRNS–COM	946271.	1572970.	1454356.	1259608.	475780.	2442910.	649590.	1118016.
12 – TRADE	861829.	315608.	280959.	259332.	115884.	253710.	94407.	1270521.
13 – MATPURCH	25927244.	8835818.	14154758.	20598918.	7700391.	15024263.	8881281.	36860619.
14 – DEPREC	4771400.	2846418.	1577109.	1571024.	568404.	1847302.	160810	958669.
15 – WAGES	29511125.	4094251.	3240911.	7763619.	2509323.	7022149.	1467617.	2951976.
16 – OTH–V.A.	21731577.	2607634.	4103171.	9927952.	2069707.	5121627.	3881781.	2881970.
17 – DEFLAFD	–420187.	–105328.	–47362.	–722413.	–331222.	–201961.	–153682.	–2928394.
18 – K–SERV	4028081.	2583159.	1283615.	1241861.	448740.	1257203.	628489.	787947.
19 – RENT	0	1699270.	0	0	0	0	0	
20 – PROFLOSS	–185922.	–324957.	–219445.	269762.	143268.	–293421.	–318157.	260339.
21 – V.A.	59456074.	13400367.	9946999.	20053805.	5408219.	14750702.	6266868.	4912507.
22 – GVO	85383310.	22236185.	24101757.	40652723.	13108611.	29774973.	15148149.	61781126.
23 –	0	0	0	0	0	0	0	0
24 – LABOR	30817030.	2172400.	1907600.	6074823.	1963477.	5593000.	1113100.	2653700.
25 – CAPITAL	71733676.	46889112.	22916599.	22144165.	8060532.	22560781.	11240317.	14049922.

Row / *Column*	*9* *LGHT–IND*	*10* *CONST*	*11* *TRNS+COM*	*12* *TRADE*	*13* *INTERSEC*	*14* *FINDEM*	*15* *GVO*
1 – AGRIC	547849.	30792.	6156	81497.	56062631.	29320688.	85383318.
2 – FUELS	839906.	724149.	5658025	260906.	37933176.	4303009.	22236185.
3 – METALS	836695.	2012637.	102994	22187.	22697638.	1404119.	24101751.
4 – M+E	423451.	1760898.	621454	117269.	14576919.	26075805.	40652723.
5 – Oth M+E	100101.	178086.	346675	17446.	4706545.	8402066.	13308611.
6 – CONNAT	1944006.	12588301.	195654	508044.	25180582.	4594391.	29774973.
7 – CHEMICAL	2506821.	617097.	480557	91455.	1748772.	2399377.	15148149.
8 – FOOD	1882162.	106254.	10096	324853.	23490528.	38290598.	61781126.
9 – LGHT–IND	26668645.	2014866.	213207	537478.	33791369.	24674225.	58465594.
10 – CONST	0	0	0	0	0	45649152.	45649152.
11 – TRNS–COM	1211659.	3986856.	568103.	333205.	16019530.	5475318.	21494848.
12 – TRADE	402115.	340503.	149688	54210.	4398761.	12906376.	17305137.
13 – MATPURCH	42763408.	24360440.	4142154	2348550.	231606449.	20349123.	435101572.
14 – DEPREC	1402858.	144600.	266000.	1226000.	21657822.	0	0
15 – WAGES	5668292.	15800000.	6014185.	6747014.	92799385.	0	0
16 – OTH–V.A.	10534676.	3055136.	6849515.	5997819.	79564736.	0	0
17 – DEFLAFD	–3178866.	–1570368.	–215091	–236021.	–10110895.	0	0
18 – K–SERV	1265871.	710280.	2486440	1162920.	17884806.	0	0
19 – RENT	0	0	0	0	1699270.	0	0
20 – PROFLOSS	9355.	1047664.	–443162	56035.	0	0	0
21 – V.A.	15702185.	21288712.	17352090	34955387.	203495123.	0	0
22 – GVO	58465594.	45649152.	21494948	17305137.	435101572.	0	0
23 –	0	0	0	0	0	0	0
24 – LABOR	5615500.	11580000.	4565000	7090200.	81146600.	0	0
25 – CAPITAL	22831889.	12671626.	45284295.	20596326.	320779241.	0	0

Source: Steven Rosefielde, *The Transformation of the 1966 Soviet Input–Output table from Producers to Adjusted Factor Cost Values*, G. E. Tempo, Washington, DC, 1975

These goods were manufactured in quadrant I, that is, the inter-industrial, intermediate input production sub-matrix. Primary inputs X_p (capital, labor and land) arrayed horizontally in quadrant III by each employing sector, are combined with counterpart intermediate inputs $a_{ij}(X_j)$ obtained from itself and other sectors to produce goods for delivery to all inter-industrial uses, and final demand. The input–output table displayed in figure 5.1 in this way maps the supply of primary inputs, their use in production, and delivery to both intermediate and final purchasers. The producing activities are arrayed vertically and the purchasing activities horizontally, allowing planners to easily observe interdependencies, and use that knowledge to analyze how changes in the composition of output demanded, or primary factors supplied might effect production possibilities and growth. Where material balances estimate input supplies on an ad hoc basis, input–output makes intermediate input production and use mathematically explicit, allowing authorities to quickly, comprehensively and consistently compute multiple plan variants.

This was accomplished by assuming that the observed intermediate input–output relationships $a_{ij} = x_i/x_j$ were "technologically" fixed, creating a system of linearities (rectangular isoquants) that applied both in the past and the future.[9] For any given vector of final demand X_f, this assumption allowed planners to compute, or at least approximate the amount of primary and intermediate inputs required to support X_f with the following equation:

$$k = b(I - A)^{-1} \tag{5.1a}$$

$$X = (I - A)^{-1}X_f \tag{5.1b}$$

where $(I - A)^{-1}$ is called the inverse matrix, solvable with standard computational methods and b is a vector of direct inputs. The results could be compared with available primary and intermediate sectoral input supplies. If provisional plan demand exceeded supply, planners would have to find ways of increasing primary inputs by stimulating labor and capital participation rates, or enhancing productivity. Where supply exceeded demand, planners would decrease X proportionally and redeploy primary inputs. These exercises could then be replicated for other final product assortments, creating a set of feasible "optima" compiled for Stalin's deliberation.

Alternatively, if Stalin were able to rank his preferences, or express them as a set of relative prices (marginal rates of commodity substitution), then the same problem could be solved by inserting prices $(p_1, \ldots p_n)$ into a linear program where gross domestic product (Y) is a linear function of activity (output) levels:

$$Y = p_1q_1 + p_2q_2 + \ldots + p_nq_n \tag{5.2}$$

where p_j the fixed price received per unit of q_j. Gosplan then could select particular activity levels such that Y is as large as possible. It is not entirely free in choosing activity levels. The sum of the amounts of the ith input used to support the n activities cannot exceed fixed primary input allocations.

$$\begin{aligned} a_{11}q_1 + a_{12}q_2 + \ldots + a_{1n}q_n &\leq x_1^0 \\ a_{21}q_1 + a_{22}q_2 + \ldots + a_{2n}q_n &\leq x_2^0 \\ a_{m1}q_1 + a_{m2}q_2 + \ldots + a_{mn}q_n &\leq x_m^0 \end{aligned} \tag{5.3}$$

The constraints are expressed as weak inequalities, since Gosplan is free to use less than Stalin's prescribed sectoral inputs. Furthermore, the activity levels must be positive:

$$q_j \geq 0 \quad (j = 1, \ldots, m) \tag{5.4}$$

Some, or all, may be zero. Stalin's linear programming problem is to maximize (5.2) subject to the constraints given in (5.3) and (5.4), computable with the simplex method.[10]

And more ambitiously, the task could be handled cybernetically through two level programming where the shadow prices generated from the dual of Stalin's primal linear program were electronically relayed to red directors to check their supply response.[11]

Clearly scientific central choice making by Stalin and Gosplan was possible, leading many to suppose that the attainment of rational planners' sovereignty was only a matter of scale. As the size of input–output tables, linear programs, and two level planning algorithms increased, Stalin's demand would govern supply and distribution in more and more detail, until in the limit they approached a communist Pareto ideal. No wonder then that L.V. Kontorovich was awarded the Noble Prize for creating linear programming, and many westerners concluded that central planning might someday rival free enterprise.

It is essential to appreciate therefore that these potentials were science fiction. Gosplan didn't have computers in Stalin's time, and the Soviet Union was never able to build a computer programming network, or comprehensive real-time database to make planners sovereign. Political adjustments to draft *tekhpromfinplans*, affecting both assortments and growth targets weren't deeply informed by menus of alternatives computed by Gosplan, and the main computing center of Gosplan never got beyond calculating a few hundred composite goods. Despite the high hopes, and technocratic wizardry, the central authorities couldn't extend their rational choice making beyond a small number of macro indicators, narrowly supported and overseen from below by the VPK, contracting networks, communist party trouble-shooters, secret police, the courts, and the prioritization of defense and heavy industry. Planning and command were real. Gosplan computed and Stalin commanded red directors to obey, but rational nano choice making crucial to market efficiency was absent at the center, and localized in party supervisors, and contracting networks connecting the VPK and heavy industry. Soviet central planning lacked mechanisms for calculating communist marginal rates of supply transformation, and optimal marginal rates of demand substitution, and thus was inherently inferior both in theory and practice. It was better than War Communism, and sustainable, but still not very good.

Administration

The transmission of draft *tekhpromfinplans* up, and approved versions down the chain of command was both a planning and administrative operation. The ministerial system which evolved out of the VSNKh immediately after forced collectivization in 1929 is displayed in figure 5.2. It had three principal components. The Council of Economic Ministers (CEM) stood at the apex. It was composed of ministers heading 30-odd industrial sectors who interfaced with, and were superior to Gosplan, a functional rather than an executive body. The CEM was subordinated to Stalin (State Economic Directorate) and took orders directly from him and his deputies. Each representative

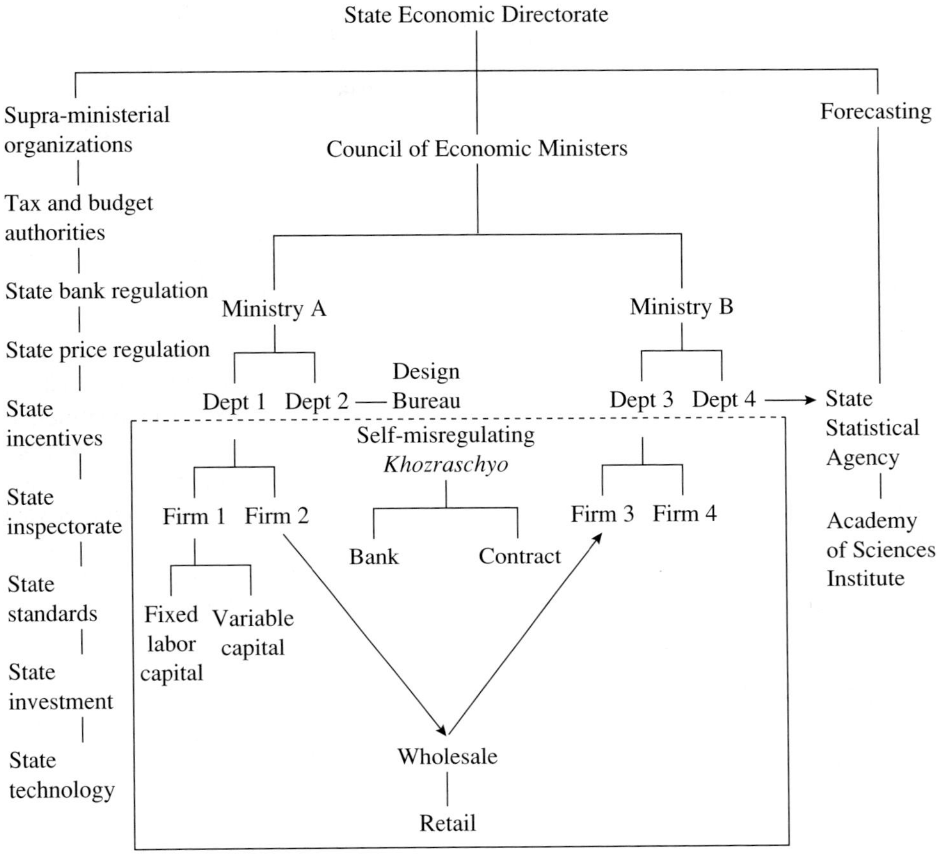

Figure 5.2 Soviet organization chart

oversaw operations in his, or her ministry, including the processing of *tekhpromfinplans* and special sectoral planning and design units attached to it. Some of this work was plan supervisory, but its most important function was sectoral plan implementation. Ministers were expected to run roughshod over red directors in their sectors, pressuring them to meet intra-sectoral needs and satisfying power centers outside their jurisdiction in other industries, branches, and the VPK. The third level of the hierarchy was called main departments, or *glavks*. These subdivisions were tasked with monitoring and implementing subsectoral planning details. The textile ministry for example was subdivided into *glavks* for cottons, woolens, silk, and synthetics. Their heads were responsible for supervising red directors producing goods under their jurisdiction. They, and their superiors all were administrative overseers and had no hand in routine enterprise management. Their activities were financed entirely from the state budget with salaries determined by rank.

Red directors by contrast were co-governed by plans, ministerial orders, party troubleshooters, VPK, secret police, and bonus incentives which rewarded them for over-fulfilling approved *tekhpromfinplans*, subject to penalties for breeching financial discipline and some state contracts. Their enterprises were self-supporting juridical entities, a status known as *khozraschyot* which gave them limited discretionary authority. Red directors could hire and fire, buy or otherwise acquire capital, contract with *khozraschyot* firms and government institutions, clear accounts through Gosbank (the state bank), borrow, pay wages, hold and disperse petty cash, prepare *tekhpromfinplans*, and obtain supplies from Gossnab or other firms via special enterprise procurement agents known as *tolkachi* (pushers). This made them masters of daily intra-enterprise operations with some room for external maneuver, but prohibited direct links with households and foreign customers. They could not advertise, contract, or negotiate with non-governmental customers and were forbidden to participate in unauthorized mergers and acquisitions, plant expansion, or entrepreneurial ventures. All transactions other than special order goods had to be consummated at state fixed prices and wages. Goods produced to contract were delivered directly to purchasers, but the rest were marketed exclusively by Gossnab.

These arrangements were less restrictive than under War Communism, but more stringent than NEP. Unlike the civil war years, red directors could negotiate and contract with state institutions as long as they refrained from other market operations including competitive price and wage setting. Gone, however, were NEP era red directors' rights to lease and price negotiate with nepmen who had been "liquidated" as a class. Nor could red directors who once wore two hats operate legally in their own private business interest. Their only opportunities for self-enrichment lay in advancing careers, maximizing bonuses tied to various aspects of plan fulfillment and over fulfillment, and dealing in gray and blackmarket operations called the "second economy."

Second Economy

The second economy is a term frequently used to describe questionable and proscribed productive activities in any economic system, running the gamut from tax evasion scams to contract killing. The phenomenon was considered particularly interesting in the Soviet Union under Command Communism and Reform Communism because private property, business, and entrepreneurship were criminalized. Consequently, a great deal of utility, income, profit, and rent-seeking behavior legal in the West was concealed in the East. There is no doubt that second economy activities were widespread. Authorities were often complicitious and notably tolerant of what could be construed as victimless crimes, but their magnitude and significance are controversial. The CIA estimated second economy activities, defined as value added operations legal in the West, at approximately 10 percent of Soviet GDP. In doing so, it assumed that the array of decentralized activities from *tekhpromfinplanning* to informal materials trading involving *tolkachi* (pushers), *blat* (bribes), and favors were part of the central planning package. Others, who thought Gosplan's reach was, or should have been more pervasive, like Gregory Grossman contended that the second economy was much larger, or even that the second economy was the first economy. Some in this camp, in contrast to the CIA, considered the steady expansion of the second economy to be a principal cause of the Soviet Union's collapse. They could be proven right, if it can be shown that Gorbachev's destructive tolerance of spontaneous privativization and resource diversion were determined by key second economy figures or networks.

The legal opportunities open to red directors are best understood as an effort mobilizing game where managerial incentives schemes fashioned by the center were employed to assure the fulfillment of certain goals regardless of the deficiencies of Gosplan's rebalancing and the ministries' *tekhpromfinplan* revisions. In the simplest case, the center's failsafe strategy was to extend the concept of piecework pay from blue-collar workers to red directors. Managers of single-product firms under this regime received bonuses based on output, where production was subject to a special set of budget constraints on quota inputs in deficit supply and non-quota inputs purchased with borrowed funds and revenues generated from the sale of outputs. Production and factor prices were fixed and the production functions expressed in conventional notation were strictly concave

$$q = f(x_1, x_2, \ldots, x_n), \tag{5.5}$$

and the quota input constraints took the form

$$w_i x_i - m_i \leq 0, \quad \forall_i^k = i, \quad k < n, \tag{5.6}$$

where m_i was the total amount the firm was permitted to spend on factor i and w_i was the price of factor i.

In addition there was an overall budget constraint equal to the receipts from sales by the firm in the last operating period plus a limited amount of credit which showed that the total expenditure on resources must not exceed the amount of money available to the firm. This sum minus fixed costs F was denoted by M and the constraint took the form

$$\sum_{j=1}^{n} w_j x_j - M \leq 0 \tag{5.7}$$

The Lagrangian for this output maximization case can be written as

$$L = f(x_1, \ldots, x_n) - \sum_{j=1}^{k} x_j(w_j w_j - m_j)\Psi\left(\left(\sum_{j=1}^{n} w_j x_j - M\right)\right).$$

The Kuhn–Tucker conditions are[12]

$$\frac{\partial L}{\partial x_i} = \frac{\partial f}{\partial x_i} - \lambda_i w_i - \Psi w_i \leq 0 \quad \forall_{i=1}^{k} \tag{5.8}$$

$$\frac{\partial L}{\partial x_j} = \frac{\partial f}{\partial x_j} - \Psi w_j \leq 0 \quad k < j \geq n, \tag{5.9}$$

$$\frac{\partial L}{\partial \lambda_i} = m_i - w_i x_i \geq 0 \quad \forall_{i=1}^{k} \tag{5.10}$$

$$\frac{\partial L}{\partial \Psi} = M - \sum_{j=1}^{n} w_j x_j \geq 0 \quad \forall_{j=1}^{n} \tag{5.11}$$

Associated with (5.8) are the equations

$$x_i\left(\frac{\partial f}{\partial x_i} - \lambda_i w_i - \Psi w_i\right) = 0 \quad \forall_{i=1}^{k} \tag{5.8a}$$

which, together with (5.8) show that a quota factor will not be used unless its marginal physical product is equal to the product of the shadow price of a relaxation of m_i, and/or the shadow price of a relaxation of M multiplied by the price of the quota factor, whichever restriction is more stringent, when they do not both hold simultaneously.

Similarly, associated with (5.9) we have

$$x_j\left(\frac{\partial f}{\partial x_j} - \Psi w_j\right) = 0 \quad k < j \leq n, \tag{5.9a}$$

which shows that a non-quota factor will not be used unless its marginal physical product is equal to the product of the factor price and the shadow price of a relaxation of M. Again the budget constraint may be non-binding. In this event the marginal physical product of the non-quota factor must be zero.

Finally associated with (5.10) and (5.11) we have

$$\lambda_i(w_i x_i - m_i) = 0 \quad \forall_{i=1}^{k} \tag{5.10a}$$

$$\Psi\left(M - \sum_{j=1}^{k} w_j x_j\right) = 0, \tag{5.11a}$$

both of which have the interpretation that the dual variable will be zero if the accompanying constraint is ineffective.

Clearly (5.4) and (5.5) permitted red directors to be potentially technically and economic efficient even though the conditions for optimization differ from the corresponding conditions in the case of a price-taking, profit-maximizing firm with no input restrictions.

If revenue maximization were the goal given to the red director, the result was the same as in the case of output maximization. This, perhaps, is obvious since the Lagrangians in the two cases differ only by a constant factor, the product price.

The aggregate output plan under this compensation scheme was irrelevant. Whether approved *tekhpromfinplans* were infeasible, just right, or too lax, red directors would always strive to maximize production regardless of cost. The more output they generated, the greater their bonuses. They never had to worry about sales because the state agreed to purchase everything they produced. The only binding constraints on their income were access to plan authorized purchases of priority intermediate inputs and enterprise revenues and credit for hiring capital and labor. The Lagrangians above tell us that if these weren't limiting, red directors were incentivized to operate at the point where the marginal physical product of capital and labor were zero. This occurs where the marginal physical productivity curve MP crosses the abscissa (stage III) at A on (TP) Stalin's total productivity feasibility curve $q = f(x)$ illustrated in figure 5.3, well to the right of the Marshallian ideal at point E. In a competitive free

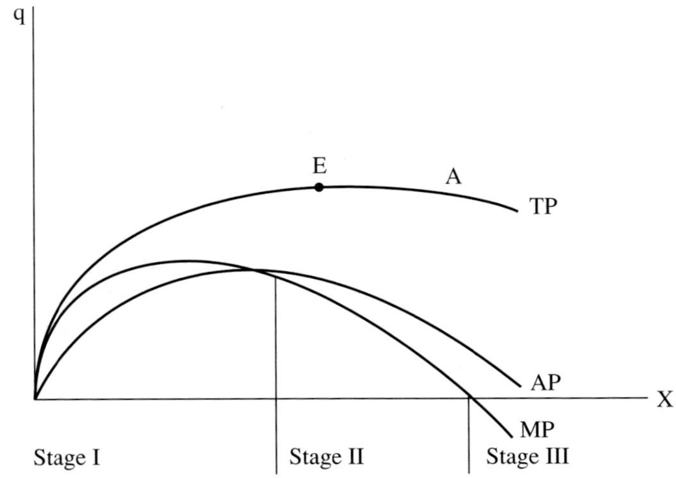

Figure 5.3 Command Communist enterprise output maximization

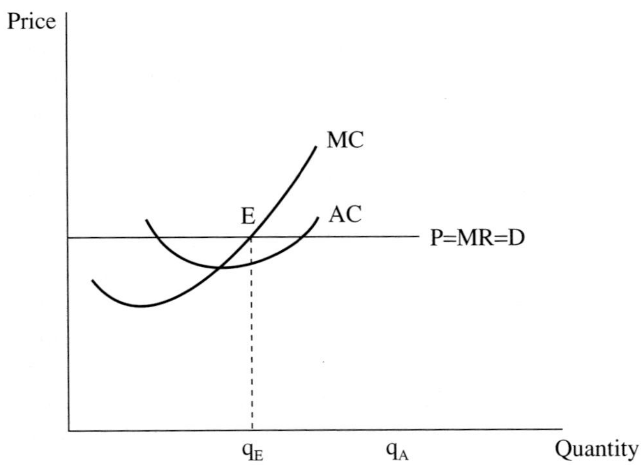

Figure 5.4 Command Communist profit maximization

enterprise economy firms profit maximize at *E* in figure 5.4, but under Stalin's bonus maximizing scheme they proceed to point q_A. They spend all revenues and credit on inputs, even though this would bankrupt their western competitive twin.

Extreme outcomes like this were exceptional because priority inputs were scarce and credit skimpy. But, it was also true that red directors only operated at *E* by coincidence. Low priority firms in figure 5.3 were clustered between the origin and *E*, and high-priority enterprises in the vicinity of *A*. A similar story moreover can be told with the same geometry, if *E* is interpreted as Stalin's second best optimum. Tying red directors' bonuses to output maximizing was clearly suboptimal because most firms subject to this rule, under or over-employed inputs, but it assured the workability of five-year planning by mobilizing resources, and harnessing output capacities.

Ratcheting

Bonus incentivization however wasn't failsafe. Red directors' bonuses often weren't triggered until current output exceeded the prior achieved level. This wasn't normally a problem unless the threshhold was ratcheted (raised) to an unattainable level, at which point red directors were best off effort minimizing. Sovietologists studied the theoretical possibilities of ratcheting from every angle (often focusing on the *tekhpromfinplan* approval process). Central authorities clearly wanted to avoid over-rewarding red directors and did ratchet bonus norms, but judging from the magnitude of bonuses paid, were cautious not to kill the goose that laid the golden egg.

Discipline

In a world without moral hazard, central planning could be limited to the plan formation, directive and incentive mechanisms just elaborated. Red directors would obey Stalin's commands and follow their material interests in the ways approved by the bonus incentive regime. The devil however was alive and well in the USSR and Stalin knew it. He understood that central planning was incomplete without strict controls and devised a host of institutions to ensure discipline. For example, if red directors could misuse their authority by purchasing caviar instead of productive inputs, they might be better off minimizing rather than maximizing output, or producing mostly for the second economy. Authorizations therefore were required for quota goods, and Gosbank wouldn't permit red directors to use funds in their bank accounts to buy items from Gossnab unless they were approved in the enterprise *tekhpromfinplan*. Few payments in the Soviet Union were anonymous. Gosbank disbursed cash for wages and little else. All other transactions were bilateral bookkeeping entries in which revenues from enterprise sales were debited against purchases. Soviet banking was less a financial institution than a payments monitoring and control device.[13] Likewise, red directors could easily be tempted to augment bonuses by adulterating products, skimping on materials and finishings. These abuses were curbed by frequent quality inspections facilitated by the state bureau of standards (Gosstandart). Every Soviet product had a nomenclature number paired with detailed product specifications. Sub-standard products were rejected and could not be used in the calculation of output bonuses or credited as sales in enterprise Gosbank accounts. Oversight in the VPK was even more stringent. Inspectors worked in military industrial enterprises around the clock. Pilferage, mysterious disappearance, or diversion into the second economy were severely punished. Enterprise accounts were "randomly" audited every fortnight.

These and a myriad of other controls reduced moral hazard, (what Stephen Kotkin calls conspiring)[14] but weren't foolproof. Central planning in the broadest sense was a perpetual battle with temptation, which was never completely won. Even when red directors and their supervisors didn't have their hands in the till, they could always work to rules.[15] The Soviet anecdotal literature is strewn with humorous stories of abuse, most of which have an element of truth.[16] Ballbearing plants for example were obligated to fulfill and overfulfill *tekhpromfinplans* even when supply exceeded demand. It was authoritatively reported that some red directors sold their surplus to smelters, which converted it back into raw metal for processing into new ball bearings. This Sisyphean cycle of value added, value subtracted, and value re-added continued ad infinitum, padding GDP and generating handsome bonuses without anything useful ever being delivered to consumers. As absurd as this was, "pre-cycling" was neither illogical nor illegal in the command system. Red directors were incentivized to maximize output, not produce goods private consumers desired. The regime was designed to be in chronic excess demand (economy of shortage, a disequilibrium economy) with the state agreeing to purchase as much output as red directors could produce. From this perspective, endlessly processing and reprocessing ballbearings wasn't fundamentally different than manufacturing products no one wanted to buy.[17]

Stalin, Gosplan, and state investment project bureaus didn't want the planning system to produce useless things, and didn't desire deficits and surplus, but they were

Red Pharaoh

Leonid Lamm, a Soviet-era dissident artist calls Stalin the Red Pharaoh to drive home the point that Command Communist discipline wasn't always coolly technocratic. It had a despotic dimension. Command Communism didn't just eliminate involuntary unemployment by superior planning. "Anti-parasite laws" compelled workers to labor (USSR Constitution 1936, Article 12: "He who does not work, neither shall he eat."). Tardiness made them vulnerable to accusations of "wrecking." They were driven to overexert themselves by "shock tactics." Aleksei Stakhanov began a movement of "heroic" norm breaking in 1935, making ordinary workers liable to standards they could not attain. And those who seemed to shirk on any of these grounds, were subject to criminal prosecution and forced servitude in Gulag. Similarly, while red directors were rewarded for exceeding achieved levels under *khozraschyot*, they were also punishable for failing to achieve impossible targets imposed from above. *Glavk* and ministerial supervisors were subject to similar pressures. All strata were bombarded by elusive promises of rewards and punitive threats, much of it beyond their control. These uncertainties violated the principles of optimal incentive theory where rewards equaled marginal value added and punishments fit every crime, but were adequate for the Red Pharaoh's purposes, enabling him to compel everyone to work harder than if they Pareto optimized.

endemic. State price fixing prevented Marshallian and Walrasian automatic equilibration and *piatiletki* could not fill the void. The leadership, however, wasn't daunted. It simply supposed that five-year plans assured supply would create its own demand; a fantasy form of Say's Law with inflexible prices. Successful industrialization on this reasoning depended solely on building additional modularized capacities and incorporating them in the plan. New automotive assembly plants required complementary component facilities contractually linked and inscribed in *tekhpromfinplans*. More cars could always be manufactured if these needs were met, primary factors were diverted from other activities and/or productivity increased, with cars rationed, sold, or gifted. And of course, it should never be forgotten that Command Communism was synonymous with resource mobilization, an aroused state of activity driven by a patchwork of inconsistent carrots and sticks.

Industrialization of this sort premised on overexertion, factor diversion, and technological modernization, complemented by forced consumer goods substitution wasn't difficult to accomplish. Forced draft modernization was the Muscovite norm from Peter the Great onwards. Stalin promulgated anti-parasite laws obligating all able-bodied working-age men and women to toil. He imposed Spartan living standards to concentrate resources on building new heavy industrial capacities and spent lavishly on acquiring foreign technologies and improving domestic know-how (in design bureaus and institutes outside the jurisdiction of red directors). And the Kremlin constructed gigantic enterprises hoping to capture economies of scale, husband scarce managerial skills, facilitate supervision, and inspire admiration at home and abroad.

These efforts dramatically transformed the Soviet Union's industrial geography. Modularly integrated, modernized industrial facilities mushroomed, capital labor ratios soared, technology and know-how improved, driving physical productivity and growth as often happens in authoritarian states. Even agriculture benefitted with the mass production of farm equipment. Just as the Soviets claimed, physical systems management could mobilize resources and orchestrate industrialization, development, modernization, and rapid output growth. Some of these goods satisfied consumer and state final demand, especially military. But most bore scant relation to demand and a great deal was merely pre-cycling. *Piatiletki* in these respects weren't entirely smoke and mirrors, but their purported triumphs too often were illusory. The real welfare impact of Soviet growth, development, and modernization was slight compared with the Western standard.

The perpetual motion of Stalin's industrialization long celebrated in the literature also gave the erroneous impression that resource mobilization vouchsafed sustainable rapid development. This was naive. There were finite limits to employment, capacity utilization, factor diversion, diminished living standards, capital widening, and centrally planned technological progress disconnected from competitive market demand. Once resource mobilization peaked and diminishing returns to capital widening set in, further advances depended squarely on state directed innovation, diffusion, and learning (including efficiency enhancement) in a cluttered and increasingly complex industrial landscape. Building new capacities (extensive growth), disconnected from consumer demand was bound to become more and more futile, with no exit. Central planning and optimal rational choice-making in complex, mature economies was an oxymoron that could only have an unhappy ending.[18]

Technology and Innovation

Soviet technology and innovation were considered critical aspects of superpower rivalry and were closely investigated by Western institutions and scholars. Studies showed that Soviet engineering and product quality often was better than anecdotes suggested, but technology broadly lagged Western standards by roughly two decades. Although there were many visible successes like the atomic and hydrogen bombs, sputnik, and rockets, ordinary household technologies were antique. This state of affairs partly reflected the Kremlin's priorities. It spent lavishly on science and technological modernization, but concentrated its efforts on military–industrial applications. William Lee (Defense Intelligence Agency) estimated that 80 percent of Soviet research and development outlays were devoted to defense. But there was another essential factor. Systems directors' sovereignty meant that innovation and technological diffusion weren't governed by consumer demand. Surrogates were employed. The Soviets borrowed Western hedonic techniques for assessing design and investment merit and experimented endlessly with organizational reform to little avail, because when the economy was finally opened under Boris Yeltsin foreign buyers for most of the goods produced with its civilian technologies could not be found.

Monkey Business

This point has been recently underscored by new archival research confirming Alec Nove's surmise that planning was far cruder and less technically efficient than Abram Bergson had conjectured.[19] Paul Gregory and associates have shown that *glavk*, ministerial, and central plans took less account of draft *tekhpromfinplans*, even when they were actually submitted in a timely way, than Bergson inferred.[20] Likewise, Stalin and "systems directors" paid little attention to Gosplan's composite goods proposals and control figures, focusing on only a few entries. Plan formation was mostly a formal exercise carried out independently at various levels detached from real constraints and optimal systems directors' choice, which ultimately became binding when Gosplan arbitrarily fixed the final control numbers, governing material balance disaggregation and final *tekhpromfinplan* setting. Each level sought to massage statistics to put its efforts in the most favorable light, leaving the task of directive oversight to the party and other specialized bodies. Bonus maximizing under this regime, which was more monkey business than a serious exercise in optimal control, still sometimes gave red directors a rational self-interest in cost-saving and efficiency, but they were frequently thwarted by exogenous interventions. These insights qualify the widely held view that Soviet growth retardation was caused by diminishing returns to combined inputs and weak technological progress, pointing to the possibility of other contributory factors like deepening disorganization and moral rot.[21] Pantomiming optimal planning and operations control may have given the illusion of organizational efficiency, but could not mollify the damage caused by monkey business plan administration.

Prometheus Unbound

Official portrayals of Stalin's strategy of communist construction concede nothing. They begin by lauding Stalin for discerning the true Leninist path, *piatiletki* and collectivization and conclude with testimonials to his success. The model is logically consistent, given the premise that economic backwardness assessed from the benchmark of full communism is caused by class obstructionism. The villains in this melodrama are nepmen and kulaks who thwart *piatiletki* and social modernization. The hero is Stalin who alone grasps the need for decapitation, eliminating anti-communist elements, pressing forward with five-year planning, industrialization, and the transformation of pre-modern farming into agricultural mega-factories. If and when technological bottlenecks emerge, smash them, quantum jumping to ever higher levels of aggregate productivity. No need to fret about optimal choice-making under constraint because the future belongs to the intrepid.

The call to battle was sounded in September 1929. Party activists lead the charge for collectivization, and industrialization was intensified. Tomorrow was always too late. Everything had to be finished ahead of schedule. Kulaks and their suspected allies had their farms, herds, and personal assets stripped[22] and were exiled to the tundra to till the permafrost.[23] Vast numbers died. One hundred and twenty million peasants were forced into collective farms and compelled to farm for the state.[24] Most of their output was requisitioned, just as it had been during War Communism, with seed set aside for the next planting. The remainder was divided among collective farm members on the basis of brigade performance.[25] The adequacy of these measures is best judged from the fact that no less than four million peasants perished prematurely (1929–38.)[26] Stalin told Winston Churchill at Yalta that collectivization had been a full fledged war for survival that cost ten million lives.[27]

Nonetheless, despite this admission, collectivization was officially portrayed as a popular groundswell. The state didn't coerce kulaks to surrender their property, the peasantry demanded that the government collectivize, inspired by Lenin's and Stalin's strategy for revolutionizing agricultural productivity.[28] Stalin himself divulged the real story in 1931 when he criticized party cadre for being "dizzy with success," that is, for stampeding peasants into collective farms faster than they could be absorbed.[29] But his tacit admission didn't matter. The main point for Stalin was that the class struggle had been won. The peasantry had been yoked to communist industrialization. Although agriculture declined instead of flourishing as predicted, urban food supplies didn't fall enough to scuttle modernization.

And non-agrarian production was declared a stupendous success. Just as during the subperiod 1926–8, industrial and GDP growth were clocked in the double digits (see chapter 7). Machine-building and heavy-industrial advances were especially rapid. To use a term made famous later by Paul Samuelson, Stalin had wisely chosen to take a turnpike to full communism. Instead of plodding along the byways as Bukharin had proposed, he had secured the future by catching up to Europe at breakneck speed. An entire generation had voluntarily sacrificed their living standards, even their lives for the cause, certain that those who followed would reap the fruits of their unselfish labor. Communism was victorious.

Turnpike Theorem

Robert Dorfman, Paul Samuelson, and Robert Solow devised a linear programming theorem in 1958 which showed that it was sometimes better to bear a sharp contraction in current consumption that expedited the attainment of a future goal than to proceed gradually in a more balanced fashion. Janos Kornai later used the concept to urge rapid post-Communist transition rather than crawling to free enterprise along country byways. During the cold war some Sovietologists believed that the turnpike theorem justified Stalin's forced industrialization. PAB theory teaches that the choice between turnpikes and byways turns on the sovereign's time preference.

The collapse of the Soviet Union, however, belies this assessment. Decapitating kulaks and their allies, corralling the peasantry in collective farms, and command five-year planning hadn't yielded Shangrila, or even a facsimile that could sustainably compete with the West. The sacrifices and suffering of the thirties were futile.[30]

This outcome speaks volumes about Marxist-Leninist dialectical divination. The Bolsheviks and many socialist sympathizers fervently believed that the path to an optimal economy lay not in markets or mathematical optimization theory, but in winning the class struggle and *piatiletki*. They characterized their exegetical doctrines as science, but indulged in liberational myth making. People were coaxed to believe that Stalin had intuited the natural order leading to pure communism and that paradise was theirs if they only kept the faith. This demagogic appeal tapped into a deep popular yearning, but it was unsound. As our analysis of five-year command planning revealed, the performance potential of the Stalinist system was manifestly inferior to democratic free enterprise. *Piatiletki* were incapable of allocating factors to best use on the supply side, or efficiently satisfying state and consumer demand. Stalin tried to compensate by overfully employing men, resources and capacities, increasing capital labor ratios, improving technology, inspiring the masses, and flailing them, but *piatiletki* didn't foster innovation and technological choice any better than static resource allocation, despite persistent claims to the contrary.

Socialism

Piatiletki and collectivization nonetheless are still sometimes venerated as socialist because they are said to be expressions of proletarian will. While it is true that Stalin did mesmerize most of the population into believing that his will was theirs, the charisma didn't last. Slowly but surely the people came to appreciate that they were subjugated by the communist party; not sovereign. Stalin's command economy therefore was never really socialist. It was Muscovy with monkey business *piatiletki* and a proletarian veneer.

Analytics of Command Communism

Standard economic geometry elaborated in chapter 2, figures 2.3–2.6 can be utilized to highlight the features of Stalin's command model. The sides of the Edgeworth–Bowley box in figure 5.5 are larger than the War Communist, NEP and Paretian cases (figure 2.3) because five-year planning and output maximizing created overfull capital, resource, and labor employment. The superscripts on the isoquants continued to be less than their Paretian counterparts because technologies were mis-selected, inputs were qualitatively suboptimal, skills weren't ideal, input acquisition untimely, and effort often reserved, although coercion and ratcheting tactics often bolstered performance. As during War Communism and NEP factors weren't employed proportionally with their marginal rates of technical substitution and in any event state fixed wage-rental ratios weren't competitively determined. Instead of efficiently producing on the contract curve at point *E*, firms operated inefficiently at *R*.

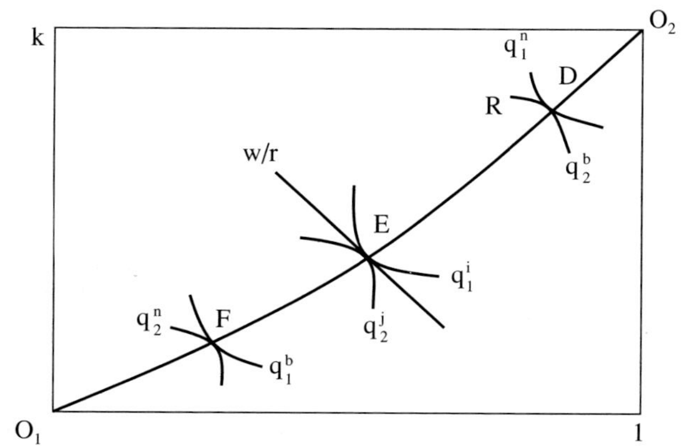

Figure 5.5 Command Communist factor-production space

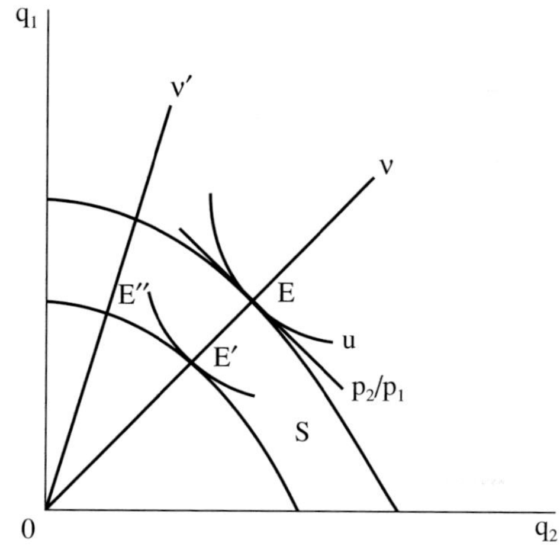

Figure 5.6 Command Communist production potential

Output in the production space depicted in figure 5.6 at point S lies on a higher production feasibilities frontier than the level achieved along the NEP expansion vector (E″). Resource mobilization allowed Stalin to produce more industrial goods than the NEP model, even after adjustment for diminished agrarian output. As in the earlier communist models, observed output at point S was far below Paretian and perfect authoritarian potential, and was economically inefficient judged both from Stalin's and the consumer utility standards.

Products were for the most part rationed, even though some goods were marketed at fixed prices in state retail stores. Figure 5.7 shows that goods weren't efficiently allocated at their marginal rates of product substitution on the contract curve, but off it at point D′.

And finally, real income distribution became more inegalitarian than ever with Stalin's and his coterie's demand controlling most outcomes. Their taste ran to guns and pyramids, rather than luxuries, but this didn't make the inegalitarianism any better. Figure 5.8 reveals that the rulers grew fat, and the people withered.

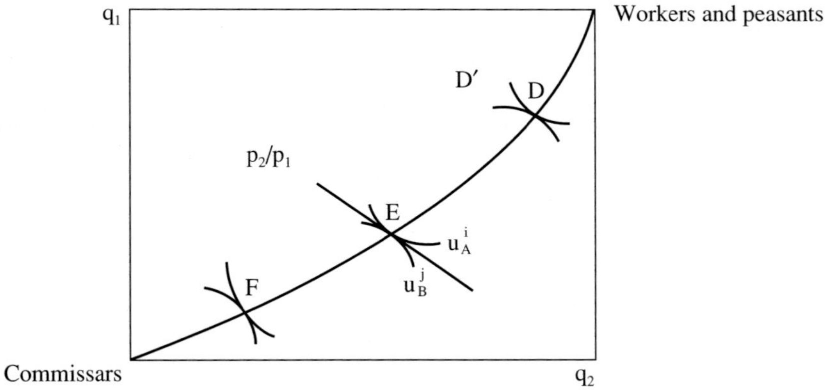

Figure 5.7 Command Communist distribution

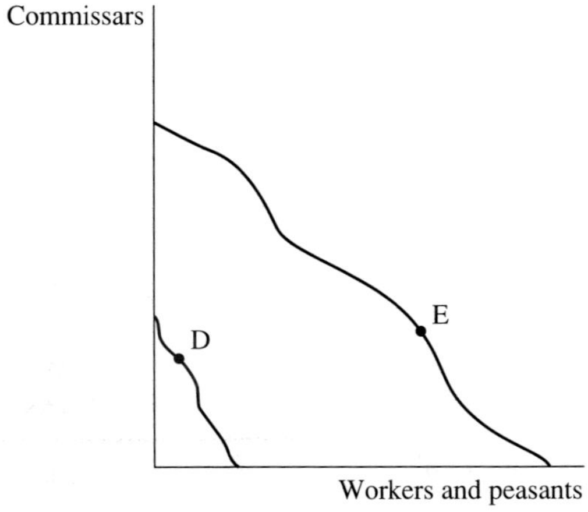

Figure 5.8 Command Communist utility possibilities

Review

The Soviet experience with War Communism and NEP confirmed Stalin's fears and reinforced his proclivity for regimes founded on strict authoritarian control. State agents and non-state actors in the first two phases of socialist construction were too unruly for his taste. He could have tightened discipline under either regime, but opted for the most restrictive alternative, where business and entrepreneurship were proscribed. And he strengthened the War Communist model by adding a powerful planning control mechanism. Its poster child was the five-year plan, but neither its scientific merit nor its nano-implementation were impressive. Other systemic components were needed for success, including managerial bonus incentives, state-supervised inter-enterprise contracting, and an informal or second economy, all mobilized by Marxist zealotry, and fear of Stalin's retribution. The results were acclaimed at the time as unprecedentedly successful, but we now know that with the exception of armaments Stalin's vaunted achievements were mostly a statistical illusion.

Systems Profile

Main features of the Command Communist economic system

- *Culture*: Muscovite authoritarian/anti-authoritarian, with a proletarian facade. Anti-authoritarianism is a mix of passivity (rationalizing subjugation) and opportunism (poor and middle peasants appropriating kulak assets).
- *Motivation*: Iron fisted party-state domination, superpower building, and opportunistic foreign expansion (Karelia, partitioning of Poland, etc.) with the assistance of the Third International, unrestrained by socialist humanist concerns.
- *Mechanism*: Natural resources, land, and the entire industrial and administrative means of production, including housing, gold, and other valuables were state owned and controlled. Agrarian collectivization obviated the peasantry's implicit land claims. Collective farmers toiled in brigades. Members were responsible for *kolkhoz* tax obligations and shared residual income, with the exception of small household plots where they were permitted to produce for their own use. There were also some *sovkhozy* (state farms), where peasants were treated like industrial laborers and received wages, instead of collective residuals. State administration over households was comprehensive. The state physically managed the economy under the banner of *piatiletki* (five-year plans), which not only entailed the formulation of enterprise production assignments, but administrative supervision, material balancing, intra-state contracting, incentivization, and discipline. The industrial sector was administered by 30-odd ministries and subdepartments. Agriculture, construction, and transportation were overseen by analogous committees. All activities were encompassed under the umbrella of central planning. Managers called red directors were appointed by the state and were granted limited, incentive-regulated

functional autonomy. Administration was separated from production on the principle of *khozraschyot*. Enterprises were required to maximize output and be self-financing. Their supervisors were salaried employees, who oversaw production, but didn't manage it on a daily basis. The state set all wages and prices, and entrepreneurship was strictly forbidden. The rule of men prevailed. The USSR was a one party state, which had sovereignty over the provision of all goods, public and private.

- *Institutions*: State ownership of means of production, land, and natural resources: industrial enterprises on *khozrachyot*, *kolkhozy* (collective farms), *sovkhozy* (state farms), machine tractor stations (MTS). Ministerial system (replacing VSNKh), including the Council of Economic Ministers (replacing the Council of People's Commissars), industrial ministeries and *glavks*. Other state control functional and control entities including Gosplan (Central Planning Agency), Gossnabsbyt' (State Material Acquisition and Distribution Agency), Gosbank (State Bank), Gosstroi (State Construction Agency), Goskomtsen (State Price Committee), Gosstandart (State Standards Bureau), Goskomstat (State Statistical Agency), Gosarbitrazh (State Contract Arbitrage Agency), and the Ministry of Foreign Trade. The state had a monopoly on nearly all non-*kolkhoz* business. Trade unions were state controlled, with subservient worker councils, and there were some cooperatives.

Main inefficiencies

- *Law of demand*: State demand sovereign over all aspects of production and distribution. Monopsony demand for labor, forced substitution, privileged access to goods and services.
- *Law of supply*: Worker supply curves were positive functions of wages for mobile workers, but not for Gulag prisoners and collective farmers who only received residual dividends. Coercion substituted for enticement. Industrial production was unresponsive to price, except to the extent that prices affected *khozraschyot* budget constraints. Absence of rule of law and private property rights created endemic moral hazard and corruption.
- *Law of equilibration*: Neither the Walrasian nor the Marshallian automatic price and quantity adjustment mechanism were operative due to state price fixing. Inter-enterprise contracting provided some useful demand/supply coordination. Gosplan attempted to resolve aggregate disequilibrium through material balancing. Ministries and *glavks* tried to do the same when disaggregating central planning assignments on a priority basis. The VPK, party activists and local officials served as troubleshooters. *Tolkachi* informally bartered critical supplies. Gosbank sometimes provided emergency financing. Collective farmers were compelled to accept residuals. Gulag prisoners took what they got. Consumers forced to substitute. Keynesian macro-excess demand was adopted creating an economy of permanent shortage. Overfull employment was persistently maintained. Inflationary pressures were combated with price controls. Hidden inflation and other moral hazards were treated with stern disciplinary measures. There were no multiplier effects because the state, not households, determined investment. There were no money markets or markets for loanable funds. The state was a monopoly investor and controlled all finance.

Tactics of Command Communist economic management

Topic	*Problem*	*State response*
State ownership	Circumscribes individual utility-seeking	Enforced with stern repression
Criminalization of business	Anti-competitive state monopoly	None
Criminalization of entrepreneurship	Red directors banned from innovating, diversifying, merging, acquiring, expanding to improve efficiency and opportunities	Planned innovation and optimal firm size
Inefficient Gosplanning	Interindustrial factor misallocation	Priority distribution, contracting
Infeasible *tekhpromfinplan* assignments	Red director, effort minimization	Incentivization tied to output maximization
Forced collectivization	Exiled or killed best farmers	Equipped collectives with machinery
kolkhoz dividends	*kolkhozniki* received meager residual labor compensation	Inegalitarian dividend distribution based on brigade performance
Worker under-compensation	Deterred effort, withdrawal from labor force	Piecework bonuses, and exhortation, anti-parasite laws, Gulag forced labor
Overfull employment	Suboptimal welfare	None
Inflationary pressure	Price distortion	Price fixing, repressed inflation
Unbalanced development	Structural militarization, over-industrialization	None
Consumer goods shortages	Deterred effort	None
Quality	Product characteristics unresponsive to demand	None
Moral hazard	Misappropriation, and misuse of state assets	Stern discipline, terror

Systemic structure	*Share of GDP*	*Productivity*	*Coercion*
Markets	0	–	–
State	70	Spectrum	High
Kolkhoz	30	Low	High

Systemic characteristics	*Degree/intensity*
State macro-regulation	None
State micro-regulation	
Pro-competitive	None
Incentives	High
Welfare/security	Moderate
Criminal dis-services	
rent-seeking, moral hazard	Moderate

Causes of macroeconomic disequilibrium (economy of shortage)	
Sticky wages and benefits	High
Sticky prices	High
Investment avoidance	None
Capital flight	None
Misinvestment	High
Liquidity preference	None
Insecure agrarian rights	Extremely high
State property rights	High
Foreign capital flows	Not applicable
State corruption	Moderate
Macro-policy mismanagement	Moderate
Class conflict	Extremely high

Main performance indicators

Per capita GDP (Bergson) (US = 100)	30–40
Maddison	20–28
Per capita GDP growth 1929–53 (Chapter 12)	1–3
Maddison	303
Over-employment	10
Retirement support burden	None
Non-working mothers and wives	Negligible

Direction of reforms

Improved planning and incentivation.

Questions

1 War Communism and Command Communism both featured the nationalization of land, resources, the means of production, housing, gold, and other assets. Both had requisition and distribution mechanisms. They were distinguished by *tekhpromfinplanning*, Gosplanning, *khozraschyot*, red director output bonus incentivization, price and wage fixing, and collectivization. Did any, some, or all of these innovations explain the difference in the performance of the two communist systems? How?

2 War Communism shared many features of the pre-1917 Muscovite system. Did any, some, or all Stalin's institutional innovations draw the Soviet Union closer, or distance it further from Muscovy? Explain.

3 Were any, some, or all Stalin's institutional innovations improvements over Czarist Muscovite arrangements? Explain.

4 What are *tekhpromfinplans*? Why were they important? How did draft and approved *tekhpromfinplans* differ from one another?

5 Did red directors take account of the supply requirements of other firms in constructing their *tekhpromfinplan*? Under what conditions was this crucial? Did contracting play a role in this regard? Explain.

6 Were red directors able to effectively build in safety margins into their *tekhpromfinplans*?

7 What was *krugovaya poruka* (family circle)? Did it help or hinder red director safety margin building?

8 What is the concept of "planning from the achieved level." How did it assist Gosplan and Stalin to counter the family circle?

9 Suppose that enterprises overstated achieved levels to augment red director bonuses? What impact would this have on subsequent *tekhpromfinplan* adjustments made by Stalin and Gosplan? (*Hint*: discuss the "ratchet effect.") Did this create a Gosplanning "twilight zone" of interdeterminism and serendipity? Explain. How would "padding" production claims affect racheting? Would this compound problems?

10 Were *tekhpromfinplans* completely detailed, or did red directors limit their reporting to composite goods, resources, and factors? Explain.

11 Was further information lost through aggregation from the bottom up the chain of command? Explain.

12 Were the 30,000-odd adjusted *tekhpromfinplans* which arrived annually at Gosplan's door mutually consistent? How did Gosplan handle the problem? Was this surrogate mechanism for Walrasian and Marshallian automatic market adjustments adequate? Explain.

13 What are material balancing, input–output planning, and linear programming? Describe their comparative merit. Were any of these techniques adequate substitutes for Walrasian and Marshallian automatic adjustment mechanism? Explain.

14 Gosplan only compiled roughly 150 composite goods plans, 5 per ministry. How were these composite plans transformed into approved enterprise *tekhpromfinplan* assignments?

15 Were approved *tekhpromfinplan* assignments feasible?

16 Might there be adverse consequences if approved *tekhpromfinplans* were infeasible? Explain.

17 Was output maximizing bonus incentivization a partial solution to this problem? Describe red director output bonus incentivization, and explain its implications.
18 Did output maximizing bonus incentivization, combined with Stalin's "high aspirational" planning and the "ratchet effect" create persistent excess aggregate excess demand and an economy of shortage? Explain these relationships.
19 What were the microeconomic consequences of output maximizing bonus incentivization? Discuss the phenomena of over-factor utilitization.
20 How precisely did Stalinist factor use differ from the free enterprise cost minimization and profit maximization? Illustrate your answer graphically.
21 How did prioritization influence enterprise input acquisition for quota and non-quota inputs, capacity utilization, and achieved output levels? Who were the winners, who were the losers?
22 What were the welfare implications of these arrangements from the perspectives of Stalin and Pareto?
23 Were ministries and *glavks* restricted to plan processing, or did they have supervisory and interventionary roles? What other state entities functioned as economic troubleshooters? Were these agencies needed because Walrasian and Marshallian automatic adjustment mechanisms were unavailable? Explain.
24 What is moral hazard? Why was Stalin's Command Communist mechanism fraught with temptation? What was Stalin's response to these perils? Were they effective. Explain their successes and limitations.
25 Official Soviet statistics indicate that Command Communism generated full employment, price stability, rapid growth, industrialization, modernization, and a moderately egalitarian distribution of income. Even allowing for significantly exaggerated growth claims, this performance contrasts favorably with that of the West during the Great Depression. Explain how the Command Communist model was able to achieve each of these macroeconomic objectives.
26 Evaluate the merit of these achievements by comparing "overfull" employment, price fixing, wage-fixing, and egalitarianism with the Pareto standard. Also evaluate the character and quality of Stalin's industrialization and modernization from the consumer utility standard. Are standard macro-success indicators misleading in the Soviet context? Explain.
27 Soviet income distribution during the Stalin's reign was moderately egalitarian, if it is assumed that his arms buildup, heavy industrialization, and Gulag were public goods. Could these outputs be considered Stalin's personal toys? Why? Similarly, the Soviet Union's inegalitarianism disregards the low incomes of *kolkhozniki* and Gulag inmates. Do all these factors suggest that Command Communism may have been strongly inegalitarian after all? Explain.
28 Vitaly Shlykov claims that Command Communism was "structurally militarized." Do Stalin's industrial priorities and output maximizing incentivization support Shlykov's characterization? Explain.
29 The "successes" of Command Communism, such as they were, are frequently attributed to Stalin's resolution of the class struggle; that is, his twin policies of *piatiletki* and forced collectivization. Based on your analysis of the properties of Stalinist central planning and output maximizing incentivization assess the necessity of forced collectivization. Does the performance of the agrarian sector during the 1930s confirm, or refute your evaluation of the power of central planning? Explain.

30 Given the poor performance of Soviet agriculture, despite heavy state investment in farm equipment, why did Stalinist consider collectivization a substantial achievement?
31 Was the Marxist–Leninist reliance on class analysis essential to Soviet industrialization and development? Explain.
32 Was Stalin's command model socialist? Explain.
33 Recent archival research revealed that Stalin had little interest in *piatiletki* and concentrated on a few specific composites. This means not only that Command Communism failed to optimize consumer preferences, but Stalin's own preferences as well. Likewise, had preferences been optimized, planning lacked mechanisms to make supply responsive to demand. Does this justify calling Command Communist planning monkey business, rather than muddling, or planned chaos? Consider the nuances and explain.

6

Terror, Homicides, and Forced Labor: 1929–1953

Summary

Economics is the science of utility seeking under constraint. It claims to illuminate the rationality of individual behavior, and social welfare. This usually can be accomplished by analyzing comparative microeconomic efficiency and per capita income on the supposition that pathologies of various kinds are subsidiary. The approach however is incomplete in the Command Communist case because economic efficiency was severely diminished by Stalin's despotism.

An inordinately large portion of the population was imprisoned and worked to death in destructive concentration camps. The labor force was decimated by millions of executions. Structural change was associated with forced collectivization that herded peasants into *kolkhozy*, and drove them into industrial employment in the cities, or Gulag. Party and ministerial discipline were bolstered with terror tactics, which mobilized effort, and contained moral hazard, but disordered economic optimization. Although none of these methods was endemic, and most did more administrative and managerial harm than good, they epitomized Stalin's dystopian brand of physical systems management, claiming more than 20 million victims, terrorizing multitudes, consigning tens of millions more to penal servitude, and wrecking most people's lives. Few Soviet families were left untouched. Gulag was part of everyone's reality from the privileged whose apartment houses were built with prison labor to the victims themselves.

These pathologies have been rationalized on various grounds: self-defense, re-education, utopia-building, expediency, and Stalin's dementia, but words don't expunge deeds. Command Communism whatever its idealistic intent was both a tool and system of devastating cruelty.

Dark Side of the Moon

The decline and fall of the Soviet empire can be chronicled without ever mentioning its dark sides: despotism, repression, oppression, suppression of personal freedom, terror, forced labor, excess deaths, structural militarization, and imperialism. This sanitized approach has the virtue of highlighting the fact that all feasible forms of physical systems management have proven inferior to free enterprise. Soviet despotism neither explains these failures, nor saves the day.

Still the inhumane aspects of Command Communism deserve recognition. They were egregious, and far outweighed any benefit that possibly could have been claimed for the system, even if it had been perfectly planned.

However, not everyone agrees. The issue is controversial. One man's self-defense may be another's murder. A large penal population may reflect persecution, or an effective justice system. Forced labor may be legal slavery, or a legitimate tool of social redemption. Conquest may be imperialism or national liberation. And facts aren't always what they seem. Analyses of the dark side thus tend to be more like judicial proceedings than straightfoward exercises in utility optimization theory, or econometrics.

Under these circumstances, it is useful to begin with demography. Census data provide valuable benchmarks, and vital statistics (natality and mortality) enabling us to gauge, albeit imperfectly, whether significant numbers of people died before their time. Premature deaths alert us to the possibility that something is awry, and suggest the need for a preliminary hearing, but aren't grounds in and of themselves for indictment because "excess" fatalities may have "natural" causes.

The data presented in table 6.1, contrasting expected and actual Soviet populations (1927–38), using the censuses of 1926–7, and 1939, together with appropriate natality and mortality statistics, reveal that there were 6.9 million fewer people alive at the beginning of 1939 than there should have been. There was also a quantum leap of 2.8 million peasant deaths above trend in 1933, bringing total excess deaths to 9.7 million during the first half of Command Communism. Additionally Robert Conquest estimates more than a million fatalities for 1939, yielding a decadal total greater than 10 million premature deaths.[1] This figure is large enough to justify an official inquest. Were those who died before their times victims of happenstance, rapid industrialization, or despotic Command Communism?

There were no wars, pandemics, plagues, or natural disasters that could explain a paper body count of this magnitude, but the numbers could be pared on statistical grounds. Censuses and vital statistics aren't completely reliable, and errors could have resulted in an over-count in 1926–7 and an under-count in 1939. No conclusive proof supporting either supposition has been adduced, but the possibility remains. However, on the other side of the coin, there are demographic grounds for believing that the discrepancy is understated. Infants who survived as long as a month were classified as stillborns in Soviet practice, prompting some to claim that infant mortality may have been millions higher than officially acknowledged, especially during the famine year of 1933. It seems reasonable to surmise therefore that the 10 million excess death figure is a sound indicator of scale.[2] And since there are no obvious innocent explanations, most of these premature deaths are plausibly attributable to the repression of nepmen, industrial discipline campaigns, suppression of dissent in the party, bureaucracy, military, NKVD and forced collectivization which can be called collectively despotic Command Communism.

Table 6.1 Excess deaths: 1927–1938

Year	*Population 1 January ('000) (1)*	*Births per '000 population (2)*	*Deaths per '000 population (3)*	*Births ('000) (4)*	*Deaths ('000) (5)*
1927	147,135	43.6	21.3	6,415	3,134
1928	150,416	42.5	18.5	6,393	2,783
1929	154,026	40.1	20.6	6,176	3,173
1930	157,030	37.9	19.7	5,951	3,093
1931	159,088	35.4	19.6	5,660	3,114
1932	162,434	31.9	20.5	5,181	3,329
1933	164,286	25.3	37.7	4,156	6,193
1934	162,248	—	—	—	—
Discrepancy	−6,915	—	—	—	—
1934	155,333	25.6	19.8	3,977	3,076
1935	156,234	33.0	17.6	5,156	2,750
1936	158,640	32.6	18.2	5,172	2,887
1937	160,925	38.7	17.9	6,228	2,881
1938	164,272	37.5	17.5	6,160	2,875
1939	167,557				
Actual increase	20,422				
Expected births	66,625				
Expected deaths	39,288				
Births minus deaths	27,337				
Discrepancy	−6,915				

Data: The population statistics for 1927 and 1939 are taken respectively from the 1926 census and Tolts, 1995. The vital statistics are a mix of previously published and newly published data uncovered by Wheatcroft. Some of the new data pertained to the European part of the USSR and have been further adjusted without explanation to the union boundaries by Wheatcroft. The statistics used here are from the first entries in columns 4 and 8.
Method: Estimates 1934–8 are extrapolated backward according to the formula $P^{t-1} = P^t/(1 + \alpha - \beta)$ where α is the birth rate and β is the death rate in year $t - 1$.
Sources: Steven Rosefielde, "Excess Mortality in the Soviet Union: A Reconsideration of the Demographic Consequences of Forced Industrialisation 1929–1949," *Soviet Studies*, 35, 3, 1983, p. 393; Steven Rosefielde, "Stalinism in Post-Communist Perspective: New Evidence on Killings, Forced Labour and Economic Growth in the 1930s," *Europe–Asia Studies*, 48, 8, 1996, table 4, p. 972; Mark Tolts, "The Soviet Census of 1937 and 1939: Some Problems of Data Evaluation," paper presented at the Conference on Soviet Population in the 1920s and 1930s, Toronto, January 27–9, 1995, p. 8; Stephen Wheatcroft, "More Light on the Scale of Repression and Excess Mortality in the Soviet Union in the 1930s," *Soviet Studies*, 42, 2, 1990, table 1, p. 358

Soviet primary sources corroborate 5.2 million of these fatalities. Table 6.2 provides the breakdown. It identifies 3.6 million peasant collectivization and famine deaths, 724,000 executions, and 868,000 assorted killings in Gulag (Chief Directorate of Corrective Labor Camps and Colonies of the NKVD) camps, prison, colonies, and among kulak exiles. There are compelling reasons to doubt the completeness of the NKVD (secret police) statistics on executions and Gulag.[3] Most of the un-ascribed fatalities should be classified under this heading. However since peasants swept up in the collectivization battle swelled the concentration camps, it may be simplest merely to surmise that collectivization, the famine that accompanied it, terror, executions, and what Alexander

Table 6.2 Documented homicides in the USSR: 1930–1939

	Documentary basis	*Compiler*	*Documentary source*	*Homicides*
Total documented homicides				
Composition:				5,204,384
1 Collectivization	Estimate	Wheatcroft	Diverse fragmentary data, NKVD	787,165
2 Famine	Enumerated samples	Wheatcroft	Official mortality rate	2,825,000
3 Executions	Enumeration	Getty, Rittersporn, Zemskov, Wheatcroft	NKVD	724,381
4 Gulag camp	Enumeration	Getty, Rittersporn, Zemskov, Wheatcroft	NKVD	360,437
5 Gulag prisons and colonies 1935–1939	Enumeration	Getty, Rittersporn, Zemskov	NKVD	69,566
6 Exiles	Enumeration	Getty, Rittersporn, Zemskov	NKVD	437,835

Homicides: Deaths directly attributable to Stalinist oppression, whether or not judicially sanctioned through execution, brutalization, forced labor and starvation. Killings of other kinds are included in official mortality rates.

Methods: *Collectivization*: (Wheatcroft, 1990) estimates collectivization deaths other than those computed directly for the famine year 1933 at 1,225,000 to 2,225,000. These figures can be compared with the Getty and Manning (1993) figure of 964,411 comprised of 437,835 known exile deaths, and 526,576 estimated peasant deaths which are neither documented by the NKVD, nor are attributable to famine. Exile fatalities are listed separately in table 1 and therefore have been subtracted from Wheatcroft's lower bound (1,225,000 – 437,835 = 787,165). Wheatcroft has also discovered 500,000 more potential collectivization victims in the NKVD material, but is inclined to interpret the discrepancy as a reporting irregularity. The data in question suggest almost 500,000 people (over two-thirds) of the Gulag population either died or ran away from camps in 1931. According to Zemskov 486,320 people vanished from the kulak exile population. Wheatcroft suggests they were transferred to Gulag, citing a report dated July 13, 1931 from Fushman (deputy chairman of TsVKh) to Molotov stating that GUITU, OGPU transferred 625,000 special exiles to Soyuzlesprom. But their return to exile is not documented and Fushman's figure does not match the 427,500 missing from the Gulag Conjuncture Reports for 1931 that Wheatcroft recognizes can be interpreted as evidence they were killed.

Famine: Computed by multiplying the estimated 1933 population by the documented mortality rate for 1932 to obtain estimated official deaths, and subtracting the natural component calculated in the same way with the mortality rate for 1932. Wheatcroft reports the same result without explaining his arithmetic (Wheatcroft, 1990).

Executions: Judicial death sentences from NKVD archive reported in Wheatcroft (1995, table 3) and Getty and Manning (1993) use the same data.

Gulag Camp: NKVD certified deaths 1934–9 reported in Getty and Manning (1993, appendix, pp. 1048–9). Estimates 1930–2 computed from Wheatcroft's Gulag end period population data for these years, and his mean Gulag camp mortality rate 1933–9 (67 per thousand). The figure for 1933 is calculated in the same way except Wheatcroft's Gulag camp mortality rate of 152 per thousand is used in place of the 1933–9 mean.

Gulag Prison and Colonies: Getty and Manning (1993, p. 1024). This figure is for the period January 1935 to the beginning of 1940, and represents a minimum enumeration. It is also stated that 86,582 people perished in prisons 1939–51, or 6,660 per annum.

Exiles: Getty and Manning (1993, p. 1024), report that 1,473,424 people died from execution, Gulag homicides in prisons and labor colonies and peasants known to have perished in exile. Exile deaths can therefore be obtained by subtraction: 1,473,424 – 724,381 (executions) – 241,642 (Gulag camp deaths 1934–9 from their appendix) – 69,566 (prison and labor colonies) – 437,835.

Sources: Rosefielde (1996b, tables A1 and A5; 1997); Getty and Manning (1993); Wheatcroft (1990, tables A1, A2 and A3); Wheatcroft (1995, table 3); Wheatcroft (1996)

Solzhenitsyn calls "destructive" labor camps were the primary aspects of despotic Command Communism that caused 10 million premature deaths before the outbreak of World War II.[4] It wasn't happenstance, *piatiletki*, the recriminalization of business, *khozraschyot*, *kolkhozy*, the economics of industrialization, or self-defense. It was despotism's harvest of sorrow reaped with Command Communism's authoritarian technologies.

There is a precedent for these homicides. Although, vital statistics aren't adequate to compute excess deaths during War Communism, the population deficit (1918–23) (projected versus actual population in 1923) is virtually the same as the Command Communist subperiod 1929–38, that is, 19.7 compared to 19.6 million people.[5] But, while War Communism's battle, terror, execution, and famine victims were inflicted during a civil war before the advent of planning, Stalin's killings were perpetrated while the nation was at peace, with a vastly improved physical management system.

Perhaps for this reason, supporters of Command Communism have been steadfastly in denial, despite Nikita Khrushchev's secret report to the 20th Communist Party Congress where he disclosed that Stalin killed millions.[6] Much of the debate on the magnitude of "the crimes of Stalin's past" centers on the size of the Gulag prison population. Estimates in the 5 million range, like the annual inmate populations reported in table 6.3, combined with official Soviet data on excess Gulag mortality dovetail with the excess death statistics in table 6.1. Figures in the vicinity of a million prisoners, like the NKVD statistics found in the State Archive of the Russian Federation (GARF) displayed in table 6.4, support the homicide totals in table 6.2. Both have strengths and weaknesses and their merit depends more on plausibility than pedigree. The NKVD figures are unconvincing. Robert Davies for example recently discovered that the NKVD prisoner count given to the 1939 Census take was 2.5 million, not 1.3 million listed in the GARF archive.[7] The GARF statistics are also internally inconsistent. It seems unreasonable to suppose, as the execution data imply, that Stalin killed 82 percent of those imprisoned in 1937.[8] Likewise, given the tumultuousness of the times, and Stalin's Orwellian bent, it is difficult to believe that the prison population in the red Pharaoh's Soviet Union amid state terror driven arrests, and collectivization was no higher in 1937 than it is in Putin's Russia today (with 28 million fewer people). Forced concentration camp labor during the 1930s undoubtedly must have been many times greater than the contemporary norm.

The second half of the 1930s is widely described as the "Great Terror," orchestrated by the state to intimidate resistors.[9] Despite their shortcomings, the NKVD execution statistics in table 6.1 confirm the characterization. Data from the same source imply that there were 14.6 million judicial penal sentences meted out (1929–45) in line with Anton Antonov-Ovseenko's earlier estimates,[10] together with an untold number of extrajudicial incarcerations by extraordinary committees of various kinds. These figures are congruent with, and further corroborate the high estimates of the Gulag population.

Public knowledge of Stalin's despotism was fragmentary. Victims, their families and acquaintances knew, others suspected, but the majorities at home and abroad were swayed in varying degrees by official utopian rhetoric. The most visible sign that something was amiss came from a series of show trials, which portrayed the wave of arrests as an effective response to subversives, traitors, "counter-revolutionaries," "capitalist roaders," and other enemies of the people bent on destroying Soviet power. The Hollywood film *Mission to Moscow* accepts this lie as gospel, and credits the NKVD for making the West's victory over Hitler possible! The proceedings began in 1930 with the trial and confession of the "Industrial Party," and became part of a tapestry

Table 6.3 Forced servitude in the Soviet Union: 1929–1977

Year	*(1)* *Industrial labour force* L_1	*(2)* *Total labour force including camp service workers* L_2	*(3)* *Population of the extended Gulag system* *P*	*(4)* *Total forced servitude including resettlement and prisoners-of-war* *S*
1927	—	0.1	—	—
1929	—	0.4	—	—
1930	0.7	0.8	0.9	—
1931	1.8	2.0	2.2	—
1932	2.7	3.0	3.4	—
1933	4.5	5.0	5.6	9.1
1934	5.0	5.5	6.2	—
1935	5.4	6.0	6.7	—
1936	5.9	6.5	7.3	—
1937	7.2	8.0	9.0	—
1938	8.6	9.5	10.6	—
1939	8.4	9.3	10.4	—
1940	9.0	10.0	11.2	—
1941	8.6	9.5	10.6	—
1942	9.0	10.0	11.2	—
1943	9.0	10.0	11.2	—
1944	9.9	11.0	12.3	—
1945	10.8	12.0	13.4	20.0
1946–50	—	12–15	—	—
1952–3	—	10–12	—	—
1954–5	—	8.0	—	—
1956 (Gulag abolished)	—	6.0	—	—
1957	—	4.0	—	—
1959	3.6	4.0	—	—
1960–76	—	—	2.5–5.0	—
1977	—	—	4.0	—

Columns 1, 3, and 4 are derived from column 2. Column 2 represents the total Gulag labour force as it is most often defined by those who have estimated its size. Since the definition typically employed deviates from usual labour force accounting conventions, total labour force should be understood as an unadjusted measure of the average number of Gulag inmates during each year specified. The term unadjusted implies that no account is taken of work-days lost for illness, incapacitation or death. It is tacitly assumed therefore, that the labour participation rate, including camp services, is always 100%. In so far as the living are concerned this is probably a good assumption. Even in freedom the male labour participation rate in 1939 for individuals aged 16–59 was 97.8%. However, had these figures been computed according to official definitions, the number of full-time employed man-year equivalent workers would have had to be reduced by perhaps 5% if it is assumed that 10% of the camp population died each year at an even monthly rate.

Source: Steven Rosefielde, "An Assessment of the Sources and Uses of Gulag Forced Labour 1929–56," *Soviet Studies*, 33, 1, 1981, table 5, p. 65

Table 6.4 NKVD Gulag camp mortality rates and population

	Mortality rates (per '000) Camps (1)	*Gulag population (2)*
1929	(67)	179,000
1930	(67)	212,000
1931	(67)	268,700
1932	(67)	334,300
1933	152	510,307
1934	60	725,483
1935	46	839,406
1936	40	820,881
1937	36	996,367
1938	97	1,317,195
1939	38	1,344,408
1940	57	1,500,524
1941	88	1,415,596
1942	210	999,738
1943	220	663,594
1944	100	715,506
1945	97	583,899

Mortality rates: Average of Wheatcroft's minimum and maximum estimates apparently derived from Zemskov.
Sources: S. Wheatcroft, "Assessing the Victims of Repression 1930–1945: Their Condition With Particular Reference to the Soviet Victims in the Famine of 1923/33", 1995, table 8; table A1. Wheatcroft cites V. N. Zemskov, "Gulag. Istorikosotsiologicheskii aspekt", *Sotsiologicheskie issledovaniya*, 1991, 6, pp. 14–15; Steven Rosefielde "Stalinism in Post-Communist Perspective: New Evidence on Killings, Forced Labour and Economic Growth in the 1930s," *Europe-Asia Studies*, 48, 6, 1996, table A2, p. 987

of purges (*chistka*) aimed at making communist party members unswervingly loyal to Stalin. Initially this meant the expulsion of dissidents real and imaged, but after Sergei Kirov's assassination in 1934, a Politburo member considered a threat to Stalin's absolutism, the script called for a steadily rising tide of arrests, confessions, and executions orchestrated by Genrikh Yagoda, head of the NKVD.[11] "Old Bolsheviks" (Lenin's comrades in arms) Grigori Zinoviev and Lev Kamenev were tried in August 1936. They were forced to plead guilty and then shot. Mikhail Tukhachevsky, Marshall of the Soviet Union, Yuri Pyatakov, Deputy Commissar of Heavy Industry, and Evgeny Preobrazhensky were arrested, tried and shot in 1937. The following year Nikolai Bukharin and Alexei Rykov (former head of VSNKh) were compelled to publicly confess and were shot.[12] Yagoda, who had been replaced by Nikolai Yezhov as NKVD chief was executed in the same year. Mikhail Tomsky, a famous Bolshevik trade union leader committed suicide to avoid arrest, as did the "revolutionary" hero Grigori Ordzhonikidze. Leon Trotsky was murdered by Stalin's agent in Mexico in 1940. The list goes on and on,[13] and the families of these "enemies" were invariably sent to Gulag.

The bloodletting at the top has transfixed most political scientists. The fratricide was important, but it also diverted attention from the mass nature of Stalin's repression. By focusing on the Bolshevik leaders, and the "political prisoners" spawned by the purges, the mis-impression was created that they primarily were the ones oppressed and unjustly imprisoned (the "revolution" devouring its children). This distorts reality. The high estimates of collectivization, exile and concentration camp premature deaths, executions, and Gulag populations are not explained by the elites, but by the ordinary people caught up in the maelstrom. As Solzhenitsyn and most of the vast memorial literature make plain, terror (*strakh*) pervaded everyone's life,[14] and is a hallmark of Command Communism. It played a decisive role in reshaping the Soviet Union's economic geography and structure[15] (see table 6.5), that cannot be countervailed by a myriad of prosaic production statistics, and must be heavily weighted in any assessment of the social welfare consequences of Soviet industrialization.

There has been a persistent effort to finesse the links between the "dystopia" of Soviet life during the 1930s and Command Communist despotism by claiming that there was a method to Stalin's madness, or by blaming terror, forced labor, premature deaths, and executions on Stalin the man rather than Bolshevik Command Communist culture, even though the two phenomena are inextricably intertwined.[16] Those who contend that Stalin's actions were lesser evils argue that terror mobilized effort, contained moral hazard, accelerated industrialization by stampeding peasants into manufacturing, while extracting grain from collective farmers to feed urban workers, and allowed vital construction, foresting, and mining projects which would have been impossible on a voluntary basis. There is no doubt that Stalin in some sense made his victims pay their own way for his benefit. But annihilating forced labor, executions, factor misallocation (tilling the tundra), squandered resources, and pervasive fear disordered rational decision-making. Despotic Command Communism was intrinsically inefficient, and although terror could produce impressive unless things like the Belomor Canal, on close scrutiny it only made matters worse.[17]

Likewise, the distinction between Stalin the psychopath and the virtue of the Bolshevik mission diverts attention from the communist obsession with winning at any cost. Command Communism was a Bolshevik model with zero tolerance for opposition. Most societies are stressed from time to time, and some succumb to despotism. But traditional cultures, especially in peace time, impose boundaries on excess. Although people are unjustly imprisoned, intimidated, oppressed and executed, these evils are contained. Command Communism, however, turned out to be morally unencumbered not just because Stalin was especially vicious and cunning, but because Lenin before him had eradicated pre-modern restraints on party authority. Old Bolsheviks, as Leon Trotsky put it, had blazed the path for Stalinist despotism by persuading themselves that Communist ends justified the means, and that they could not be right against the party; that they had to surrender their will to the leader. Command Communism consequently cannot be separated from its pathology. The Bolshevik authoritarian martial police state created a culture of expediency, and Stalin carried it to the logical extreme within the physical systems management paradigm.[18]

Stalin's reign of terror which should be dated from forced collectivization in 1929, rather than Kirov's death in 1934, never abated during his lifetime. The Gulag population remained high throughout World War II despite the intensive use of prisoner suicide brigades. Most Soviet soldiers captured by German and Allied forces after victory in Europe were repatriated directly to Gulag for the crime of "surrendering to the enemy." They were joined by millions of Axis prisoners of war, including more than 700,000 Japanese. Along the way from 1939 to 1953 there were more than 10 million additional non-war related civilian casualties. And at the time of his death, Stalin was planning another massive purge.[19] The hallucinatory dimension of Command Communism came in waves, but never really subsided until the great despot was carted off to Hades.[20]

Review

The hallmark of Command Communism wasn't just state ownership, the recriminalization of leasing, business and entrepreneurship, physical systems management, structural militarization, and *piatiletki*. It was the despotism of Stalin's brand of an authoritarian martial police state. Physical systems management and oppression were dominant features of War Communism, NEP, and the post-Stalin reform era. Terror, Gulag, forced labor, repression, executions, and excess deaths were observable throughout. But Stalin's dystopian version of physical systems management, built on the Leninist culture of expediency, was special. It was more unscrupulous, more intense, and more encompassing than its predecessors and successors, which is why it is inextricably associated with the Great Terror and Orwellian totalitarianism. It was Bolshevik fanaticism co-opted by Stalin's fears and complexes.

The macaber arithmetic is indicative. There were more than 20 million non-war excess deaths during Stalin's rule. Tens of millions were arrested and consigned to annihilating forced labor. Additional tens of millions were terrorized, and ensnared in the hallucination called Soviet reality, with little other than mis-industrialization, structural militarization and the delusion of progress to show for it. Despotism, when it wasn't squandering human capital (homicides) could coerce effort, but brute force was not only immoral, it was inimical to rational, constrained economic optimization.

Questions

1 Why do terror, repression, oppression, despotism, wrongful imprisonment, forced labor, excess deaths, and executions violate Pareto optimality? Explain.
2 Should these pathologies be formally included in "social welfare functions" when evaluating comparative systems merit? Explain.
3 How can the pathology of an individual like Stalin be distinguished from the mechanics of Command Communism? (*Hint*: compare the intensities and context of oppression under Stalin with those under Lenin, Khrushchev, and Gorbachev.)
4 Is there anything in Stalin's version of physical systems management that made it more murderous than Lenin's, Khrushchev's, or Gorbachev's? Explain, and then reconsider your answer to question 3.
5 Does perfect planning require despotism? Explain.
6 Are economists justified in treating Stalin's despotism as an aberration of Bolshevik physical systems management? State and justify your premises and judgments.
7 List the rationales offered to justify Stalin's crimes against humanity. Take sides, and defend your judgments.
8 Who was worse, Stalin or Hitler? Were their crimes on a par? Take a position, and justify it.
9 Why are Stalin's crimes treated more indulgently in Russia and abroad than Hitler's? Speculate and explain.

10 Does the Muscovite model play a role in Stalin's excesses? Explain.
11 Are socialist oriented physical managed systems at special risk of terror, repression, oppression, despotism, wrongful imprisonment, forced labor, excess deaths, and executions? State your grounds and defend your position. (*Hint*: consider the record in Eastern Europe, North Korea, China, Cambodia, North Vietnam, and Cuba.)
12 Socialism is derived from the Enlightenment and the idea of the West. It is humanistic in intent. Could the "cultural revolutions" which accompanied the emergence of physical managed systems have destroyed the inhibitions in pre-modern and western societies protecting them against fanatic excess? Consider the mitigating role of pre-modern and Enlightenment cultures in defending society against extremism. State your premises and defend your position.

7

Economic Performance: 1929–1953

Summary

The consensus view of western Sovietologists was that Stalin's industrialization strategy had been remarkably successful, despite some lamentable excesses. Abram Bergson's authoritative adjusted factor cost recalculations of Soviet national income revealed double-digit Soviet growth (1928–37), and an accompanying radical structural transformation from an agrarian to an industrial economy. Richard Moorsteen clarified Bergson's finding, showing that this rapid growth was along Stalin's preferred trajectory. He had set out to eradicate economic backwardness, and Simon Kuznets declared Stalin had succeeded. These results seemed to impressively confirm the merit of administrative command planning, particularly so because Bergson famously argued that his estimates measured supply-side efficiency (see chapter 2). His adjusted factor cost prices couldn't shed light on the "consumer utility standard," but were second best, given Stalin's (systems directors') preferences. His despotism was seldom mentioned, or incorporated into a net assessment, nor were structural militarization and excessive heavy industrialization seriously taken into account. They weren't denied, just brushed under the rug.

Official Soviet national income data suggested even better performance with net material product growing 16.7 percent per annum, doubling every four years (1929–37). But they had little credibility because published growth rates could not be replicated with official sub-sectoral statistics; a discrepancy ascribed variously to "free invention" or inadvertent error.

Western Sovietological estimates were clearly better than the official fantasies. But the picture they painted, together with interpretive commentaries were too rosy. The assumption that sub-aggregates weren't significantly padded, or distorted by spurious innovation was never adequately justified. The presumption should have been just the reverse. Likewise, the growth reported didn't measure either consumers' or systems directors' preferences (the demand side), nor did it reflect neoclassical supply-side production potential as Bergson misleadingly asserted. The improvement in welfare wasn't proportional to the growth of "real output." And perhaps most important of all, Stalin's development goals were perverse, characterized by structural militarization, excessive heavy industrialization, repression, forced labor, terror, catastrophic premature deaths, and despotism. Moorsteen is almost certainly correct that Stalin rapidly achieved his ends, but he should have looked more critically at the human consequences.

Pre-war Soviet economic development proved that Five Year Planning was the best strategy for constructing socialism. During the first three five-year plans, 1928–1940, the USSR built the material technical foundations for industrialization, achieved the highest tempos of socialist investment, and significantly improved the people's material and cultural living standards, while strengthening national defense.

(*Narodnoe khoziaistvo SSSR za 70 let (Iubileinyi statisticheskii ezhegodnik)*, Finansy i Statistika, Moscow 1987), p. 41

Stalin ruled the Kremlin for nearly a quarter century from 1928 to 1953. The foundations of Soviet industrial socialism were forged under his watch during the first two five-year plans, 1928–37, continuing through 1940, followed by more than four years of Nazi occupation, economic recovery, and a quinquennium of "cold war." For many, these were the Soviet Union's glory years, when Moscow showed the world that its workers' state could achieve both economic and military miracles. Supporters abroad were elated, while Western governments strove to take the measure of this nuclear superpower.

Tables 7.1–7.5 purportedly document these economic claims. The State Statistical Bureau reports that Soviet national income (NMP) more than quadrupled during the

Table 7.1 Basic indicators of Soviet economic development: 1928–1949 (1928 = 100)

	1932	*1937*	*1940*
NMP	1.6	3.4	4.5
Capital stock	1.1	1.7	2.4
Industry			
Producer goods	2.7	6.5	10.0
Consumer goods	1.6	3.1	4.2
Agriculture	0.9	1.1	1.3
Workers	2.1	2.5	3.0
Labor productivity			
Industry	1.3	2.4	3.1
Agriculture	1.1	1.6	1.7
Construction	1.0	1.9	2.5

Source: *Narodnoe khoziaistvo SSSR za 70 Let*, Finansy i Statistika, Moscow, 1987, p. 41

Table 7.2 Soviet industrial growth: 1928–1940 (1928 = 100)

	1932	*1937*	*1940*
Industry	202	446	650
Electricity	375	1,049	1,444
Fuel	211	357	457
Ferrous metals	184	528	617
Chemical	319	992	1,511
Machinery	399	1,128	1,985
Light	161	260	348
Food	157	302	411

Source: *Narodnoe khoziaistvo SSSR za 70 Let*, Finansy i Statistika, Moscow, 1987, p. 34

Table 7.3 Agricultural collectivization

Year	*% of households*
1927	0.8
1928	1.7
1929	3.9
1930	23.6
1931	52.7
1932	61.5
1937	93.0
1939	95.6

Source: *Narodnoe khoziaistvo SSSR za 70 Let*, Finansy i Statistika, Moscow, 1987, p. 35

first half of Stalin's tenure catapulting forward at a compound annual rate of 12.3 percent. Industrial producer goods grew even faster at 19.4 percent per annum, while consumer goods also put in a good show at 11.7 percent per annum. And even though labor was rapidly transferred from agriculture to industry, agrarian output increased 2 percent per annum. These spectacular gains moreover weren't attributed solely to "perspiration," (capital widening) that is, adding fixed and variable capital, land, and labor. The proletariat was also "inspired." Working better with the assistance of rapid technological progress, industrial labor productivity advanced at a 9.1 percent annual clip, agriculture 4.1, and construction 7.3 percent.

Table 7.2 provides insight into the structure of industrial performance. The laurel goes to machine-building which grew at an astonishing 25.8 percent per annum, doubling every three years. This reflected the Marxist view that aggregate growth could be maximized by concentrating development in the industrial capital goods sector. But the strategy didn't mean that current consumption was neglected. Light industrial consumer goods expanded 10.1 percent per annum.

All of these accomplishments were attributed in substantial part to Stalin's brilliant agrarian collectivization. Table 7.3 shows that within the brief span of eight years, 1929–37, more than 90 percent of agriculture was converted from private farming to *kolkhozy* (collective farms). The task was immense, and encountered fierce resistence,

Table 7.4 Gross crop (millions of tons)

	1909–13	*1928–32*	*1933–7*	*1938–40*
Grain	65.2	73.6	72.9	77.9
Sugar	9.7	9.8	14.6	15.8
Cotton	0.7	1.0	1.8	2.5
Potatoes	22.4	45.9	49.8	47.9

Source: *Narodnoe khoziaistvo SSSR za 70 Let*, Finansy i Statistika, Moscow, 1987, p. 35

Table 7.5 Animal products (millions of tons)

	1908–13	*1928–32*	*1933–7*	*1938–40*
Meat	3.9	4.3	2.7	4.5
Milk	24.1	26.3	22.2	27.6

Source: *Narodnoe khoziastvo SSSR za 70 Let*, Finansy i Statistika, Moscow, 1987, p. 35

but the inherent superiority of collective farming is revealed in the crop statistics (table 7.4). The only blemish is the severe decline in livestock during 1933–7, caused by kulaks slaughtering their herds. Everything else is peachy.

But were any of these claims true? Western Sovietologists committed themselves to discovering the answer.

Their approach, particularly that of Abram Bergson, the leading figure in the field, was influenced by the development of Western national income accounting which accompanied the Keynesian revolution. He transformed TsSU's data into "shadow" series in precise conformance with American accounting practice, paying attention to the minutest accounting detail, with prices adjusted to what he believed to be a surrogate "market" standard by deleting turnover taxes, subsidies, and profits, and imputing a uniform rate of return on capital.[1]

These calculations supported the claim that the Soviet Union had rapidly industrialized (1928–40), but painted a soberer picture of the effectiveness of Moscow's growth model. They found that the moderate growth accomplished was due to "perspiration" rather than "inspiration;" that growth was decelerating and the Kremlin's long-term prospects were inferior. The West had nothing to fear from its erstwhile communist competitor.

The tables below derived from Abram Bergson's and Simon Kuznets' *Economic Trends in the Soviet Union* prepared for the Rand Corporation in 1963 vivify these summary findings.[2] Table 7.6 arrays the supply side evidence. Output is measured as net national income and doubles as a proxy for GNP because the two series grow identically. Results are reported in Laspeyres and Paasche form valued at 1928 prices (composite) and 1937 ruble factor cost. Both are legitimate, but the latter (1937 factor cost series) is said to be preferable because the industrial base is more compatible with other western nations at similar stages of development.

Labor is measured in man hours, capital at 1937 prices, land in acres, and are applied in succeeding panels to guage the growth of factor productivity. The Laspeyres

Table 7.6 Soviet national product, factor inputs, and factor productivity (1928 = 100)

Item	*Measure*	*1937*	*1940*
NNP	1937 factor cost	149.5	164.6
NNP	Composite	262.5	289.5
Employment	Adjusted for non-farm hours	137.9	154.2
Fixed capital	1937 rubles	243.9	308.3
Farm land	Acres	120.5	121.8
Livestock	1937 rubles	67.9	79.8
Inputs	1937 weights	139.1	155.6
NNP/worker	1937 factor cost	108.7	107.3
NNP/capital	1937 rubles	61.1	53.3
NNP/worker	Composite	190.1	187.6
NNP/capital	Composite	188.7	186.0

NNP is net national income. The composite is the 1937 output bundle weights, valued at 1928 prices. Inputs are capital, labor, land, and livestock.
Source: Abram Bergson, "National Income," in Bergson and Simon Kuznets, *Economic Trends in the Soviet Union*, Harvard University Press, Cambridge, MA, 1963, table 1.1, p. 4

productivity series grow at 5 percent per annum due to improved labor skills, capital deepening, and other facilitating advances (technological progress). These "inspirational" results appeared to bode well. But, the Paasche statistics were contra-indicative. Labor productivity growth was negligible and capital productivity growth severely so, implying that Soviet industrialization was "perspirational." Factor productivity diminished rapidly as labor, capital, and land were added, and since there were distinct limits to capital deepening, labor force participation and the addition of new lands, living standards had little or no upside potential in the long run.

Warren Eason's research on the composition of the Soviet labor force illuminates matters further (table 7.7). It reveals that labor "perspiration" was achieved by hastily transferring peasants to industrial activities, rather than by mobilizing untapped labor reserves after unemployment was eradicated in the early 1930s. Soviet labor force growth inched ahead in 1928–39 at only 0.3 percent per annum, but the non-agricultural component more than doubled, advancing at a 7 percent rate. This is the "other shoe." On one "foot" Stalin's collectivization and "dekulakization" delivered savage blows to agricultural, but on the other they drove 19.3 million people into non-agricultural employment providing the sweat for forced industrialization.[3]

Raymond Powell's data in table 7.8 demonstrate that industry was a bright spot. Value added per man hour in 1928–40 was "inspired," increasing at 3.9 percent per annum even using the slow growth 1937 Paasche indicator. Capital widening and perhaps capital deepening appeared to pay off handsomely in this sector. But they weren't costless. Powell's net industrial capital series grows substantially faster than valued add calculated in 1937 prices, confirming Bergson's judgment that Stalin's economic successes were mainly a matter of perspiration, even in industry.

The same story applies to agriculture (table 7.9). Gale Johnson showed that the increase in total man-days, capital and land employed in agriculture greatly exceeded the rise in official total output on his adjusted figures. The input–output ratio declines significantly

Table 7.7 Soviet labor force composition

	Millions			*%*	
Year	*Total*	*Non-agric.*	*Agric.*	*Non-agric.*	*Agric.*
1928	86.1	15.5	70.0	18.0	82.0
1929	87.4	16.4	71.0	18.8	81.2
1930	89.5	18.1	71.4	20.2	79.8
1931	88.0	21.4	66.6	24.3	75.7
1932	88.6	24.1	64.5	27.2	72.8
1933	88.8	26.0	62.8	29.3	70.7
1934	89.1	25.9	63.2	29.1	70.9
1935	89.3	27.4	62.2	30.3	69.7
1936	90.0	28.6	62.3	31.5	68.5
1937	89.6	32.6	57.0	36.4	63.6
1938	89.7	34.7	55.0	38.7	61.3
1939	89.8	34.8	55.0	38.8	61.2
1940	100.8	40.8	60.0	40.5	59.5
1950	99.7	43.0	54.0	44.3	55.7

The labor force increase in 1940 is primarily due to territorial acquisitions.
Source: Warren Eason, "Labor Force," in Abram Bergson and Simon Kuznets (eds.), *Economic Trends in the Soviet Union*, Harvard University Press, Cambridge, MA, 1963, table II.10, p. 77

Table 7.8 Soviet value added in industry (1928 = 100)

Year	*1928 Rubles*	*1937 Rubles*	*Man-hours*	*Net capital*
1928	100.0	100.0	100.0	100.0
1929	130.8	114.8	105.9	105.9
1930	178.5	128.1	119.8	121.0
1931	226.2	146.4	136.0	151.7
1932	238.5	139.5	146.8	186.4
1933	233.8	132.3	136.2	211.9
1934	290.8	148.3	148.8	231.1
1935	413.8	203.8	164.5	259.1
1936	538.5	237.3	173.2	295.8
1937	583.1	262.0	180.2	327.3
1938	678.5	295.1	189.2	363.6
1939	778.5	356.7	191.0	405.6
1940	830.8	354.0	214.4	444.1
1945	781.5	417.2	221.7	388.1
1950	1,164.6	467.7	293.7	664.3
1953	1,501.5	635.0	340.5	958.0

Source: Raymond Powell, "Industrial Production," in Abram Bergson and Simon Kuznets (eds.), *Economic Trends in the Soviet Union*, Harvard University Press, Cambridge, MA, 1963, table IV.10, p. 187, table IV.11, p. 188, table IV.12, p. 190

Table 7.9 Soviet agricultural production and total man-days (1928 = 100)

			Official		
Year	*Official total*	*Johnson total*	*Crops*	*Livestock*	*Total inputs*
1913	80.6	86.2	85.5	73.0	
1917	71.0		69.2	73.0	
1921	48.4		47.0	48.9	
1928	100.0	100.0	100.0	100.0	100.0
1929	97.6		99.1	94.2	
1930	94.4		107.7	73.0	
1931	91.9		107.7	67.9	
1932	86.2		106.8	54.7	
1933	81.4	87.1	103.4	47.4	
1934	85.4		106.8	52.6	
1935	95.7		117.9	62.8	
1936	87.9		106.8	70.1	
1937	108.1	101.7	128.2	79.6	
1938	96.8		102.6	87.6	141.0
1939	97.6		106.8	86.9	
1940	125.8	105.2	132.5	83.2	
1945	69.4		79.5	52.6	
1950	112.9		129.1	86.1	153.7
1953	124.0		126.5	102.9	

Source: Gale Johnson, "Agriculture," in Abram Bergson and Simon Kuznets, *Economic Trends in the Soviet Union*, Harvard University Press, Cambridge, MA, 1963, table V.1, p. 205, table V.3, p. 208, table V.6, p. 216

(1928–38), but increased slightly from 1938 to 1950. The increase in total sown area and the substitution of mechanical for animal power were cited as the two most important factors in the rise of gross agricultural output since 1928; increases in crop yields were next, while improvements in feeding efficiency played only a minor role.

Confirmation of these low returns on investment is provided by Janet Chapman's estimates of per capita consumption and communal services computed in 1937 adjusted market prices. Table 7.10 reveals that the payoff to the people for their substantial sacrifices was meager. Living standards rose less that 1 percent per annum (1928–37) and over the extended period 1928–50. And she finds that even as late as 1958, American living standards were treble those of the Soviets (table 7.11).

Part of the blame can be laid at the doorstep of the USSR's trade policy. Nations with a comparative advantage in manufacturing capital durables usually are able to accelerate per capita consumption growth by exchanging them for consumer goods. Franklyn Holzman however found that Stalin distained foreign trade, following an autarkic policy of domestic self-sufficiency (table 7.12), exporting whatever Moscow could to acquire vital inputs for industrialization (table 7.13).

Chapman's living standard statistics however should not be considered the bottom line. Industrialization also contributed to national security. Raymond Powell's and Abram Bergson's tables, 7.14 and 7.15, show that the military was the primary beneficiary of

Table 7.10 Soviet living standards and real wages

Year	*Index*
1928	100.0
1932	—
1937	109.9
1940	105.5
1944	75.8
1950	120.9
1955	175.3
Growth (%)	
1928–37	0.9
1928–50	0.7

Per capita consumption and communal services: 1937, adjusted market prices (1928 = 100).
Sources: Janet Chapman, "Consumption," in Abram Bergson and Simon Kuznets (eds.), *Economic Trends in the Soviet Union*, Harvard University Press, Cambridge MA, 1963, table VI.1, p. 238

Table 7.11 Per capita consumption and communal services in the USSR and USA: 1958 (1954 dollars)

USSR	*USA*	*USSR/USA (%)*
475	1,423	33.4

Source: Janet Chapman, "Consumption," in Abram Bergson and Simon Kuznets (eds.), *Economic Trends in the Soviet Union*, Harvard University Press, Cambridge MA, 1963, table VI.3, p. 252

Table 7.12 Share of exports in Soviet national income: 1913–1959

Year	*%*
1913	10.4
1929	3.1
1930	3.5
1931	3.0
1932	2.6
1933	2.3
1934	1.8
1935	1.3
1936	0.8
1937	0.5
1955	1.9

Source: Franklyn Holzman, "Foreign Trade," in Abram Bergson and Simon Kuznets (eds.), *Economic Trends in the Soviet Union*, Harvard University Press, Cambridge, MA, 1963, table VII.3, p. 290

Table 7.13 Soviet export structure (% of total)

Year	*Food*	*Raw materials*	*Industrial goods*
1913	60.0	34.4	5.6
1929	21.5	62.7	15.8
1930	31.6	53.2	15.2
1931	35.2	47.7	17.2
1932	22.5	53.5	24.0
1933	19.0	58.1	22.9
1934	16.1	60.3	23.6
1935	19.0	62.0	19.0
1936	13.4	66.8	19.8
1937	22.9	58.6	18.5
1938	30.5	50.4	19.1

Source: Franklyn Holzman, "Foreign Trade," in Abram Bergson and Simon Kuznets (eds.), *Economic Trends in the Soviet Union*, Harvard University Press, Cambridge, MA, 1963, table VII.6, p. 294

Table 7.14 Soviet munitions spending

Year	*1928 rubles*	*1937 rubles*	*1928 index*	*1937 index*	*1928 burden*	*1937 burden*
1928	0.2	0.4	100	100	0.6	0.2
1929	0.3	0.5	150	125		
1930	0.4	0.7	200	175		
1931	0.4	0.8	200	200		
1932	0.4	0.8	200	200		
1933	0.5	0.9	250	225		
1934	1.7	2.9	850	725		
1935	2.8	4.8	1,400	1,200		
1936	4.8	8.2	2,400	2,050		
1937	5.7	9.5	2,800	2,375	6.7	3.4
1938	7.4	12.3	3,700	3,075		
1939	11.9	19.9	5,950	4,975		
1940	16.1	26.8	8,050	6,700	17.0	6.5
Growth (%)						
1928–37			39.5	37.3		
1937–40			42.2	41.3		

Powell's munition data were provided by Bergson, who in turn derived the figures in current rubles as a residual from the official defense budget by subtracting soldiers' wages and subsistence. The ruble figures are factor cost in 1928 and 1937 prices respectively. The burden is computed as the munitions share of Bergson's estimates, in corresponding prices.

Sources: Raymond Powell, "Industrial Production," in Abram Bergson and Simon Kuznets (eds.), *Economic Trends in the Soviet Union*, Harvard University Press, Cambridge, MA, 1963, table IV.9, p. 178. Abram Bergson, "National Income," in Bergson and Kuznets, *Economic Trends in the Soviet Union*, Table, table 1.1. Abram Bergson, *The Real National Income of the Soviet Union Since 1928*, Harvard University Press, Cambridge, MA, 1961, table 3, p. 46, table 17, p. 88

Table 7.15 Soviet defense spending (billions, shares, thousands)

Year	*Current rubles*	*1937 rubles*	*Current burden*	*1937 burden*	*Military manpower*
1928	0.8	1.9	2.4	1.0	562
1937	17.4	17.4	6.2	6.2	1,750
1940	56.5	45.8	13.0	13.8	3,500
1944	135.7	118.0	30.2	38.8	12,000
1950	80.8	42.4	8.9	10.3	4,000
1955	105.4	62.0	8.9	10.2	5,500

Source: Abram Bergson, *The Real National Income of the Soviet Union Since 1928*, Harvard University Press, Cambridge, MA, 1961, table 3, p. 46, table 4, p. 48, p. 61, p. 364

Stalin's five-year plans. Munitions grew at a compound annual rate of 40 percent (1928–37), more than doubling every two years. The initial base was low, but the rapid growth raised the defense burden (share of defense outlays in GNP) well into the double digits by 1937, where it remained until the system imploded.

Not all Sovietologists saw things this way. Bergson's own composite GNP series (1928 ruble prices) grew at 11.9 percent per annum (1928–37), twice as fast as the

Command Communism: 1937–1953

The high water mark of Soviet growth was 1937, the year of the Great Terror. Thereafter official national income slowed to a few percent per annum. Civilian growth plummeted after Hitler occupied large swathes of the country during World War II, and a significant portion of the capital stock constructed (1928–37) was destroyed. Postwar reconstruction was swift, despite the consignment of returning POWs to Gulag (for the treasonous act of surrendering), Soviet hegemony over Eastern and Central Europe, and the famine of 1947. National income recovered to prewar levels by 1950, but per capita consumption never reached the 1928 level before Stalin's demise. Along the way the USSR lost another 30 million lives, 9 million to battle casualties. At least 10 million of this total were victims of despotism, bringing Stalin's terror killings to 20 million, the figure widely cited in the popular literature. Stalin's Muscovite ambitions never flagged. He was thwarted from occupying half of Japan (Hokkaido to Tokyo) by the American navy, but energetically promoted communist expansion in Korea and Europe, acquiring the atomic and hydrogen bombs along the way in 1949 and 1951. A spate of recent publications allege that he didn't die of natural causes, but was killed to preempt his launching World War III. Even if he weren't plotting to do so, the possibility fits the profile. His Muscovite version of administrative command planning was archetypically despotic and militaristic, without any sign of transitioning to western social democracy.

series featured in the Bergson–Kuznets volume (table 7.6), as did Powell's industrial series valued in 1928 prices (table 7.8). And Moorsteen showed elsewhere that the Laspeyres measure better reflected the change in production potential along Stalin's preferred growth trajectory (appendix 7.1), but interesting as this demonstration was, Soviet performance after 1937 conformed to the "perspirational" pattern displayed by the Paasche series. Even if Soviet industrialization had begun with a bang as officially asserted, it ended (1937–53) with a sigh.

And of course, there was always the possibility that the official sub-aggregated data on which the Bergson school relied were padded in ways that could not be detected by auditing their internal consistency, or remedied by Western accounting. Objective observers therefore were able to interpret the "heroic" years of early industrialization in shades from dark grey to sky blue, but beyond 1937 the spectrum narrowed. Since Western scholars were never able to replicate the growth rates officially claimed with the published sub-aggregate data, it could be reasonably concluded that economic growth during the full Stalin period 1928–53 had been uninspired. Blame could be laid at the door of World War II, but the Bergson–Kuznets school had defined the problematic differently. By stressing the perspirational aspect of Soviet growth, they advanced the testable hypothesis that post-Stalin growth would be anemic and in the limit could be immiserizing, unless the Kremlin found a way to dramatically improve labor skills and technological progress. Few Sovietologists predicted that economic performance after 1953 would be poor, or that the system would collapse. But this wasn't the essential point. The Bergson school had crafted statistics and marshaled supply-side theory supporting the proposition that command communism would prove to be economically inferior, just as the detailed analysis of *piatiletki* implied, placing the burden on the Kremlin's shoulders to prove that western Sovietologists were wrong.

Review

The Bolsheviks believed that all was fair in love and class warfare. During the 1920s it was claimed not only that the economy recovered from the ravages of World War I and War Communism by 1926, but that national income grew at more than 30 percent per annum (1926–8) precisely at the time Stalin was lamenting that industrialization was imperiled by the kulak menace. This cognitive dissonance has many potential explanations, not the least of which is statistical misrepresentation. Given the substance of the "great industrialization debates 1924–28" it is inconceivable that national income could have grown faster than 30 percent per annum (1926–8).

The statistical claims of the communist command era 1929–53 follow the same template. They are grossly implausible. There is no basis for believing that rapid advances in administrative command planning and embodied science and technological progress could have propelled industrial growth and gross national product ahead at the rates reported, especially against the backdrop of forced collectivization. NMP did not grow at 16.7 and industry at 21.1 percent per annum (1928–40) as officially asserted, with agriculture humming along, marred only by a brief dip in meat production (1933–7).

But if the Bolsheviks exaggerated, what were the true figures? There is a strong possibility that the answers will never be known. The numbers could have been concocted before they reached the central statistical authorities, or they could have been freely invented. Most western specialist however persuaded themselves that the raw data could be adjusted and made "reliable" enough. They reasoned that Soviet authorities needed accurate data for internal control. Bolshevik statisticians could have operated with two sets of books, one for internal and another for external consumption, but it was argued that there was no evidence that this was the case. Since the accused under Western law is innocent until proven guilty, the presumption was that there was only one set of honestly constructed statistics, which were reliably reported unless there were exceptional political or national security reasons for doing otherwise. This implied that red statistics could only be distorted on mechanical grounds, or because of Marxist price fixing.

After a period of protracted debate, a consensus was reached that the Soviets had mishandled new goods pricing, mistakenly treating inflation as if it were value added. NMP growth adjusted for this error was closer to 11.9 percent per annum (1928–37). Recalculations were also made using a technique known as adjusted factor costing which was supposed to transform Marxist fiat prices into market equivalents. They corresponded closely with official series and therefore seemed to buttress the notion that the Kremlin's numbers were reliable, as did the more moderate growth computed with official late year price weights. Although the disparity between Soviet GDP growth computed in 1926–7 prices and prices of 1937 seemed extreme, Raymond Powell and Richard Moorsteen showed that the behavior was consistent with "index number relativity" under conditions of rapid economic growth.

The consensus estimates reported in tables 7.6–7.15, computed at "late year" ruble prices, thus appear to reveal that command communism was an effective engine of economic growth which allowed the Soviet Union to partially catch up with the United States (1928–53) despite the ravages of World War II. Military and heavy industrial performance were clearly superior, but advances were made on all fronts including living standards and agricultural production, leaving open the possibility not only that Command Communism was viable, but that it might even be superior to free enterprise. The only potentially fatal blemish was negative factor productivity growth, which implied that the benefits of science and technological progress might someday be offset by diminishing returns to capital widening. Official Soviet data did not confirm this finding, making it impossible to definitively judge whether diminishing returns posed a serious challenge to Command Communism.

All of these inferences however are premised on the supposition that the statistical misrepresentation flagrantly evident during NEP was curtailed thereafter; that Stalin himself had a change of heart. Also, one must somehow believe that Stalinist administrative command planning in an era of forced collectivization and terror was able to perform better than free enterprise; that administrative muddling unassisted by markets was better than economic competition under the rule of law. Arguments have been crafted to support this position by glossing over the reality of *piatiletki* and the disconnection between most aspects of supply and demand in the Command Communist economic system. But in retrospect, as partisanship fades, such arguments seem increasingly mistaken.

Appendix 7.1 The Moorsteen Effect

Richard Moorsteen contended that Bergson's fast growing Laspeyres series was a good indicator of Stalin's preferred path. His geometric demonstration is reproduced in figure A7.1. Industry is arrayed on the ordinate, agriculture on the abscissa. Points A and B represent the combined product of manufactures and agricultural goods in 1929 and 1937 respectively. Each point lies on the production feasibility frontier prevailing in the designated year. The distance B′B along the output vector for 1937 measures the improvement in Russia's ability to produce the late year mix compared with 1929. The distance AA′ depicts the counterpart change along the 1929 vector. B′B is clearly larger than AA′ indicating that production potential grew more along the vector preferred by Stalin than along the route Bukharin favored. Since the Laspeyres growth exceeds the Paasche, it corresponds more closely with B′B than AA′, a relationship confirmed by inserting the 1937 price line through point A, leading to B″ (the equivalent value of A along the 1937 vector), and the 1929 line through B to point A″ (the equivalent of B along the 1929 vector). Note that the Laspeyres growth AA″ is similar to the change in production potential B′B, and the Paasche growth B″B is similar to the change in production potential AA′.

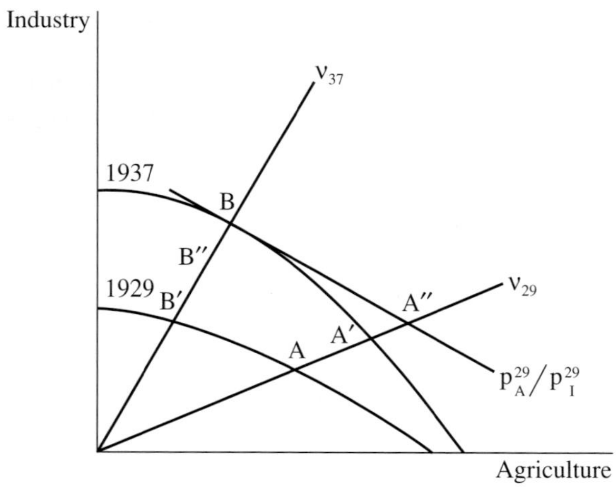

Figure A7.1 Soviet growth: 1929–1937

Questions

1 Why were NEP growth statistics implausible, viewed from the perspective of the "great industrialization debates 1924–8?"
2 Should Stalin have been able to grasp that forced collectivization was unjustified, given the rates of industrial growth the Bolsheviks officially claimed? Should his failure in this regard be attributed to cognitive dissonance, analytic incompetence, or Stalin's knowledge that the industrialization statistics were exaggerated? Explain.
3 Why should we believe that Stalin became more scrupulous about the cosmetic enhancement of official statistics after NEP?
4 What culture-based premises induced Western economists to suppose that command communist statistics were reliable? Assess the plausibility of these premises in retrospect, based on your knowledge of *piatiletki* and Soviet despotism.

5 Free enterprise theory from Adam Smith onward teaches that competitive exchange under the rule of law is more efficient than administrative muddling. What implicit assumptions therefore had to be made in order for western analysts to infer that Soviet growth claims were plausible? Distinguish between growth calculated at 1926–7, and 1937 ruble factor cost prices. Given your knowledge of *piatiletki* and Soviet despotism, were these implicit assumptions justified?
6 The Command Communist model has been shown to be capable of generating physical growth of goods and services. Do official Soviet economic statistics validate this inference? Explain.
7 Could Command Communist growth have been immisering? (*Hint*: pre-cycling, consumer dissatisfaction, overfull employment, Gulag.)
8 Scrutinize Western estimates. What evidence can you find that this may have been the case? Suppose official growth claims were exaggerated as they were during NEP. How would this affect your assessment of the probable economic consequences of Command Communism?
9 Is there evidence that the Soviet Union quickly became over-capitalized? Explain, what the social welfare implications are of over-capitalization?
10 Is there evidence that the Soviet Union was structurally militarized during Command Communism? Is this evidence plausible? Explain.
11 Based on your preceding responses, would you characterize Command Communism as a great success, mediocre, a failure, or a catastrophe judged from the standpoints of social welfare and alternative possibilities? Explain.

Part III

Soviet Communism: Hope and Disenchantment

The Command Communist era was epitomized by rapid industrialization, socialist central planning, terror, the "Great Patriotic War" (World War II), and the American nuclear monopoly 1945–9 which prevented Stalin from using the Red Army to pursue his imperial ambitions in Japan and the West. He relied instead on subversion and guerrilla tactics resulting in the infamous "cold war," which might have taken a more menacing turn after the Kremlin acquired the hydrogen bomb in 1951 had Stalin not died soon thereafter.[1]

The post-Stalin epoch took on a markedly different character. Moscow partially distanced itself from the seamier, unscrupulous sides of Command Communism ("the thaw", "socialism with a human face"),[2] while preserving its allegiance to the Leninist cause. Nikita Khrushchev inaugurated a policy of "*mirovaya sosuchestvovannia*" (peaceful coexistence) in 1955,[3] denouncing Stalin's crimes against humanity at the 20th Communist Party Congress the next year.[4] And while the criminalization of business, entrepreneurship, and private property remained sacrosanct, Moscow sought to challenge the West by improving the technology, administration, and incentives of central planning to the point where it outshined democratic free enterprise.

The West responded cautiously. There was considerable hand ringing over the possibility that central planning might prove to be a superior engine of growth,[5] mitigated by the diminished prospect of superpower hot war. For a while both sides reduced military expenditures, but then the upward spiral resumed, with the Soviets leading the pace of advance.[6] This created a latent instability that was the hallmark of the epoch. Both sides strove to peacefully turn the "correlation of forces" in their favor, while preserving their military options, including fighting and winning a nuclear war (team B).[7] They simultaneously managed perceptions of comparative systems merit, and struggled with the issue of military pre-emption; a drama that colored public discourse. During the 1950s and much of the 1960s, it seemed as if the Soviets were winning the growth race, as well as the hearts and minds of people attracted to socialist principles across the globe. But then perceptions changed. Even though the statistics continued to show Soviet economic performance in a favorable light, the correlation of forces turned,[8] leading to a loss of faith within the Soviet elite which culminated in its self-destruction. The Command Communist economy never ceased "working," but hope for the good life vanished, bringing a colossal social experiment to an ignominious conclusion.

8

Reform Communism: 1953–1991

Summary

The Communist Party of the Soviet Union during the Stalin era repeatedly asserted that Command Communism was the world's best economic system. There was room for modernization as science and technology progressed, but not fundamental reform except the drastic curtailment of terror, Gulag, and forced labor, since the best was best and everything else inferior. Stalin successors for this and other reasons viewed fundamental systemic change such as the decriminalization of private property, business, and entrepreneurship, or the dissolution of central planning as a political third rail. They were prepared to rein in terror and Gulag, and to contemplate further methodological and organizational "rationalization," including computers, cybernetics, optimal planning, and incentivization, but marketization of any sort was considered heretical until Mikhail Gorbachev cut the Gordian knot.

The process of Command Communist economic metamorphosis, or more concisely "Reform Communism," began immediately after Nikita Khrushchev's coronation, when he arrested Lavrenti Beria, head of the NKVD and signaled milder repression in a secret speech to the Twentieth Party Congress. He launched a campaign to till "virgin lands" and radically reorganized state and party administrative jurisdictions (*sovnarkhozy*) for which he was subsequently deposed as a "hare-brained schemer." Alexei Kosygin, his immediate successor, continued more cautiously with a program for reforming enterprise incentives, including tying bonuses to profit maximization. This initiative attempted to improve performance by applying Western efficiency standards to state production. Soviet leaders concomitantly attempted to modernize Command Communism through computerization, cybernetics, and optimal planning controlled or assisted from the center. As Gertrude Schroeder correctly opined, all these efforts were little more than a treadmill of reform. They addressed cosmetic issues, but studiously avoided Command Communism's original sin: the separation of supply from consumer demand. The Communist Party was prepared to undertake fixes that enhanced its control, but none that devolved power to consumers and hence its efforts at improving economic efficiency were futile. This didn't mean that the economy couldn't grow. Technological advances permitted the system to produce more goods no one wanted, but even here results were unsatisfactory. The official (exaggerated) growth rate declined persistently after the late 1960s leading to what Mikhail Gorbachev described as "*zastoi*" (stagnation). Although, the Communist Party continued to insist that Reform Communism was best, Gorbachev's accusation was tantamount to admitting that physical systems management had failed.

During his brief tenure as First Secretary of the Communist Party and President of the Soviet Union, reform was tacitly abandoned in favor of the more radical goal of building "market communism." The program began restoring elements of NEP leasing and entrepreneurship and then swerved toward Muscovite market privilege by allowing managers to use enterprise revenues for personal consumption and to privatize assets to themselves ("spontaneous privatization"). The initiative, if well intended, was poorly conceived because it failed to create conditions for equal opportunity and the rule of contract law. Instead of fostering "*uskorenie*" (acceleration), it caused a hyper-depression as plunder swiftly disorganized production. A viable form of market socialism could have been constructed, but Gorbachev either didn't know how, or didn't want to do it, triggering the systems collapse.

Treadmill of Reform

Command Communism had three distinctive features that were softened and modified in the post-Stalinist era up to 1987: terror, autarky, and planning. During Stalin's reign the economy was centrally planned, regulated and administered; terror was pervasive and the Soviet Union was a marginal participant in the global economy. Although Western liberals never despaired that the Kremlin might some day turn to democratic free enterprise, most understood that this could take decades, or even centuries. The postwar era inevitably was to be a contest between two rival systems: plans versus markets,[1] East versus West, or more grandiosely, communism versus capitalism, and included a hegemonic dimension as the superpowers sparred for global influence. Both acknowledged the rivalry, but interpreted it differently. The Soviets sought to prevail by expanding the principles of Command Communism to Eastern Europe and the Third World, and by improving the efficiency of central planning, while constructing socialism with a human face. This meant jettisoning, or at least tempering terror and autarky, without incorporating markets. The West responded by imagining the possibility of a globally integrated, social democratic USSR that could be gradually nudged away from its authoritarian martial police state to free enterprise. The West's game was to simultaneously "contain" Soviet communism, and prove the superiority of liberal market globalization within the Soviet framework of "peaceful coexistence."

Gulag: 1953–1991

There were ten to twelve million inmates incarcerated in Gulag when Stalin died in 1953. Two to four million were reportedly released in 1954–5, and another four million shortly after Khrushchev's secret speech to the Twentieth Party Congress. This left approximately four million inmates in 1959. CIA studies using national technical means counted, and estimated, that there were roughly four million prisoners in 1977, about half in Gulag. These statistics show that while repression was drastically reduced during Reform Communism, it didn't vanish, even though some scholars attribute extraordinary incarceration levels to judicial efficiency.

The success of this "engagement" from both perspectives hinged significantly on the Soviet Union's micro- and macroeconomic performance. The global rivalry and even the battle within would depend not just on cosmetically enhanced statistics, but on direct perceptions of comparative life quality, including personal liberty. The contest was likely to be won or lost on the Soviet leadership's ability to humanize, and substantially improve the low economic efficiency of central planning. This involved an element of double think on both sides. If official statistics were taken at face value, momentum clearly favored Moscow. There was no objective basis for Stalin's successors contemplating radical reform (other than dispensing with terror), or the West's faith in free enterprise. The endless succession of economic reforms which followed revealed that the Kremlin wasn't confident in either its numbers or the merit of the results. Although Nikita Khrushchev proclaimed that Soviet communism would "bury" Western capitalism (because free enterprise was marked for extinction), by the late 1960s the USSR's industrial and GDP growth rates began to conspicuously decelerate casting doubt not only on the micro-failings of physical systems management, but on its long-run macroeconomic prowess. Whatever the true rate of aggregate growth, Soviet growth "retardation" became the litmus test of Reform Communism's merit for both contestants. Unless the slide were arrested, the economy sooner or later would become stagnant or worse. The battle lines were crisply drawn. Western economists, most notably Abram Bergson after 1962 stressed negative factor productivity growth as central planning's Achilles' heel, while the Kremlin repeatedly promised "*uskorenie*" (acceleration) driven by technological progress and improved micro-efficiency.

Soviet reforms during this era are classifiable into two broad archetypes: perfect command and perfect regulation. The political-economic literature refers to these tendencies as "centralization" and "decentralization." The former can be conceived as "computopia," where Kremlin supermen direct Gosplan to solve an economy-wide linear, or non-linear program and devise a complementary perfect enforcement mechanism to assure its realization. The sci-fi version devised by Dr. "Frank N. Stein" is a leadership controlled, interactive, cybernetic, supply side Pareto simulation which replaces managers and consumers with artificially intelligent cyborgs. Sci-fitopia outshines computopia by substituting perfectly rational, artificially intelligent robots for humans flawed by unruly emotions. They electronically profit and utility maximize under a series of leadership-guided regulations which allow the autocrat to compute his grand utility possibilities frontier and choose the supreme optimum.[2]

Decentralization, a halfway house toward formally legitimizing some individual initiative, devolves loosely regulated decision-making authority from the center to the periphery. Red directors operate as agents rather than state servants and consumers may be granted a modicum of sovereignty. The corresponding sci-fi variant gives cyborgs a degree of agent and consumer sovereignty. Otherwise, perfect command and perfect regulation are alternative routes to the same sorts of socialist ends.

Computerization

The possibilities of powerful physical systems management reforms, computopic, sci-fi and practical were artefacts of the computer revolution. Planning during Stalin's time was done initially on abaci, and then later on rudimentary mechanical calculating machines. Modern computers and electronic calculators with ever-expanding memories didn't appear in the Soviet Union until the mid-1950s, accompanied in swift succession by developments in dispersed processing, cybernetics, operations research, and the internet. Whereas reform hitherto had meant improved administration, management, organization, enforcement, and incentive rationalization; the emergence of superior forms of data acquisition, processing, storage and retrieval, optimal programming, interactive optimization, decompositional algorithms, and remote monitoring and surveillance vastly expanded possibilities for both centralized and decentralized physical planning. Reform became not only synonymous with best bureaucratic practice, but with revolutionary advances in optimal control.

Centralization

The Soviet computopic command development strategy was built around a national computer pyramid.[3] The capstone (engraved with an all seeing eye) was the main computing center of Gosplan, which was connected to every module of the central planning hierarchy from head to toe in a comprehensive network. It supposedly allowed 42 full-time employees to perform 600,000 computational operations involving 30,000–40,000 *tekhpromfinplan* data items in the Moscow Ballbearing Works No. 1.[4] Full connectivity assured that every red director could electronically report his *tekhpromfinplan*, coordinate with contractors, and receive centrally approved assignments. V. F. Pugachev estimated that the entire national economy could be optimally planned with a quadratic program using five million equations and constraints.[5] In relatively short order many Soviet enterprises, organizations, and research institutes were computerized, and it seemed for a moment as if Lenin's premature vision in *State and Revolution* might actually come true.[6] But reality quickly set in. Although information could be acquired, processed, distributed, stored, and retrieved for direct central planning, or decomposed modular subplanning and aggregation, it soon became embarrassingly clear that the center hadn't a clue what to do with its newfound computer capabilities. Systems directors remained opposed to consumer sovereignty, and displayed little interest in household satisfaction. The computer pyramid did nothing to change this. Nor was it much help in micro-controlling production for state purchase. The leadership could not choose preferred output mixes for more than a few hundred composite goods and the prevailing administrative and control structures continued to use traditional material balance procedures with only marginal benefit from computerization. Try as it might, the main computer center of Gosplan couldn't substitute real-time internet enterprise control for bonus-powered *khozraschyot*. Electrons whirled and draft paper plans spewed forth in ever-greater volumes, but comprehensive, centralized, cybernetic, computopic, or sci-fi (servo-mechanistic) microeconomic control always eluded the USSR's systems directors.

A succession of administrative overhauls was no more effective. Ministries were expanded, consolidated, and reorganized. State committees came and went, enterprises were amalgamated and arranged into science and production associations, linking research and development directly to manufacturing. Each bureaucratic and managerial reform had its pros and cons, but none were, nor could they have been panaceas. The root problems of Reform Communism were the same as they had been from the outset of the Bolshevik coup d'etat. The criminalization of private business, entrepreneurship, and ownership, combined with physical systems management, central planning, and state price fixing precluded Marshallian and Walrasian automatic demand and supply equilibration[7] without providing an effective surrogate. Administrative reform altered the framework of disequilibrium management, but didn't address the source.

Decentralization

Computopic decentralization was similarly impractical, but expanding the scope of red director discretion proved feasible. The physical management system was broadened by liberalizing *khozraschyot* with sophisticated enterprise bonus incentivization schemes effectively transforming red directors into managers.[8] The idea wasn't novel. Profit was employed as one of many bonus reward criteria during the late 1920s and revenue was often utilized thereafter together with output as a cardinal incentive, but output remained king throughout until Alexei Kosygin chose to make Evgeny Liberman's concept of profitability the foundation stone of enterprise reform on September 27, 1965.[9]

Western liberals were heartened, interpreting Libermanism as a harbinger of democratic free enterprise and party watchdogs worried that they might be right, compelling Liberman to tortuously explain the distinction without a difference between profit and profitability.[10] But this scholasticism was a minor distraction. What mattered was that some enterprise managers henceforth would be rewarded for maximizing positive net revenue instead of output, mimicking the Western textbook maximand. Utilizing the same notation and constraints as in the output maximizing case, red directors would receive a fixed ruble reward for every ruble of profit earned up to the point where profit was maximized.

The corresponding Lagrangian is

$$\hat{L} = px - \sum_{r=1}^{n} w_r v_r - F - \sum_{i=1}^{k} \hat{\lambda}_i (w_i v_i - m_i) - \hat{\psi}\left(\sum_{r=1}^{n} w_r v_r - M \right)$$

and the Kuhn–Tucker conditions are:

$$\frac{\partial L}{\partial v_i} = p\frac{\partial x}{\partial v_i} - w_i - \hat{\lambda}_i - \psi w_i \leq 0 \quad \forall_{i=1}^{k} \tag{8.1}$$

$$\frac{\partial \hat{L}}{\partial v_j} = p\frac{\partial x}{\partial v_j} - w_j - \hat{\psi} w_j \leq 0 \quad k < j \leq n \tag{8.2}$$

$$\frac{\partial \hat{L}}{\partial \hat{\lambda}_i} = m_i - w_i v_i \geq 0 \quad \forall_{i=1}^{k} \tag{8.3}$$

$$\frac{\partial \hat{L}}{\partial \hat{\psi}} = M - \sum_{r=1}^{n} m_r v_r \geq 0 \quad \forall_{r=1}^{n} \tag{8.4}$$

Assuming that factor i is used (8.1) allows us to write

$$p\frac{\partial x}{\partial v_i} = (1 + \hat{\lambda}_i + \hat{\psi}) w_i \tag{8.1a}$$

Since $\hat{\lambda}_i$, $\hat{\psi} > 0$, it is clear that the factor is underused by the usual Pareto standard, but the Kuhn–Tucker conditions provide no theoretical reasons to suppose that Soviet enterprises are either inherently technically or economically inefficient, assuming quota restrictions are designed to optimize planners' preferences. Similarly, if factor j is used (8.2) enables us to write

$$p\frac{\partial x}{\partial v_j} = (1 + \hat{\psi}) w_j \tag{8.2a}$$

and to conclude that these factors are also underused by the Pareto criterion.

Like their Western counterparts, maximization required red directors to produce only to the point where marginal revenue was equated with marginal cost at E in figures 8.1 and 8.2. They would never produce more than output-maximizing enterprises did because to do so would reduce their bonuses. This result was Pareto improving compared to the typical output maximizing case because it meant that capital and labor would always be put to better use instead of being overfully employed. Red directors in the Liberman world still might under produce at A because constraints on quota inputs were binding, but this problem could be solved merely by eliminating quotas. The Lagrangian appears to suggest that the inefficiency of Soviet enterprise micro supply could be eliminated by simply adopting Western profit maximizing.

An appreciation of the possibilities can be deepened by considering the example of a multi-product Soviet enterprise. In doing so, assume that the firm has specific amounts of fixed factors of production. The amount of a fixed factor that is used cannot exceed the total available to the firm in the short run. Thus if z_{jr} is the amount

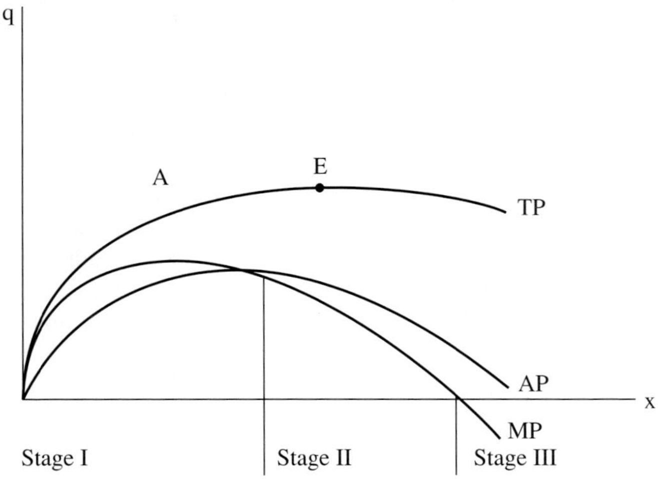

Figure 8.1 Command Communist constrained output maximization

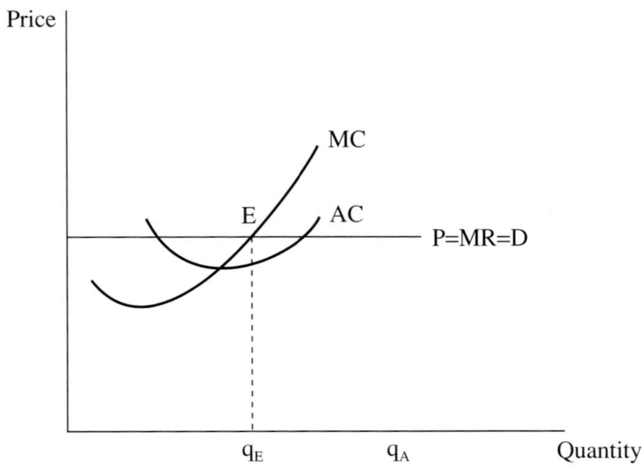

Figure 8.2 Reform Communist profit maximization

of fixed factor r used in producing product j and Z_r is the total amount of the fixed factor available to the firm, it must be true that

$$\sum_{j=1}^{m} z_{jr} - z_r < 0.$$

In addition when units of a fixed factor are put into a new use, there are start-up costs that will be incurred by the firm. Machines must be adjusted or calibrated when they are used, storage spaces must be cleaned, etc. These costs are shown by

$$K(z_{ji}, \ldots, z_{mq}),$$

which is convex and has positive first derivatives.

Under the conditions of the multi-product firm the production function is shown as

$$x_j = f_j(v_{j1}, \ldots, v_{jn}, z_{j1}, \ldots, z_{jq}), \quad \forall_{j=1}^{m}$$

Here x_j is the quantity of product j produced, while v_{ji} is the amount of variable factor i used in producing product j and z_{jr} is the amount of fixed factor r used in the production of j. The production function of each product is strictly concave.

For the purpose of simplifying the notation we assume that there are no quota factors. Because of the multi-product nature of the firm, the planning authorities can require that a particular assortment of outputs be produced. That is, they can require that a minimum amount of each good be produced. If an assortment requirement is imposed, the profit maximizing Lagrangian is:

$$\tilde{L} = \sum_{j=1}^{m} p_j x_j - \sum_{j=1}^{m} \sum_{i=1}^{n} w_i v_{ji} - K(z_{11}, \ldots, z_{mq})$$

$$-F - \sum_{j=1}^{m} \tilde{\theta}_j (\tilde{x}_j - f_1(v_{i1}, \ldots, v_{in}, z_{j1}, \ldots, z_{jq}))$$

$$-\sum_{r=1}^{q} \tilde{u}_r \left(\sum_{j=1}^{m} z_{jr} - z_r \right) - \hat{\psi} \left(\sum_{j=1}^{m} \sum_{i=1}^{n} + K(z_{11}, \ldots, z_{mq}) - M \right)$$

The assortment constraints show $\bar{x}_j$ as the minimum amount required and thus can be written as

$$\tilde{x}_j - f(v_{j1}, \ldots, v_{jn}, z_{j1}, \ldots, z_{jq}) \leq 0$$

The Kuhn–Tucker conditions are:

$$\frac{\partial \tilde{L}}{\partial v_{ji}} = p_j \frac{\partial f_j}{\partial v_{ji}} - w_i + \tilde{\theta}_j \frac{\partial f_j}{\partial v_{ji}} - \hat{\psi} w_i \leq 0 \quad \forall_{j=1}^{m}, {}_{i=1}^{n} \tag{8.5}$$

$$\frac{\partial \tilde{L}}{\partial z_{jr}} = p_j \frac{\partial f_j}{\partial z_{jr}} - \frac{\partial K}{\partial z_{jr}} + \tilde{\theta}_j \frac{\partial f_j}{\partial z_{jr}} - \tilde{\mu}_r - \hat{\psi}_r \frac{\partial K}{\partial z_{jr}} \leq 0 \quad \forall_{j=1}^{m}, {}_{r=1}^{q} \tag{8.6}$$

$$\frac{\partial \tilde{L}}{\partial \tilde{\theta}_j} = f_i(v_{j1}, \ldots, v_{jn}, z_{j1}, \ldots, z_{jq}) - \bar{x}_j \geq 0 \quad \forall_{j=1}^{m} \tag{8.7}$$

$$\frac{\partial \tilde{L}}{\partial \tilde{\mu}} = Z_r - \sum_{j}^{m} z_{jn} \geq 0 \quad \forall_{r=1}^{q} \tag{8.8}$$

$$\frac{\partial \tilde{L}}{\partial \hat{\psi}} = M - \left(\sum_{k=1}^{m} \sum_{i=1}^{n} w_i v_{ji} + K(z_{11}, \ldots, z_{mq}) \right) \geq 0$$

An assortment constraint is binding if the quantity of the product required by unconstrained profit maximzing is less than the amount required in the assortment. In this case $\tilde{\theta}_j > 0$ and (8.8) can be shown as

$$(p_j + \tilde{\theta}_j)\frac{\partial f_1}{\partial v_{ji}} = (1 + \hat{\psi})w_i \quad \forall_{i,j} \tag{8.8a}$$

Similarly (8.9) may be written as

$$(p_j + \tilde{\theta}_j)\frac{\partial f_j}{\partial z_{jr}} = (1 + \hat{\psi})\frac{\partial K}{\partial z_{jr}} + \tilde{\mu}_r \quad \forall_{j,r} \tag{8.9a}$$

if the assortment constraint is binding on good *j*. Thus the rule for dividing fixed factors among different products differs from the Pareto rule.

Of course, it can be argued that legitimate social goals may require a minimum output of goods or of some goods that would be greater than the output provided by profit maximization at established parametric prices.

The upshot of these exercises is the revelation that while profit based bonus incentivization eliminates the extreme wastefulness of output based rewards, it isn't a panacea unless input and output prices reflect the sovereign's marginal rates of product substitution (the set of relative prices which maximize the sovereign's utility), or are optimally modified with input and output assortment quotas. Since as previously explained this could not be accomplished under Soviet command planning arrangements, then the advantage of profit over output-based incentives was unevaluable. While profit incentives no doubt curbed waste, it is difficult to fathom how it could have dramatically improved economic efficiency. Soviet wages, rents, and output prices were "false prices." They were disconnected from utility by design and were deliberately set sufficiently high above *sebestoimost'* (prime cost) to assure overfull factor utilization, mimicking the effect of output maximizing. There is no basis consequently for assessing whether the utility of aggregate Soviet output determined by this ersatz profit maximizing with Marxist labor cost prices was greater than the utility generated from output maximizing, both from the systems directors' and the Paretian consumers' perspectives, an insight which illuminates the deficiency of Bergson's production potential concept. The same principle applies to micro-quota setting. Since the state could not assess the merits of this or that micro-quota array, it could only happen upon an optimum by accident and even then would not know it.[11]

Soviet Marxist Labor Value Price-setting

Price-fixing was a corollary of the criminalization of business. Marx taught that negotiated money exchange was the mechanism capitalists used to extract surplus value from workers and the Soviets sought to preempt its recurrence by requiring that all exchanges be transacted at official state set prices. Negotiating prices was a criminal offense with few exceptions under War Communism, Command Communism, and Reform Communism until 1987. Official labor cost prices for 25 million products were fixed by the State Price

Committee (Goskomtsen). Marx claimed that all value was created by labor, implying that the value of any product could be determined by computing its labor cost (wages, plus the past wage cost of non-labor inputs). This was called prime cost (*sebestoimost'*). Soviet price setters started with *sebestoimost'* and added overhead charges, profit mark ups, as well as wholesale and retail turnover taxes (sales taxes). Abram Bergson used these protocols to argue that Soviet ruble prices had meaning because they were based on labor factor cost, and could be made more meaningful by deleting profit mark ups and turnover taxes, and adding back a uniform interest rate return as a proxy for capital services, a procedure compatible with Western national income accounting. His claim however was overstated. Neither Marxist labor value, nor Bergsonian adjusted factor cost prices are compatible with Pareto. Soviet prices (and wages) weren't determined by utility maximizing demand, and therefore aren't jointly tangent to isoquants at any point on the Pareto contract curve in figure 2.3. They neither measure Paretian marginal rates of transformation, nor substitution, and therefore are merely opaque fiat factor cost proxies for the kinds of demand-responsive prices that make Western GDP values meaningful. Relatedly, *tekhpromfinplans* computed by bonus maximizing red directors were co-determined by official fiat prices and line item budgetary constraints, not Paretian equilibrium prices, and consequently were suboptimal.

Moreover, bonus incentivization raised a series of further perplexities. What was the optimal bonus reward and how should it be funded?[12] What should be done, if for example, red directors violated quota and or assortment constraints in maximizing outputs, or profits? Suppose exogenous constraints prevented enterprise managers from producing profitably. Should managers be rewarded for loss minimizing? How could managers be deterred from falsifying their accomplishments to enhance their bonuses? Who cared if a suboptimal mix were generated or red directors overstated their achievements? The further one delves into the practicalities of bonus incentivization, red management versus red direction, the more one discovers a wilderness of indeterminism that accurately reflects what Friedrich von Hayek called "planned chaos." Perpetual bonus "reform" became a fixture of Reform Communism, but it never was more than an exercise in futility.

The same inference applies to more ambitious efforts at reforming and cybernetically regulating decentralized economic relationships. An "algorithm" (road map) as Richard Judy put it was needed to cut through the maze of possibilities separating Soviet planning practice from the optimum.[13] Management-system design, planning, and operations all "had to be" connected and coordinated by key bits of information reflecting supplies and demands. A vast research and reform effort called the automatic system of management and planning (ASUP) emerged from this humble origin during the 1960s.[14] It focused on the construction of standardized management and planning indicators; decision-making aids for utilizing them, mechanisms for distribution, coordination, and supervision. The endeavor was couched as cybernetic, but the feedback dimension was feeble. Algorithms made little inroads into displacing people, and since the entire operation was only tenuously related to the sovereign preferences of the leadership, or consumers, it was mostly pretense.

An endless succession of administrative organizational reforms followed a similar pattern. Nikita Khrushchev dis-enthroned Stalin's ministerial hierarchy in May 1957 and replaced it with a regional plan-supervisory mechanism based on new territorial units, rather than established republican jurisdictions called "*sovnarkhozy*" (regional economic councils). The change had no discernible aggregate benefit, caused considerable resentment, and led in short order to the Kosygin reforms of 1965 which restored the ministerial system and established Goskomtsen (State Committee for Prices), Gossnab (State Committee for Material-Technical Supply) superseding ministerial supply networks, and GosTekhnika (State Committee for New Technology). The State Committee for Labor and Social Questions was granted expanded authority. The Soviets toyed with placing economic ministries on *khozraschyot* during the late 1970s, as they had been earlier under NEP. Proposals were vetted for the creation of special regional development agencies, consumer goods coordination, and a ministry for inter-sector machinery production, etc. Another broad area of initiative was the merger of industrial enterprises into large associations, including "science-production" associations, and for transforming some ministerial *glavks* into industrial associations. The number of science-production associations in industry rose from 1,101 at the beginning of 1973 to 3,670 at the end of 1977, when they accounted for 44.3 percent of sales and 45 percent of employment. As usual the initiative began with a bang and ended with a whimper. It often amounted to little more than changing the names on the doors. Besides over-dosing on giantism and mergers, managerial training programs were expanded and ministries were required to develop plans for retraining managers at least once every six years. In May 1978 the Academy of the National Economy of the USSR was established to provide senior executive training. The next year, in July 1979, the Communist Party of the Soviet Union (CPSU) and the Council of Ministers adopted an omnibus Decree No. 695 refocusing incentives on the fulfillment of five-year plans, authorized a major industrial price reform January 1, 1982, adjusted incentives to emphasize net rather than gross output, adopted a "programmatic" approach to planning, restated the desirability of placing industrial ministries on *khozraschyot*, limited five-year plan revisions, and expanded enterprise access to bank investment credits. In June 1982 Gosplan de facto took on the status of a ministry, directly planning and allocating resource flows to enterprises and associations. Gorbachev followed suit in 1985 expanding enterprise self-financing (*samofinansirovanie* and *samookupaemost'*) and increasing managerial discretionary authority over administrative expenditures. Two years later he vested authority over enterprise target setting in the Council of Ministers and permitted enterprises to sue their ministries and allowed labor collectives to elect permanent enterprise councils. The merry-go-round whirled over and over again, but it never overcame planned chaos or reinvigorated the Command Communist system.[15]

Innovation

It is likely that Soviet economists were more keenly aware than their Western colleagues that rationalizing the irrational through sundry reforms was chasing rainbows. Tauter plans, cybernetics, and better incentives could not save the day for Leninist microeconomics. But there was more hope that victory could be seized from the jaws of defeat through scientific and technological progress. If Reform Communism couldn't produce things anyone wanted efficiently, it could perhaps flood society with many more of them.

The task seemed tractable precisely because it depended more on applied engineering than specific demand. Imagine a universal technology that could improve productivity in all activities. The inability of the systems directors to supply desired characteristics and assortments in this instance wouldn't prevent GDP from growing rapidly because the rising tide would raise all boats. Systems directors need only finance research, development, testing and evaluation (RDT&E) to increase physical productivity and save input costs. Where technological progress was product specific, or benefits were qualitative rather than quantitative, a battery of hedonic indicators could be employed to evaluate comparable worth. Opportunities for buying, leasing, borrowing, copying or illegally acquiring advanced technologies from abroad also were considered a plus because foreign innovations met the market test. The rate of scientific and technological progress from this perspective seemed to be a function of the scale of the RDT&E effort and reforms designed to enhance research efficiency.

The scope of the Soviet endeavor in both regards was prodigious. According to official statistics, the Kremlin spent 6 percent of GDP on science in 1988, up from 4 percent in 1970.[16] The USSR Academy of Sciences had a staff of 62,363 scientists.[17] There were 5,111 scientific institutions, employing 4.2 million workers.[18] And the results were impressive. Profit was increased by 5 billion rubles, costs lowered by 3.7 billion rubles,[19] and GDP productivity growth was several percent per annum.

Direct outlays on RDT&E were buttressed by reform and rationalization. These spanned administrative reorganizations, rules for pricing new goods, and above all else bonuses for inventing, producing, and adopting superior technologies. As with other aspects of microeconomic behavior, systems directors decided to simulate Western optimization, and mimic its incentives. Workers, scientists, and managers were allowed to utility seek for their personal benefit like entrepreneurial lessees under NEP by innovating, producing new goods, and adopting advanced technologies, instead of obeying authoritarian commands. Although the government preferred comprehensive control, it recognized that few inventors in enterprises or institutes would spend their time creating without the prospect of adequate reward. Output and profit maximizing red directors would resist manufacturing better goods whenever changing product lines disrupted production and had no interest in enhancing enterprise productivity because they correctly anticipated that norms governing bonuses would be ratched upward by supervisors to reflect improvements in output capacities.

The solution was a myriad of innovation and technological diffusion schemes, which were patterned on core microeconomic bonuses. Designers and engineers in institutes and bureaus were compensated according to the number of new blueprints they devised. In-house enterprise inventors were promised a share of the prospective profits, or cost savings attributable to their innovations. Red directors were similarly incentivized for promoting technological progress and diffusion by augmenting the size of the bonus fund for improving "quality" and compensating them for idle production time entailed.

But the payoff to these reforms was invisible. Although science expenditure as a share of GDP rose 50 percent (1970–88), GDP growth benefits didn't increase as might have been expected if innovation reforms had been effective. Likewise, Soviet technology exports were imperceptible. Whereas, Japanese cars and electronic exports bespoke success, Russian civilian manufactures seldom passed muster in the West.[20] This is hardly surprising and has little to do with Western trade restrictions as often claimed. Command Communism was customer unfriendly and deceptive. Innovation often improved goods in some measurable technical sense. New products might be lighter and stronger. But, if these characteristics were secondary, or undesirable from the customer's perspective, the "progress" was spurious. Change had occurred, "productivity" had risen, output grew, but value hadn't been added. With some exceptions, particularly weapons, the Soviet innovation effort was a mirage. Wags rhetorically asked what was the difference between four-star and one-star Soviet cognac, replying – the number of stars on the label! Reform communism didn't enhance macro-performance any more than it did microeconomic rationality. As Paul Krugman put it, "perspiration" initially conveyed an illusion of vigorous welfare enhancing growth, but could not generate the "inspiriation" (high-value innovation) to sustain it.[21]

False Positives

During the cold war, it was considered churlish to harp on the demand side failings of Reform Communism. Setting aside Goskomstat's and the CIA's problematic statistics, the Soviet Union encountered by foreign visitors was reassuringly familiar, despite its greyness. Planes, trains, buses, cars, hotels, public housing, schools, factories, hospitals, restaurants, retail stores, clothes, food, books, records, while shoddy, were nonetheless recognizable. Some services like the ballet were excellent. People were literate and seemed to go about their business as usual. Citizens consumed enough calories, enjoyed access to public entertainment, married, divorced, and life expectancy gradually rose.[22] If one blinked, the poverty of Soviet existence could almost seem normal, leading to the surmise that the distortions of Reform Communism in the grand scheme of things didn't greatly matter, especially if the negatives were rationalized as the price for full employment, price stability, steady growth and egalitarianism. Indeed it could even be shown that the Soviet economy behaved better than America's judged from the standpoint of Heckscher–Ohlin theory.[23] The USSR in accordance with its comparative advantage exported capital-intensive and imported labor-intensive goods, but America did not. Despite the demand insensitivity of Soviet labor cost prices, they guided planners in the Ministry of Foreign Trade to behave "rationally."

But these appearances in differing ways were deceptive. The utilitarian value of similar appearing goods often diverges enormously. A facsimile of a Rembrandt etching, although good enough to fool amateurs, nonetheless is worthless compared with the original in the marketplace. Likewise, a serviceable, but inferior Soviet fur coat was unsaleable in Paris. Soviet products by and large were no frills. They were suitable for Spartans, but not Athenians. The fact that Reform Communism provided a semblance of civilized existence therefore shouldn't be misconstrued. Soviet border guards were needed to prevent Soviet citizens from fleeing, not to keep Westerners from flooding into the USSR to enjoy "la dolce vita." Few sane individuals who experienced life East and West would have chosen physical systems management.

Likewise, the fact that the Ministry of Foreign Trade behaved rationally in the global marketplace insofar as the system allowed, shouldn't be surprising. Reform Communism wasn't inefficient because its citizens were incapable of utility maximizing. It was under-productive because the state prohibited private demand from influencing supply. In the few instances where the state acted like a utility maximizing transactor in the foreign marketplace, trading at world market prices, it could behave appropriately, but these exceptions couldn't be extrapolated into the rule.

Eulogy for Planning

During the cold war the West associated itself with markets, and the East with planning. When Gorbachev rescinded Gosplan's directive authority and Yeltsin dismantled the ministerial productive control mechanism, including *tekhpromfinplanning*, the battle between markets and plans conclusively ended in free enterprise's triumph. There is no longer any political support for computopia in its many guises, regardless of whether it features systems directors' or consumer's sovereignty. The market's victory is total. But, of course, this doesn't imply that governments, corporations, and individuals shouldn't plan. The PAB rule requires everyone to optimally plan to the point where the procedure increases utility, ceasing thereafter. In this sense the cold war debate was always misleading. The issue never was impulse versus foresight. The market and planning motif was just a slogan that captured an important aspect of the dichotomy between productive systems that legalized and those that criminalized private property, business, and entrepreneurship.

Market Communism: Second Wave

Reform communism until the advent of Mikhail Gorbachev had been a technocratic shell game (computopic monkey business), but it didn't have to be. Khrushchev and his successors could have devised innumerable schemes partially transferring economic sovereignty from the Politburo to the people. This would have necessitated markets that allowed consumers to entice suppliers to adjust production for their satisfaction, without abandoning Leninist principles. As during NEP, the state could have retained ownership of the means of production, allowing citizens to lease assets for profit. Stalin's brutal liquidation of nepmen as a class had made this taboo until Gorbachev decided it was time for more radical measures. His strategy of "*perestroika*," literally "reconstruction," differed from "*reforma*" (reform) and, was a Market Communist second wave, achieved by partly rehabilitating certain kinds of markets rather than simulating them solely from the supply side (Liberman-style bonus incentivized profit maximizing and state inter-enterprise contracting.) The initiative was dangerous from a Marxist point of view because it raised the specter of popular economic sovereignty overturning the dictatorship of the vanguard of the proletariat. More practically, like NEP, it was fraught with moral hazard that called for caution and finesse.

Gorbachev, as other socialists before him, tacitly supposed that people could be trusted to engage in some types of voluntary negotiated business transactions, subject to communist party controls, rules, oversight, and discipline. The litmus tests were exploitation and welfare. The Marxist state was obligated to assure that workers were paid their full value added and to produce goods that maximized social well-being. As Oscar Lange demonstrated in the mid-1930s these goals could be achieved even in a regime which criminalized private property, business, and entrepreneurship by adopting state auctions, perfect competitive profit maximizing, and lump-sum social dividends.[24] Other schemes including partial privatization, cooperatives, and leasing were also feasible, but there were four essentials. First there must be equal opportunity, with fair property allocation and equal market access. Second, unregulated exchange must be governed by the rule of contract law. Principles 1 and 2 preclude monopoly, oligopoly, and other forms of unequal exchange. Third, the state must deter misconduct, especially insider moral hazards that threaten equal opportunity and competitiveness. And fourth, the vanguard of the proletariat should not only develop socially optimal programs, but vigilantly suppress regulatory corruption. Market socialism as Stalin understood wasn't so much infeasible as it was prone to abuse.

Social Democracy

The only form of market socialism that has gained wide acceptance in the West is EU social democracy which refrained from criminalizing private property, business, and entrepreneurship; accepts the legitimacy of Pareto utility seeking, and pursues a socialist agenda through public programs and tax-transfer schemes. This was the approach advocated by the Czarist era Menshevik Party. It was scorned by Lenin who insisted on criminalizing private property, business and entrepreneurship. Lenin relaxed his prohibition against some business and entrepreneurial activities, but retained state ownership under NEP. The Lange model adhered to Lenin's original position, deviating only insofar as managers were compelled to produce the goods consumers demanded through a modified Marshallian quantity-adjustment process, mediated by the State Price Board. Gorbachev's Market Communism was internally inconsistent. He tried to blend NEP leasing, Reform Communist controls, spontaneous privatization, private and public entrepreneurship, and insider privilege and wound up with Market Muscovy, a market system operating under the rule of men controlled by rent granting.

It isn't clear whether Gorbachev failed to grasp the danger, naively discounted it, or deliberately set out to enrich his circle. Perhaps the correct answer is all of the above. But whatever the motives, he launched a series of "radical" market building reforms without paying heed to the fundamentals. He introduced "*arenda*," leasing and franchising for small cooperatives, especially restaurants. Foreign joint ventures like McDonalds were permitted and were allowed to settle accounts in dollars. Foreign currency could be converted in local kiosks with rates supposedly set by the forces of supply and demand. Commodity exchanges were authorized, currency controls reduced, entrepreneurship was legalized, central planning was abolished, enterprises freed from ministerial oversight, managers were given access to cash in their firms' accounts, and were permitted in many instances to spontaneously privatize. By 1990 prices had become partially decontrolled, and the USSR was beset by Ponzi schemes and financial fraud. In less than a quinquennium Gorbachev had put in place most of the ingredients for a well-functioning market system *except an equitable distribution of assets, equal opportunity, free entry, the rule of contract law, appropriate controls and regulations, safeguards against moral hazard, and a disciplinary mechanism to suppress corruption.* Although the Soviet Union's mineral wealth and land was reserved to the "people" and key industries including the military-industrial complex remained state owned, this wasn't enough to offset the tidal wave of plunder that soon undid the USSR. Red directors, schooled in the second economy, now suddenly resurrected as managers diverted enterprise revenues to their private consumption. Firms not only were spontaneously privatized, but were pillaged. Valuable assets were spun off, or sold for cash, leaving workers with the debts. Contracts were shredded,[25] and production disorganized. The economy plummeted like a stone, and just kept falling – to the applauds of Western "shock therapists" who construed the debacle as "creative destruction."

Shock Therapy

Shock therapy is a metaphor borrowed by economists from psychiatry suggesting that the best way to shift from a controlled productive order like Reform Communism is to abruptly terminate price and currency controls, abolish state subsidies, and immediately liberalize by decriminalizing private property, business, and entrepreneurship. The approach, strongly advocated by Yeltsin's Western advisors including Anders Aslund and Jeffrey Sachs could have been best if there were a pre-existing democratic tradition and rule of law to help govern business, privatization, and entrepreneurship. Rutaro Komiya, former director of METI has ridiculed the concept as shock without therapy, when these prerequisites are missing, a point validated by Russia's failed transition to democratic free enterprise.

Westerners widely hailed Gorbachev for "biting the bullet," "taking strong medicine," and other antique virtues. "*Perestroika*" in their view was part and parcel of a suite of policies including "glasnost" (candor), "*demokratizatsia*" (democratization), "*novoe myshlenie*" (new thinking), and "*uskorenie*" (acceleration) which were intended to achieve "*perekhod*" (transition) to peaceful, democratic free enterprise, and was therefore seen as progressive. But it wasn't anything like what it seemed.[26] It was "destructive destruction," a Muscovite, anti-Bolshevik usurpation leading back to the future.

Muscovite Markets

Russia markets have distinctive Muscovite features visibly displayed under Czarism, NEP, Gorbachev's Market Communism, and post-Communism. First and foremost, they aren't founded on the rule of law that assures contractual justice. The right to Pareto utility seek is degraded when the judicial system serves the autocrat and the powerful first and everyone else as an afterthought. This principle extends to implementation because even when courts render fair verdicts, they mean nothing if the state fails to enforce them. Second, rent-grantees (those given the right to use the autocrat's assets) enjoy a privileged, anti-competitive status, exerting formidible market power. Third, the weak are economically exploited, persistently paid less than the value of their marginal product. And, fourth, the autocrat has the right to confiscate properties and reallocate grants at his or her whim, violating the sanctity of property and diminishing incentives to innovate and invest. These principles collectively make Muscovite markets autocratically sovereign.

Review

Soviet leaders continuously tinkered with Stalin's Command Communist model after 1953. Although the system was supposed to be perfect, the Kremlin knew better. All of the changes undertaken, during the Reform Communist era were intended to improve the efficiency of planning, not to supplement or replace the Muscovite authoritarian martial police state natural economy with NEP-type socialist markets, until Gorbachev inaugurated Market Communist "*perestroika*." The Reform Communist strategy was sound as far as it went. Moscow would exploit scientific advances in computerization, optimal programming, and cybernetics to improve plan formulation and processing. From a computopic perspective, the systems directors aspired to achieve a supreme optimum on the nation's utility possibility frontier using centralized or dispersed computing. Had they succeeded Muscovy would have been superseded by computopia or more fancifully "sci-fitopia." This effort was supplemented by a rationalized agency approach whereby red directors were trained in the latest western efficiency methods including optimal investment choice procedures and incentivized to maximize profits and technological progress. An "automatic system of management and planning" was also devised to facilitate centrally guided agent optimization with timely and accurate information. And Moscow never tired of initiating administrative control reforms.

The Soviets tried, but failed, because Bolshevism in all its guises was designed to disregard consumer preferences in favor of leadership command. Supply was disconnected from demand and prices had no economic content. The Kremlin to its regret discovered that it could mimic markets, but could not match their efficiency. It could simulate quality enhancement, but could not achieve any real economic benefit, and of course computopic and sci-fi planning were only psychedelic monkey business.

Mikhail Gorbachev tried to escape this merry-go-round of physical systems management reform. But like Khrushchev before him he was part hare-brained schemer, and part self-serving opportunist. While, he prattled about markets, he never lifted a finger to assure equal opportunity, or the rule of contract law. And he played with fire by allowing managers to use state revenues for personal consumption, and to spontaneously privatize enterprises. He spoke about market communism, but laid the foundations of new millennium Market Muscovy.

Western scholars for the most part beguiled themselves with the thought that Command Communism theoretically was the equal of free enterprise, or performed well enough to survive Western competition. Their attitude reflected too high a regard for abstraction and a series of fads that made optimal planning and incentive schemes seem more important than they really were by failing to discern the reality of rent-granting Muscovy behind the rhetoric of "scientific socialism." When the dust finally settled the Soviet not only faded into oblivion, it left behind a horrendous legacy of mis-industrialization and of ecological devastation as testament to the prescience of Robert Burns: "The best laid plans o' mice an' men Gang aft agley."

Ecocide

Murray Feshbach calls the toxic consequences of Command and Reform Communism "ecocide" to stress the life-threatening potential of Soviet industrial and environmental mismanagement. This problem and the cognate issue of remedying Soviet technological mis-selection remain endemic not just because Muscovy has changed less than commonly supposed, but because embodied Soviet-era technologies were infungible. Existing plant and equipment cannot be easily and cheaply retooled, increasing the costs of environmental and structural repair.

Analytics of Reform Communism

The geometry of Reform Communism is as follows. The sides of the Edgeworth–Bowley box in figure 8.3 are larger than the War Communist, NEP, and Paretian cases (elaborated in chapter 2) because of excess systems directors' and managerial demand for capital, resources, and labor. Planners commanded firms to over-produce and set prices artificially high to over-motivate profit-maximizing red directors. The superscripts on the isoquants continued to be less than their Paretian counterparts (figure 2.10) because technologies were mis-selected, inputs were poor, skills deficient, input acquisition untimely, and effort often reserved, despite the use of sophisticated incentives. As during War Communism and NEP factors weren't employed proportionally with their marginal rates of technical substitution and state fixed wage-rental ratios weren't

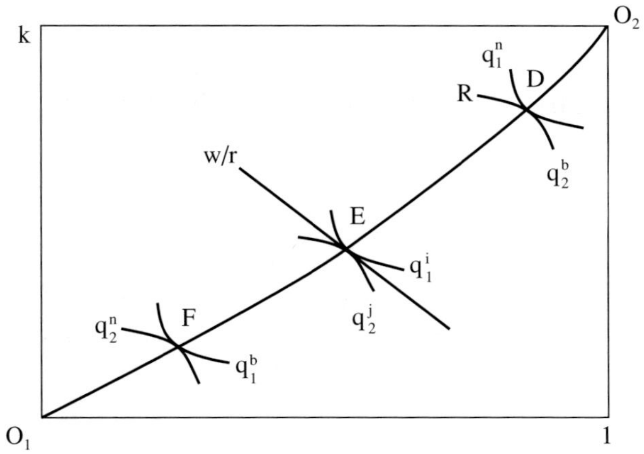

Figure 8.3 Reform Communist factor-production space

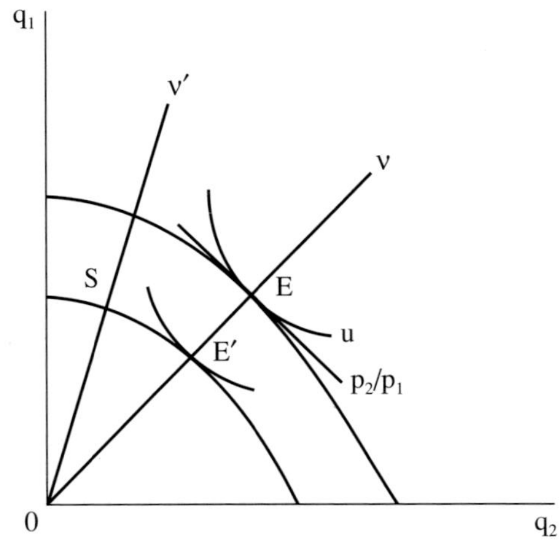

Figure 8.4 Reform Communist production possibilities

competitively determined. Instead of efficiently producing on the contract curve at point E, firms operated inefficiently at R.

Output in the production space depicted in figure 8.4 at point S lies on a similar production feasibilities frontier to the one achieved along the Command Communist expansion vector. Planning and incentive reforms had little impact on Soviet output structure and potential. As in all Soviet communist models, observed output levels were far below Paretian and perfect authoritarian potential, and were economically inefficient judged both from the systems directors and the consumer utility standards.

Products were for the most part rationed, even though some goods were marketed at fixed prices in state retail stores. Reforms didn't greatly improve retail shortages. Figure 8.5 shows that goods weren't efficiently allocated at their marginal rates of product substitution on the contract curve, but off it at point R.

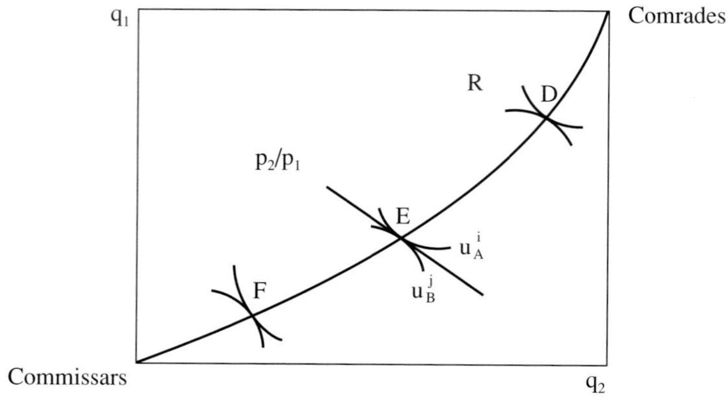

Figure 8.5 Reform Communist distribution

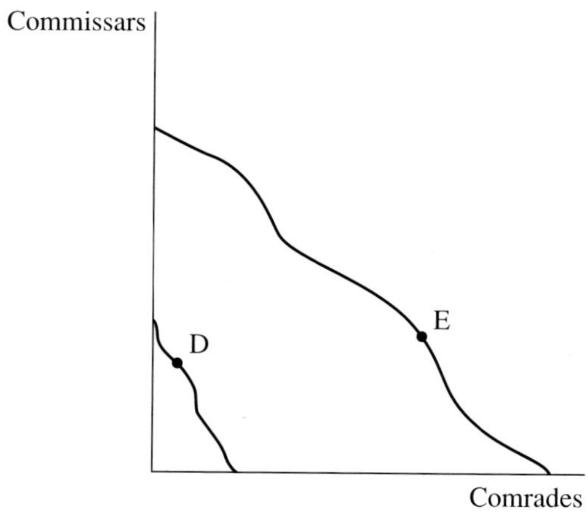

Figure 8.6 Reform Communist utility possibilities

And finally, real income distribution remained extremely inegalitarian with leaders', administrators', party activists' and red directors' demand controlling most outcomes. Their taste ran to guns, pyramids, and discretely consumed luxuries, but this didn't make the inegalitarianism any better. Figure 8.6 reveals that the powerful and corrupt prospered at the people's expense at point D.

Systems Profile

Main features of the Reform Communist economic system

- *Culture*: Muscovite authoritarian/anti-authoritarian, with a proletarian facade. Anti-authoritarianism is a mix of passivity and opportunism.

- *Motivation*: Iron-fisted party-state domination, superpower building, and opportunistic foreign expansion (Third World).
- *Mechanism*: Natural resources, land, and the entire industrial and administrative means of production, including housing, gold, and other valuables were state owned and controlled. Agrarian collectivization obviated the peasantry's implicit land claims. Collective farmers toiled in brigades. Members were responsible for *kolkhoz* tax obligations, and shared residual income, with the exception of small household plots where they were permitted to produce for their own use. *Sovkhozy* (state farms), where peasants were treated like industrial laborers and received wages, instead of collective residuals, expanded. Household choice was severely restricted by the state. The state physically managed the economy under the banner of *piatiletki* (five-year plans), which not only entailed the formulation of enterprise production assignments, but administrative supervision, material balancing, intra-state contracting, incentivization, and discipline. The industrial sector was administered by 30-odd ministries and subdepartments. Agriculture, construction and transportation were overseen by analogous committees. All activities were encompassed under the umbrella of central planning. Managers called red directors were appointed by the state, and were granted limited, incentive regulated functional autonomy. Administration was separated from production on the principle of *khozraschyot*. Enterprises were required to initially maximize output, but profit maximizing gradually displaced it. They were also obligated to be self-financing. Their supervisors were salaried employees, who oversaw production, but didn't manage it on a daily basis. The state set all wages and prices, and entrepreneurship was strictly forbidden. The rule of men prevailed. The USSR was a one-party state, which had sovereignty over the provision of all goods, public and private. Reform was focused on improving central planning techniques and methods with computerization, optimal programming, and cybernetics. These advances were later shared with enterprises, and efficiency methods and incentives were borrowed from the West. Information generation, processing, and distribution were facilitated by the automatic system of management and planning. During Gorbachev's reign, these mechanisms were supplemented with "*arenda*" (leasing), some specialized markets like foreign exchange and managers were given limited latitude to innovate and market outside the plan. Then toward the end, Gorbachev restricted administrative oversight, gave managers broad discretion over the use of enterprise assets, and finally abolished Gosplan, reducing state guidance to guaranteed state purchase, contracting, incentives, and price fixing.
- *Institutions*: State ownership of means of production, land, and natural resources: industrial enterprises on *khozrachyot*, *kolkhozy* (collective farms), *sovkhozy* (state farms), machine tractor stations (MTS). Ministerial system, including the Council of Economic Ministers, industrial ministries and *glavks*. Other state-control functional and control entities included Gosplan (Central Planning Agency), Gossnabsbyt' (State Material Acquisition and Distribution Agency), Gosbank (State Bank), Gosstroi (State Construction Agency), Goskomtsen (State Price Committee), Gosstandart (State Standards Bureau), Goskomstat (State Statistical Agency), Gosarbitrazh (contract adjudication), and the Ministry of Foreign Trade. The state had a monopoly on nearly all non-*kolkhoz* business. Trade unions were state controlled, with subservient worker councils and there were some cooperatives. Gorbachev expanded the role of cooperatives, introduced some markets, and gave managers the "right" to misuse state funds, and spontaneously privatize state assets to themselves.

Main inefficiencies

- *Law of demand*: State demand sovereign over all aspects of production and distribution. Monopsony demand for labor, forced substitution, privileged access to goods and services. During the Gorbachev period moral hazard was ascendant. The economy was disorganized by rent-seeking and asset-grabbing. Demand was mostly a function of price in only a few markets. In most instances it was determined by requisition, power, and privilege.
- *Law of supply*: Worker supply curves were positive functions of wages for mobile workers, but not for Gulag prisoners and collective farmers. Coercion substituted for enticement. Industrial production became responsive to fiat price, as the role of profit maximizing expanded. Absence of rule of law and private property rights created endemic moral hazard and corruption. Gorbachev's reforms only worsened matters.
- *Law of equilibration*: Neither the Walrasian nor the Marshallian automatic price and quantity adjustment mechanism were operative due to state price fixing. This remained more or less true throughout the Gorbachev period. Inter-enterprise contracting provided some useful demand/supply coordination, bolstered by Gosarbitrazh. Gosplan attempted to resolve aggregate disequilibrium through material balancing. Ministries, and *glavks* tried to do the same when dis-aggregating central planning assignments on a priority basis. The VPK, party activists, and local officials served as troubleshooters. *Tolkachi* informally bartered critical supplies. Gosbank sometimes provided emergency financing. Collective farmers were compelled to accept residuals. Gulag prisoners took what they got. Consumers forced substitutex. Keynesian macro-excess demand was adopted creating an economy of permanent shortage, until Gorbachev's policies disorganized the system. Overfull employment was persistently maintained until *perestroika*. Inflationary pressures were combated with price controls, but these too eroded in the late 1980s. Hidden inflation. and other moral hazards were tolerated and then indulged when Gorbachev arrived. There were no multiplier effects because the state, not households, determined investment. There were no money markets, or markets for loanable funds. The state was a monopoly investor and controlled all finance, except during the late Gorbachev years.

Tactics of Reform Communist economic management

Topic	*Problem*	*State response*
State ownership	Circumscribes individual utility-seeking	Enforced with stern repression
Criminalization of business	Anti-competitive state monopoly	None
Decriminalization of cooperative business, and some other initiatives under Gorbachev	Moral hazard	None

Criminalization of entrepreneurship	Red directors banned from innovating, diversifying, merging acquiring, expanding to improve efficiency and opportunities	Planned innovation and optimal firm size. Innovation incentives given to red directors
Decriminalization of entrepreneurship under Gorbachev	Moral hazard	None
Inefficient Gosplanning	Inter-industrial factor mis-allocation	Priority distribution, contracting, computerization, optimal planning, cybernetics, ASUP
Infeasible *tekhpromfinplan* assignments	Red director, effort minimization	Incentivization tied to output maximization, later profit maximization
Abolition of central planning	Moral hazard, disorganization	None
Kolkhoz dividends	*kokhozniki* received meager residual labor compensation	Inegalitarian dividend distribution based on brigade performance, shift to *sovkhozy*
Worker under-compensation	Deterred effort withdrawal from labor force	Piecework bonuses, and exhortation, anti-parasite laws, Gulag forced labor
Overfull employment	Suboptimal welfare	None
Mass unemployment under Gorbachev	Depression	None
Inflationary pressure	Price distortion	Price fixing, repressed inflation, under Gorbachev open inflation tolerated
Unbalanced development	Structural militarization, over-industrialization	None
Consumer goods shortages	Deterred effort	None
Quality	Product characteristics unresponsive to demand	Quality improvement incentives. Under Gorbachev leasing and partial marketization were supposed to help
Moral hazard	Misappropriation, and misuse of state assets	Strict financial controls until Gorbachev. Then toleration

Systemic structure, 1953–88	*Share of GDP*	*Productivity*	*Coercion*
Markets	0	–	–
State	80	Spectrum	High
Kolkhoz	20	Low	High

Systemic characteristics, 1953–88	*Degree/intensity*
State macro-regulation	None
State micro-regulation	
Pro-competitive	None
Incentives	High
Welfare/security	Moderate
Criminal dis-services	
Rent-seeking, moral hazard	Moderate

Causes of macroeconomic disequilibrium (economy of shortage)	
Sticky wages and benefits	High
Sticky prices	High
Investment avoidance	None
Capital flight	None
Misinvestment	High
Liquidity preference	None
Insecure agrarian rights	Extremely high
State property rights	High
Foreign capital flows	Not applicable
State corruption	Moderate
Macro-policy Mismanagement	Moderate
Class conflict	Extremely high

Main performance indicators

Per capita GDP (US = 100)	
Rosefielde	20
Maddison	30
Per capita GDP growth 1953–91 (ch. 12)	1–3
Over-employment	10
Retirement Support burden	None
Non-working Mothers and wives	Negligible

Direction of reforms

Improved planning and incentivation.

Questions

1. What is reform? How is reform distinguished from systemic change?
2. Should post-Stalin changes in administrative organization, planning, and incentivization 1953–87 be characterized as reforms, or the construction of a new system? Explain.
3. What is optimal programming? Can it be undertaken in a firm, or must it be carried out at a central planning agency?
4. Does the central planning agency have to acquire all information about enterprises to optimally plan, or can it allocate parts of the task to the firms?
5. If the central planning agency permits firms to solve some tasks themselves, but still controls the outcomes, should the operation be considered decentralized? Distinguish two types of peripheral activity, one where agents are indirectly controlled, and the other where they have some degree of autonomy. Does this distinction matter if planners and agents (consumers) have different tastes? Should the term decentralization be reserved for the latter case?
6. Suppose in a computopic supply-side universe that central planners were able to compute the nation's production "capabilities" frontier (without ever taking account of competitive input supply and output demand) for 25 million products. Would this be of much help, if systems could only form transitive preference fields for a few hundred composite goods? Is this why perfect planning is best suited for cyborgs?
7. Incentive reform supplemented Soviet attempts to create computopic planning. It was considered promising because Stalin's scheme of tying red director bonuses to output maximizing was said to be inefficient. Illustrate and explain the distortions caused by output maximizing.
8. Evgeny Liberman claimed that these distortions could be overcome by profit maximizing at state fixed prices. Illustrate and explain the advantages of rewarding red directors for profit maximizing.
9. Do these advantages mean that the welfare consequences of Soviet and Western profit maximizing are the same? Explain. Are the distinctions important?
10. In theory, systems directors could impose constraints on red director profit maximizing that enabled a precise replication of free enterprise outcomes. Does this insight have any practical importance in the Soviet case? Explain.
11. Science and technological progress make it possible for nations to produce more, at lower cost, regardless of their economic systems. If America and the Soviet Union initially were twins with identical tastes and identical outputs (but different systems), does this mean that their growth potential would be the same if they innovated at the same rate? Explain. (*Hint*: would they choose the same innovations?)
12. How would technological choice be made in the US? How would it be made in the USSR? Would one be more efficient than the other? Explain.
13. Is there any reason to believe that Reform Communist systems can do any better solving the efficiency problems for science and technological progress (and diffusion) than for the static problems of optimal supply? Explain. Does it follow that the dynamic performance of Reform Communist systems shouldn't be any better than their static efficiency performance? Explain.
14. What was Gorbachev's version of "*arenda*" (leasing). How did it differ from leasing under NEP.

15 Could leasing have been used as a way station to equitable privatization by permitting successful lessees to purchase facilities and real estate? Explain.
16 Gorbachev extended the autonomy of managers by rescinding controls over the uses of state enterprise revenue. Why had his predecessors resisted this devolution of authority? Did it raise the specter of moral hazard? Explain.
17 Did Soviet managers succumb to moral hazard?
18 Are Western managers susceptible to the same temptations? If so, what institutions are in place to discipline them? Were parallel institutions developed in the Soviet Union?
19 James Buchanan once observed that privatization is only useful when assets are vested in competent hands, and institutions support free, competitive enterprise. Gorbachev tolerated "spontaneous privatization" where brazen managers privatized enterprises to themselves. Was this approach likely to satisfy Buchanan's conditions for constructive privatization? Explain.
20 Gorbachev abolished Gosplan as an administrative control institution in the spring of 1991. Could the *khozraschyot* system, including price fixing survive without its "head." Explain the efficiency consequences of Gorbachev's action.
21 If Boris Yeltsin never existed, would Gorbachev's radical initiatives have led to "Market Muscovy?" Explain.
22 Sometime in the late 1920s Stalin decided that NEP had to be aborted. Could Stalin's ghost have restored the pre-Gorbachev status quo? Explain.
23 Was the collapse of Soviet socialism inevitable? In what sense? Explain.
24 Gorbachev had talked a great deal about a smooth transition to market communism, yet he never attempted to create the necessary and sufficient conditions for a Pareto efficient system. Why then were Western specialists so sure that his actions were progressive?
25 Does Gorbachev's Market Communist debacle prove that market socialism is undesirable? Relying on Oscar Lange, appraise what really went wrong with Gorbachev's *perestroika*.
26 How was *khozraschyot* and decentralization connected with Muscovite rent-granting?
27 In what sense was the rhetoric of Reform Communism merely a cover for the reality of the Muscovite authoritarian martial police state?

9

Structural Militarization

Summary

The Soviet Union acquired the atomic bomb in 1949 and the hydrogen bomb two years later. These weapons, combined with full-spectrum armed forces, manned by more than five million soldiers made it a superpower. Despite all the failings of Soviet central planning, the performance of the military-industrial sub-economy was impressive.

The Deputy Chairman of Yeltsin's Russian Defense Council contends that the Soviet command economy served the military first. The defense sub-economy's contribution to GDP exceeded 30 percent (Academician Yuri Yaremenko), and weapons were the fastest-growing component of industry. These assertions, broadly supported by the American Office of the Secretary of Defense, if correct, cast Reform Communism in an illuminating perspective. They indicate that post-Stalinist economic performance was profoundly influenced by "structural militarization;" the bifurcation of the system into an embedded, priority military sub-economy where supply was responsive to the Ministry of Defense's micro-demand, operating only loosely under Gosplan's control, insulated from post-Stalin reforms, and a civilian segment guided by Gosplan, ministries, *glavks*, ASUP, profit maximizing, and contracting. Their performance was separable. The military-industrial component was relatively efficient and grew rapidly; the civilian sector wasn't and didn't. Profligate military expenditures didn't destroy the Soviet Union. The failings of the consumer sector were endogenous to the Reform Communist system, but too many guns did worsen living standards.

Post-Stalin reforms shed considerable light on the productive possibilities of Soviet central planning, but do not tell the whole story because they omit one important sector: the military industrial complex (VPK). Defense production in these enterprises was overseen and controlled by the Ministry of Defense, with little or no red directorial discretion over volumes and assortments. Assignments and output maximization were preeminent, not profit maximization, and military planners paid scant attention to budgetary constraints. Inspectors monitored defense production around the clock and operations were technically efficient within the constraints of the system. Arms procurements were financed by the Fund for the National Economy, rather than the official defense budget (acknowledged by Mikhail Gorbachev in 1989), a procedure adopted to deceive Western security analysts.[1] Gosplan had little control over the VPK. The General Staff (Genshtab) considered all defense industrial information top secret and revealed only what it wanted to civilian statisticians and planners.[2] We still do not know the military's share of Soviet GDP (the "defense burden"), its absolute magnitude,[3] and growth characteristics.[4]

These uncertainties cloud judgments about the merit of Reform Communism. Some like Franklyn Holzman contended that Soviet defense spending was smaller than America's absolutely and relatively, and close to West European norm.[5] Since the Soviet Union was an acknowledged superpower, Holzman's analysis implied that the weapons sector was hyper-efficient,[6] allowing the Kremlin to achieve military parity with America, while devoting most of the nation's resources to civilian purposes. The relative constrained technical efficiency of the VPK spiced aggregate performance on this interpretation, and could not have caused Reform Communism's devitalization.

The Central Intelligence Agency has staked claim to the opposite view. Its calculations indicated that the Soviet defense burden was in the vicinity of 15 percent, nearly treble America's, and argued that these excessive outlays were an important cause of Reform Communism economic malaise.[7] Factor productivity growth in the weapons sector it contended was strongly negative. Although input growth kept pace with GDP growth, weapons didn't grow at all during 1970–89, disregarding cyclical oscillations. Absent defense overspending, Reform Communism might have given the West a strong run for the money in determining comparative merit.

Both positions however are vigorously disputed by Vitaly Shlykov, Deputy Chairman of Yeltsin's Russian Defense Council, and consummate VPK/GRU (military intelligence) insider who argues that "structural militarization" was a principal source of Soviet GDP growth, and of the system's futility.[8] Shlykov contends that defense constituted more than 30 percent of aggregate Soviet value added, and weapon procurements grew at double digit rates from the mid-1950s onward, driven by rapid factor productivity growth, associated with priority RDT&E outlays, and contraband military industrial technology transfers. Soviet GDP growth as he sees it was closer to official claims than the CIA's (before adjustment for inflated consumer goods production). The problem with the Soviet system wasn't the military sub-economy. It was the ineffectuality of the civilian sector under Reform Communism, and the meager benefits of excessive security services.

Downsizing the Soviet VPK to an optimal level in Shlykov's view was impossible because defense in the Command Communist and Reform Communist eras was structurally militarized. The VPK, Genshtab, Ministry of Defense, and the Politburo all concurred that there could never be too much defense. They felt duty bound to prepare for worst case scenarios, and then added resources to deal with the unthinkable. This excessiveness was "structural." It wasn't a whim, or a reflection of the external threat.

The economy was defense intensive because this is what the leadership and the VPK desired. The supply mechanism was complementary. The VPK was given priority access to inputs. It had first dibs both on the quantity and quality of available supplies, and military contracts took precedence over civilian claimants. The VPK also received the lion's share of RDT&E services, and new capital formation, and was self-sufficient. It had the production capacities to assure that the economy served the needs of the armed forces first, leaving the civilian sector with a Spartan minimum.

The illusion of economic success fostered by structural militarization in Shlykov's opinion rendered the post-Stalin system doubly deficient. Technocratic central planning didn't provide a competitive standard of living, and excessive defense spending made matters worse by diverting resources from consumption to dubious military undertakings. His perception is confirmed by studies carried out by the American Office of the Secretary of Defense.[9] Holzman's assessment that weapons production was a small and subsidiary aspect of the Reform Communist production scheme was disproven by Gorbachev's revelation that defense spending was more than twice the official figure. The military industrial complex was the centerpiece, not the stepchild of the post-NEP economic system. The CIA's analysis while closer to the truth is marred by a critical costing error[10] that made the military industrial complex erroneously appear as an impediment to sustainable GDP growth, instead of its driving force.

No valid summary judgment on the merit of Command and Reform Communism can be rendered without dispelling the fog caused by Holzman's and the CIA's mis-characterizations. The post-NEP Soviet Union was a formidable authoritarian martial police state that allowed the leadership to realize some of its superpower aspirations. Command and Reform Communism weren't just about central planning, terror and autarky. They were about imperial Muscovy in Bolshevik garb. Structural militarization in this respect was an asset, not a liability that killed two birds with one stone – it increased the aggregate growth rate and buttressed national defense, even though military expenditures were prodigal. While the CIA correctly claimed that resources diverted from civilian activities curtailed consumer goods production, and were a social burden, no Bolshevik leader with the possible exception of Gorbachev believed that the cost exceeded the benefit. They, like Putin today, considered the burden placed on ordinary people morally, economically, and politically tolerable. Yeltsin alone defied this consensus for mixed motives including allowing his cronies to divert VPK resources to themselves, but even he left the military-industrial complex intact, ready to resume its traditional role when the Kremlin's imperial ambitions revived.

Review

Every nation has the right of self-defense and most retain armed forces. Given the Leninist view that the Soviet Union was encircled by hostile capitalist forces, and the USSR's experience in World War II, no one should be surprised that the Kremlin had prodigious military-industrial capacities, even though the official defense budget indicated otherwise. Vitaly Shlykov, however, contends that the Soviets did more than devote a large share of the nation's resources to defense; he asserts that the economy was structurally militarized. This term means that weapons production became an end in itself, divorced from external threat. The structure of Soviet production was skewed toward guns, at the expense of butter, by excessive allocation of resources to defense and war mobilization entailments on civilian production capacity. The evidence strongly supports his hypothesis and provides a powerful, if partial, explanation for Gorbachev's dissatisfaction with Reform Communism. Shlykov insists as well that Putin's Market Muscovy is heading down the same slippery slope.

Questions

1 How does Vitaly Shlykov define "structural militarization"?
2 What is the difference between a run-of-the-mill militarized economy, and one where militarization is structurally embedded?
3 Structurally militarized economies do not contract when external threats diminish. In the Soviet case, Shlykov contends that the defense burden continuously rose during the Reform Communist period, even though the American defense burden steadily declined after the Vietnamese War. What does this imply about the social welfare worth of Soviet defense expenditures?
4 America's GDP exceeded the Soviet Union's during the 1980s by more than 50 percent (according to Soviet statistics), yet its armed forces were at least twice as large as America's. What does this imply about the comparative productivity of the Soviet military machine-building sector and/or the scale of the Kremlin's military spending? Does this seem plausible? Explain.
5 Franklyn Holzman claimed that the Soviets were able to achieve military "parity" with America at one-third the cost. This is an extreme form of the hyper-productivity theory. Does this seem plausible? Explain.
6 Holzman based his argument on the reliability of official Soviet defense budgetary statistics. How was his theory falsified?
7 The American Central Intelligence Agency contended that the Soviet defense burden was approximately 15 percent of GDP, remaining nearly constant while national income grew. It also asserted that real weapons growth was stagnant for nearly two decades. What do rising real costs and stagnant production imply about productivity growth. Is it negative or positive?
8 If Shlykov is right about the VPK's privileged position in the Soviet economic system, is the CIA's hypothesis of negative military machine-building productivity growth plausible? Explain.
9 Is "structural militarization" compatible with the Muscovite model? Explain.
10 What does the superiority of the Soviet Union's military sub-economy imply about the civilian potential of the Reform Communist model, based on the post-Stalin experience? Explain.
11 What role did "structural militarization" play in the Soviet Union's collapse? Explain.
12 The CIA believed that arms control and disarmament were keys to Soviet revitalization; that the Reform Communism and democratic free enterprise could coexist in perpetuity. Given your preceding replies, why was this theory implausible? Was the Agency engaging in wishful thinking, or merely trying to coax the Soviets into reducing their arsenal?

10

Delusions of Adequacy

Summary

Few foresaw the Soviet Union's collapse because the telltale signs weren't in Goskomstat's or the Sovietologists' numbers. Wall Streeters are fond of saying that "the trend is your friend," and anyone who applied this maxim to the "facts" could not have concluded scientifically that the Soviet Union was failing. The evidence was there, but not in the numbers Goskomstat published or the CIA reconstructed. Broadly speaking, the Agency's series showed the USSR to be a "normalizing," "structurally de-militarizing" economy, performing on a par with America (1955–89) both in terms of national income and per capita consumption growth. It and the broader Sovietological community had confidence in these numbers because they had been adjusted downward for "padding" in the national income aggregate and for "hidden" machine-building inflation, and following Bergson it was widely believed that the CIA's adjusted ruble factor cost series was compatible with aspects of neoclassical theory. Moscow was faulted because given its relative backwardness it could have done better, and much was made of its growth retardation, a gradually decelerating pace of advance which began in 1968. But these observations pointed to the system's inferior long-term potential, not its imminent demise. The Goskomstat story was rosier, claiming that Gorbachev had reversed the USSR's flagging vitality, until GDP started to mysteriously plummet in 1990. Many Sovietologists too were initially enthused by "*perestroika*."

To have appreciated the handwriting on the wall, analysts would have had to probe more deeply into fundamentals. They would have had to have treated Mikhail Gorbachev's complaints about "stagnation" prophetically, recognizing that physical systems management wasn't producing things people wanted, and that the consumption statistics were more exaggerated than the CIA's "physical" adjusted estimates indicated, a point well supported by copious anecdotal evidence. And they would have had to fully come to terms with the Soviet Union's structural militarization, a phenomenon that satisfied the leaderships desire for power, but frustrated its Muscovite quest for "la dolce vita" (the sweet life). The USSR's rulers shed crocodile tears for the people's material squalor, but were intensely dissatisfied with the limits imposed by the system on their personal lifestyle, initiating Gorbachev's counter-revolution from above. Had proletarian sovereignty really been his Market Communist goal, transition would have taken a very different course.

Almost seventy years ago our Leninist party raised over the nation the victorious banner of the socialist revolution, the struggle for socialism, freedom and equality, for social justice and societal progress, against oppression and exploitation, poverty and national subjugation.

For the first time in human history, the interests and needs of the workers were placed at the center of the state's agenda. There have been many successes during socialist construction of the Soviet Union in the political, economic, social and spiritual realms. Under party guidance, the Soviet people have built socialism, defeated fascism in the Great Patriotic war, established and strengthened the national economy, and transformed their homeland into a great power.

Our achievements have been immense and indisputable, and the Soviet people are justifiably proud of their successes. They are the true guarantee of the realization of the current plan, and our future dreams.

Materials from the Plenum of the Communist Party Central Committee, January 27–9, 1987, Politizdat, 1987, pp. 6–7, quoted in Narodnoe Khoziaistvo SSSR za 70 Let, Iubileinyi Statisticheskii Ezhegodnik, Finansy i Statistika, 1987, p. 12

The Enigma of Reform Communist Growth

The Communist Party on the seventieth anniversary of the Bolshevik coup d'etat boasted that Soviet socialism under its guidance had been an enormous success. The nation had rapidly developed and become a prosperous workers' state, with liberty, equality, and justice for all to the amazement and dismay of its adversaries. Although neoclassical theorists by the mid-1930s recognized that perfect planning was conceivable,[1] and could under ideal circumstances be as efficient as perfect competition, most Westerners doubted that central planning could be very effective in an economy that criminalized business, entrepreneurship, and private property. They presumed that the absence of automatic Marshallian and Walrasian market adjustment mechanisms would prevent the satisfaction of both systems directors' and consumer's demands; that goods and factors would have inferior characteristics, that the wrong product bundles would be produced and mis-distributed, and that inputs would be inefficiently allocated and employed. Productivity, living standards, and welfare would be low and growth prospects dismal because systems directors would be unable to make the right complex technological choices. They could transfer technology, innovate, and simulate Western investment criteria, but could not attain a Pareto optimum based on consumers' or planners' preferences with state ownership, suppressed entrepreneurship,[2] price, wage, interest, foreign exchange rate fixing, patchwork incentives, and monkey business planning. Growth didn't just depend on the march of science. As Irving Fisher explained more than eight decades ago,[3] it required inter-temporal competitive consumption maximization, something beyond the reach of Reform Communism.

How could these positions be reconciled? The Communist Party's statistics could be accepted as proof that Western pessimism was misplaced, either because the numbers were true as reported, or performance on a discounted basis was still satisfactory. Alternatively, the Western presumption could be upheld either by arguing Soviet statistics were misleading, or more subtly, that they masked negative productivity growth, which might allow good results at first, but presaged inferior performance in the long run.

Although specialists were divided, a consensus was forged in the late 1940s and early 1950s that Soviet statistics were usable and reliable, unless there were credible grounds for suspicion in specific instances.[4] This caveat came to mean that some downward adjustments to Soviet claims was required for "hidden inflation" (bogus claims of quality enhancement, misclassified in national income statistics as value added). The magnitude of these markdowns varied from analysts to analyst, but in most instances supported a net assessment closer to the Communist Party's than the skeptics' position.

The compromise solution for those who considered this an enigma was first vetted in the early 1960s by Abram Bergson who discovered that Soviet combined factor (capital and labor) productivity growth was negative, using Goskomstat subaggregate data that were supposed to be hidden inflation free.[5] This led him and the profession to surmise after Khrushchev that the Soviet model was dynamically inferior and would in due course persistently underperform the Western norm.

The hypothesis was appealing because the story told seemed rooted in neoclassical aggregate economic growth theory, which postulated that changes in Pareto equilibrium activity depended on input volumes and technological progress, given fixed tastes and endowments:

$$y = \lambda(F(k,1)) \tag{10.1}$$

where y is output, λ is technological progress, F the aggregate production function, k is capital and l is labor.

The production function F could take innumerable forms, but the Cobb–Douglas specification which assumed constant returns to scale, constant factor shares, and a unitary elasticity of capital labor substitution was considered especially convenient and instructive:

$$y = (F(\alpha k + (1 - \alpha)1) \tag{10.2}$$

where α and $(1 - \alpha)$ are constant capital and labor shares respectively.

Total factor productivity growth $\dot{\lambda}$ can be expressed and estimated directly as[6]

$$TFP = \dot{y}/(\alpha \dot{k} + (1 - \alpha)\dot{1}) \tag{10.3}$$

a formula which makes its easy to see that the sources of growth can be partitioned into variations in input volumes and technological progress, weighted by Pareto equilibrium capital and labor value added.

And there is an interesting intermediate case where technological progress is greater, but the net effects of input growth volumes are less than 1. Here the benefits of what Krugman calls "inspiration" is partially or whole negated by excessive "perspiration," conditions that could easily result in secular growth retardation.[7]

These relationships, corroborated with other specifications like the CES (constant elastic of factor substitution) production function,[8] applied to Soviet data indicate that growth during the Command Communist period was driven both by perspiration and inspiration (mostly the former computed at 1937 prices; mostly by the latter at 1928 prices). But Abram Bergson found using his own Soviet data initially, and CIA statistics thereafter that combined factor growth productivity was negative throughout the Reform Communist period.

The miracle claimed by the Communist Party in this way was debunked by arguing that rapid industrialization was primarily attributable to factor mobilization (perspiration) having little or nothing to do with the superiority of Soviet physical systems management, and when this source of growth evaporated due to slow labor force growth and rapidly diminishing returns to investment, inferior technological prowess consigned the Kremlin to a degenerate growth trajectory.

This explanation isn't infallible. It doesn't prove that Soviet technological prowess was destined to be eternally subpar,[9] although theory suggests that this would be the most likely outcome. It mis-assumes that estimated Cobb–Douglas factor shares actually reflect marginal technical rates of factor substitution, with or without adjusted factor costing.[10] And more importantly, with the exception of 1990 and 1991, combined factor productivity growth computed with official statistics was always positive during the Reform Communist years using unadjusted official statistics.

Apparently there is no way to escape the quandary of official Soviet statistics. If they are "usable" and "reliable" then the Communist Party is right. If not, then how "unusable" and "unreliable" are they? Those who read Gorbachev's laments about "stagnation" and the Soviet Union's collapse as evidence of overstated growth, tend to argue on systems grounds that combined factor productivity growth was more negative than Bergson estimated; that aggregate growth was correspondingly slower, and other forces like moral hazard and systemic disorganization also played a role in the USSR's demise. Those who accept CIA-type adjustments, portray the Soviet experience in a brighter light, but don't have any plausible economic explanation for its implosion.[11]

Official Soviet Record

The Communist Party's triumphal assessment of Soviet economic accomplishments is allegedly substantiated with the data presented in the tables in this chapter:

Table 10.1 shows national income computed with a Laspeyres type index rising 5.5 percent per annum 1960–86, well above the comparable mean for the developed West. Admittedly NMP growth had decelerated beginning at 6.8 percent per annum in the 1960s, diminishing to 5.3 during the 1970s and falling to 3.6 in the period 1980–6,

Table 10.1 Basic indicators of Soviet economic development: 1960–1986 (1960 = 1)

	1970	*1980*	*1986*
NMP	1.9	3.2	4.0
Capital stock industry	2.0	3.2	4.1
producer goods	2.4	4.4	5.6
consumer goods	2.0	3.4	4.4
Agriculture	1.4	1.5	1.8
Workers	1.5	1.8	1.9
Labor productivity			
industry	1.6	2.6	3.1
agriculture	1.7	2.0	2.5
construction	1.6	2.2	2.6

Source: *Narodnoe Khoziaistvo SSSR za 70 Let*, Finansy i Statistika, Moscow, 1987, p. 8

Table 10.2 Comparative national income, USSR and USA (%: USSR/USA)

1960	58
1970	65
1980	67
1986	66

Although not explicitly stated, the comparison in table 10.2 is computed in dollars.
Source: *Narodnoe Khoziaistvo SSSR za 70 Let*, Finansy i Statistika, Moscow, 1987, p. 13

but thanks to Mikhail Gorbachev's brilliant strategy of "*uskorenie*" (acceleration), this trend would soon be reversed.[12] Moreover, contrary to Bergson's conjecture, factor productivity growth had not turned negative (measured per unit of labor), and had moved ahead briskly in all sectors including industry, agriculture, and construction. And Goskomstat could have easily constructed a series of "combined" inputs (labor and capital) which would have disconfirmed Bergson's hypothesis.

This robust performance allowed the Soviet Union to make headway in catching up with America. Table 10.2 claims that the USSR's national income rose from 58 percent of the United States' in 1960, to 66 percent by 1986, confirming that planning was a viable, and perhaps superior alternative to free enterprise, depending on whether Soviet performance was discounted for its relative backwardness (table 10.3).

Sectoral data on Soviet industrial performance corroborates these impressions. Growth throughout is impressive, especially in machine-building, the backbone of the Marxist model, with little devoted to weapons. The military burden (defense share of GNP) falls from 10.2 percent in 1955,[13] to under 3 percent in 1988,[14] a figure well below the concurrent American defense burden. Moreover the nation enjoyed full employment, just as it had done since 1930,[15] and inflation was less than 2.8 percent (table 10.4).[16] No wonder the Communist Party, the vanguard of the workers was in a celebratory mood. Socialism had surpassed and confused its competitors.

Table 10.3 Soviet industrial growth: 1960–1986 (1960 = 100)

	1970	*1980*	*1986*
Industry	2.3	4.0	5.0
Electricity	2.6	4.9	6.1
Fuel	1.8	2.8	3.1
Ferrous metals	2.1	3.1	3.5
Chemical	2.4	4.5	5.8
Machinery	3.1	8.0	11.6
Light	1.7	2.5	2.8
Food	2.0	2.7	2.4

Source: *Narodnoe Khoziaistvo SSSR za 70 Let*, Finansy i Statistika, Moscow, 1987, p. 130

Table 10.4 Soviet inflation: 1986–1990 (increase from the preceding year: %)

	1986	*1987*	*1988*	*1989*	*1990*	*1960–90*
Industrial wholesale (before turnover tax)	1.0	0.5	0.9	1.7	3.0	1.4
Retail (including cooperatives)	2.0	1.0	1.0	2.0	4.7	2.1
GNP	0.4	0.4	0.6	4.5	8.6	2.7

The GNP inflation series is computed as the implicit deflator.
Source: *Narodnoe khoziaistvo 1990*, Goskomstat, Moscow, 1991, pp. 107, 109

Western Estimates

But not so fast. Just as during the Stalin era, Sovietological recalculations told a very different tale, and this time the Laspeyres and Paasche measures were mutually confirming.

Figure 10.1 provides the CIA's image of Soviet economic performance across the expanse of the post-Stalin era. At first glance it seems to support the Communist Party's triumphal assessment. The GNP, industrial and agricultural growth trajectories are all straight up, without the business cycle fluctuations marring Western series, but the devil is in the detail. Not only are the Central Intelligence Agency's output growth rates slower than the official series, more importantly factor productivity growth is "uninspired." The data presented in table 10.5 reveal that combined factor productivity growth was negative during the entire Reform Communist period from Khrushchev to Yuri Andropov until it turned briefly positive before plummeting (1989–91).

These findings cast the merit of the post-Stalin reform planning model in an instructive light. They inform us that Soviet economic growth not only decelerated, but strongly imply that the cause was systemic; that the Achilles' heel of administrative command planning was feeble technological progress. The post-Stalin reform mechanism had shown initial signs of vitality, but these proved to be false positives. As Bergson surmised three decades earlier, physical systems management turned out to be inferior to free enterprise in the long run. Although the CIA's numbers do not demonstrate that the Soviet Union had to implode, they illuminate one profound source of devitalization. James Noren and Laurie Kurtzweg summarized matters this way:

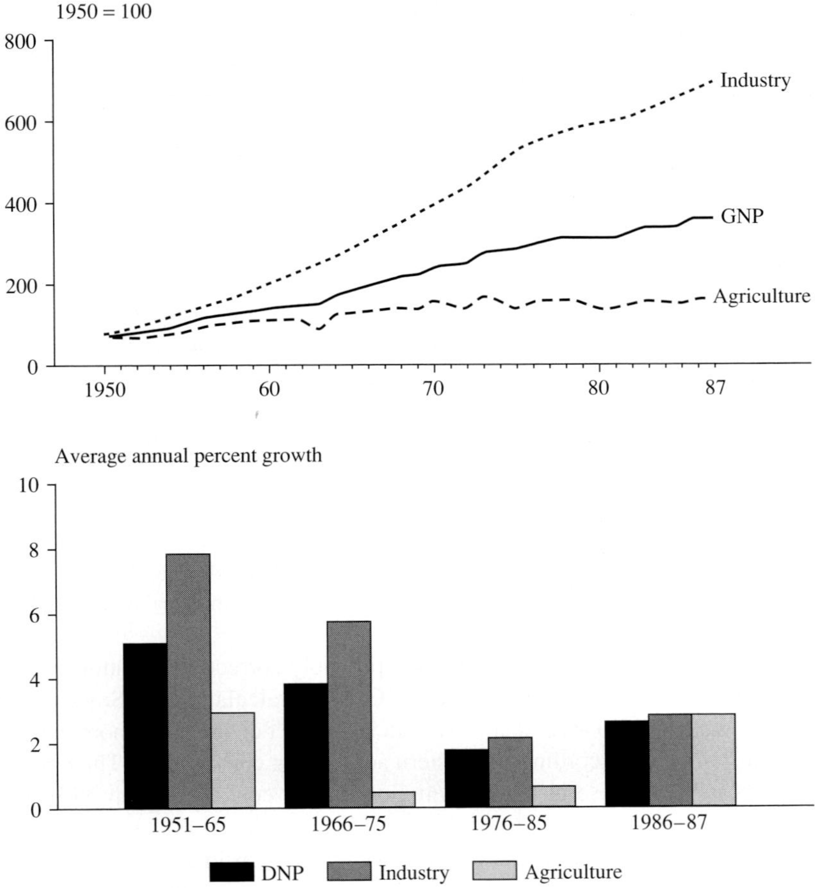

Figure 10.1 USSR: Trends in GNP and industrial and agricultural output: 1950–1987
Source: *Measures of Soviet Gross National Product in 1982 Prices*, Joint Economic Committee of Congress, Washington, DC, 1990, p. 5

Table 10.5 Soviet factor productivity trends: 1961–1988 (CIA estimates)

	1961–70	*1971–80*	*1981–5*	*1986–8*	*1989–90*
GNP	4.9	2.4	1.7	2.4	–0.5
Combined Inputs	–0.3	–0.6	–1.4	1.3	—

Sources: *Measures of Soviet Gross National Product in 1982 Prices*, Joint Economic Committee of Congress, Washington, DC, November 1990, pp. 54–7. James Noren and Laurie Kurtzweg, "The Soviet Economy Unravels: 1985–91," in *The Former Soviet Union in Transition*, Joint Economic Committee, Washington, DC, February 1993, pp. 14 and 17

Table 10.6 CIA and Goskomstat GNP growth estimates: 1981–1987 (%)

	1981–5	*1986*	*1987*
GNP			
Soviet	4.0	4.6	3.3
CIA	1.8	4.0	1.3
NMP			
Soviet	3.6	4.1	2.3
CIA	1.6	3.5	1.4

Source: *Measures of Soviet Gross National Product in 1982 Prices*, Joint Economic Committee of Congress, Washington, DC, November 1990, p. 3

> The readers of successive Joint Economic Committee compendia on the Soviet economy since the 1950s will be familiar with the story told there of growing weakness evidenced in declining rates of growth, sharply falling productivity gains, and a wide and probably increasing gap between Soviet and Western levels of technology. During this period institutions that planned and administered the economy changed little, and policies that successive governments adopted to improve matters proved to be marginal changes at best.[17]

Noren and Kurtzweg's summary judgment is probably correct, but cannot be accepted as the final word because it assumes that the CIA's recalculations of Soviet GNP and industrial growth were unbiased; that its statisticians didn't do anything more than recompile Goskomstat's data according to Western accounting conventions. The opportunity to test this possibility arose in 1987 when Goskomstat converted from NMP to GNP accounting and published a truncated series permitting direct comparison. Table 10.6 prepared by the CIA shows that the disparity between its estimates and official Soviet statistics isn't primarily explained by Soviet accounting conventions. The Agency's figures for 1981–5, 1986, and 1987 are often less than half Goskomstat's. Nor is the disparity the result of differences in indexing. The official index is chain linked, and the prices for the period 1980–7 for the most part should be the same as the CIA's.

Some of the mystery harks back to the perennial issue of "reliability." Sovietologists were never able to replicate official national income growth rates from published sub-serial statistics. But another equally problematic cause was the Agency's decision to use physical sub-series indices, rather than value data as proxies for hidden inflation. Physical indexes by definition take no account of product and service improvement, and hence are downward biased to the extent characteristics improve. And more subtly, they lower the index weights of sectors the Soviets claimed were fast growing. Tables 10.7 and 10.8 reveal that the effect of the CIA's preference for physical series is particularly strong in services (approximately 17 percent of GNP at 1982 factor cost),[18] and industry (32.2 percent of GNP at 1982 factor cost).[19] The disparity is precisely 50 percent in the critical machine-building sector (11 percent of GNP at 1982 factor cost) where Goskomstat claims output grew 11.2 percent per annum (1951–87). This adjustment alone is sufficient to turn industrial-factor productivity from the negative to the positive column, and is particularly controversial because it is driven in large part by the Agency's weapons estimates derived independently of Goskomstat's data. The CIA's weapons adjustment doesn't comply with American accounting standards and its use of physical series runs counter to US recent practice.[20] During the late 1990s

Table 10.7 USSR: Comparisons of CIA and alternative estimates of services growth: 1951–1984 (%)

	1951–60	*1961–70*	*1971–80*	*1981–4*
Housing				
CIA[a]	4.0	3.5	2.5	2.5
Prell[b]	7.7	5.6	5.2	4.9
Education				
CIA[a]	2.8	4.8	2.4	0.9
Prell[b]	4.1	5.5	3.8	2.5
Health				
CIA[a]	4.5	3.7	2.0	1.6
Prell[b]	5.9	4.7	4.0	3.6
Science				
CIA[a]	10.2	7.7	4.6	1.8
Prell[b]	7.7	6.9	4.6	2.2
Government administration				
CIA[a]	−4.2	3.5	3.5	1.5
Prell[b]	−2.1	4.3	3.9	1.7

[a] Estimates cited by Prell, based on earlier data than the rest of estimates in this paper.
[b] See Mark Prell, *The Role of the Service Sector in Soviet GNP and Productivity Estimates* (Ph.D. dissertation. Massachusetts Institute of Technology, 1987), pp. 218–24, 231–2.

American GNP growth statistics were explicitly raised to recognize qualitative advances in goods and services where prices had fallen, such as the computational power of personal computers. The CIA assumed precisely the opposite.

Sovietologists who mastered these technicalities before things fell apart tended to split the difference. They discounted official Soviet claims because they weren't verifiable, and the CIA's because its adjustments had gone too far. Consequently victory could not be awarded to Bergson solely on the basis of "unvarnished" facts. He was probably right that the Soviet model would prove to be "perspirational," but up to the end no conclusive verdict could be rendered without invoking the possibility he rejected, that hidden inflation made Soviet sub-aggregate data "unreliable."

And there were other mixed signals. Bergson and Kuznets found that the Stalinist model had two other flaws. Its consumer welfare dividend was meager, and growth had been driven in significant part by munitions production (weapons). Per capita consumption (1928–50) had barely improved despite enormous industrial investment, and the economy seemed structurally militarized.

Were these negative trends perpetuated, or did Stalin's death alter economic priorities?

Insofar as Soviet officials concurred with either assessment for the Stalin era, the evidence for the post-Stalin USSR is entirely favorable. Table 10.9 presents comparative official and CIA per capita income and per capita consumption data compiled by Gertrude Schroeder and Elizabeth Denton for the period 1951–80.[21] Both per capita income series display substantial progress, Goskomstat's measure growing at 5 percent per annum, more than quadrupling over thirty years, and the CIA's advancing at 3.5 percent per annum. Enhanced living standards on these numbers weren't the leadership's first priority, but the performance was better than America's. As with

Table 10.8 USSR: Comparison of CIA estimates of industrial growth with official Soviet statistics: 1951–1987 (%)

	1951–60	*1961–70*	*1971–80*	*1981–7*	*1951–7*
Total industry					
CIA[a]	8.6	6.3	4.0	2.2	5.5
Soviet[b]	11.7	8.6	5.9	3.9	7.8
Ferrous metals					
CIA[a]	9.5	6.4	2.5	1.3	5.2
Soviet[b]	10.4	6.8	3.5	1.9[c]	6.3[c]
Fuels					
CIA[a]	9.3	6.0	4.2	1.4	5.5
Soviet[b]	9.3	6.2	4.4	1.6	5.6
Electric power					
CIA[a]	12.3	9.7	5.8	3.3	8.1
Soviet[b]	13.7	10.6	6.1	3.7	8.9
Machinery					
CIA[a]	7.4	6.6	5.1	2.4	5.6
Soviet[b]	15.4	12.1	9.9	6.3	11.2
Chemicals					
CIA[a]	10.7	10.0	5.6	3.8	7.8
Soviet[b]	14.7	13.3	8.1	5.0	10.6
Wood, pulp, and paper					
CIA[a]	6.4	2.7	1.0	2.7	3.2
Soviet[b]	8.0	5.3	3.3	3.6	5.2
Construction materials					
CIA[a]	15.7	5.9	3.1	2.3	7.0
Soviet[b]	18.4	8.6	4.5	3.4	9.0
Light industry					
CIA[a]	8.0	4.5	2.5	1.6	4.3
Soviet[b]	9.6	5.5	4.0	1.5	5.4
Food industry					
CIA[a]	9.1	6.4	2.7	1.1	5.1
Soviet[b]	8.9	6.6	3.4	3.8	5.8

[a] Growth of total industry is calculated from indexes of branch growth, weighted by value added at 1982 factor cost. Branch growth is calculated from indexes of gross output by subbranch, weighted by value added in 1982 producers' prices (established prices, excluding turnover taxes and subsidies).
[b] Growth of total industry and its branches is calculated from values of gross output in comparable producers' prices (established prices, excluding turnover taxes and subsidies) of a series of linked base years (1952, 1955, 1967, 1975, and 1982).
[c] End year is 1984.

GNP, per capita consumption growth slowed during the 1980s (the CIA consumption growth rate was 1.9 percent)[22] but remained respectable, and Gorbachev seemed to be intent on making things better. Perhaps socialism with a human face really was possible, erasing one of the principal blemishes of Stalin's model.

Table 10.9 Comparison of official and CIA measures of Soviet per capita consumption (%)

Indexes (1950 = 100)	*Soviet index of real incomes per capita*[a]	*CIA index of real per capita consumption*[b]	*Average annual rates of growth (%)*	*Soviet index*	*CIA index*
1950	100	100			
1955	142	125	1951–5	7.3	4.5
1958	173	143	1956–60	5.6	4.0
1960	187	151	1961–5	3.6	2.4
1964	209	163	1966–70	5.9	5.1
1965	223	171	1971–5	4.4	2.9
1966	236	179	1976–80	3.4	2.2
1967	252	189			
1968	268	200	1951–60	6.5	4.2
1969	281	210	1961–70	4.7	3.8
1970	297	219	1971–80	3.9	2.5
1971	310	226			
1972	323	229	1951–80	5.0	3.5
1973	339	236			
1974	352	244			
1975	368	252			
1976	384	257			
1977	397	263			
1978	408	269			
1979	419	276			
1980	435	282			

[a] The index was put together from indexes for various periods given in *Narkhoz* 1965, p. 593; Narkhoz 1967, p. 674; *Narkhoz* 1970, p. 537; *Narkhoz* 1975, p. 567; and *Narkhoz* 1980, p. 380.
[b] Table A.2. Growth rates were calculated from unrounded data.

Official data on defense were similarly reassuring. Where Bergson, relying on the published defense budgetary statistic, had found the military burden from the late 1930s onward to be mostly in the double digits, the defense share of GNP declined to 5.5 percent in 1960 and then to less than 3 percent in the 1980s.[23] This good record was marred in 1989 when Gorbachev revealed, contrary to Bergson's assumption, that weapons were excluded from the official "defense" budget, and revised the figure to 7.5 percent of GNP after which it began declining again.[24] Accepting this corrected figure as a benchmark, it seems that the Soviet Union hadn't significantly reformed since Stalin's days, even though some improvement is implied.

The Central Intelligence Agency however took a very different position. It found the USSR's defense burden (1970–90) to have increased by 50 percent above Bergson's figure for 1955.[25] Structural militarization hadn't abated, it had intensified. Indeed on some measures the burden had doubled.[26] But this was offset in part by the CIA's claim that the burden was gradually declining after 1970, and weapons were decreasing as a share of defense spending.[27] Sorting out this tangle of contradictions is too difficult here for our purposes,[28] but the bottom line for the Agency was that the military component of the Soviet economy was gradually declining. It was a burden, but not menacing either to its economic future or Western security.[29]

Table 10.10 Average annual rate of growth of national product for selected OECD countries (GDP) and the USSR (GNP) (%)

	1951–5[a]	*1956–60*	*1961–5*	*1966–70*	*1971–5*	*1976–9*	*1951–79*[b]
Total OECD	*NA*	*NA*	*5.2*	*4.8*	*3.1*	*4.0*	*NA*
Of which							
Canada	5.2	4.0	5.7	4.8	5.0	3.7	4.8
United States	4.2	2.3	4.6	3.1	2.3	4.4	3.4
Japan	7.2	8.6	10.0	12.2	5.0	5.9	8.3
Australia	3.8	4.0	4.8	6.0	3.5	2.4	4.2
New Zealand	3.8	4.0	4.9	2.7	4.0	0.3	3.3
Finland	5.0	4.1	4.8	4.8	3.9	2.5	4.2
France	3.7	5.0	5.8	5.4	4.0	3.7	4.6
West Germany	9.2	6.5	5.0	4.4	2.1	4.0	5.1
Italy	5.6	5.5	5.2	6.2	2.4	3.8	4.8
Netherlands	5.9	4.0	4.8	5.5	3.2	3.1	4.4
Norway	3.8	3.3	4.8	3.7	4.6	4.2	4.1
Spain	5.2	3.2	8.5	6.2	5.5	2.5	5.3
Sweden	3.4	3.4	5.2	3.9	2.7	1.1	3.4
Switzerland	4.9	4.3	5.2	4.2	0.8	0.9	3.5
Turkey	8.1	4.6	4.8	6.6	7.5	4.1	6.0
United Kingdom	3.9	2.6	3.1	2.5	2.0	2.4	2.7
USSR	5.5	5.9	5.0	5.2	3.7	3.0	4.8

[a] Data in column 1 for Japan and the United Kingdom are for 1953–5: for Finland, France, West Germany, Italy, and the Netherlands – 1952–5; and for New Zealand and Spain – 1955 only. The corresponding data in column 7 are for 1953–79, 1952–79, and 1955–79, respectively. NA = not available.

Sources: OECD data are from *National Accounts of OECD Countries*, OECD, Paris, 1981, except for the value for total OECD for 1961–65. The latter value is from the 1980 edition of the same publication USSR data are from table A-5

On balance therefore Bergson seems to have batted 0.667. He correctly anticipated the retardation in Reform Communist growth driven by negative combined factor productivity and the continuing high defense burden, but living standards improved more rapidly than he expected.

No report card however would be complete without some indication of class rank. How did the post-Stalin physical management system perform compared with its free enterprise peers?

Much of the answer is provided in tables 10.9 and 10.10 which compare the CIA's estimates of Soviet national income and per capita consumption growth with counterpart statistics compiled by the OECD for its member states (1951–79). The Soviets beat the simple numerical GNP growth average and greatly surpass the European mean. Per capita OECD GDP data derived from United Nations sources show that even during the "wretched" 1980s the Soviet Union outperformed the United States and Europe on its official series, but did only half as well on the Agency's numbers.[30] However, during the next five-years, per capita GDP growth in America, Japan, and Europe fell to the Soviet level (CIA measure) during the 1980s.

As figure 10.1 initially suggested when all was said and done, Soviet economic performance, even on the Agency's numbers hardly painted a picture of an economy on life-support.

The per capita consumption data tell broadly the same story, and raise the question of whether the CIA's figures were sufficiently discounted. How could an economy which criminalized business, entrepreneurship, and private ownership have kept pace with OECD market economies for 35 years before collapsing. As we saw earlier, Gorbachev and his advisors thought the CIA's estimates were too high! They spoke of stagnation (zero growth) starting as early as 1980. The CIA rejected this grimmer picture because it believed that the physical indexes it employed in lieu of value sub-aggregate series captured most of the overstatement. But their belief was ill founded for two reasons. First, nothing prevented those who falsified the value statistics from similarly overstating physical production.[31] Second, contrary to the assumptions of neoclassical growth theory, Soviet and Western statistics are fundamentally non-comparable. Soviet value estimates neither measure production potential, nor consumer utility, regardless of adjusted factor costing.[32] They are opaque fiat statistics. The production of ever more goods and services that no one really wants only constitutes progress for those prepared to assume that this is the case.[33] Students steeped in neoclassical production theory are inclined to disregard these fatal deficiencies because for them there is no technological regress, or productive disorganization. If input utilization is unchanged, outputs should be constant. If inputs grow, so should GNP. But these abstractions don't apply straightforwardly in non-transparent systems where "principal agents'" interests are misaligned with their supervisors, and moral hazard can topple the house of cards. The Soviet Union was secretive at all levels because there was a lot to hide, and the false assumption that its economic statistics were "reliable" led Sovietologists to mis-suppose that "seeing" (the numbers) was "believing" (perceiving the truth). As the collapse compellingly shows, the system was less bountiful and more fragile than they surmised.

OECD Post Mortem

Perceptions of the Soviet communist experiment in the West until recently were shaped by debates within the Sovietological profession, but these concerns are being gradually superseded by a new generation of scholars and institutional actors interested more in global development than socialist natural economy. Many of these studies, especially Angus Maddison's cast the Soviet development model in an adverse light. His series, computed in dollars for the period 1913–91, show the USSR losing ground to the United States despite what should have been substantial benefits of relative backwardness. Its performance during the last two communist decades in terms of GDP and GDP per capita were poor, and disastrous if the hyper-depression of 1992–8 is blamed on the old regime (tables 10.10, 10.11, 10.12, 10.13, figures 10.2 and 10.3). After all the sound and fury, living standards in 1998 were only 14.5 percent of America's, not 66 percent as Goskomstat claimed in the late 1980s. The verdict of history, at least from the standpoint of the OECD, World Bank, IMF, and United Nations therefore is likely to be that the Soviet Union proved the competitive inferiority of communist administrative command planning.

Table 10.11 Average annual rate of growth of per capita consumption in selected OECD countries and the USSR

	1951–5[a]	*1956–60*	*1961–5*	*1966–70*	*1971–5*	*1976–9*	*1951–79*[a]
Total OECD	*NA*	*NA*	*3.7*	*3.7*	*2.8*	*3.1*	*NA*
Of which							
Canada	2.5	2.1	2.6	2.7	5.2	2.4	2.9
United States	1.5	1.0	2.8	2.7	2.0	3.4	2.2
Japan	7.0	6.8	7.9	8.6	4.8	3.9	6.6
Australia	0.4	0.9	2.5	2.9	2.5	1.1	1.7
New Zealand	NA	NA	1.5	0	1.2	0.1	0.7
Finland	3.7	2.0	5.0	4.1	3.6	1.5	3.4
France	3.7	3.2	4.5	4.0	4.1	3.6	3.9
West Germany	8.1	5.5	4.1	4.0	2.6	3.7	4.6
Italy	3.9	4.1	5.3	6.1	1.8	2.6	4.0
Netherlands	3.4	2.3	4.9	4.9	2.3	3.3	3.5
Norway	1.8	2.2	2.6	2.9	3.2	1.9	2.5
Spain	4.6	1.5	7.3	4.8	4.8	1.6	4.1
Sweden	1.8	1.8	3.6	2.3	2.3	0.9	2.2
Switzerland	1.4	2.3	3.1	3.0	1.4	2.1	2.2
Turkey	5.4	1.9	1.8	3.0	4.5	1.7	3.1
United Kingdom	3.9	2.2	2.0	1.6	2.0	2.4	2.2
USSR	3.1	3.8	2.1	4.3	2.6	1.7	3.0

[a] Data in column 1 for Japan and the United Kingdom are for 1953–5: for Finland, France, West Germany, Italy, and the Netherlands – 1952–5; and for Spain – 1955 only. The corresponding data in column 7 are for 1953–79, 1952–79, and 1955–79, respectively. The value in column 7 for New Zealand is for 1961–79. NA = not available.

Sources: See sources to table 1 for the OECD consumption data. The USSR consumption data are from table A-9. The population data for all countries are from *World Population 1979*. US Bureau of the Census, Government Printing Office, Washington, DC, 1980, and *Demographic Estimates for Countries With a Population of 10 Million or More: 1981*. US Bureau of the Census, Government Printing Office, Washington, DC, 1981, and *World Population 1977*. US Bureau of the Census, Government Printing Office. Washington, DC, 1978

Table 10.12 Comparative GDP size, USSR and USA: 1913–1998 (USA = 100)

	USSR	*USA*
1913	44.9	100
1930	32.8	100
1938	50.7	100
1950	35	100
1960	41.2	100
1973	42.8	100
1980	40.4	100
1991	32.3	100
1998	15.3	100

Table 10.13 Comparative per capita GDP, USSR and USA: 1913–1998 (USA = 100)

	USSR	*USA*
1913	28.1	100
1930	23.3	100
1938	35.1	100
1950	29.7	100
1960	34.8	100
1973	36.3	100
1980	34.6	100
1990	29.6	100
1991	28.1	100
1998	14.5	100

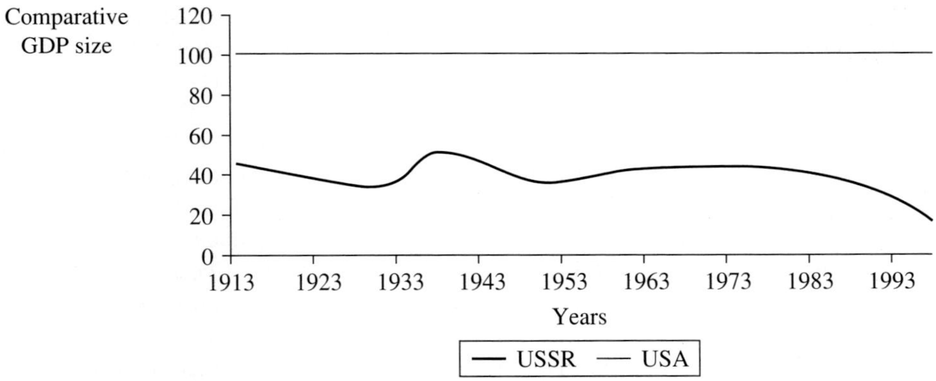

Figure 10.2 USA–USSR: Comparative GDP and per capita GDP: 1900–2000
Source: Angus Maddison, *The World Economy: Historical Statistics*, OECD, Paris, 2003

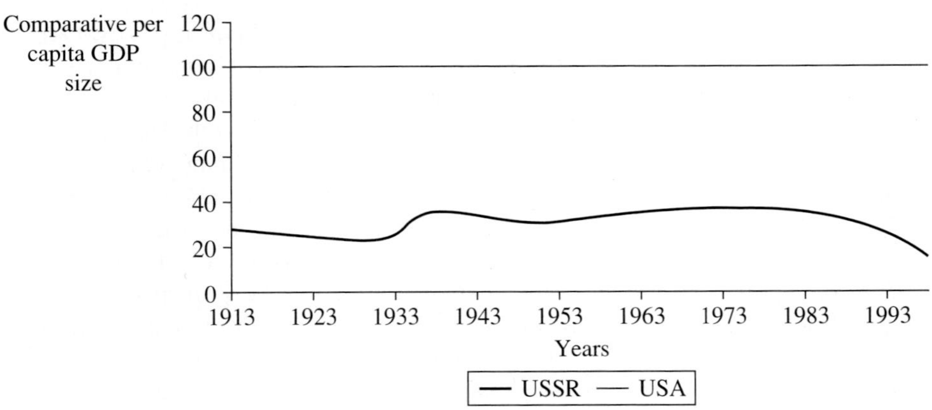

Figure 10.3 USA–USSR: Comparative per capita GDP size: 1900–2000
Source: Angus Maddison, *The World Economy: Historical Statistics*, OECD, Paris, 2003

Review

Kremlin leaders from November 7, 1917 to the Soviet Union's waning moments never publicly displayed any doubts about the ultimate triumph of socialism, although Putin is said to have done so in private,[34] and with the exception of War Communism crafted statistics corroborating their claims. Western economists, including John Maynard Keynes considered Bolshevik economic concepts absurd and expected Soviet rule to quickly crumble, but attitudes changed as hopes for liberal alternatives faded. Western governments were gradually compelled to recognize Soviet Russia, and economists soon revised their judgments. For a time, under the radicalizing influence of the Great Depression, some Western economists adopted the Bolshevik position, but most like Abram Bergson sensibly kept an open mind, even going so far as to elaborate the formal conditions under which Command Communism could simulate Pareto efficiency. Marxist economists such are Maurice Dobb during the early postwar period more or less accepted official Soviet statistics at face value,[35] while neoclassicists contended that reliable estimates could be derived by filtering and reprocessing the raw data. This openminded attitude held sway during the 1950s when "take offs" and the "Soviet challenge" were in vogue, but as the communist tide in Western Europe ebbed, a new orthodoxy emerged. After Bergson concluded in 1963 that the distinctive feature of the Soviet model was negative factor productivity growth, the consensus unwaveringly insisted that Command Communism would underperform free enterprise in the long run, even though official statistics and western adjustments thereof using Bergson's own rules didn't bear out the prediction. The only way that consensus could be reconciled with evidence was to drastically adjust ruble factor cost data downward for "hidden inflation." Bergson had resisted this expedient in his earlier work arguing that the subseries on which he relied were "usable," but did not object when the CIA started discounting Soviet growth on the suspicion that inflation was being disguised as value added (quality improvement). The gap between Western perceptions and Soviet claims increased throughout the 1970s and 1980s. Experts placed less and less confidence in the official numbers, but continued to assert the reliability of their own counter-estimates. The collapse of the Soviet Union shows that the direction of their ad hoc adjustments was correct, but probably not the magnitude. Soviet leaders and people couldn't have been as disgruntled as events revealed had the growth of living standards really kept pace with America's as official statistics indicate. The poor performance of Command Communism wasn't attributable to its inability to mobilize resources. Employment was overfull from 1929 to 1989. The problem lay in the systems failure to effectively innovate and diffuse new technologies which retarded physical growth and the radical severance of supply from demand which diminished the impact of greater physical abundance. In the final analysis Bolshevik statistics almost always reported huge successes that were mostly illusory or warped. Theory and practice were in fact consistent once the statistical code was deciphered. Command Communism was an inferior economic system.

Questions

1 It has been argued by Mark Harrison that while Soviet statistics were seriously distorted by hidden inflation before 1955, they were mostly distortion free thereafter. Did Gorbachev agree with this assessment? (*Hint*: would "perestroika" have been necessary based on official growth statistics?) If Gorbachev disbelieved the numbers, why should we believe them?

2 Although the Kremlin often spoke about reform after Nikita Khrushchev, little was done about it. Could this passivity have been partly explained by Goskomstat's buoyant statistics? Consult the tables in this chapter in constructing your answer. In fooling others did Moscow fool itself?

3 Most Western scholars have insisted that official Soviet economic subseries statistics were "reliable" and "usable," especially when converted from established ruble prices to adjusted factor cost. What are subseries? Why are they said to be more reliable than official national income aggregates. How reliable and usable did official Soviet statistics turn out to be? What is adjusted factor costing? Why did Bergson imagine that Marxist labor value prices could be transformed mechanically into equilibrium market prices?

4 Did Western scholars abide strictly by Bergson's judgment that official Soviet subseries data were reliable and usable enough not to require further adjustment for hidden inflation?

5 What is hidden inflation? Why is it so hard to estimate?

6 If the Soviets did mis-ascribe price increases to value added, what prevented them from adjusting their supposed "physical" series accordingly on the pretext of standardizing "physical units"?

7 If the Soviets did mis-ascribe price increases to value added, what prevented them from misreporting output and output growth?

8 Western economists have shifted their ground over the decades regarding just how much Soviet statistics should be discounted. Was this explained primarily by the discovery of new evidence or shifting political attitudes? Explain.

9 What does the Soviet Union's collapse tell us about the accuracy of Western estimates?

10 Was the West's failure attributable solely to mis-estimating quantitative growth, or was an insensitivity to the inferior utilitarian significance of Soviet numbers also a factor? Explain.

11 If Soviet growth were lower than the CIA estimated, what does this imply about planned scientific and technological progress and diffusion? The Soviets invested a fortune in research, development, testing, and evaluation. Given your knowledge of *piatiletki* broadly construed, explain why the paltry return on this investment seems plausible.

12 Based on your prior responses, do you believe that the Soviet Union made substantial headway catching up with America as the CIA's estimates suggest?

13 Should the Soviet Union have made substantial headway catching up with the United States given its relative economic backwardness? Explain.

14 Despite the advantages of economic backwardness and the spectrum of statistics presented in this chapter, could the Soviets have lost substantial ground to America (1917–91)? Isn't this the most likely outcome? Explain.

Part IV

Russia

Although Gorbachev's position as President of the Soviet Union weakened steadily after the abortive August 1991 coup d'etat, the dissolution of the USSR was nonetheless a surprise because Yeltsin might have succeeded to the throne later that year had he chosen to do so. Instead Yeltsin, in his capacity as President of the Russian Federation, allowed the Soviet Union to dissolve, charting new waters. As during War Communism there was considerable hope that, despite the chaos of the moment, Russia would shed its Muscovite heritage in favor of democratic free enterprise or social democracy. Political and economic liberals East and West heralded the forthcoming transition and predicted superior results after a brief consolidation.

This was wishful thinking. Not only did Yeltsin opt for Muscovy, authoritarian rent-granting with a mixture of markets and state ownership, his shock therapeutic policies tolerating asset-grabbing, revenue diversion, Ponzi schemes, and capital flight sent production into a hyper-depressive free fall. The economy finally reached rock bottom during the financial crisis of 1998 and began rebounding shortly thereafter as Vladimir Putin gradually restored central authority, the military, and secret police. The World Bank and IMF put on a brave face throughout, contending that Russia was successfully transitioning instead of modernizing Muscovite style, until 2004 when they acknowledged their error. One can hope that this setback will be ephemeral, but the trend toward renationalization, planning, and tight central control doesn't bode well. Despite nationalization and nearly a century of continuous convulsion and hardship, Russian progress toward westernization remains thin.

11

Post-Communism

Summary

Denigrating central planning was considered small-minded during the cold war. But as soon as the Soviet Union expired, free marketers didn't hesitate to say I told you so. They lambasted physical systems management and extolled democratic free enterprise while advocates made excuses. Just as few predicted the Soviet demise, many now were certain that westernization was the only viable way forward and perhaps could be achieved in as little as 500 days. However, what was said wasn't what was meant. The Yeltsin administration didn't want democracy and consumer sovereignty any more than Lenin, and Western market enthusiasts were only confident that their vision would prevail in the long run.

Post-Communism evolved amid these contradictions. Boris Yeltsin officially embraced "*perekhod*" (transition from communism to democratic free enterprise) and took dramatic measures to prove it. He accelerated the decriminalization of private property, business, and entrepreneurship while simultaneously terminating compulsory state purchases, abolishing price, wage, interest and foreign exchange fixing, and pared restrictions on international capital flows. Enterprises were no longer required to acquire inputs from, and deliver outputs to, Gossnabsbyt' and were free from Gosbank oversight. These initiatives and others demolished coercive central planning and control and built some new structures, but left Reform Communist institutions and organizations mostly intact. Gosplan, ministries, *glavks*, state enterprises, the apparat, the state bank, the state price committee, the state standards committee, Goskomstat, the VPK, all survived, but have been reorganized and retasked. As a consequence the substance of post-Communism cannot be deduced simply by comparing organization charts. What counts is whether "*perekhod*" reforms promote or impair democracy and consumer sovereignty.

Close observation reveals that post-Communism has followed a Muscovite course. Russia's constitution is authoritarian and the president rides roughshod over the parliament much like a Communist Party General Secretary. Privatization has been an exercise in plunder instead of an equitable denationalization. The economy has been divided into enclaves with anti-competitive oligarchs on top. Second is the "virtual economy," composed of remnants of the physical management system including much of the Soviet era "rust belt" and the military-industrial complex (VPK). Subsistence markets of various kinds serving the poor are a third echelon, followed by a small competitive sector. The boundaries dividing these various market categories however are blurring, pointing to the eventual emergence of a blended oligopsonistic market where preserves are allotted and protected by the autocrat, bureaucracy, and mafia. Like all Muscovite systems, the Kremlin rules by granting and rescinding property rights and privileges to rival factions. The rule of men supersedes the rule of law and society is partitioned into estates of a few "haves" and a multitude of "have-nots." For a time it appeared as if oligarchs might transform themselves into pro-competitive entrepreneurs with secure property rights, but the Yukos Affair has shattered this illusion. Oligarchy is in retreat and the influence of the security services and military is strengthening. Russia appears to be drifting back to the future, even though the Putin administration and some transitologists deny it.

After the Fall

The Soviet Union's demise wasn't inevitable. Market Communism could have been reversed just as ruthlessly as NEP if someone with Stalin's mettle had seized the day. The population would have supported a Brezhnev-type Reform Communist restoration. But this time around Boris Yeltsin was an anti-communist committed to ridding Russia of Bolshevik economic control. The die was cast. The only real question (not fully apparent at the time) was whether the Muscovite transition was going to occur within the political framework of the Soviet Union or within Russia and the Commonwealth of Independent States (CIS).

On December 21, 1991 the verdict was rendered. Although Gorbachev held the upper hand, controlling the KGB and armed forces, he capitulated to Yeltsin in his capacity as President of the Russian Federation without a struggle and dissolved the Soviet Union by executive decree with tacit Communist Party consent. The dubious legality of his action didn't matter because Yeltsin was the only viable ruler after Gorbachev abdicated.

Chto delat'? What was to be done? Politically the answer was unequivocal – "*perekhod*." Gorbachev was identified with *perestroika*, that is, Market Communism. Yeltsin had successfully stigmatized this policy devised by Alexander Yakovlev as a half measure which destabilized the economy without cleansing it of Bolshevism.[1] No half measures for Yeltsin. He promised a swift and complete transition to a Western "social" market economy, understood as an entrepreneurially vigorous, free enterprise system based on private ownership, with a non-communist state social safety net.

There is no reason to doubt that Yeltsin believed his formula pointed Russia toward the best of all possible worlds, in the same sense Lenin was cocksure about the virtues of War Communism. But it is equally obvious that he had no sober understanding of what was entailed. Like the Bolsheviks before him, democracy didn't really mean popular rule, nor free enterprise consumer sovereignty founded on a Lockean social compact. *Perekhod* meant Market Muscovy, (see chapter 10), Muscovite-style balloting,[2] crony privatization, and insider sovereignty. There was a chance post-Communism might turn out better than this with the right coaching; that Russia might at long last westernize,[3] but prospects for a brighter future weren't promising, unless he had the right advisors.

Which group would be the most influential? Would the security services, armed forces, administrative bureaucracy, and the state executive dominate as they had for much of Russia's history? Would power shift to rentier insiders like the emerging natural resource oligarchs, or to liberal advocates of a westernizing cultural revolution? The first round appeared to go to the westernizers.

Shock Therapy

Reform Communism didn't instantly perish with the USSR. While spontaneous privatization gathered steam in 1991, much of Soviet enterprise including the military-industrial complex remained state owned. And the abolition of compulsory central planning hadn't relieved the government of its obligation to purchase everything red directors produced. The decapitated *khozraschyot* enterprise bonus incentive mechanism therefore kept chugging along, placing a floor under Russia's deepening depression. This posed the Yeltsin administration's first challenge. It could cut the umbilical cord, canceling state contracts and guaranteed purchase, forcing fledgling private enterprises to fend for themselves (transition), or it could gradually phase in the new rules mitigating unnecessary hardship. Zealots counseled "shock" (therapy) (see chapter 8), moderates temperance. It was no contest. The Yeltsin team refused to temporize. It insisted that any dip caused by shock therapy would lead to a rapid rebound up the "J" curve, with full transition completed as Stanislav Shatalin predicted in 500 days.[4] By early spring 1992 most state contracts were canceled, and enterprises were compelled to sell their wares in the market. Many managers refused to believe their ears. Products like Sukhoi 27 fighter aircraft couldn't be freely sold, and red directors couldn't accept that the state was telling them to shut down. So they kept on producing until their supplies were exhausted, expecting a bailout that never materialized.

Shock therapy's impact was swift and catastrophic, exacerbating the depression of 1989–91 attributable to the internal disorganization caused by Gorbachev's Market Communist toleration of "spontaneous privatization" and managerial misappropriation of enterprise materials and revenues. No Western government could cavalierly cancel its procurement contracts without causing a wave of bankruptcies, and a severe depression driven by negative Keynesian multiplier effects (see chapter 2). Yeltsin's "shock" methods (without therapy) had to be worse because the state was the nation's prime contractor, red directors lacked market experience, and there was no effective institutional support. Soviet enterprises were rudimentary production facilities. They had no credit, or in-house expertise in pricing, recruitment, benefits, advertising, sales, or product design. Even if managers secretly aspired to become entrepreneurs, they lacked the means to do it quickly. No one therefore should have been surprised by the morning after. GDP fell more than 50 percent (1989–98), leaving more than 20 percent of the labor force unemployed and claiming more than three million lives.[5]

Systems Building

The debacle was partially acknowledged. National income statistics compiled by the Russian government, the World Bank, IMF, and OECD were doctored,[6] but nonetheless showed Russia in the grips of a hyper-depression nearly twice as severe as America's (1929–33). The Yeltsin administration initially claimed that unemployment was less than 2 percent, but after a few years accepted the OECD's methodology which generated joblessness figures in the low double digits. The Kremlin rejected Sergei Glazyev's charge that Yeltsin's policies were "genocidal," but admitted that the demographic situation was dire.[7]

Having bit the bullet however, the issue was no longer whether "transition" would entail hard times, but what could be done as Karl Marx might have phrased it to shorten the "birth pangs." Moscow could have partially restored selected Soviet era controls, substituted Keynesian surrogates like public works spending and deficit finance, placed its faith in accelerating the demolition of Soviet institutions, or constructing new ones. It rejected controls because they risked a reversion to communism and Keynesian methods for encouraging dependency on the state, leaving institutional demolition and systems building as the instruments of choice. These went hand in glove if the goal were democratic free enterprise. The Kremlin could have installed the rule of contract law and completed the decriminalization of business, entrepreneurship, and private property by fully privatizing, breaking up residual barter networks (Gaddy's virtual economy), simplifying business start-up procedures, and paring government to the Paretian ideal. With the communist legacy behind it, Moscow could then have built a durable framework for free enterprise by transforming anti-competitive into pro-competitive institutions. Market-facilitating laws could have been fashioned to replace legislative directives, with the rule of contract law supplanting state judicial subordination. Banks could have provided finance to the creditworthy instead of insiders, economic regulations could have been designed to promote equal opportunity instead of privilege, and the government officials could have been made responsive to the popular will.

Figure 11.1 illuminates this twofold process.[8] It depicts an ideal social democratic, post-Communist organization chart (cf. the Command Communist organization chart in chapter 5). Institutional demolition is concentrated within the State Economic Directorate, the Council of Economic Ministers, the ministries, the marketing network, and the State Price Committee. The mandatory central planning component of the State Economic Directorate is eliminated, and other functions including indicative planning are transferred to policy cabinet-type ministries (e.g. the Ministry of Economics, the Ministry of Economics, Development and Trade, the Ministry of Finance etc.). The Council of Economic Ministers is abolished as a directive body. Ministries and *glavks* are pared and transformed into custodial agencies for the state's productive assets. *Khozraschyot* enterprises become fully self-governing by eliminating state guaranteed

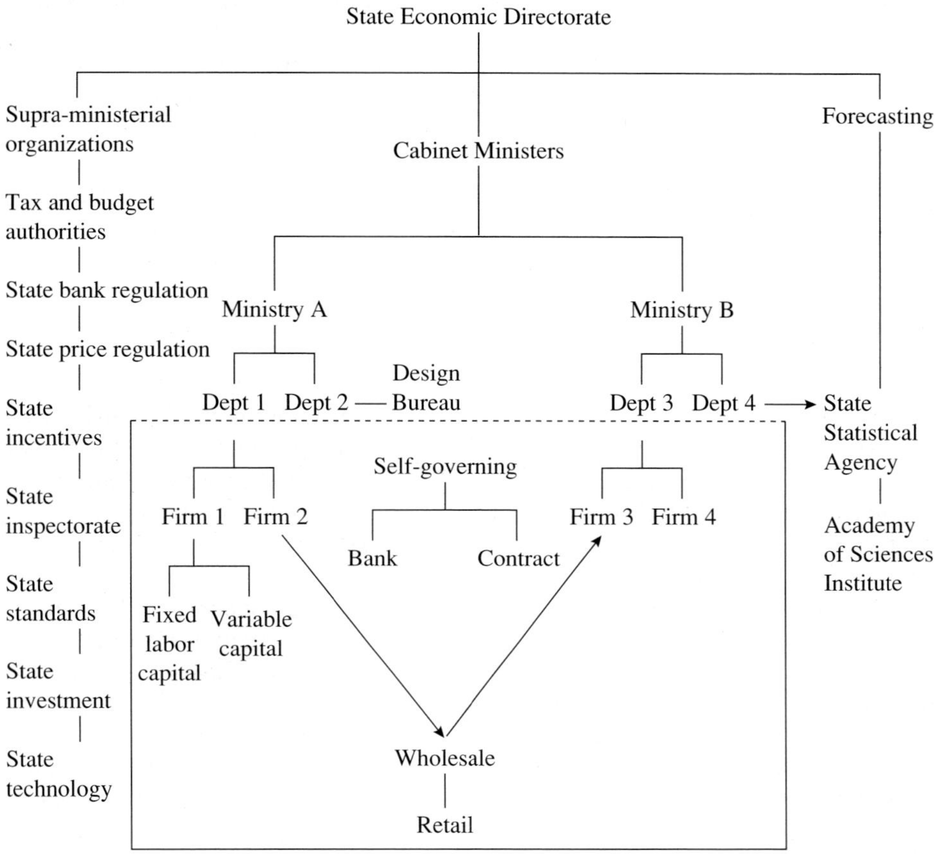

Figure 11.1 Russian organization chart

purchase, rationed input supply, and by privatizing. Wholesalers and retailers are converted to *khozraschyot* and hence private self-sufficiency. Banks cease being agents of plan control, are privatized, and forced to become commercially viable. Price and wage fixing are mostly ended, but the large majority of other former supra-ministerial organizations and support agencies like Goskomstat and the Academy of Sciences function as before.

Demolition in short meant abandoning coercive planning and control, managerial incentives and guaranteed state purchase; installing self-governance more than abolishing organizations and institutions. This had been the latent potential of NEP leasing, which re-emerged seven decades later supplemented by private ownership. Like Lenin's criminalization of business it symbolized a seismic change, but the devil was in the detail of institutional, organizational, and agency transformation. State entities and diverse types of private business can serve many masters, as NEP clearly revealed, making it imperative to distinguish the substance of Yeltsin's system building from lofty declarations.

The first hint of his administration's priorities occurred on September 21, 1993 when Yeltsin unilaterally scrapped Russia's constitution, disbanded the Duma, forcibly replacing his opponents including Ruslan Khasbulatov and Alexander Rutskoi with more pliant legislators; an action reminiscent of Lenin's dissolution of the Russian Constituent Assembly in January 1918. He then swiftly imposed a Muscovite-style constitution more to his liking that conferred authoritarian powers on the presidency, permitting him to rule by decree without effective checks and balances. The continuity with the Bolshevik "dictatorship of the proletariat" and Czarist arrangements has been widely noted, but supporters insisted that a strong hand was necessary to assure westernization even though this meant sacrificing democratic control over public programs.

Privatization

The new regime set about using its systems building authority in very peculiar ways. Instead of concentrating on a commercially oriented rule of contract law, an independent judiciary, and supportive culture, the cart was put before the horse. Priority was given to privatization instead of current operations encouraged by the desire of Yeltsin's inner circle, former red directors, *apparachniki*, and scoundrels to grab, strip, and loot.

The plundering was conducted under legal cover. Legislation was enacted in 1992 distributing enterprise shares in a seemingly equitable manner. Ownership was divided into four categories: state, citizens, managers, and workers. The first two were described as outside, and the latter as inside shareholders. Outside shares were non-voting (like preferred stock in the West) and insider shares were voting (common stock). The government and citizens initially received 25 percent stakes (the exact amount varied by sector), but workers fared best otherwise. They were given 80 percent of the inside shares (40 percent of the total), with the remainder allocated to senior management.[9] The preferential treatment accorded former red directors wasn't explained, except for the oblique assertion that Russia's market system should be predicated on "private" rather than workers' ownership and control.

This pretext was telltale. Managers not only received a too generous share of state enterprises, but were granted the Soviet era right of "*edinonachalie*" (one-man-rule). Although workers were the majority shareholders with the right to choose management at annual shareholders meetings, managers had a free hand in daily operations (an arrangement paralleling Yeltsin's power over parliament). This allowed executives to divert enterprise revenues for personal use, liquidate variable capital for the same purpose, and spin off lucrative fixed assets to wholly management-owned companies at nominal cost (asset-stripping). Wherever managers doubted their ability to control enterprise-earning streams, they mis-appropriated workers' and outside shareholders' assets. Had Yeltsin begun his crisis management regime by establishing a benevolent rule of law, managerial malfeasance could have been discouraged, but this wasn't his intent and in short, order asset control was mostly in the hands of former communist red directors.

Outside shares were subject to similar "abuses." Every Russian citizen was issued a voucher for his or her share in 25 percent of the peoples' assets (about $50 at the time). Workers in the state administrative sector, farmers, and soldiers received only these vouchers, while industrial employees and managers double dipped because they also received 80 percent of the insider shares. Vouchers were convertible in complex ways into shares, but most were accumulated by disreputable mutual funds whose directors defrauded shareholders by purchasing companies for their own account, and vanishing. These ill-gotten stakes became the "primitive capital accumulation" for some fledgling oligarchs. The state for its part reserved the right to issue new shares, a loophole facilitating backdoor re-nationalization, but chose instead to gradually sell its equity to private outsiders under the auspices of the State Privatization Fund administered by Anatoly Chubais. These lucrative assets, many in the natural resource processing sector, were channeled to the Yeltsin clan at bargain-basement prices (bid rigging), often allowing "purchasers" to pay by picking the state's pocket. In the notorious "loans for shares" scam the government-owned firm Norilsk Nickel, worth billions of dollars, borrowed money from Vladimir Potanin with the proviso that he would be compensated with shares at token prices in case of default. The government then needlessly defaulted (funds could have been acquired to pay the debt) giving Potanin a 51 percent state for $170 million. Expanding on this success with similar methods, Potanin eventually acquired control of thirty companies including Sidanko Oil, Sviazinvest (telecommunications), Perm Motors, Northwest Shipping, Magnitogorsk Steel, the GAZ automobile plant, Izvestiia, Komsomolskaia Pravda, and Expert. In the same fashion Menatep, a bank controlled by Mikhail Khodorkovsky, followed suit with a $350 million loan of the same sort giving him an 88 percent stake in the formerly state-owned oil company Yukos worth $2 billion. Menatep risked nothing having received the funds it loaned to the state from the government in the form of low interest bearing bank deposits.[10]

The Yeltsin regime never wearied of plunder. In the early years it tolerated a hyperinflation which wiped out the peoples' savings for the enrichment of officials who got their hands on newly issued currency first. It turned a blind eye to public Ponzi schemes (chain-letter-type frauds) like the MMM case,[11] which fleeced millions, with no recourse under Yeltsin's rule of men.

MMM Ponzi Scheme

The 1990s was a swindler's paradise in Russia. Ponzi schemes were pandemic. The largest of these pyramid scams was perpetrated by Sergei Mavrodi, his brother Vyacheslav Mavrodi, and his future wife Marina Muravieva who founded the MMM company (Mavrodi, Mavrodi, and Muravieva). They managed to entice at least two million people to invest possibly as much as 1.5 billion US dollars by offering to pay dividends up to 1,000 percent per annum before the scheme collapsed in 1994. Fifty investors having lost everything committed suicide. The company declared bankruptcy on September 22, 1997. Sergei Mavrodi was arrested in 2003 and is still being prosecuted.

The government delayed paying its debts and built up large wage arrears to state employees, which together with arrearages in the private sector lead to the barterization of large segments of the economy.

Wage Arrears

The Yeltsin government's withdrawal for state industrial control and management, especially its rescision of guaranteed state purchase sent production into a tailspin in the early 1990s, playing havoc with state tax revenues. The government responded by printing money, causing hyperinflation, and delaying wage payments to state employees. Only one-third of Russian workers private and state, received wages in full and on time in 1997; one-fourth had their wages delayed, while 30 percent had to wait months to get paid. This caused enormous hardship among industrial, administrative, and military workers, whose inflation-adjusted wages dwindled in the interim. Other kinds of arrears were pandemic. Any debtor who could, did delay payment counting on inflation to lessen their real obligations. Total arrears of all kinds was estimated at 80 billion dollars on January 1, 1997 by the ILO. The problem remained an impediment to recovery, until it was gradually overcome during the Putin era.

Later in 1997 government officials perpetrated a GKO state-borrowing scam which culminated the next year in the financial crisis of 1998.

GKO

GKO (*Gosudarstvennoe Kratkosrochnoe Obyazatelstvo*) is an acronym for short-term Russian government bonds which played a decisive role in the infamous financial crisis of August 1998. The Yeltsin government enticed foreign investors into purchasing GKOs with extraordinarily high interest rates that were paid Ponzi scheme-style out of the proceeds of new GKO sales. When the pyramid could no long be sustained the state defaulted, causing a financial panic that devalued the ruble by more than 50 percent.

Throughout it leased state natural resources to favored processors at a small fraction of their market value. Although Putin subsequently confiscated the empires of some oligarchs like Boris Berezovsky and Vladimir Gusinski, the merry chase for plunder never abated, with assets seized being transferred to the next generation of insiders. The privatization of agrarian land provides a bonanza for oligarchs who have avidly bought up millions of hectares from financially pressed peasants.[12] And movements are afoot to grant private firms the land they currently rent from the state and grandfather (forgive) past criminal transgressions.[13]

Rent-seeking

Westernizers were dismayed but not disheartened. Although they hadn't anticipated that privatization would in Marshall Goldman's term degenerate into "piratization," they nonetheless sought solace in the belief that once everything had been stolen, buccaneers (roving bandits) would construct an equitable rule of law for their self-protection. Russian liberals noted that America survived its robber barons, and argued Russia would have the same happy ending, even though the analogy was contrived. Some progress has been made. Many contractual conflicts have been amicably adjudicated in post-Communist arbitration courts.[14] But as one eminent Russian jurist wryly observed, it remains true that "If you don't know what else to do, obey the law!"[15]

Russia has yet to provide the business sector with a level playing field, despite much vaunted campaigns for enterprise restructuring. From the outset Yeltsin's administration fostered Muscovite rent-seeking instead of fair competition. It is better to be well connected than smart. Insiders are permitted to sell state services and bureaucratic access for private gain (as they did during NEP), and grant lucrative contracts to intimates for services that may never be rendered. An anti-monopoly agency has been established, but it doesn't foster competition, and the state helps oligarchs defend their turf with two consequences. First, much of what passes for government contracting, regulation and business promotion is thinly veiled transfers from state coffers that would be criminal in the West. Second, the government has institutionalized market discrimination, segmenting the economy into four spheres. Oligarchic controlled businesses like natural resource processing, utilities, and grain storage stand at the apex. They are anti-competitive and often violently deter new entrants with tactics like contract killings. The virtual economy including the VPK, operating mostly within the Soviet era physical systems management framework, comes next. It relies heavily on barter. It too is anti-competitive and will remain so even if fully privatized as currently contemplated (but the trend in the VPK is the other way). Then there is Russia's subsistence markets composed in large part of rust-belt industrial firms that were once the core of the Soviet physical management system, but now are the Kremlin's stepchildren, bereft of credit, often operating hand-to-mouth. They serve Russia's poor (roughly one-third of the population).[16] And finally, there is a hatchling upscale service sector catering to Russia's rich and aspiring middle class, which accounts for a small percentage of GDP.

Enterprise Restructuring

Soviet enterprises were more like production plants than Western corporations. They didn't design and innovate. They neither negotiated prices, nor wages. They had little need for credit, no shareholders, and no need for salesmen because the state purchased everything they produced. Although firms were required to at least break even with revenues from sales covering variable costs (*khozraschyot*), managers weren't concerned with marketing. Gorbachev's brief experiment with Market Communism and Yeltsin's Muscovite Market systems which ensued, compelled post-Communist enterprises to adapt or perish. The process was haphazard. In the initial phase most workers were given majority ownership of inside shares (those held by manager and workers) without however achieving operational control. Restructuring here mostly meant a process of gradually increasing management's ownership share and the reassertion of one-man rule (*edinonachalie*). Elsewhere it meant adjusting finance, organization, mergers and acquisitions, corporate governance, factor allocation, production, and distribution to market demand. Firms gradually learned to master barter, and then moved beyond virtual economy networks to heighten their demand responsiveness when the oil bonanza effectively re-monetized the economy. There are many conflicting measures of these accomplishments, but whatever the score, they weren't enough to make Russian industrial goods globally competitive.

This is hardly the transition westernizers had in mind. Post-Communism is a compartmentalized economic system partitioned into privileged and disadvantaged estates, thwarting equal opportunity and Pareto-efficient development. Corruption is rampant, and business is throttled by bureaucrats and the mafia. Some enterprises have succeeded despite these obstacles in transforming themselves into modern, profit-maximizing concerns, but they are exceptional. Most are pre-Smithian. State enterprises like their cousins everywhere are dominated by insider preferences and moral hazard, despite a patina of market responsiveness. Oligarchic firms are the same. Their prosperity depends on defending and expanding privileges, not enhancing long-term competitiveness. The virtual economy is rough and tumble Soviet physically managed barter, and subsistence markets are primitive. This hasn't stopped the Kremlin from encouraging liberals to dream that today's inefficiencies are a prelude to tomorrow's Pareto ideal. But this will remain wishful thinking even if these components eventually blend into a monetized, less sharply regimented, anti-competitive market, where preserves are allotted and protected by the autocrat, bureaucrats, and the mafia, until the leadership changes its stripes, withdrawing from the private sector, and suppressing privilege.

Not even globalization can save Russia from Muscovite marketization without a fundamental Kremlin change of heart. Russian enterprises in every sphere to date have failed to develop the corporate culture needed to successfully penetrate western markets with high value added goods. Of course, they can sell crude petroleum, natural gas and unprocessed timber, but they cannot design, manufacture, and merchandise industrial exports effectively, a problem compounded by the "Dutch disease" ("resource curse"), an overvalued currency caused by petro-exports. Nor can foreign investment save the day. Capital has steadily fled Russia (1991–2005),[17] but even if this pattern were reversed, Western firms can only partner with domestic oligarchy. They cannot seriously compete with it under the prevailing rules of the game. Post-Communist Market Muscovy is anti-competitive because the leadership is in league with privilege, above the rule of law, not because Western investors are too timid to seize a golden opportunity.

Oligarchic Interlude

For a time it seemed as if the oligarchs were the victors of post-Communism;[18] that a handful of buccaneers and cronies had captured the state, routing both Russia's liberals and the security services. They cooperated with both factions when it suited them on tax cuts and military reform, but oligarchic priorities seemed paramount even after Putin confiscated the empires of some of Boris Yeltsin's rogue proteges. As late as the Spring of 2003, some specialists lauded oligarchs as progressive businessmen and advocated amnesty against past transgressions to assure the inalienability of their property and the security of their future investments.[19] Of course there were counter-signs. Full-spectrum rearmament is scheduled to commence in 2006, modernizing Russia's armed forces with fifth generation, state of the art equipment by 2010.[20] And Putin conspicuously packed his government with retired military and intelligence officers. But these straws in the wind weren't taken seriously until July 2003 when Putin launched his attack on Russia's richest man, Mikhail Khodorkovsky for illegally accumulating his wealth.[21] Observers recognized immediately that what became known as the "Yukos Affair" (Khodorkovsky's Yukos petroleum company), was a thinly disguised campaign of intimidation to assert the primacy of state power over private interests, confirming a pattern established earlier in Putin's repression of the media oligarchs Vladimir Gusinski and Boris Berezovsky.[22] In a flash it became clear that post-Communism hadn't been about democratic free enterprise or "crony capitalism." It heralded the third coming of Muscovy.

Yukos Affair

On July 2, 2003 Platon Lebedev, Chairman of the Board of the financial group MFO Menatep and a major shareholder in Yukos oil company (headed by Russia's wealthiest oligarch, Mikhail Khodorkovsky) was arrested and charged with stealing a 20 percent stake in Apatit, a company worth \$283 million in 1994. Vasily Shakhnovsky, a billionaire Yukos shareholder, was indicted for tax evasion. Vladimir Gusinsky, a media oligarch in exile, was arrested August 24, 2003 all actions widely interpreted as warnings to Khodorkovsky to cease opposing Vladimir Putin's rent-granting and authoritarian politics. Khodorkovsky was pushing for oil pipeline deals against Putin's wishes and using democratic rhetoric to build a formidible political power base at home and abroad; a tactic that Viktor Yushchenko subsequently employed successfully in Ukraine's Orange Revolution. On October 26, 2003, Khodorkovsky's plane was stormed by security agents in Novosibirsk. He was hauled off to prison in Moscow, charged among other things with defrauding the state of \$5 billion in revenue. Yukos was forced to pay \$6.4 billion in back taxes on July 1, 2004. In December the government virtually confiscated Yukos's assets for unpaid taxes and transferred them roundabout to Gazprom. Finally Khodorkovsky was convicted for a series of economic crimes and sentenced to a nine-year prison term in May 2005. Although he undoubtedly acquired his wealth disreputably, the moral of the story is neither justice served, nor justice denied. The message of the Yukos Affair understood by all and sundry is that the Czar's power cannot be threatened without evoking a despotic response. Russia's other oligarchs now know with certainty that if they challenge Putin their assets will be confiscated and they will be imprisoned or killed. It is rent-granting that is sacrosanct, not private property.

Third Coming

The signature feature of the Russian style of political economic rule is revokable entitlement. Privilege in the Kremlin court isn't a right. The Czar (or supreme Communist leader) claims all assets in his name, or the state's, and demands obedience even though he recognizes that subjects are fractious and unruly. He effectuates his will not with totalitarian micro-management, but by keeping factions weak without secure assets and playing them off against each other. Property rights may be nominally granted in perpetuity, but without the rule of law, everyone is supposed to understand that gifts and privileges can be rescinded. Fortunate souls like Yeltsin's Prime Minister and Chairman of Gazprom Viktor Chernomyrdin may be appointed to administrate cash cows, skimming much of the cream, but only at their liege's pleasure.[23]

Some of Russia's Post-Communist oligarchs misconstrued Yeltsin's and Putin's westernizing rhetoric, or became too big for their britches.[24] They forgot that the Czar is only secondarily concerned with welfare and national power; that keeping the wolves at bay is the primary goal, and therefore momentarily imagined that they were indispensable, or could operate with impunity above the unwritten law.

By arresting Khodorkovsky, freezing 42 percent of Yukos's shares,[25] and ultimately expropriating the company for "unpaid taxes," Putin put all oligarchs on notice that he will not tolerate challenges to his authority from anyone foolish enough to believe that property "rights" and privileges are inalienable. The head of state alone is ultimately sovereign; oligarchs, plutocrats, capitalists, workers, peasants, consumers, even clan supporters are nothing, an attitude that precludes democratic free enterprise, whatever the ideology of the day. Just as Bolshevism wasn't communist or socialist in any ideal sense, so too Russia's post-Communist westernization has been a sham. The Kremlin predicably has chosen to construct the third coming of Moscovy with a protean set of rules intended simultaneously to curry favor with allies, while disciplining wayward spirits regardless of the consequences for efficiency and national welfare.

The security services, VPK, and even the Genshtab (the general staff of the Russian armed forces) are no exceptions. Although, their allegiance to, and dependence on the state makes them more reliable than rival princes and oligarchs, and hence usually more influential, presidents keep them on a short leash to forestall conspiracies. Putin's pronounced tilt toward the *silovki* (power elite),[26] reflected in bureaucratic staffing, military modernization goals, and the elimination of liberal parties from the parliament in the December 2003 elections doesn't symbolize his capture by these groups, merely a return to the traditional Muscovite power agenda with the Czar firmly in control.

Russia's future remains prefigured in its past. The Kremlin will continue being ruled by an autocrat whose power reposes not in the strength of Russia's economy and armed forces, but in the fragility of rival's claims on property and privilege. The strategy is logical, but non-Western because it subordinates Paretian welfare to Muscovite political countervailance. Russian rulers don't Pareto optimize. They satisfice, foregoing some military might and prosperity to safeguard their hegemony. And this time around Moscow seems bent on shredding traditional social safety nets, making tens of millions doubly vulnerable to predation.

Structural Militarization

During the Yeltsin years, the Kremlin chose to downplay the military aspect of Muscovite rule. Weapons production plunged approximately 90 percent, a significant portion of military-industrial enterprises were privatized (a process now being reversed), and there was a great deal of talk about eradicating structural militarization (see chapter 9). The sharp curtailment in demand for VPK services and the concomitant de-prioritization of the military-industrial sub-economy seemed to confirm that Russia was on the way to becoming a normal, civilian focused system.

But there are good reasons to believe that this judgment is premature; that curtailment and de-prioritization were tactical policies rather than a rejection of the authoritarian martial police state. The OPK (Defense Industrial Complex) as the VPK is now sometimes called had 1,700 enterprises and organizations located in 72 regions in 2002, just as it did a decade earlier. Although weapons factories in 2004 were officially operating at only 42 percent of the 1991 level, the capital stock has been carefully maintained. Should Putin desire, full-capacity utilization could be achieved in relatively short order. The Reform and Development of the Defense Industrial Complex Program (2002–6) signed by Prime Minister Mikhail Kasyanov in October 2001, together with the Security Council in the State Armaments Program for 2001–10, approved by President Vladimir Putin on January 20, 2002, indicates that the Putin administration intends to achieve this goal, with full-spectrum modernized weaponry by 2010.[27]

Perhaps this is a pipe dream. But, if it isn't, then structural militarization was merely cocooning during the Yeltsin years, readying itself for the next challenge.

Muscovite Economic Potential

Putin's Market Muscovy thus is closer to pre-Bolshevik Russia than Western democratic free enterprise. It is comprehensively inefficient. The division of estates and diverse anti-competitive enclaves prevent factors from being allocated to best use. Satisficing assures that preferences and demand don't take adequate account of individual and societal possibilities. Disregard for profit maximizing distorts supply. Market segmentation warps product distribution, and privilege makes inequality and injustice intractable. The system in a nutshell is autocratically sovereign, under-productive, and globally uncompetitive. However, like Command Communism, Reform Communism, and Czarism before it, inefficiency doesn't preclude resource mobilization. The Kremlin can employ multiple instruments to achieve full employment and can grow by transferring foreign technology, investing in research, development, testing, and evaluation, diffusing new technology, and improving education, training, and management. Inferior systems are prone to stagnate, underperform, and malfunction, but conjunctural factors sometimes allow spurts like the Command Communist industrialization drive of the 1930s. This is where Putin finds himself today. After a decade of hyper-depression and the financial crisis of 1998, Russia has rebounded 80 percent of the way back to 1989. Growth rates off the bottom are anemic given the severity of its hyper-depression, but impressive if taken out of context. There could be a few more good years of growth that benefits few and immiserizes many, especially if high natural resource prices fill the Kremlin's coffers, but the Market Muscovy model like its predecessors is vulnerable to growth retardation, stagnation, depression, periodic crises, and collapse.[28] Western democratic free enterprise isn't immune from these afflictions, but is self-healing.

The "third coming" is also susceptible to structural militarization (see chapter 10). Muscovite autocrats are inclined to erect military-industrial complexes and indulge the Genshtab's insatiable resource demands because a strong military kills three birds with one stone. It provides the Kremlin with superpower prestige, defense, and popular support. If oligarchs can't be trusted, and privilege is incompatible with equality, military might often serves as a handy "second best." This wasn't the case during NEP when Lenin and Stalin were leery of Trotsky, nor during the Yeltsin years when plunder was the main national pastime, but Putin's actions suggest a reversion to the Muscovite norm.[29]

If so, the military will become an increasing source of strength and weakness. It will deter foreign encroachment, but heighten global instability. It will revive heavy industry, but reduce competitiveness. It will become the backbone of growth, and a guarantee of inferior living standards. Losing by winning has been a cardinal feature of the Muscovite model, which is unlikely to change.

Fate and Attitude Management

The Kremlin believes in public attitude management and guardian angels. History shows that merchandising dreams convinces enough people that black is white to sustain Muscovite rule and muddle through. Although the system has never been optimal, things have worked themselves out often enough to encourage leaders to ignore the details and place their trust in fate. The failure of Reform Communism hasn't altered these reflexes. The search for magical administrative and policy solutions that will make Market Muscovy supreme continues unabated. During post-Communism the Kremlin not only failed to westernize its bureaucracy and administrative mechanisms along Weberian lines, but promoted one panacea after another. First hope was placed in Ronald McKinnon's "order of financial liberalization," which was supposed to jump start transition by taming inflation.[30] Ruble convertibility, competitive foreign exchange rates, and free capital flows were next, followed by G-7 assistance, foreign investment, enterprise restructuring, tax reduction for the rich, elimination of social benefits in kind for the poor, the "dictatorship of law," fiscal federalism, WTO membership, EU accession, and globalization.[31] All these initiatives had the potential for enhancing efficiency, but none addressed the deficiency of the Muscovite system itself. Just like Reform Communism, Market Muscovy's economic potential remains severely constricted by authoritarian controls and monkey business.

The path of least resistance for the West has been to acknowledge minor errors and implementational failures, while affirming the worthiness of transition.[32] Most transitologists contend that Pareto efficient marketization is "path dependent," that once begun cannot be reversed, while denying that distortions caused by "shock therapy" could have a path dependence of their own, or that Muscovite culture could be immune to westernization. Even Joseph Stiglitz who has criticized IMF and World Bank mis-advice and believes the consequences are path dependent feels that lost ground can be retrieved with modest policy changes.[33] But this can't be accomplished by turning a blind eye to the deeper systemic problem. Russia's micro-reality as under Reform Communism is still more disjointed than Pareto efficient, while serving the needs of the authoritarian martial police state. Consequently it will continue to drift back toward a soft Orwellian Muscovite future, leading to a geo-political repolarization closer to the cold war than EU accession, or a globalized new world order.

Post-Communist Performance

It will take decades before the contradictions of post-Communist Muscovy work themselves out. All that can be said with certainty now is that the Muscovite system sustained and survived hyper-depression in the 1990s (figure 11.2), and is recovering more slowly than the Soviet Union under NEP. Table 11.1 presents the basic facts.

Grigorii Khanin insists that they aren't to be trusted,[34] but the big picture is plain. Russia has staged a mild partial recovery after 1998 driven primarily by high oil prices, despite a declining and obsolescing net capital stock (table 11.2).[35]

The labor force has shrunk due to excess deaths and the discouragement of those unable to find jobs for many years (table 11.3). There were 7.9 million discouraged workers in 1998,[36] who were previously employed, but have given up after several years of fruitless searching.

The unemployment rate excluding discouraged job seekers is shown in table 11.4. For many years Goskomstat only reported "registered" unemployed, a preposterous figure given the hyper-depression graphed in figure 11.2. The new official survey estimates based on ILO definitions and methods are five times higher, but still implausibly in

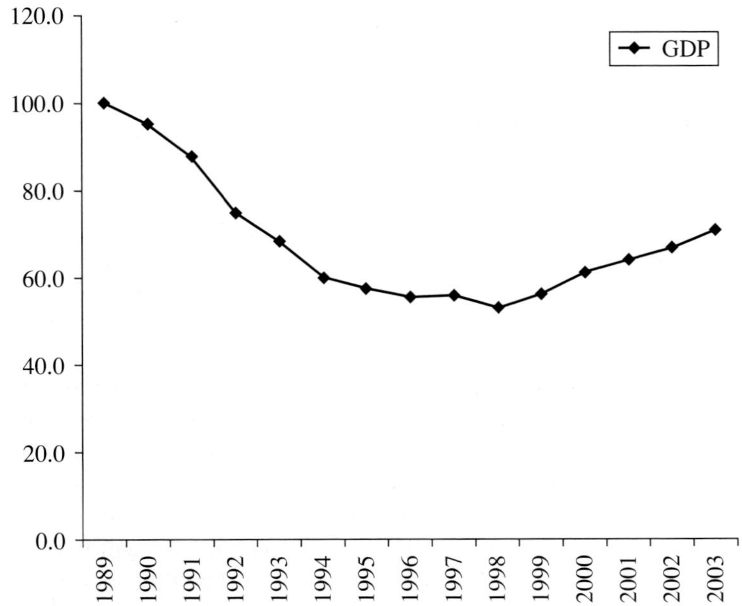

Figure 11.2 Russian hyper-depression: 1989–2002

Table 11.1 Post-Communist Russian performance, selected indicators (1989 = 100% inflation)

	GDP	*Consumption*	*Capital formation*	*Industry*	*Employment*	*Consumer Prices*
1980	78.1	—	—	74.4	96.9	—
1989	100.0	—	—	100.0	99.9	—
1990	97.0	100.0	100.0	99.1	100.0	5.2
1991	92.2	93.9	84.5	91.9	99.6	160.0
1992	78.8	89.0	49.4	75.4	97.7	1,528.7
1993	71.9	88.1	36.7	64.7	95.3	875.0
1994	62.8	85.4	27.1	51.2	93.7	309.0
1995	60.2	83.1	25.1	49.5	90.6	197.4
1996	58.2	80.5	20.8	47.5	87.8	47.8
1997	58.7	82.9	19.1	48.5	87.2	14.7
1998	55.9	81.7	17.3	46.0	85.6	27.8
1999	58.9	79.7	18.2	51.0	84.4	32.9
2000	64.2	85.6	20.1	57.1	84.6	38.6
2001	67.4	90.9	22.5	66.0	85.1	12.2
2002	70.2	—	—	70.6	85.3	—
2003[a]	74.6	—	—	—	—	—

[a] Author's estimate

Source: *Economic Survey of Europe*, United Nations, no. 1, 2003, tables B1, B2, B3, B4, B5, B8, pp. 224–7, 230

Table 11.2 Real gross fixed capital formation and capital stock growth in the Russian Federation (1990 = 100)

1990	*1991*	*1992*	*1993*	*1994*	*1995*	*1996*	*1997*	*1998*	*1999*
New capital formation									
100	84.5	49.4	36.7	27.1	24.6	20.4	18.9	17.7	17.4
Capital stock growth									
105.6	103.3	101.9	100.5	99.7	100.2	100.2	—	—	—

Source: *Economic Survey of Europe*, United Nations, no. 2/3, 2000, table B.3, p. 161. *Rossiskii statisticheskii ezhegodnik, statisticheskii sbornik*, Moscow, 1997, table 7.10, p. 294

line with the European Union norm. The real figure, including workers discouraged by hyper-depression was approximately 25 percent in 1998 and 15 percent in 2003.

The export structure is dominated by natural resources (table 11.5), while imports are consumer-goods intensive. This low value-added export pattern is likely to persist, reflecting the uncompetitiveness of the Muscovite model, but consumer goods imports will contract if and when Russia remilitarizes. Beyond this we will have to wait and see. The systemic deficiencies of Reform Communism should be greater than its successor because Market Muscovy is more liberal, but the evidence to date is inconclusive. The micro and macroeconomic welfare costs of plunder, rent-seeking, and

Table 11.3 Civilian labor force in the Russian Federation (millions of workers)

	1985	*1990*	*1991*	*1995*	*1998*	*Change 1990–8*
UN-Goskomstat	75.3	75.7	—	72.3	73.1	−2.6
Predicted	75.3	75.7	76.7	79.2	81.4	5.7

The predicted labor force was computed by applying Stephen Rapawy's growth estimates to the UN's concept of labor force.
Sources: Steven Rosefielde, "The Civilian Labour Force and Unemployment in the Russian Federation," *Europe–Asia Studies*, 52, 8, 2000, table 3, p. 1436

Table 11.4 Registered and surveyed unemployment in the Russian Federation (% of the civilian labor force: 1994–8, excluding discouraged workers)

	1994	*1995*	*1996*	*1997*	*1998*	*2003*
Registered	2.1	3.2	3.4	2.8	2.7	—
Survey (ILO definitions)	7.5	8.9	10.0	11.2	13.3	8.6

Source: United Nations Economic Commission for Europe, *Economic Survey of Europe*, 1999, 2 (New York, 1999), table B6, p. 69. "Economically Active Population Makes 50 Percent," *Johnson's Russia List*, no. 8003, Article 2, January 6, 2004

Table 11.5 Commodity composition of Russian trade with non-CIS partners: 2000 (%)

Exports	
Fuels	60
Primary commodities	16
Labor and resource intensive	3
Other manufactures	21
Imports	
Fuels	1
Primary commodities	32
Labor and resource intensive	8
Other manufactures	59

Source: *Economic Survey of Europe*, United Nations, no. 1, 2003, chart 6.2.5, p. 177

anti-competitive privilege, and increased moral hazard could outweigh the benefits of enclave marketization.

Russia is also beset by a host of social problems arising from the catastrophic impact of the Soviet Union's collapse and the predatory character of Yeltsin's *perekhod*. A rapidly falling population symbolizes this distress. Adjusted for net migration, the Federation's population declined by more than four million during the 1990s from 147 to 143 million. The rate of decrease has accelerated more recently to nearly a million per annum, and Murray Feshbach foresees the possibility of a decline to 80 million

Table 11.6 Russia population trend: 1990–1998 (adjusted for migration: millions)

1990	147.3
1991	147.8
1992	147.7
1993	147.3
1994	146.2
1995	145.7
1996	144.9
1997	144.1
1998	143.8

Source: Steven Rosefielde, "Premature Deaths: Russia's Radical Economic Transition in Soviet Perspective", *Europe-Asia Studies*, 53, 8, 2001, 1159–76

by 2050. Low birth rates and high rising mortality rates support his forecast (see table 11.6 and figure 11.6). If it materializes, the Kremlin will find it difficult to orchestrate sustained economic growth and adequately protect its national security.[37]

Finally a word is in order about comparative size. Estimates range widely. Russia's GDP in 1991 dollars has been computed between 3.9 and 17.9 percent of America's, with per capita figures from 6.8 to 31.5 percent in 1995.[38] Similar figures should apply today, but higher numbers are possible due to the opaque international politics of purchasing power parity formulation.

Analytics of Market Muscovy

The Market Muscovy factor space has shrunken (figure 11.3) compared with the Pareto ideal elaborated in chapter 2. Hyper-depression diminished capital along the vertical sides of the Edgeworth–Bowley box and labor along the horizontals. The labor force

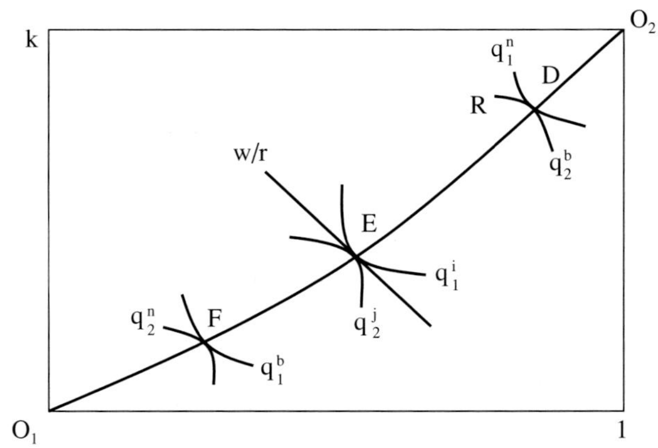

Figure 11.3 Post-Communist factor-production space

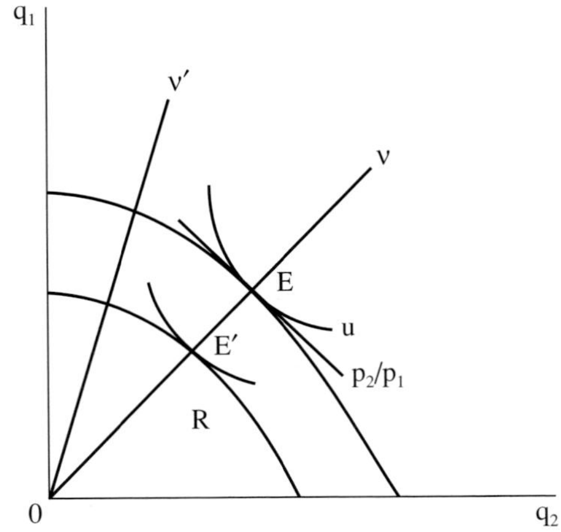

Figure 11.4 Post-Communist production possibilities

has contracted, and involuntary unemployment increased compared with both the Reform Communist and free enterprise norms. Superscripts on the isoquants are lower than before because predatory management and hyper-depression related labor mis-employment intensified. They are lower than their Paretian twins because technologies were mis-selected, inputs are qualitatively deficient, skills aren't ideal, input acquisition is untimely, and effort is often reserved. Factors aren't employed at their marginal rates of technical substitution because most managers are disinterested (satisficing takes precedence over profit maximizing) and residual physical systems management constrains performance in the "virtual economy." Enclave barriers also prevent factors from being allocated to best use. Instead of constrained efficiently producing on the contract curve at point E, firms operate inefficiently at R.

Output in the production space depicted in figure 11.4 lies at point R along a new disequilibrium expansion path (not shown), but below the Reform Communist production feasibility frontier (the lower concave curve). The hyper-depression depicted at point R replicates the War Communist outcome with a different output structure. It is premature to locate the Market Muscovy production feasibility frontier, or its ruler sovereign optimum, but it must lie well beneath the Paretian ideal at point *E* because Muscovy's Marshallian and Walrasian adjustment mechanisms are defective.

Products are distributed differently in each enclave. Barter predominates in the "virtual economy" and anti-competitive distribution in oligarchic operations. Transactions between these preserves, the subsistence, and emerging luxury services markets are inefficient in varying degrees. Some improvements should occur over time, but figure 11.5 reveals that goods typically won't be allocated at their marginal rates of product substitution on the constrained contract curve, but off it at point R.

And finally, income inequality is as extreme as it was before 1917, aggravated by Putin's conversion of communist-era social benefits in kind to cash payments in 2004 that will soon be eroded by inflation. The demand of oligarchs, Muscovite rulers, clans, predatory ex-red directors, and assorted scoundrels dominates consumption.

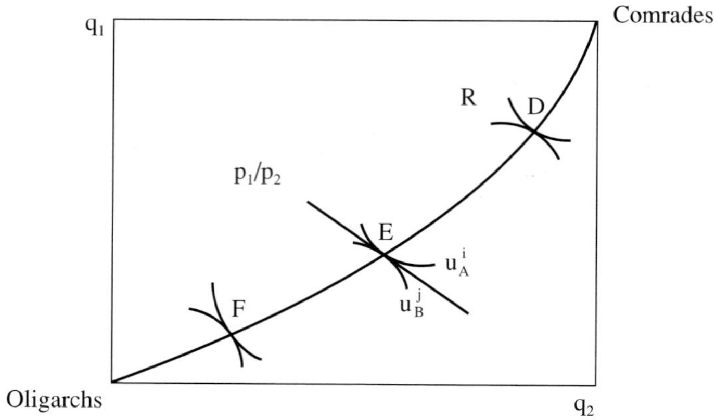

Figure 11.5 Post-Communist retail distribution

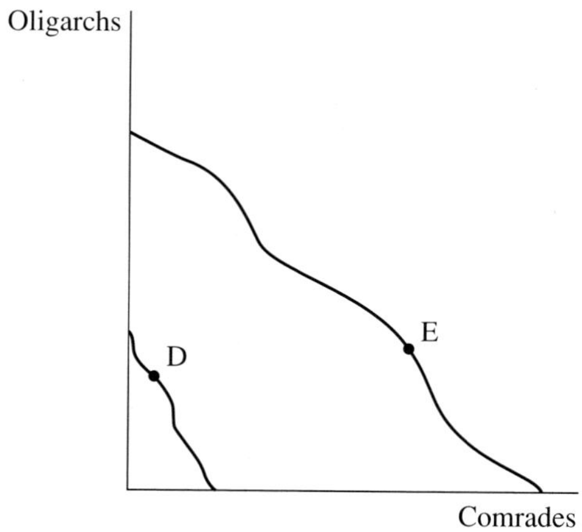

Figure 11.6 Post-Communist utility possibilities

The majority received neither guns (defense services) nor butter during the Yeltsin years at point D on a low utility feasibility frontier (figure 11.6). The situation has improved since then and there are signs that guns will soon be the featured item on the people's platter.

Systems Profile

Main features of Market Muscovy

- *Culture*: Muscovite authoritarian/anti-authoritarian with a democratic free enterprise facade. Anti-authoritarianism is a mix of passivity and opportunism.

- *Motivation*: Survival, empowerment, enrichment, superpower building, and opportunistic foreign expansion in the former Soviet Republics achieved by manipulating factions through the judicious use of revokable privileges and property rights.
- *Mechanism*: Natural resources, land and the entire industrial and administrative means of production, including housing, are "managed" and/or owned by the state. Natural resources remain the people's property. Much of Russia agriculture voluntarily preserves the *kolkhoz* organization. Farmers are free to exit and sell their plots. Compensation for commons is on a case by case basis. *Sovkhozy* have been privatized. Households have enhanced economic liberty. Physical systems management has been circumscribed to the "virtual economy," which includes large elements of the VPK. *Piatiletki*, and coercive planning aspects of economic ministries, *glavks* and Gossnabsbyt' have been abolished, together with administrative supervision, intervention, material balancing, guaranteed state purchase of industrial output, state managerial incentivization, and discipline. The economy is divided into enclaves of various types of markets and residual physical systems management. Oligarchs anti-competitively satisfice (rather than profit maximize) in the natural resource sectors and other lucrative activities. Some parts of the VPK operate similarly, but others continue on the Reform Communist pattern. State administration functions largely as before, but with greater opportunities for legal and illegal private benefit. Subsistence markets are hand to mouth affairs, but the small market in upscale services is modernizing. Interaction among enclaves is sub-optimal. The state no longer sets wages, prices, interest, and foreign exchange rates, but manipulates them. The rule of men persists. Russia is no longer a one-party system (although informally it is close to it), but the president is constitutionally empowered to rule autocratically disregarding parliament, the judiciary, and political parties. Soviet-era micro-reforms have been partially displaced by private corporate governance. Business, entrepreneurship, and private property are all legalized in approved activities. Leasing is commonplace in the natural resource and real estate sectors, but cooperatives are in decline.
- *Institutions*: Russia is a mixed Muscovite economy with state ownership of natural resources, public land, urban real estate, some utilities, industrial enterprises in the VPK, the state savings bank (Sberbank) with 70 percent of all private deposits, and the administrative apparatus; and a private sector with oligarchic, subsistence, and competitive markets, and residual physical systems management in the virtual sub-economy. Business, entrepreneurship, and private ownership, including cooperatives have been re-legalized for approved activities. *Kolkhozy* have been privatized but remain communal. *Sovkhozy* have been converted to private farms. The ministerial system, including the Council of Economic Ministers, industrial ministries and *glavks* have been pared, re-tasked, and transformed into less coercive and more regulatory entities. Other state functional agencies like Gosplan (Central Planning Agency), Gossnabsbyt' (State Material Acquisition and Distribution Agency), Gosbank (State Bank), Gosstroi (State Construction Agency), Goskomtsen (State Price Committee), Gosstandart (State Standards Bureau), Goskomstat (State Statistical Agency), Gosarbitrazh (contract adjudication), and the Ministry of Foreign Trade have been similarly modified. The Soviet state production monopoly has been rescinded and trade unions have become autonomous. Many enterprises voluntarily preserve workers councils, but as before they have little power over management. The expansion of cooperatives under Gorbachev has been reversed, and moral

hazard remains rampant because the system is still governed by the rule of men, rather than the rule of law.

Main inefficiencies

- *Law of demand*: Insiders' (rulers') preferences dominate high-value production and distribution. Hyper-depression has created a buyers' market for labor. There will be monopsony demand for labor in some sectors after recovery. Forced substitution and privileged access to goods and services has been greatly reduced. Demand isn't a function solely of prices and incomes. It is warped by rent-seeking, asset-grabbing, moral hazard, coercion, and commandeering in the virtual sub-economy.
- *Law of supply*: Worker supply curves are positive functions of wages outside the virtual sub-economy. Gulag work conditions have normalized. Industry and agricultural supplies are price responsive, and the role of profit seeking has expanded. Absence of the rule of law and alienable property rights adversely affect supply.
- *Law of equilibration*: Neither Walrasian nor Marshallian automatic price and quantity adjustment mechanisms operate effectively, causing more than a decade of hyper-depression. Insofar as Keynesian pump-priming has been tried, it too has been ineffective. The alternative monetarist money supply expansion method hasn't done any better. It caused hyperinflation and contributed to economic collapse. Hidden inflation is no longer discussed, but according to Khanin has not disappeared. Soviet material balancing, contracting, bonus incentivization, and assignment continue to operate on a reduced scale in the virtual sub-economy. Troubleshooter and *tolkachi* activities have diminished. Credit is mostly available to oligarchs and insiders, and therefore plays a limited role in micro- and macroeconomic adjustment processes. The economy has flipped from one of chronic excess demand to one of persistent deficient demand despite rampant inflation. Overfull employment has been replaced by double digit under-employment (with an extraordinary number of discouraged workers who haven't found jobs in years), but this problem is abating. Disinvestment and capital flight are culprits in Russia's hyper-depression. Money and foreign exchange markets as well as markets for loanable funds have been created, but function inefficiently.

Tactics of post-Communist economic management

Topic	*Problem*	*State response*
State ownership	Circumscribes individual utility-seeking	Sharply reduced, proposed end 2005, but is increasing
Decriminalization of private ownership	Asset-grabbing, moral hazard	Selective prosecution
Decriminalization of business	Moral hazard	None
Decriminalization of entrepreneurship	Moral hazard	None

Inefficient Gosplanning	Inter-industrial factor misallocation	Abolished coercive planning
Abolition of central planning	Moral hazard, disorganization	None
Infeasible tekhprom finplan assignments (virtual subeconomy)	Red director effort minimization	Firms made self-sufficient, assignment by contract only
Kolkhoz dividends	*kolkhozniki* receive residual compensation	Members can set new rules for communal labor
Worker under-compensation	Deterred effort, labor force withdrawal	Voluntary wage negotiation, but ineffective due to hyper-depression
Double-digit unemployment	Under-capacity utilization, distress	No jobs programs
Protracted unemployment (discouraged workers leave labor force)	Poverty	None
Hyperinflation	Economic disorganization	Gradual application of monetary discipline
Unbalanced development	Structural militarization, over-industrialization	Sustained, but weapons production drastically reduced, de-industrialization
Consumer goods shortages	Deterred effort	Persist in virtual sub-economy and subsistence markets, foreign imports for those with money
Quality	Product characteristics unresponsive to demand	Persists in virtual sub-economy, but demand responsive in the competitive sub-economy
Moral hazard	Mis-appropriation and misuse of state and company assets	None

Systemic structure, 1992–2004	*Share of GDP*	*Productivity*	*Coercion*
Markets	55	Mostly low	Moderate
State	30	Spectrum	Moderate
Virtual	15	Spectrum	Moderate

Systemic characteristics, 1992–2004	*Degree/intensity*
State macro-regulation	Low
State micro-regulation	
pro-competitive	Low
incentives	Low
welfare/security	Low
administrative regulation	High
Criminal disservices	High

Causes of macroeconomic disequilibrium (hyper-depression)	*Degree/intensity*
Sticky wages and benefits	Low
Sticky prices	Low
Investment avoidance	Extremely high
Capital flight	Extremely high
Misinvestment	High
Liquidity preference	Low
Insecure agrarian rights	Moderate
State property rights	High
Foreign capital flows	Low
State corruption	High
Private corruption	Extremely high
Macro-policy management	Extremely high
Class conflict	High
System disorganization	Extremely high
Plunder	Extremely high

Main performance indicators

Per capita GDP	10
US = 100	
Rosefielde	10
Maddison	20
Per capita GDP growth 1992–2004	–2
Unemployment	12
Discouraged workers (no job for years)	8
Retirement support burden	None
Non-working mothers and wives	Negligible

Direction of reforms

Muscovite superpower restoration

Review

Key elements of Mikhail Gorbachev's circle grew weary of structurally militarized Reform Communism and successfully lobbied for a Market Communist experiment tolerant of asset seizing and revenue misappropriation. This radical reform, called *perestroika*, ultimately destroyed Soviet rule.

In the aftermath, the demons Gorbachev had unleashed generated a hyperdepression, including a 90 percent contraction in weapons production. The trauma was unnecessary. The Kremlin could have adopted democratic free enterprise, or social democracy, but was addicted to Muscovy. Russia has survived the adversity and is now recovering thanks to Putin's sterner authoritarian martial police state, but the system's potential is inferior. Westernization is much discussed, but only the trappings of modernization are visible.

Questions

1 Mikhail Gorbachev called his radical market reforms "*perestoika*" (radical reconstruction). Boris Yeltsin considered Gorbachev's efforts too timid and insisted on "*perekhod*" (transition). How did these concepts differ? Do the distinctions in their declaratory goals matter? Explain.

2 Could Yeltsin have combated the Russian depression in 1990–1 by restoring control over red director's discretionary use of state revenues and assets and halting privatization? Explain.

3 Was the scope of Yeltsin's legalization of business, entrepreneurship, and private property sufficient to assure consumer sovereignty, Arrow democracy, and Pareto optimality? Explain.

4 What steps were required to assure that post-Communist markets and government administration optimized Paretian social welfare?

5 What steps did Yeltsin take to achieve this goal? Elaborate using organization charts.

6 Why does Marshall Goldman call Russian privatization, "piratization"? Explain. Discuss the "loans for shares" scandal.

7 What was voucher privatization? What was its rationale? Was it fair? Why didn't it work?

8 Under Anatoly Chubais' privatization scheme insiders (managers and workers) were the effective owners and controlled all corporate decisions. As rational economic actors, what should have been their outside dividend payout policy? Explain. Western finance theory teaches that outside shares are worth the present discounted value of dividends paid. Did this make vouchers worthless for ordinary citizens? Could vouchers have been worth more to managerial and worker insiders seeking control? Explain.

9 What is "*edinonachalie*"? How did it abet "asset-stripping" and other moral hazards? Workers had the right to change management policy and dismiss managers at

annual shareholder meetings. Was this an adequate check, or was the prospect of managerial dismissal destabilizing? Explain.

10 What is "rent-seeking"? How does it differ from money laundering? How does it differ from mafia extortion? Should "compensation" paid rent-seekers be treated as value added and included in national income? Explain.

11 Joseph Stiglitz contends that the IMF's and World Bank's "monetarist" transition strategies, which adhered to the precepts of Ronald McKinnon (Order of Economic Liberalization) predictably caused Russia's hyper-depression, and made the post-Communist system anti-competitively path dependent. His position is an assault on the "Washington Consensus." What is the "Washington Consensus"? Outline Stiglitz's criticism. Does it take adequate account of the Muscovite economic model? Explain.

12 Some have claimed that Yeltsin's demolition and market-building efforts were Muscovite half measures which modernized autocracy and privilege without westernization. Elaborate their position and provide supporting evidence.

13 What was shock therapy? (Be sure to discuss wholesale cancellation of state contracts). Was Rutaro Komiya, former Minister of METI, correct when he described Yeltsin's contract cancellation strategy as "shock" without "therapy?" Explain.

14 What role did "guaranteed" state purchase play in the Soviet system? Why was guaranteed state purchase especially critical after the abolition of Gosplan? Why was it more difficult for Russian firms to adjust to the elimination of guaranteed state purchase and the abrogation of state contracts than it would have been for Western firms? Explain.

15 If actions speak louder than words, what do Yeltsin's actions tell us about the hidden agenda behind his policy of "*perekhod*?"

16 Policies don't always work as intended. Wise policy-makers "learn by doing." Were Yeltsin's policies wise? Describe Russia's macroeconomic performance (1992–8), and evaluate whether Kremlin policy-makers showed any signs of learning. Can a case be made for their persistence from either a Paretian or Muscovite standpoint? If yes, outline your arguments.

17 What are oligarchs? Did they acquire their wealth the old fashioned way through hard work? Elaborate.

18 Are their property rights and privileges secure compared with Western billionaires like Bill Gates? Discuss the "Yukos Affair" and analyze its implications.

19 Western corporations, operating on their shareholders' behalf, strive to maximize the present discounted value of their firms. This maximizes shareholder wealth and benefits society because they must competitively profit maximize to achieve their objective. If oligarchs have insecure property rights, would it be sensible for them to maximize corporate present value? If oligarchic businesses are anti-competitive can their profit seeking be socially optimal? Are oligarchs prone to satisfice instead of profit maximize? Assess the comparative productivity and merit of oligarchic and competitive firms.

20 The Yeltsin administration reduced defense activities by approximately 90 percent. It preserved the VPK and retained its huge arsenal, but expenditure cuts diminished military readiness and jeopardized the long-run technological competitiveness of its armed forces. How should these actions be interpreted? Do they reflect "*novoe myshlennie*" (new thinking) and westernization, or a re-weighting of insider influence within the Muscovite paradigm?

21 What is the "virtual economy"? How does it work? (*Hint*: interpret barter as a continuation of the Soviet-era physical management system.) Are there tax advantages for participants in the virtual economy operating outside the money exchange system? Explain. Can local governments, regional authorities, and the VPK leverage their cash operations by encouraging the virtual economy? Explain. What are the efficiency costs of the barter-physical systems management sub-economy?

22 What is the "subsistance" market sub-economy? Does it have access to credit? What are its prospects for expansion?

23 Does Russia have a competitive market sub-economy? What is its scope and limitations?

24 Do the virtual and subsistence sub-economies enhance competitiveness and facilitate Russia's integration into the global market system? Explain.

25 Theory teaches that foreign investment should flow from rich to poor countries where costs are low and business opportunities are promising. Capital has persistently flowed out of Russia to the West. Does this invalidate the theory? If not, how can the phenomenon be explained?

26 Is it reasonable to suppose that Russia will catch up with the West without foreign investment and technology transfers? How then does Putin expect to overtake Portugal soon? Is his expectation realistic?

27 How has post-Communism evolved since 1991 from the transitological and Muscovite perspectives? Are there grounds for optimism for partisans of Muscovy and westernizers? What would be the best outcome of the Yukos Affair for supporters of each persuasion? Elaborate.

28 What has been the human consequences of post-Communism in terms of education, health, excess deaths, population size, social safety net, income and wealth inequality, equal opportunity, social justice, political voice and personal liberty? What is your net assessment of nation welfare under Reform Communism and Market Muscovy? Has social welfare improved or diminished?

29 What is Russia's economic potential if the Muscovite consolidation continues? Can it be a superpower? Can living standards rise? Can it achieve full employment? Can hyper-depression be overcome? Can it be globally competitive? Can it be Pareto efficient? Can it converge with the West's high frontier, if it doesn't westernize? Explain.

30 During the cold war transitologists deferred to Sovietologists, accepting the viability of physical systems management, without relinquishing their faith in the superiority of democratic free enterprise. When the Soviet Union collapsed, they instantaneously reversed themselves. Were they justified? Did Sovietologists get things all wrong? Explain.

31 If Putin continues along the Muscovite path, and is able to report superior performance as the Communists did (by hook or crook), are transitologists vulnerable to another rude awakening? Explain. Is it impossible to tell whether Putin's Russia is Muscovite or Western, or are transitologists just ignoring the evidence?

12

Prospects

Muscovy After the Age of Miracles

The twentieth century was to be the age of miracles. The invisible hand was supposed to transform Czarist Muscovy into democratic free enterprise; or into utopian communism as Bukharin and Preobrazhensky saw it in 1919. Lenin confused heaven with a post office, Trotsky with a red labor army. Stalin tried administrative command planning and terror. Khrushchev and Kosygin opted for incentives and a treadmill of administrative reforms. Brezhenev (and many Western economic theorists) embraced computopia. Gorbachev wagered on a communist market; Yeltsin on cronyism and communist liquidation, and the World Bank on shock therapy. All failed, despite cosmetically enhanced statistics which said it wasn't so, generating a soberer mood. Many now hope that a pragmatic approach to westernization, firmly rejecting miracles, based on honest statistics where the Federation accedes to the European Union and becomes a full fledged participant in Paretian globalization will do the trick.

But this expectation is a-historical. While Soviet Communism is dead, Muscovy is alive and well. The traditional culture is re-crafting a unique version of a mixed economy that only superficially resembles European social democracy or American free enterprise. The Kremlin embraces Western liberal rhetoric in its entirety. It supports free and fair elections and representative democracy. It applauds an equitable social contract, the rule of contract law, free enterprise, equal opportunity, minority empowerment, consumer sovereignty, an open economy, small government, social justice, laws which reflect the will of the people, and an independent judiciary. Pareto is its ideal.

However, this rhetoric like the Soviet constitution of 1936 is mendacious. Russian leaders haven't any intention of scrupulously abiding by it. They are cynical. Pareto is either only what they want him to be, or a convenient foil to disarm democratic opposition. This is very difficult for westerners to accept. They equate the idea of the West with reason and are reluctant to believe nations knowingly conduct themselves differently. Likewise, tolerance inclines them to believe that since all countries deviate from their ideals, and everyone should be given the benefit of the doubt, Muscovy isn't really abnormal.

The notion that Russia's flaws aren't cause for concern is culturally misplaced. While Western societies on both sides of the Atlantic are sometimes cynical and opportunistic, they are committed to democratic free enterprise and social justice. The Kremlin is not. Russia's leaders whatever they say remain autocratic. They are committed to the rule of men rather than the rule of law, and hence are inveterately anti-democratic, and anti-Paretian. The Kremlin occasionally tips its hat to the "Russian Idea" community and mutual support,[1] but its real commitment is to Muscovite hegemony. Privilege, preferential opportunity, and inequality are embedded in the system, degrading social welfare in all aspects.

These defects are sometimes masked by macroeconomic aggregates. Nothing prevents oppressive societies from achieving full employment, price stability, high levels of investment and growth. They can even provide subsistence social safety nets and public goods.

But they fail in two fundamental respects: efficiency and social welfare. Unequal opportunity necessarily means that resources cannot be put to best micro- and macroeconomic use from the sovereign's perspective. Productivity and productivity growth both suffer, problems exacerbated by other dysfunctional attitudes fostered by privilege. And matters are worse from the victims' point of view. These illiberal traits have made Russia economically backward, and there is nothing in the third coming of Muscovy that suggests a marked change for the better.

The same criticism applies to social welfare. The good society provides prosperity for the vast majority, not the unscrupulous and undeserving. Russia has always failed this crucial test, and the prospect is for more of the same, with even less consideration for the disadvantaged than under communism. This is clearly bad for most Russians, but not necessarily for outsiders. Foreign investors who escape being defrauded, exporters, importers, and consumers may selectively benefit. The afflictions of some may be the boon of others. But these special considerations don't alter the big picture.

Market Muscovy is likely to be severely Pareto inferior for Russia and the globe, even if high oil prices continue to provide fortuitous windfall gains. The majority of Russians and the rest of the world would be better off with Russian democratic free enterprise (or European social democracy) than autocratic "mercantilism" as Alexander Gershenkron describes the core Russian system. And of course, few at home or abroad see structural militarization and Soviet-scale rearmament as virtues. Communism is gone, but the deeper conflict between the idea of the West and Muscovy remains. The true "end of history" may yet be on the bright shining horizon, but it hasn't arrived, despite the claims of some.

Andrei Schleifer and Daniel Triesman contend that Russia already has become a normal middle income, democratic capitalist market economy like Mexico. While they admit that "democracies in this income range are rough around the edges: their governments suffer from corruption, their judiciaries are politicized and their press is almost never entirely free. They have high income inequality, concentrated corporate ownership, and turbulent macroeconomic performance," but will outgrow these teething problems as per capita incomes converge towards the West's high frontier. Shleifer and Treisman justify this optimism by insisting that Russian GDP reachieved the 1991 level;

inequity peaked in 1994 and is receding as wages become more competitive, Russia ranks "right in the middle of its post-communist peers" in the "burden of bribery" and "state capture"; its entrepreneurs have become world class like John D. Rockefeller and J. P. Morgan, and "Russia's politics has been among the most democratic in the region." Most of these assertions are untrue, and the norms applied are inconsistent with Pareto-efficient democratic free enterprise. Since diverse pathologies have things in common, it can always be said that any specific pathology is a "normal" abnormality. Putin plagiarized his Ph.D. thesis.[2] All Third World leaders do so. Hence plagiarism is normal. But the wordplay can't transform Muscovy into American free enterprise, or core EU social democracy.[3] Nor at this late date are there any grounds for imagining a virtuous, still undiscovered Muscovite ideal. The Kremlin experimented with Utopian Communist, Command Communist, and Reform Communist; physical management systems and subservient markets under NEP, Market Communism and post-Communism, all to no avail because authoritarianism and democratic free enterprise are mutually exclusive.

Notes

Preface

1 David Engerman, *Modernization from the Other Shore*, Harvard University Press, Cambridge, MA, 2003. Engerman not only recounts evolving attitudes, but condemns the "universalism" which arose after World War II for blinkering many academics to the importance of cultural particulars.

2 This approach emphasizes the technical economic consequences of Russian exceptionalism rather than larger meta-economic issues raised by slavophils and westernizers, "totalitarians" and "revisionists," or institutionalists and universalists. "Isms" in the text aren't primary, they are subordinate to Russia's cultural continuities. For a discussion of current academic debates on these matters see Alice Gomstyn, " 'Totalitarian' and 'Revisionist' Historians Debate Who Was Right: Some Say It's Time to Move On," *Johnson's Russia List*, no. 8045, Article 2, February 2, 2004.

1 Muscovy and the West

1 Geoffrey Hosking, *Russia and the Russians*, Harvard University Press, Cambridge, 2001. Cf. Stefan Hedlund, *Russian Path Dependency*, Routledge, London, 2005, and Alexander Yakovlev, *A Century of Violence in Soviet Russia*, Yale University Press, New Haven, 2002, pp. x–xi. "The land of Rus accepted Christianity from Constantinople in AD 988. Characteristics of Byzantine rule of that era – baseness, cowardliness, venality, treachery, overcentralization, apotheosis of the ruler's personality – dominate Russia's social and political life to this day. In the twelfth century the various fragmented Russian principalities were conquered by the Mongols, Asian traditions and customs with their disregard for the individual and for human rights and their cult of might, violence, despotic power, and lawlessness became part of the Russian people's way of life. The tragedy of Russia lay first and foremost in this: that for a thousand years it was ruled by men and not by laws. They ruled ineptly, bloodily. The people existed for the government, not the government for the people. Russia avoided classical slavery. But it has not yet emerged from feudalism; it is still enslaved by an official imperial ideology, the essence of which is that the state is everything and the individual nothing.

2 Samuel Huntington, "The West: Unique, Not Universal," *Foreign Affairs*, 75, 6 (1996), pp. 28–46.

2 Economic Fundamentals

1 Vilfredo Pareto, *Cours d'economie politique professe a l'Universite de Lausanne*, 3 vols., 1896–97; *Manual of Political Economy*, 1906. Kenneth Arrow, *Social Choice and Individual Values*, Wiley, New York, 2nd edn., 1963; "Optimal and Voluntary Income Distribution," in Steven Rosefielde (ed.), *Economic Welfare and the Economics of Soviet Socialism*, Cambridge University Press, Cambridge, 1981, pp. 167–88. Abram Bergson, "A Reformulation of Certain Aspects of Welfare Economics," *Quarterly Journal of Economics*, 52, 1 (1938), pp. 210–34; "Socialist Economics," in H. Ellis (ed.), *A Survey of Contemporary Economics*, Richard D. Irwin, Homewood, IL, 1948, pp. 412–48; "The Concept of Social Welfare," *Quarterly Journal of Economics*, 68, 2 (1954), pp. 233–53; *Essays in Normative Economics* Harvard University Press, Cambridge, MA, 1966; "Market Socialism Revisited," *Journal of Political Economy*, 75, 4 (1967), pp. 655–73; "Social Choice and Welfare Economics under Representative Government," *Journal of Public Economics*, 6, 3 (1976), pp. 171–90. Paul Samuelson, "Reaffirming the Existence of a 'Reasonable' Bergson–Samuelson Social Welfare Function," *Economica*, 44 (1977), pp. 81–8; "Bergsonian Welfare Economics," in Steven Rosefielde (ed.), *Economic Welfare and the Economics of Soviet Socialism*, Cambridge University Press, Cambridge, 1981, pp. 223–66. James Meade, *The Just Economy*, George Allen and Unwin, London, 1978. Amartya Sen, *Collective Choice and Social Welfare*, Holden–Day, San Francisco, 1971. Jan van de Graaf, *Theoretical Welfare Economics*, Cambridge University Press, Cambridge, 1957.

2 For a fuller treatment of micro- and macroeconomic principles see Steven Rosefielde, *Comparative Economic Systems: Culture, Wealth and Power in the 21st Century*, Blackwell, Oxford, 2002, chs. 2, 5, and 6.

3 Irving Fisher, *The Theory of Interest*. Fisher argued that the interest rate was determined by the principle of time preference, where current individual consumption and investment behavior is affected by the size and sequencing of future consumption possibilities. People who care little for the future, and consume intensively today are said to have high time preferences; whereas patient people have low rates of time preference. Fluctuations in interest rates are demand led in Fisher's conception. Interest rates rise when the community wants to accelerate its time profile of consumption (reducing savings and investment), and fall when it chooses to defer and augment future consumption (increasing savings and investment).

4 Robert Solow, "A Contribution to the Theory of Economic Growth," *Quarterly Journal of Economics*, 70, February (1956), pp. 65–94.

5 Abram Bergson, "A Reformulation of Certain Aspects of Welfare Economics," *Quarterly Journal of Economics*, 52, 1 (1938), pp. 310–34; *The Real National Income of Soviet Russia Since 1928*, Harvard University Press, Cambridge, MA, 1961. Steven Rosefielde, "Neoclassical Norms and the Valuation of National Product in the Soviet Union and Its Postcommunist Successor States," *Journal of Comparative Economics*, December (1995), pp. 375–89. Steven Rosefielde and Ralph W. Pfouts, "The Mis-specification of Soviet Production Potential: Adjusted Factor Costing and Bergson's Efficiency Standard," in Steven Rosefielde (ed.), *Efficiency and Russia's Economic Recovery Potential to the Year 2000 and Beyond*, Ashgate, Aldershot, London, 1998, pp. 11–31.

6 Adjusted factor costing deleted turnover taxes from industrial wholesale prices, together with profits, and added back a uniform interest charge on capital. These adjustments are consistent with national income accounting principles, and have merit in this respect, but do not create accurate measures of production potential. Also, it should be noted that since wholesale turnover taxes were small, their distortionary effect was slight.

3 War Communism: 1917–1921

1 James Billington, *The Icon and the Axe*, Vintage Books, New York, 1966, pp. 447–56. "But the path of liberalization was not the path taken by Russia" (p. 456).

2 Alexander Gerschenkron, "Russia: Patterns and Problems of Economic Development, 1861–1958," in Gerschenkron, *Economic Backwardness in Historical Perspective*, Harvard University Press, Cambridge, MA, 1962, pp. 119–51.

3 Russia had 7.8 million workers before the Bolsheviks took power; 5.2 million were employed in small workshops and artisan establishments. Despite the influx of substantial foreign capital Russia failed to keep pace with its European rivals' development from 1860 to 1913. See Alec Nove, *An Economic History of the USSR*, Pelican, Baltimore, 1972, pp. 14–17.

4 Alexander Chayanov, *The Theory of Peasant Economy*, Richard Irwin, Homewood, IL, 1996. Jerome Blum, *Lord and Peasant in Russia from the Ninth to the Nineteenth Century*, Atheneum, New York, 1969, pp. 504–35. Nove, *An Economic History of the USSR*: "The peasants did not achieve equality before the law . . . Their land was held by the village community . . . the *mir* or *obshchina*. The heads of families . . . controlled land utilization . . . they periodically redistributed strips within a three-field system familiar to students of medieval farming. The peasant was not allowed to leave his village without authority . . . and all the households . . . were jointly liable for taxes and for redemption dues" (p. 21).

5 Mikhail Tugan-Baranovsky, *The Russian Factory in the 19th Century*, Richard Irwin, Homewood, IL, 1970, p. 270. "All these (modern) mills work chiefly on state orders." According to Lyashchenko, 28.5 percent of Russian investment was owned by foreign nationals, concentrated in heavy industry. See Nove, *An Economic History of the USSR*, p. 18.

6 Robert Levy, *Mesocosim: Hinduism and Organization of a Traditional Newar City in Nepal*, University of California Press, Berkeley, CA, 1984. Levy stresses the metaphor of a ceremonial ballet.

7 Both in economics and diplomacy negotiated rules of conduct are often treated as instruments of influence rather than solemn obligations, declarations to the contrary notwithstanding.

8 Stefan Hedlund, *Russian Path Dependence*, London, 2005. Cf. Nove, *An Economic History of the USSR*, "by the late eighteenth century the gentry had the right to become merely parasitic landlords (though in fact many of them did continue to serve the state in various capacities), while the majority of the peasants were reduced to a state of slavery. The belief survived among them that 'they were the lord's but the land was God's.' They disputed the legitimacy of the ownership of the land by the lords, and considered that those who cultivated the land should have the full use of it."

9 Vladimir Ilyich Lenin, *State and Revolution*, International Publishers, 1917. *Modern History Sourcebook: Vladimir Ilyich Lenin: State and Revolution*, 1918, www.fordham.edu/halsall/mod/lenin-statere v.html., p. 8.

10 Nikholai Bukharin and Evgeny Preobrazhensky, *The ABC's of Communism*, Penguin Books, Baltimore, MD, 1969.

11 Robert V. Daniels, *The Conscience of the Revolution*, Harvard University Press, Cambridge, MA, 1965. Nove, *An Economic History of the USSR*, pp. 56–9. A decree on "workers' control" was issued on November 27, 1917. Factory committees, which already existed under the Provisional government, were given stronger powers. Railways were operated for the first few months by trade unions, but all this eventually gave way to the Bolshevik control. Nove, *An Economic History of the USSR*, pp. 50–1.

12 Inna Lamm, *Face of Square: Mysteries of Kazimer Malevich*, Pinakotheke, Moscow, 2004. John Milner, *Vladimir Tatlins and the Russian Avant-Garde*, Yale University Press, New Haven, 1983. Christina Lodder, *Russian Constructivism*, Yale University Press, New Haven, 1983.

13 Nove, *An Economic History of the USSR*, table, p. 68.

14 Steven Rosefielde, "Premature Deaths: Russia's Radical Economic Transition in Soviet Perspective," *Europe–Asia Studies*, 53, 8 (2001), table 4, p. 1164. The underlying source is E. Z. Volkov, *Dinamika naseleniya SSSR za vosem' desyat let* (Moscow, 1930). The reliability of Volkov's estimate is uncertain because of the poor quality of the data, and the usual problems with assumptions about trends in natality and mortality. However, there is broad agreement that Volkov's estimate is in the ballpark. See R. W. Davies, Mark Harrison, and S. G. Wheatcroft, *The Economic Transformation of the Soviet Union, 1913–1945*, Cambridge University Press, Cambridge, 1994, pp. 62–4.

15 Emma Goldman, *My Disillusionment in Russia*, Apollo, New York, 1970.

16 Dis-equilibrium is automatically resolved in market economies by managers adjusting production to maximize profits (Marshallian quantity adjustment mechanism), and by transactors negotiating price to maximize utility (Walrasian price adjustment mechanism).

4 NEP: 1921–1929

1 Alec Nove, *An Economic History of the USSR*, Pelican, London, 1972, pp. 59–63, 85.

2 Ibid. A small number of exceptions were made to this rule. Vladimir Putin is considering reintroducing leasing in the Russian oil sector. He is contemplating re-nationalizing the industry and contracting out its management. See "Putin in USA: Khodorkovsky in Exchange for America's Support," *Pravda*, September 24, 2003, reprinted in *Johnson's Russia List*, no. 7336, Article 4, September 24, 2003.

3 Nove, *An Economic History of the USSR*, p. 106.

4 Ibid., pp. 93–6. The "scissors" refers to the shape formed by plotting terms of trade with one good in the denominator, and then plotting the reciprocal. There is no analytic rationale for doing this, but the image of a scissors conveyed a menacing impression, which would be frequently invoked in subsequent discussions of worker–peasant economic relations.

5 Ibid., p. 98.

6 Oscar Lange, "On the Economic Theory of Socialism," in Benjamin Lippincott (ed.), *On The Economic Theory of Socialism*, McGraw-Hill, New York, 1964. Abram Bergson, "Socialist Economics," in H. Ellis (ed.), *A Survey of Contemporary Economics*, Richard D. Irwin, Homewood, IL, 1948, pp. 412–48. The Lange model, like NEP, features state ownership of the means of production, with industrial supply responsive to consumer market demand. It is designed to achieve "socialist" consumer sovereignty by assigning managers to produce to the point where marginal cost equals price, and manipulating income through lump sum taxes. The NEP model is very close in spirit, even though it substitutes leasing for direct state market supply. Both are vulnerable to moral hazard. See Steven Rosefielde, "Competitive Market Socialism Revisited: Impediments to Efficient Price-Fixing," *Comparative Economic Studies*, 27, 3 (1986), pp. 17–23.

7 See Nove, *An Economic History of the USSR*, pp. 93–6.

8 Ibid., p. 100.

9 Cf. Marshall Poe, *The Russian Moment in World History*, Princeton University Press, Princeton, NJ, 2003, who argues that the Muscovite way was as valid as democratic free enterprise. Gabriella Gershenson, "Moscow, on Its Terms," *San Francisco Chronicle*, September 21, 2003, reprinted in *Johnson's Russia List*, no. 7331, Article 6, September 21, 2003.

10 Alexander Erlich, *The Soviet Industrialization Debate, 1924–1928*, Harvard University Press, Cambridge, MA, 1960.

11 Nikolai Bukharin, "Novoe otkrovenie o sovetskoi ekonomike ili kak mozhno pogubit' raboche–krest'yanski blok" ("New Revelation of the Soviet Economy or How Can the Workers–Peasant Bloc be Destroyed, Bolshevik"), December 10, 1924; *Kvoprosu o trotskizme (On Trokskyism)*, Moscow–Leningrad, 1925; *Building Up Socialism*, London, 1926. Bukharin's advocacy of individual farming echoed Stolypin's pre-war initiatives.

12 Evgeny Preobarzhensky, *Novaya ekonomika* (*New Economy*), Moscow, 1926. Available in English, from Oxford University Press, London, 1965.

13 Lev M. Shanin, "Ekonomicheskaya priroda nashevo beztovariya," ("The Economic Essence of Our Commodity Shortage"), *Ekonomicheskoe obozrenie*, November 1925.

14 G. A. Feldman, "K teorii tempov narodnogo dokhoda," ("On the Theory of the Rate of Growth of the National Income"), *Planovoe khoziaistvo*, November and December, 1928. Evsei Domar, *Essays in the Theory of Economic Growth*, New York, 1957.

15 James Millar argues that this strategy failed. More resources had to be transferred to agriculture to support collectivization, than flowed back to industry. See Millar, "Soviet Agricultural Development and the Agricultural Surplus Hypothesis," *Soviet Studies*, 22, 1 (1970), pp. 77–93; "Mass Collectivization and the Contribution of Soviet Agriculture to the First Five-Year Plan: A Review Article," *Slavic Review*, 33, 4 (1974), pp. 750–66. James Millar and Alec Nove, "A Debate on Collectivization: Was Stalin Really Necessary?" *Problems of Communism*, 25, 4 (1976), pp. 56–7. Michael Ellman, "Did the Agricultural Surplus Provide the Resources for the Increase in Investment During the First Five Year Plan?" *Economic Journal*, 85, 340 (1975), pp. 844–63.

16 Erlich, *The Soviet Industrialization Debate*, pp. 189–92, provides the following chronology:
1923: Twelfth Communist Party Congress: Trotsky warns on the lag of industry behind agriculture and calls for an extension in the scope of planning as well as for drastic austerity measures; Bukharin denounces concepts of industrialization promoted at the expense of the peasantry.
1924: Thirteenth Communist Party Congress: leftist opposition led by Preobrazhensky and Pyatakov attacks the policy of lowering industrial prices and calls for accelerated industrialization; adopted resolution denounces Trotskyism as a "petty bourgeois deviation."
1925: Fourteenth Communist Party Congress: industrialization oriented toward economic independence proclaimed as the major task; Stalin repudiates Bukharin's "get rich" formula, and defends moderate agricultural policies against the "Leningrad opposition" led by his former associates, Kamenev and Zinov'ev.
1926: Fifteenth Communist Party Congress: Stalin and Bukharin in all-out attack against the "oppositionist bloc" headed by Trotsky, Kamenev, and Zinov'ev; policies of the opposition denounced as "social-democratic deviationism" and as a grave threat to the worker–peasant alliance.
1927: Grain collections drop to less than half of their level of the last two months of 1926; industrial "goods famine" reappears. Fifteenth Communist Party Congress: the whole leadership of the left-wing opposition expelled from the party; general directives for the future Five Year Plan emphasize the need for speed as well as for balance, and urge greater support for collective farming.
1928: Plenary session of the Central Committee: "rightist deviation," denounced as chief danger.
1929: Trotsky deported: Joint plenary session of the Central Committee and of the Central Control Commission. Stalin openly breaks with Bukharin and Rykov and identifies them and Tomsky as leaders of the "rightist deviation"; Bukharin removed as head of the Communist International and as editor of *Pravda*, Tomsky as head of the trade unions. All-out collectivization begins in the fall.

17 Nove, *An Economic History of the USSR*, quotes E. H. Carr as follows: "It was no longer true that class analysis determined policy. Policy determined what form of class analysis was appropriate to the given evident" (p. 107).

18 Alec Nove, *Economic Rationality and Soviet Politics, or Was Stalin Really Necessary*? Praeger, New York, 1964. As always Soviet data can be contradictory and confusing. The data reported in table 4.1 compare 1928 with 1917 rather than 1913. Robert Davies has argued that production in 1916 was higher than 1913, but growth comparisons with 1917 as the base are much faster than those for 1913. See *Narodnoe khoziaistvo SSSR za 70 let*, Finansy i

statistiki, Moscow, 1987, p. 32. Also, see R. W. Davies, "Changing Economic Systems: An Overview," in R. W. Davies, Mark Harrison, and Stephen Wheatcroft (eds.), *The Economic Transformation of the Soviet Union, 1913–1945*, Cambridge University Press, Cambridge, 1994, p. 9, and Davies, "Industry," in Davies, et al., *The Economic Transformation of the Soviet Union*, pp. 135–6. Based on this benchmark, Davies reports that industry recovered from a mere 20 percent of the 1913 level in 1920 to above 4 percent in 1926–7. The 1917 benchmark is 80 percent higher. Paul Gregory examines estimates around the 1928 benchmark, and settles on a range between 0.93 and 1.07 for the comparison 1913–28, using western national income accounting conventions. See Paul Gregory, "National Income," in R. W. Davies, *From Tsarism to the New Economic Policy: Continuity and Change in the Economy of the USSR*, Macmillan, London, 1990, pp. 237–48, tables 62–5, pp. 332–7. Davies et al. favor 1.11, implying a complete recovery in per capita income. He observes that the acceleration in 1924–5, variously put at 52 or 61 percent for large-scale industry, was entirely unexpected, according to V. S. Groman, a prominent non-party official in Gosplan, "there was not a single mind in the USSR which would have foreseen this." And the rate of growth 1925–6, variously put at 34 to 29 percent for all industry, also exceeded expectations. He fails to discuss performance for the full subperiod 1925–9.

19 Nove, *An Economic History of the U.S.S.R.*, pp. 110–13. Moshe Lewin, *Russian Peasants and Soviet Power*, Northwestern University Press, Evanston, IL, 1968, p. 174.

20 Nove, *An Economic History of the U.S.S.R.*, p. 115. Cf. *Narodnoe khoziaistvo SSSR za 70 Let*, Finansy i statistiki, Moscow, 1987, p. 11.

5 Command Communism: 1929–1953

1 Abram Bergson, *The Economics of Soviet Planning*, Yale University Press, New Haven, CT, 1964, pp. 133–44. Alec Nove, *The Soviet Economic System*, George Allen and Unwin, London, 1977.

2 *Narodnoe khoziaistvo SSSR za 70 Let*, Finansy i statistiki, Moscow, 1987, p. 115.

3 American forces captured plan documents confiscated by the Nazis from Smolensk during World War II. The size of the *tekhpromfinplans* are inferred here from approved final plans.

4 A candy firm might report jelly beans as one of its composite goods, but not varieties and different sizes.

5 This interpretation is based on the author's discussion with Vladimir Bezrukov, Director of the Main Computing Center, Gosplan, 1976. Vladimir Popov and Nikolai Shmelev, *The Turning Point: Revitalizing the Soviet Economy*, Doubleday, New York, 1989. See the reference to M. Yun in *Turning Point*. Gosplan was responsible for 2,000 material balances; Gossnab for 15,000. Industrial branch ministries compiled 60,000 material balances, paired with 50,000 contracts that were then disaggregated by a factor ranging from 10 to 15. Personal communication with Vladimir Popov, June 2004.

6 Eugene Zaleski, *Stalinist Planning for Economic Growth, 1933–1952*, University of North Carolina Press, Chapel Hill, 1980, table 27, p. 157. Michael Ellman, *Soviet Planning Today*, Cambridge University Press, Cambridge, 1971; see appendix 1, "Aggregation as a Cause of Inconsistent Plans," pp. 95–100. Pro-forma compliance however didn't signify that Stalin's aspirations were technically feasible. He had no knowledge of enterprise production functions, input supply, and output distribution possibilities. The more ambitious his aspirations, and the greater the aggregate structural adjustments demanded, the lower the probability that Gosplan's paper re-balancing and subsequent assignment setting by ministries and *glavks* would permit red directors to muddle through. Even in the best case, where Gosplan merely accepted thirty thousand-odd *tekhpromfinplans* as submitted, prospects for reconciling inconsistencies and compiling feasible enterprise micro-programs were slight, and diminished rapidly with political intervention.

7 Contracts were enforced by state arbitration courts (gosabitrazh). See Eugenia Belova, "Legal Contract Enforcement in the Soviet Economy," *Comparative Economic Studies*, 47, 2 (2005), pp. 387–401. Heidi Kroll, "Decentralization and the Pre-contract Dispute in the Soviet Industry," *Soviet Economy*, 2 (1986), pp. 51–71.

8 Steven Rosefielde, *The Transformation of the 1966 Soviet Input–Output Table from Producers to Adjusted Factor Cost Values*, G. E. Tempo, Washington, 1975; *The Complete Soviet Producers' Price Soviet Input–Output Table for 1966*," Duke–UNC Occasional Papers on Soviet Input–Output Analysis, Durham-Chapel Hill, June 1974; *Soviet International Trade in Heckscher–Ohlin Perspective*, Heath Lexington, Lexington, MA, 1973. Wassily Leontief, "Quantitative Input–Output Relations in the Economic System of the United States," *Review of Economic Statistics*, 18, 3 (1936); *The Structure of the American Economy*, Oxford University Press, Oxford, 1941; *Input–Output Economics*, Oxford University Press, New York, 1966. Vladimir Treml, Dimitri Gallik, Barry Kostinsky, and Kurt Kruger, *The Structure of the Soviet Economy: Analyses and Reconstruction of the 1966 Input–Output Table*, Praeger, New York 1972. Vladimir Treml (ed.), *Studies in Soviet Input–Output Economics*, Praeger, New York, 1977.

9 Paul Samuelson, "Abstract of a Theorem Concerning Substitutability in Open Leontief Models," in T. C. Koopmans (ed.), *Activity Analysis of Production and Allocation*, Wiley, New York, 1951.

10 Robert Dorfman, Paul Samuelson, and Robert Solow, *Linear Programming and Economic Analysis*, McGraw-Hill, New York, 1958. L. V. Kantorovich, *The Best Use of Economic Resources*, Harvard University Press, Cambridge, MA, 1965.

11 Janos Kornai, *Mathematical Planning of Structural Decisions*, Amsterdam: North-Holland Publishing Company, 1967. Michael Ellman, *Soviet Planning Today, Proposals for an Optimally Functioning Economic System*, Cambridge University Press, Cambridge, 1971. John Hardt et al., *Mathematics and Computers in Soviet Economic Planning*, Yale University Press, New Haven, CT, 1967. Martin Cave, *Computers and Economic Planning: The Soviet Experience*, Cambridge University Press, Cambridge, 1980. Martin Cave and Paul Hare, *Alternative Approaches to Economic Planning*, St. Martin's Press, New York, 1981. Michael Ellman, *Socialist Planning*, Cambridge University Press, Cambridge, 1979. David Dyker, *The Process of Investment in the Soviet Union*, Cambridge University Press, Cambridge, 1981.

12 H. Kuhn and A. Tucker, "Nonlinear Programming," in J. Neyman (ed.), *Proceedings of the Second Berkeley Symposium on Mathematical Statistics and Probability*, University of California Press, Berkeley and Los Angeles, CA, 1951, pp. 481–92.

13 Steven Rosefielde, "Klepto-Banking: Systemic Sources of Russia's Failed Industrial Recovery," in Howard Stein, Olu Ajakaiye, and Peter Lewis (eds.), *Deregulation and the Banking Crisis in Nigeria: A Comparative Study*, Palgrave, Houndmill, Basingstoke, 2002, pp. 193–210. George Garvey, *Money, Financial Plans and Credit in the Soviet Union*, Ballinger, Lexington, MA, 1977.

14 Stephen Kotkin, "A Conspiring So Immense," *New Republic*, February 13, 2006, pre-printed in *Johnson's Russia List*, no. 36, Article 29, February 7, 2006.

15 Eugenia Belova and Paul Gregory, "Dictator, Loyal, and Opportunist Agents: The Soviet Archives on Creating the Soviet Economic System," *The Public Choice*, 113 (2002), pp. 265–86.

16 Jan Winiecki, *The Distorted World of Soviet-Type Economies*, University of Pittsburgh Press, Pittsburgh, 1988.

17 Paul Gregory (ed.), *Behind the Facade of Stalin's Command Economy*, Princeton University Press, Princeton, NJ, 2002. Gregory, *The Political Economy of Stalinism*, Cambridge University Press, New York, 2003.

18 Cf. Paul Krugman, "The Myth of Asia's Miracle," *Foreign Affairs*, 73, 6 (1994), pp. 62–78. Welfare enhancing growth requires that technological progress improve utility, not just output nobody wants.

19 Nove, *An Economic History of the USSR*. Bergson, *The Economics of Soviet Planning*.

20 Paul Gregory, *The Political Economy of Stalinism: Evidence From the Soviet Secret Archives*, Cambridge University Press, London, 2003; "Bergson's Basic Hypothesis and the Soviet Archives: Insights from the Political Economy of Socialism," *Comparative Economic Studies*, 2 (2005), pp. 402–17. Andrei Markevich and Paul Gregory, "Soviet Planning Archives: The Files That Bergson Could Not See," *Comparative Economic Studies*, 47, 2 (2005), pp. 364–86.

21 Steven Rosefielde, "Tea Leaves and Productivity," *Comparative Economic Studies*, 47, 2 (2005), pp. 259–73.

22 From Stalin's standpoint land wasn't expropriated because it was claimed by the Soviet state. Land was merely transferred to alternative users.

23 Alexander Solzhenitsyn, *Gulag Archipelago*, 3 vols.,YMCA, Paris, 1973–5.

24 Warren Eason, "Labor Force," in Abram Bergson and Simon Kuznets, *Economic Trends in the Soviet Union*, Harvard University Press, Cambridge, MA, 1963.

25 *Kolkhozniki* were organized into groups called brigades which were collectively responsible for meeting quotas. This was a variant on the Czarist practice in the *obshchina*.

26 See ch. 6.

27 W. S. Churchill, *The Second World War, Vol. IV: The Hinge of Fate*, London, 1951, pp. 447–8.

28 Moshe Lewin, *Russian Peasants and Soviet Power*, Northwestern University Press, Evanston, IL, 1968, p. 174.

29 Joseph Stalin, "Dizzy With Success," *Pravda*, no. 60, March 2, 1930.

30 Stalin could have built an adequate defense against Hitler with the NEP economic mechanism.

6 Terror, Homicides, and Forced Labour: 1929–1953

1 Steven Rosefielde, "Stalinism in Post-Communist Perspective: New Evidence on Killings, Forced Labour and Economic Growth in the 1930s," *Europe–Asia Studies*, 48, 8 (1996), table 4, pp. 959–87. Robert Conquest, "Communications to the Editor," *American Historical Review*, June (1994), p. 1039. Anne Applebaum, *GULAG: A History*, Doubleday, New York, 2003. Galina Ivanova, *Labor Camp Socialism: The Gulag in the Soviet Totalitarian System*, M. E. Sharpe, Armonk, NY, 2000. Stephane Coutois, Nicolas Worth, et al., *Black Book of Communism*, Harvard University Press, Cambridge, MA, 1999.

2 Winston Churchill reported that Stalin told him that as many as 10 million peasants were dealt with during 1929–33, and that the "great bulk were very unpopular and were wiped out by the labourers," Churchill, *The Second World War, Volume IV: The Hinge of Fate*, pp. 447–8. Jerry Hough reports a figure half as large based on outdated calculations by Frank Lorimer; see Jerry Hough and Merle Fainsod, *How the Soviet Union is Governed*, Harvard University Press, Cambridge, MA, 1979, p. 152.

3 Rosefielde, "Stalinism in Post-Communist Perspective," p. 969. The NKVD data are seriously internally inconsistent. Cf., Walter Laqueur, *The Dream that Failed. Reflections on the Soviet Union*, Oxford University Press, 1994, New York, 1994.

4 Steven Rosefielde, "Documented Homicides and Excess Deaths: New Insights into the Scale of Killing in the USSR During the 1930s," *Communist and Post-Communist Studies*, 30, 3 (1997), pp. 321–31.

5 Steven Rosefielde, "Premature Deaths: Russia's Radical Economic Transition in Soviet Perspective," *Europe–Asia Studies*, 53, 8 (2001), table 4, p. 1164. Population deficit estimates often exceed excess death statistics because families tend to desire fewer children as nations modernize. The gap between predicted and observed populations in these instances does not imply foul play, only changing parental tastes. Premature deaths are computed differently. Instead of projecting natality, actual births are tallied from annual registries. The predicted population therefore is determined by mortality trends alone, for all cohorts

including those born after the subperiod began, and shortfalls mean that more people died than actuarially expected. This isn't a matter of parental taste. The problem is one of missing persons.

6 Nikita Khrushchev, *Crimes of the Stalin Era, Special Report to the 20th Congress of the Communist Party of the Soviet Union*, annotated by Boris Nicolaevsky, New Leader, New York, 1956.

7 Robert Davies, "Closing the Bergson Gap: New Data on a Problem in Soviet Statistics," *Comparative Economic Studies*, 47, 2 (2005), pp. 274–88. The census count is compatible with a top secret memo prepared by Sautin for Voznesenskii (Deputy Head of Gosplan) August 6, 1940.

8 Rosefielde, "Stalinism in Post-Communist Perspective," table A1, p. 986.

9 Robert Conquest, *The Great Terror: Stalin's Purge of the Thirties*, Macmillan, New York, 1980; *The Great Terror: A Reassessment*, Oxford University Press, London, 1990.

10 Rosefielde, "Stalinism in Post-Communist Perspective," table 3, pp. 969–70. Anton-Ovseenko, *The Time of Stalin: Portrait of a Tyranny*, Harper and Row, New York, 1980.

11 Robert Conquest, *Stalin and the Kirov Murder*, Oxford University Press, London, 1989.

12 Robert Tucker and Stephen Cohen (eds.), *The Great Purge Trial*, Grosset and Dunlap, New York, 1965.

13 Alec Nove, *Stalinism and After*, George Allen and Unwin, London, 1975. Alexander Uralov (Abdurakhman Avtorkhanov), *The Reign of Stalin*, Bodley Head, London, 1953. David Dallin, *From Purge to Coexistence: Essays on Stalin's and Khrushchev's Russia*, Regnery, Chicago, 1964. Alexander Orlov, *The Secret History of Stalin's Crimes*, Random House, New York, 1953. Leonard Schapiro, *The Communist Party of the Soviet Union*, New York, Random House, 1959; "The Great Purge," in B. H. Liddell Hart (ed.), *The Soviet Army*, Weidenfeld and Nicolson, London, 1956, pp. 65–72. *The Case of the Anti-Soviet Trotskyite Centre*, Report of Court Proceedings Heard before the Military Collegium of the Supreme Court of the U.S.S.R., Moscow January 23–30, 1937, People's Commissariat of Justice of the U.S.S.R., Moscow, 1937. *The Case of the Trotskyite–Zinovivite Terrorist Centre*, Report of Court Proceedings Heard before the Military Collegium of the Supreme Court of the U.S.S.R., August 24, 1936, People's Commissariat of Justice of the U.S.S.R., Moscow 1936. Donald Rayfield, *Stalin and His Hangmen: An Authoritative Portrait of a Tyrant and Those Who Served Him*, Viking, New York, 2004. Also see the story of L. D. Yaroshenko, a Gosplan economic specialist who was sent to Gulag for criticizing a draft textbook, and then refusing to recant after Stalin noted his "error," N. S. Khrushchev, *Vospominannia*, Vremia, pp. 106–9, 112–14, recounted in Stephen Shenfield, *Johnson's Russia List*, no. 8127, March 19, 2004. For an assessment of Putin's security services, see Simon Montefiore, "Democratic Despot," *New York Times*, (Op-Ed), March 14, 2004.

14 Solzhenitsyn, *Gulag Archipelago*. Nadezhda Mandelstam, *Hope Abandoned*, Random House, New York, 1974. Roy Medvedev, *Let History Judge*, Alfred Knopf, New York, 1972. Lev Kopelev, *To Be Preserved Forever*, J. B. Lippincott, Philadelphia, 1977. Victor Herman, *Coming Out of the Ice*, Harcourt Brace Jovanovich, New York, 1979. Evgeniia Ginzburg, *Into the Whirlwind*, Harcourt Brace and World, New York, 1967.

15 Steven Rosefielde, "The First 'Great Leap Forward' Reconsidered: Lessons of Solzhenitsyn's Gulag Archipelago," *Slavic Review*, 39, 4 (1980), pp. 559–87.

16 Avraam Shifman, *Chetvertoe izmerenie*, Posev, Frankfurt/Main, 1973. Robert Conquest, *Reflections on a Ravaged Century*, Norton, New York, 1999. D. D. Guttemplan, "The Holocaust on Trial," *Atlantic Monthly*, 285, 2 (2000), pp. 45–66. Cf. Moshe Lewin, *The Soviet Century*, Verso, London, 2005.

17 Anne Applebaum, *Gulag: A History*, Doubleday, New York, 2003. Edwin Bacon, *The Gulag at War*, Macmillan, Birmingham, 1994. Paul Gregory and Valery Lazarev (eds.), *The Economics of Forced Labor: The Soviet Gulag*, Hoover Institution Press, Stanford, 2003. O. Khlevnyuk, "Why Did the Terror Take Place? The Objectives of the 'Great Terror',"

in Christopher Read (ed.), *The Stalin Years*, Palgrave, New York, 2003. Barry McLoughlin and Kevin McDermott (eds.), *Stalin's Terror*, Palgrave, New York, 2003. E. A. Rees, *The Nature of Stalin's Dictatorship*, Palgrave, New York, 2003. Simon Ertz and Leonid Borodkin, "The Labor Economics of the Soviet Gulag: Forced Labor and the Search for Incentives," *Comparative Economic Studies*, 47, 2 (2005), pp. 418–36.

18 Conquest, *Reflections on a Ravaged Century*. D. D. Guttemplan, "The Holocaust on Trial," *Atlantic Monthly*, 285, 2 (2000), pp. 45–66.

19 Abdurakhman Avtorkhanov, *Zagadka Smerti Stalina*, Posev, Frankfurt/Main, Germany 1976.

20 On Stalin's megalomania see Albert Weeks, *Stalin's Other War: Soviet Grand Strategy 1939–1941*, Rowman and Littlefield, Lanham, MD, 2003.

7 Economic Performance: 1917–1953

1 "The measurement of national income, it has been said, is an art rather than a science. If this is so (and few practitioners would disagree), for Russian national income it may be felt the art must even assume an occult character. Is it really worth while to attempt such measurements in this case? . . . Great as the difficulties are, they do not appear to be overwhelming. With sufficient care and industry, it should be possible to limit the range of conjecture, and even uncertain knowledge may be highly valuable on a vital theme." Abram Bergson, *The Real National Income of Soviet Russia Since 1928*, Harvard University Press, Cambridge, MA, 1961. Cf., Steven Rosefielde, "Tea Leaves and Productivity."

2 (CIA), *Measures of Soviet Gross National Product in 1982*, Joint Economic Committee of Congress, Washington, DC, November 1990, p. 2. Research on Soviet GNP was pioneered by Abram Bergson in the 1940s and developed by him and his colleagues under the sponsorship of the RAND Corporation during the 1950s and 1960s. Bergson's initial work involved estimating GNP in current established prices and adjusting those estimates in an effort to correct some of the distortions of the Soviet pricing system. His adjusted factor cost values were intended to reflect the costs of labor and capital resources used in the economy – the factors of production – better than established prices could. Subsequently, RAND scholars estimated price indexes that were used to derive measures of GNP growth in constant prices. Bergson also has used these building-block studies of GNP as a basis for comparing levels of economic activity in the USSR and other countries and for analyzing Soviet productivity. After the RAND Corporation's research on Soviet GNP concluded in the late 1960s, the CIA – where classified work on the subject began in the early 1950s – became the principal source of western estimates. Recent CIA efforts have concentrated largely on constant price measures of Soviet economic growth, although Soviet GNP in current prices also is estimated for selected years. Because of changes in the availability of data, our present approach to estimating growth differs from that used by Bergson and his associates in two major ways. First, we primarily use data on changes in quantities of output weighted by base-year values, rather than data on changes in current values of output deflated by price indexes. Second, our estimates of the growth of total GNP are determined as a weighted average of growth rates estimated for industry and other sectors in which GNP is produced. In contrast, in the Bergson–RAND approach, total GNP growth was a weighted average of estimates of the growth of purchases for consumption and other uses of GNP. The RAND studies are summarized by Bergson in *The Real National Income of Soviet Russia Since 1928*, Harvard University Press, Cambridge, MA, 1961, pp. vii–ix, and by Abraham Becker in *Soviet National Income, 1958–64*, University of California Press, Berkeley and Los Angeles, 1969. *USSR: Measures of Economic Growth and Development* (pp. 11–12, 26) also discusses estimates of Soviet GNP by RAND Corporation and other researchers outside the CIA.

3 Simon Kuznets asserts that the driving force was increased female labor participation rates, basing his conclusion on Warren Eason, but misreading him. The female labor force grew only 2.5 percent 1926–39, and the female participation rate dropped precipitously because

of a shift in the demographic structure. See Warren Eason, "Labor Force," in Abram Bergson and Simon Kuznets (eds.), *Economic Trends in the Soviet Union*, Harvard University Press, Cambridge, MA, 1963, table II.3. Cf. Simon Kuznets, "A Comparative Appraisal," in Bergson and Kuznets, *Economic Trends in the Soviet Union*, p. 341. Professor Eason's estimates indicate that the rise was due largely to the increasing engagement of women (and perhaps also of some men in agriculture) in full-time occupation.

Part III Soviet Communism: Hope and Disenchantment

1 Leonida Krushelnycky, "The Mystery of Stalin's Death," BBC News, February 24, 2003. According to the Russian Historian Edvard Radzinsky, "All the people who surrounded Stalin understood that Stalin wanted war – the future World War III – and he decided to prepare the country for this war."
2 Ilya Ehrenburg, *The Thaw*, 1954. Socialism with a human face was the political program of the Czech Communist Party chairman Alexander Dubceck. Promulagated in 1968, the program called for greater freedom of the press and culture.
3 Peaceful coexistence was a concept promoted in early 1953 immediately after Stalin's death, proclaiming that communist and capitalist states could non-belligerently coexist during the cold war.
4 Nikita Khrushchev (First Secretary of the Communist Party), *Crimes of the Stalin Era: Special Report to the 20th Congress of the Communist Party of the Soviet Union* (closed session), February 24–5, 1956, published by the *New Leader*, 1962, www.trussel.com/hf/stalin/htm.
5 CIA, *Economic Impact of Soviet Military Spending*, (CIA), ER-IR-75-3, April 1974, pp. 6, 12. Steven Rosefielde, *False Science, Underestimating the Soviet Arms Buildup*, Transactions, Brunswick, New Jersey, 1987.
6 Rosefielde, *False Science*.
7 Team B was an expert panel established by the Director of Central Intelligence, George H. W. Bush, chaired in its third version by Richard Pipes. The panel included Paul Nitze, Albert Wohlstetter, Paul Wolfowitz, I. Lewis Libby, William Casey, John Connally, John Foster, Clare Booth Luce, Edward Teller, and Zbigniew Brzezinski.
8 George Hansen, *Correlation of Forces: For Decades of Soviet Military Development*, Praeger, New York, 1987.

8 Reform Communism: 1953–1991

1 George F. Kennan, in his Mr. X containment article argued for the long-term superiority of the "idea of the west," "The Sources of Soviet Conduct," *Foreign Affairs*, 29, 3 (1951), pp. 351–70.
2 On the grand utility possibility frontier, see Jan van de Graaf, *Theoretical Welfare Economics*. A single cyborg could be programmed to play all roles.
3 Richard Judy, "Information, Control, and Soviet Economic Management," in John Hardt et al. (eds.), *Mathematics and Computers in Soviet Economic Planning*, Yale University Press, New Haven, 1967, pp. 1–67. The main thrust was toward the creation of a state system of computer centers. Late in 1963, a special commission of the Chief Administration on Introduction of Computer Technology into the National Economy of the State Committee on Coordinating Scientific Research Work of the USSR reported that the purpose would be to perform computations related to formulating optimal national economic plans, re-computations of state prices, operational control, banking finance and statistics (p. 36).
4 G. Popov, *Elektronnye mashiny i upravlenie ekonomikoi*, Moscow, 1963, p. 142.
5 V. F. Pugachev, "Voprosy optimalnovo planirovaniia narodnovo khoziaistvo s pomoshchiu edinoi gosudarstvennoi seti vychislitelnykh isentrov," *Voprosy ekonomiki*, 7 (1964), p. 103.

6 Nikolay Fedorenko, *Optimal Functioning System for a Socialist Economy*, Progress, Moscow, 1974. Martin Weitzman, "Iterative Multi-Level Planning with Production Targets," *Econometrica* (1970), pp. 50–65.

7 Alan Abouchar (ed.), *The Socialist Price Mechanism*, Duke University Press, Durham, NC, 1977.

8 Martin Weitzman, "The New Soviet Incentive Model," *Bell Journal of Economics*, 7, (1976), pp. 251–7. Evsei Liberman, *Ekonomicheskie methody povysheniya effektivnosti proizvodstva*, 1970 (*Economic Methods and the Effectiveness of Production*), New York, 1972. Evsey Domar, "On the Optimal Compensation of a Socialist Manager," *Quarterly Journal of Economics*, 88, 1 (1974), pp. 1–18. David Granick, "The Ministry as a Maximizing Unit in Soviet Industry," *Journal of Comparative Economics*, 4, 3 (1980), pp. 255–73. Bengt Holmstrom, "Design of Incentive Schemes and the New Soviet Incentive Model," *European Economic Review*, 17, 2 (1982), pp. 128–48. N. Ireland, and Peter Law, "Incentive and Efficiency in the Kosygin Reforms," *Journal of Comparative Economics*, 4, 1 (1980), pp. 33–9. Michael Keren, I. Miller, and J. Thornton, "The Rachet Effect: A Dynamic Managerial Incentive Model of the Soviet Enterprise, *Journal of Comparative Economics*, 7, 4 (1983), pp. 347–67. Heidi Kroll, "Decentralization and Precontract Dispute in Soviet Industry," *Soviet Economy*, 2, January–March (1986), pp. 51–71. M. Loeb and W. Magat, "Success Indicators in the Soviet Union: The Problem of Incentives and Efficient Allocations, *American Economic Review*, 68, 1 (1978), pp. 173–181. V. Danilin, K. Lovell, I. Materov, and S. Rosefielde, "Measuring and Improving Enterprise Efficiency in the Soviet Union," *Economica*, 52, 206 (1984), pp. 225–34. John Bonin, "On the Design of Managerial Incentive Structures in a Decentralized Planning Environment," *American Economic Review*, 66, 4 (1976), pp. 682–7. John Bonin and Wataru Fukuda, "Controlling a Risk-averse, Effort-selecting Manager in the Soviet Incentive Model," *Journal of Comparative Economics*, 11, 2 (1987), pp. 221–34. David Conn, "A Comparison of Alternative Incentive Structures for Centrally Planned Economic Systems," *Journal of Comparative Economics*, 3, 3 (1979), pp. 235–53. David Conn, "Effort, Efficiency and Incentives in Economic Organizations," *Journal of Comparative Economics*, 6, 3 (1982), pp. 223–34.

9 A. Kosgyin, "Ob uluchshenii upravleniia promyshlennostiu sovershenstvovanii planirovania i usileniia ekonomicheskovo stimulirovanii promyshlennovo proizvodstva" ("On Improving Industrial Management, Perfecting Planning, and Increasing Economic Incentives for Industrial Production"), *Pravda*, September 28, 1965. There were many other aspects of the Kosygin Reform. For a detailed discussion see Eugene Zaleski, *Planning Reforms in the Soviet Union, 1962–1966*, University of North Carolina Press, Chapel Hill, 1967, pp. 141–83.

10 Liberman, *Economic Methods*, ch. 2, "Concerning the Operation of the Law of Value," pp. 43–63.

11 Martin Weitzman famously argued in the 1960s that optimization with prices and quantities gave the same result. This was a restatement of the well known systems "duality" principle claiming the equivalence of optimal plans and markets. But in retrospect, the concept should be restated as an impossibility theorem; that Soviet practice precluded the achievement of optimality by any means. See Martin Weitzman, "Prices versus Quantities," *Review of Economic Studies*, 41 (1974), pp. 477–91. Cf. Mark Harrison, "Command and Collapse: The Fundamental Problem of Command in a Partially Centralized Economy," *Comparative Economic Studies*, 47, 2 (2005), pp. 296–314.

12 Joseph Berliner, *The Innovation Decision in Soviet Industry*, MIT Press, Cambridge, 1976, pp. 400–27.

13 Judy, "Information, Control and Soviet Management," p. 6.

14 S. A. Kuznetsov, V. L. Makarov, and V. D. Marshak, *Informatsionnaia Baza, Perspektivnovo Planirovaniia v OASU*, Ekonomika, Moscow, 1982. K. A. Bagrinovsky and

V. S. Prokopova, *Imitatsionnye Sistemy Priniatia Ekonomicheskikh Reshennii*, Nauka, Moscow, 1989. A. Iu. Sheviakov and A. Ia. Kiruta, *Modelirovanie Sbalansirovannosti i Soglasovaniia Planovykh Reshenii v Sfere Narodnovo Blagosostoianiia*, Nauka, 1986. A. Modin, N. V. Makhrov, and V. I. Danilin, *Dinamika Proizvodstvennykh Ob"edinii i Modeli Planirovaniia Ikh Deiatel'nosti*, Nauka, 1984.

15 Abram Bergson, *The Economics of Soviet Planning*, Yale University Press, New Haven, 1964. Gertrude Schroeder, "The Soviet Economy on a Treadmill of 'Reforms'," in *Soviet Economy in a Time of Change*, Joint Economic Committee of Congress, Washington, DC, October 10, 1979, pp. 312–66. Joseph Berliner, "Planning and Management," in Abram Bergson and Herbert Levine (eds.), *The Soviet Economy: Toward the Year 2000*, George Allen and Unwin, London, 1983, pp. 350–90. Gertrude Schroeder, "Soviet Economic 'Reform' Decrees: More Steps on the Treadmill," *Soviet Economy in the 1980s: Problems and Prospects*, vol. 1, Joint Economic Committee of Congress, Washington, DC, 1982, pp. 79–84; "Organizations and Hierarchies: The Perennial Search for Solution," *Comparative Economic Studies*, winter (1987), pp. 7–28; "Post-Soviet Economic Reforms in Perspective," in *The Former Soviet Union in Transition*, vol. 1, Joint Economic Committee of the United States, February 1993, pp. 57–80. The treadmill of reform inspired a great deal of black humor. For example Sergei Roy recalls that "True, there were quirky bureaucratic twists to Khrushchev's resurrection of the *sovnarkhozy*, like their division into urban and rural ones. The resulting confusion was not inconsiderable . . . A woman kills her husband, but as the couple isn't local, the police chief is at a loss who to report the case to, the urban or rural public prosecutor. Then he has a bright idea: 'What did she use to slit his throat, a sickle? Sure that's in the rural department. If she had bashed his head in with a hammer, it would've been urban.' " Or the following yarn is symptomatic: "Walking in winter through vast fields of unharvested, snow-covered maize . . . I caught another tractor driver in the act of emptying sacks of fertilizer into a stream: He didn't like the smell, so he opted for the easy way, killing any life in the stream. During harvest time, all dirt tracks and roads leading to the elevators were covered thick with grain pouring out of the holes in the trucks, providing ample food for butter-fat doves and turtle doves." "Planned production targets, that were not achieved in real life, could always be achieved on paper: *Pripiski* 'falsified reports' became practically universal and automatic." See Sergei Roy, "Brezhnev Era Economy," in *Moscow News*, February 11–17, 2004.

16 *Nauchno-Tekhnicheskii Progress v SSSR, Statisticheskii Sbornik*, Goskomstat SSSR, Moscow, 1990, p. 14.

17 *Nauchno-Tekhnicheskii*, p. 17.

18 *Nauchno-Tekhnicheskii*, p. 18.

19 *Nauchno-Tekhnicheskii*, p. 8.

20 Robert C. Allen, *Farm to Factory: A Reinterpretation of the Soviet Industrial Revolution*, Princeton University Press, Princeton, NJ, 2003; "A Reassessment of the Soviet Industrial Revolution," *Comparative Economic Studies*, 47, 2 (2005), pp. 315–32. Allen claims that Soviet industrialization was more successful than Japan's by ignoring the competitive test, and accepting official statistics.

21 Paul Krugman, "Myth of Asia's Miracle," *Foreign Affairs*, 73, 6 (1994), pp. 62–79.

22 Elizabeth Brainard, "Reassessing the Standard of Living in the Soviet Union: An Analysis Using Archival and Anthropometric Data," *Comparative Economic Studies*, 47, 2 (2005), pp. 333–45. Irwin Collier, "The 'Welfare Standard' and Soviet Consumers," *Comparative Economic Studies*, 47, 2 (2005), pp. 333–45.

23 Steven Rosefielde, *Soviet International Trade in Heckscher–Ohlin Perspective*, Heath Lexington, Lexington, MA, 1973.

24 Oscar Lange and Fred M. Taylor, *On the Economic Theory of Socialism*, University of Michigan Press, 1938. Abram Bergson, "Socialist Economics," in H. Ellis (ed.), *A Survey of Contemporary Economics*, Richard D. Irwin, Homewood, IL, 1948, pp. 412–48.

25 Cf. Eugenia Belova, "Legal Contract Enforcement in the Soviet Economy," *Comparative Economic Studies*, 47, 2 (2005), pp. 387–401.

26 Gertrude Schroeder captures the prevailing sentiment. She reduces Gorbachev's reforms to a few fundamentals. First, Gorbachev started a discussion about property ownership and expanded the private sector, especially through the use of cooperatives. Second, he began dismantling the monopoly on foreign trade. Third, he initiated the "Presidential Plan" adopted by the federal legislature on October 19, 1990, which adhered to the "Abalkin Blueprint" (fall of 1989), and Shatalin's "500 day" program for free enterprise, featuring privatization of state property, and price decontrol. "Unlike its predecessors, this official document outlined measures appropriate to that goal. Under its general authority, the government in early 1991 sharply increased both wholesale and retail prices, but also freed some 40 to 45 percent of them to be determined through contractual negotiations." It also contemplated radical changes in property ownership, land, enterprise operating rules, promotion of small businesses, suppression of monopoly, western banking reforms, a uniform system of profit taxes, the establishment of joint stock companies, securities markets, foreign investment, and entrepreneurship. All this in her opinion translated into a transition program featuring: stabilization, liberalization, privatization, regulation, new institutions, and the restructuring of production. See Gertrude Schroeder, "Post-Soviet Economic Reforms in Perspective," in *The Former Soviet Union in Transition*, vol. 1, Joint Economic Committee of the United States, February 1993, pp. 57–80. Cf. Padma Desai, who portrays Gorbachev as the hero of Russia's globalist future. Padma Desai, *Perestroika in Perspective: The Design and Dilemmas of Soviet Reform*, Princeton University Press, Princeton, NJ, 1989.

9 Structural Militarization

1 Noel Firth and James Noren, *Soviet Defense Spending: A History of CIA Estimates, 1950–1990*, Texas A&M University Press, College Station, 1998, pp. 188–90.

2 Some scholars have wrongly assumed that weapons can be gauged from the residual "other machinebuilding" sector of Soviet input–output tables.

3 Dmitri Steinberg, *Reconstructing the Soviet National Economic Balance, 1965–1984: An Alternative Approach to Estimating Soviet Military Expenditures, Vol. 1: Technical Discussion Decision-Sciences Applications*, DSA Report no. 692, March 11, 1986; *Vol. 2: Compilation of Working Tables*, March 21, 1986; "Estimating Total Soviet Military Expenditures: An Alternative Approach Based on Reconstructed Soviet National Accounts," in Carl Jacobsen (ed.), *The Soviet Defense* Enigma, SIPRI, New York, 1987, pp. 27–58. Also see Steinberg, "Trends in Soviet Military Expenditures, *Soviet Studies*, 42, 4 (1990). Steven Rosefielde, "Soviet Defense Spending: The Contribution of the New Accountancy," *Soviet Studies*, 42, 1 (1990), pp. 59–80.

4 For a full account of the Soviet spending controversy see Steven Rosefielde, *Russia in the 21st Century: The Prodigal Superpower*, Cambridge University Press, London, 2005, ch. 3.

5 Franklyn Holzman, *Financial Checks on Soviet Defense Expenditures*, Lexington Books, Lexington, MA, 1975; "Are the Soviets Really Outspending the U.S. on Defense?" *International Security*, 4, 4 (1980), pp. 86–104; "Soviet Military Spending: Assessing the Numbers Game," *International Security*, 6, 4 (1982), pp. 78–101; "Politics and Guesswork: CIA and DIA Estimates of Soviet Military Spending," *International Security*, 14, 2 (1989), pp. 101–31; "Politics, Military Spending, and the National Welfare," *Comparative Economic Studies*, 36, 3 (1994), pp. 1–4.

6 The CIA vetted a similar hypothesis in the mid-1970s, claiming that the Soviet military machinebuilding sector was hyper-productive. See *Economic Impact of Soviet Military Spending*, ER-IR-75-3, April 1974, pp. 6, 12.

7 Firth and Noren, *Soviet Defense Spending*. Rosefielde, *Prodigal Superpower*, tables 3.7 and 3.8, footnote 38. Advocates of arms control and disarmament generally shared the CIA's

view that the Soviet leadership sought to curb defense spending in order to reinvigorate flagging growth and improve consumer welfare. See Julian Cooper, *The Soviet Defense Industry: Conversion and Reform*, Royal Institute of International Affairs, London, 1991.

8 Vitaly Shlykov, *Chto Pogubilo Sovetskii Soiuz? Amerikanskaia Razvedka o Sovetskikh Voennykh Raskodakh (Who Destroyed the Soviet Union? American Intelligence Estimates of Soviet Military Expenditures)*, Voennyi Vestnik, no. 8, Moscow, April 2001; *Chto Pogubilo Sovetskii Soiuz? Genshtab i Ekonomika*, Voennyi Vestnik, no. 9, Moscow, September 2002.

9 David Epstein, "The Economic Cost of Soviet Security and Empire," in Henry Rowen and Charles Wolf, Jr. (ed.), *The Impoverished Superpower: Perestroika and the Soviet Military Burden*, Institute for Contemporary Studies, San Francisco, 1990. Cf. Steven Rosefielde, *False Science: Underestimating the Soviet Arms Buildup*, Transaction, Rutgers, NJ, 1987. William Lee, *The Estimation of Soviet Defense Expenditures, 1955–1975*; *CIA Estimates of Soviet Military Expenditures: Errors and Waste*, American Enterprise Institute, Washington, DC, 1995. Lev Dudkin and Anatol Vasilevsky, "The Soviet Military Burden: A Critical Analysis of Current Research," *Hitotsubashi Journal of Economics*, 28, 1 (1987).

10 Rosefielde, *Prodigal Superpower*, ch. 3.

10 Delusions of Adequacy

1 Harold Hotelling, "Edgeworth's Taxation Paradox and the Nature of Demand and Supply," *Journal of Political Economy*, 40 (1932), pp. 577–616; "Demand Functions with Limited Budgets," *Econometrica*, 3 (1935), pp. 67–78.

2 Abram Bergson, "Managerial Risks and Rewards in Public Enterprise," *Journal of Comparative Economics*, 2, 3 (1978), pp. 211–25.

3 Irving Fisher, *The Theory of Interest*, Augustus M. Kelley, New York, 1970.

4 Abram Bergson, "Reliability and Usability of Soviet Statistics: A Summary Appraisal," *American Statistician*, 7, 3 (1953), pp. 13–16. "Contrary to a common supposition, the Russians seem generally not to resort to falsification in the sense of free invention and double book-keeping. I have explained that there is falsification of a local sort . . . I am now concerned primarily with falsification of a comprehensive character at the center. This distinction, I fear, is a fine one. Almost all the deficiencies that have been discovered lead to unduly favorable impressions of the Soviet economy. If the Russians do not wilfully introduce such deficiencies to create such impressions, they are at least notably tolerant of them" (p. 15). "While it has seemed in order to distinguish in this essay between falsification by lower echelons and falsification at the center, it will be evident that a number of the grounds for thinking that the latter is not a general practice must also apply to the former. As a result, there is some upper limit to the margin of error introduced by falsification by lower echelons" (p. 16). For a fuller discussion of this issue see Steven Rosefielde, "Tea Leaves and Productivity."

5 Abram Bergson, "National Income," in Bergson and Simon Kuznets (eds.), *Economic Trends in the Soviet Union*, Harvard University Press, Cambridge, MA, 1963, pp. 1–35.

6 Abram Bergson, "Technological Progress," in Abram Bergson and Herbert Levine (eds.), *The Soviet Economy Toward the Year 2000*, George Allen and Unwin, London, 1983; *Planning and Productivity under Soviet Socialism*, Columbia University Press, New York, 1968; "Productivity Under Two Systems: The USSR versus the West," in Jan Tinbergen, Abram Bergson, Fritz Machlup, and Oskar Morgenstern (eds.), *Optimal Social Welfare and Productivity: Comparative View*, Barnes and Noble, New York, 1972; "Productivity and the Social System: The USSR and the West, Harvard University Press, Cambridge, MA, 1978; "Comparative Productivity: The USSR, Eastern Europe and the West," *American Economic Review*, 77, 3 (1987), pp. 342–57. Cf. Steven Rosefielde, "Comparative Production Potential in the USSR and the West: Pre-Transition Assessments," in Rosefielde (ed.), *Efficiency and Russia's Economic Recovery Potential to the Year 2000*

and Beyond, Ashgate, Aldershot, London, pp. 101–35. Positive growth in the Cobb–Douglas world can be achieved when technological progress and input growth volumes, or their net effects are greater than 1. When the sign is reversed, growth is negative.

7 Paul Krugman, "The Myth of Asia's Miracle."

8 Martin Weitzman, "Soviet Postwar Economic Growth and Capital-Labor Substitution," *American Economic Review*, 60, 4 (1970), pp. 676–92. Steven Rosefielde, *Efficiency and Russia's Economic Recovery Potential to the Year 2000 and Beyond*, Ashgate, Aldershot, 2000.

9 During the early 1960s Bergson believed that the application of western investment criteria might allow the Soviet Union to achieve rapid technological progress. See his discussion of *Tipovaia metodika opredeleniia ekonomicheskoi effektivnosti kapital'nykh vlozhenii i novoi tekhniki (Typical Method of Determining the Economic Effectiveness of Capital Investment and New Technology)* in Abram Bergson, *The Economics of Soviet Planning*, Yale University Press, New Haven, CT, 1964, pp. 252ff. T. S. Khachaturov, "Capital Investment Decisions in the USSR," *American Economic Review*, 48S (1958), pp. 368–84. David Granick, "On Patterns of Technological Choice in Soviet Industry," *American Economic Review*, 52S (1962), pp. 149–57.

10 Steven Rosefielde and R. W. Pfouts, "The Mis-specification of Soviet Production Potential: Adjusted Factor Costing and Bergson's Efficiency Standard," in Rosefielde, *Efficiency and Russia's Economic Recovery*, pp. 11–31.

11 Bergson also was influenced by his analysis of the great debate on socialism's feasibility which raged during the 1930s among Ludwig von Mises, Friedrich von Hayek, Lionel Robbins, and Oscar Lange. Two questions were at issue: (1) must a system that criminalizes business, entrepreneurship and private property collapse? (2) Can such a system be as efficient as market economies? Bergson concluded in a 1948 article (based partly on the survival of the USSR) that the answer to the first question was no. He waffled on the latter, erroneously arguing that a board of supermen could allocate resources rationally without markets (agreeing with Lange that they could solve Walras's general equilibrium equations), and on a less ethereal plane explaining that it was premature to judge the comparative merit of real, as distinct from textbook socialism and capitalism. See Abram Bergson, "Socialist Economics," in Abram Bergson, *Essays in Normative Economics*, Belknap Press, Cambridge, MA, 1965, pp. 234–36. The fallacy in his supermen argument lies in the absence of a mechanism to reconcile their conflicting preferences elucidated later by Kenneth Arrow, *Social Choice and Individual Values*, Wiley, New York, 2nd edn, 1963. Cf. Arrow, "Optimal and Voluntary Income Distribution," in Steven Rosefielde (ed.), *Economic Welfare and the Economics of Soviet Socialism*, Cambridge University Press, Cambridge, 1981, pp. 167–88. Then in a follow-on essay published 17 years later, "Socialist Calculation: A Further Word," in *Essays in Normative Economics*, pp. 237–8 he judges that "in view of the experience with socialism to date, the critics of this system have turned out to be nearer the mark than its proponents." Somewhere along the way Bergson concluded that the Soviet system in practice was comparatively inefficient. Cf. Friedrich von Hayek, *Collectivist Economic Planning*, London, 1935; "Socialist Calculation: The Competitive Solution," *Economica*, May 1940; "The Use of Knowledge in Society," *American Economic Review*, September 1945. Ludwig von Mises, *Socialism*, London, 1936. Lionel Robbins, *Nature and Significance of Economic Science*, London 1935. Steven Rosefielde, "Tea Leaves and Productivity."

12 Abel Aganbegyan, *The Economic Challenge of Perestroika*, Indiana University Press, Bloomington, 1988, p. 2. Aganbegyan was Gorbachev's chief economic advisor. Cf. *Narodnoe Khoziaistvo SSSR za 70 Let*, 1987, Finansy i Statistika, Moscow, 1987, pp. 52–3.

13 Abram Bergson, *The Real National Income of Soviet Russia Since 1928*, Harvard University Press, Cambridge, MA, 1961, table 14.2, col. 5, p. 217. Bergson's military burden figure is the official defense budgetary statistic.

14 *Narodnoe khoziaistvo SSSR 1990*, Moscow, Goskomizat, 1991, p. 16.

15 *Narodnoe khoziaistvo SSSR 1990*, p. 97. There were approximately 2 million unemployed in 1990 which was less than 2 percent of the labor force. According to American conventions, these job seekers in a large country like the Soviet Union are considered transitorily unemployed, and are not counted in the definition of normal "full employment." Full employment in the United States is customarily defined as 5.5 percent "transitory" unemployment.
16 No explanation was offered for the large disparity between the implicit GNP deflator, and the component industrial wholesale and retail price indexes. Official series measure open inflation, without adjustment for hidden inflation.
17 James Noren and Laurie Kurtzweg, "The Soviet Economy Unravels: 1985–91," in *The Former Soviet Union in Transition*, vol. 1, Joint Economic Committee, Washington, DC, February 1993, pp. 11–12.
18 *Measures of Soviet Gross National Product in 1982 Prices*, Joint Economic Committee of Congress, Washington, DC, November 1990, p. 26.
19 *Measures of Soviet Gross National Product*, p. 23.
20 Rosefielde, *Prodigal Superpower*, ch. 3.
21 Gertrude Schroeder and Elizabeth Denton, "An Index of Consumption in the USSR," in *USSR: Measures of Economic Growth and Development*, Joint Economic Committee of Congress, Washington, DC, December 8, 1982, pp. 317–401.
22 Noren and Kurtzweg, *The Soviet Economy Unravels*, table 4, p. 17.
23 Steven Rosefielde, *False Science: Underestimating the Soviet Arms Buildup*, Transaction Press, Rutger, NJ, 1987, table 14.2, p. 201.
24 *Narodnoe khoziaistvo SSSR 1990*, p. 16.
25 Abram Bergson, *The Real National Income of Soviet Russia Since 1928*, table 14.2, col. 5, p. 237.
26 David Epstein, "The Economic Cost of Soviet Security and Empire," in Wolf and Rowan, *Impoverished* Superpower, pp. 155–84.
27 Raymond Firth and James Noren, *Soviet Defense Spending*.
28 Rosefielde, *Prodigal Superpower*.
29 Firth and Noren, *Soviet Defense Spending*.
30 Rosefielde, *Comparative Economic Systems*, table 15.2, p. 210, and n. 1, p. 211. Noren and Kurtzweg, "The Soviet Economy Unravels."
31 Bergson's counter-argument that distortions in sub-aggregate series weren't too large and in line with the "reliability" of the aggregate series is belied by his own finding that Soviet GNP growth 1928–37 couldn't have exceeded 11.9 percent, when the official figure was 16.7 percent. Bergson, "The Reliability and usability of Soviet Statistics: A Summary Appraisal," *American Statistician*, 7, 3 (1953), pp. 13–16. See Sergei Roy, "Brezhnev Era Economy," *Moscow News*, February 17, 2004. "Planned production targets, that were not achieved in real life, could always be achieved on paper: *pripiski*, falsified reports became practically universal and automatic."
32 Bergson, "Socialist Calculation: A Further Word," in Bergson, *Essays in Normative Economics*, Harvard University Press, Cambridge, MA, 1966, pp. 237–42 where this point is acknowledged.
33 Bergson, "Socialist Economics." While Bergson denied that Soviet prices reflected the consumer utility standard, he left open the possibility that they measured "planners" preferences, even though "Arrow's paradox" meant that this couldn't be microeconomically so. The distinction encouraged many to give the CIA's numbers a more rational, utilitarian significance they didn't deserve.
34 According to Vladimir Ulsoltsev who spied together with Vladimir Putin in East Germany, Putin is said to have foreseen the inevitable collapse of the Soviet Union in 1985, at the time of Konstantin Chernenko's death. See Robin Munro, "Friend: Putin Saw U.S.S.R. in Decline," *St. Petersburg Times*, October 31, 2003.
35 Maurice Dobb, *Soviet Economic Development Since 1917*, International Publishers, New York, 1949.

11 Post-Communism

1 *Johnson's Russia List*, December 2, 2003. Yakovlev was the head of the Communist Party's propaganda division.

2 Stalin is alleged to have said "The important thing to know is not how they voted, but how we count them," Boris Kagarlitsky, "Tricks of Vote Fixing Trade," *Moscow Times*, December 18, 2003, reprinted in *Johnson's Russia List*, no. 7474, Article, 16, December 18, 2003. Peter Reddaway and Dmitri Glinski, *The Tragedy of Russia's Reforms: Market Bolshevism Against Democracy*, US Institute of Peace Press, Washington, DC, 2001. They argue that Yeltsin's "authoritarian modernization ruined the nation and despoiled the idea of democracy in the popular mind."

3 Anatoly Korolev, RIA Novosti, December 22, 2003, "Solzhenitsyn Proves Right Again," reprinted in *Johnson's Russia List*, no. 7484, Article 3, December 23, 2003. "Mass impoverishment, broken families, neglected children and a declining birth rate are just some of the facts of modern Russian life to point to an ongoing crisis in the state and society. Russia is on the brink of collapse and its national history may come to an end before we know it, Solzhenitsyn warns . . . the nation will be able to save itself only if it rediscovers its spirituality, rooted in the folk notion of social justice. The worship of money and emphasis on exploitation of one person by another, within reasonable limits, are alien ideas to the Russian mentality. It will therefore be self-destructive for Russian society to refashion itself after the Western model, adopting the principle of the survival of the fittest and turning its individual members into raw material for one another's civilized consumption. Even if it has proved efficient in the West, capitalist democracy will not work on Russian soil. It will only add to Russia's host of economic and social problems. Free market is an economic system absolutely unacceptable to Russia, as merciless competition will bring the nation to dehumanization, hostility and ultimately ruin. As Solzhenitsyn sees it . . . democracy in the liberal camp's reading of the notion is harmful and dangerous for Russia. Democratic ideas and principles may only be applied to some elements of the government, not the whole of it – otherwise the vessel will become uncontrollable. The crushing defeat in the latest elections of Russia's two major pro-reform parties – Yabloko and the Union of Right Forces – proved Solzhenitsyn right yet again. The public voted down the vision of the entire nation being pulled out of the mire by a bunch of oligarchs and oil magnates."

4 Josef Brada and Arthur King, "Is There a J-curve for Economic Transition from Socialism to Capitalism?" *Economics of Planning*, 25, 1 (1992), pp. 37–53. Stanislav Shatalin et al., *Transition to the Market: 500 Days*, part I, Moscow, Arkhangelskoe, August, 1990. For the English edition see St. Martin's Press, New York, 1991.

5 Steven Rosefielde, "The Civilian Labour Force and Unemployment in the Russian Federation," *Europe–Asia Studies*, 52, 8 (2000), pp. 1433–47; "Premature Deaths: Russia's Radical Economic Transition in Soviet Perspective," *Europe–Asia Studies*, 53, 8 (2001), pp. 1159–76. At the end of 2003 8.6 percent of Russia's economically active population (6.2 million people) was unemployed. The labor force was 65.2 million. But adjustment for discouraged workers puts the figure in the teens. Current Goskomstat statistics show "only" a 44.1 percent GDP decline 1989–98, but these numbers were improperly upwardly revised using implausible assumptions (23 percent of GDP was based on no evidence whatsoever), and committing serious arithmetic errors.

6 Goskokomstat and the World Bank jointly revised Soviet GNP upward by approximately 10 percent in 1995 with implausible assumptions and gross arithmetic errors. When Rosefielde corrected the arithmetic, and notified Alan Gelb the errors were left uncorrected. See *Rossiskaia Federtsiia: Doklad o natsional'nykh schetakh*, Goskomstat, October 1995.

7 Sergei Glazyev, Genotsid (October 1993–August 1998), *Rossiya i novyi mirovoi poryadok, Strategiya ekonomicheskogo rosta na poroge XXI veka*, 2nd edn., TERRA, Moscow, 1998.

8 For an alternative interpretation see Paul Gregory and Wolfram Schrettl, "Administration

and Reform of the Russian Economy," in *Russia's Uncertain Future*, Joint Economic Committee of Congress, Washington, DC, December 2001, pp. 81–96.

9 Y. Perevalov, I. Gimadi and V. Dobradei, "Vliiaet li privatizatsiia na deiatel'nost' predpriitatii, ("Has Privatization Influenced Enterprise Performance?") *Voprosy ekonomiki*, June 1999, pp. 76–89. A. Radygin, "Pererasspredelennie prav sobstvennosti v postprivatizasionnoi Rossii ("The Redistribution of Property Rights in Post-Privatized Russia"), *Voprosy ekonomiki*, June 1999, pp. 54–75. Saul Estrin and Mike Wright, "Corporate Governance in the Former Soviet Union: An Overview," *Journal of Comparative Economics*, 27, 3 (1999), pp. 398–421. Trevor Buck, Igor Filatotchev, Mike Wright, and Vladimir Zhukov, "Corporate Governance and Employee Ownership in an Economic Crisis: Enterprise Strategies in the Former USSR," *Journal of Comparative Economics*, 27, 3 (1999), pp. 459–74. J. David Brown and John Earle, "Privatization, Competition, and Transition Policy Strategies: Theory and Evidence from Russian Enterprise Panel Data," paper presented at the American Economics meetings, New Orleans, January 5, 2001. J. Blasi, M. Kroumova, and D. Kruse, *Kremlin Capitalism: The Privatization of Russia*, Cornell University Press, Ithaca, 1997. Klaus Segbers (ed.), *Explaining Post-Soviet Patchworks: Pathways from the Past to the Global*, vol. 2, Ashgate, Aldershot, 2001. As of 1995 insiders held 58.5 percent and outsiders excluding the state held 31.7 percent of industrial corporate shares. The state retained a 9.5 percent stake. Workers owned 48.5 percent of the total, directors 10 percent. Outsiders respectively held the following positions: banks 1.6 percent, investment funds 7.2 percent, holding companies and financial industrial groups (FIGs) 8.1 percent, individuals 9.6 percent, and foreigners 1.7 percent. Others accounted for 0.3 percent. See S. Aukutsionek, R. Kapliushnikov, and V. Zhukov, "Dominant Shareholders and Performance in Industrial Enterprises," *The Russian Economic Barometer*, 1 (1998), 1, pp. 8–41. The authors forecast a decline in workers' ownership to 36.3 percent and the state's share to 2.7 percent in 1999, with the primary gainers being managers (15 percent), FIGs (11.8 percent), and individuals (15.6 percent).

10 See Joseph Blasi, Maya Kroumova, and Douglas Kruse, *Kremlin Capitalism: Privatizing the Russian Economy*, Cornell University Press, Ithaca, New York, 1997. David Remnick, "Can Russia Change?" *Foreign Affairs*, 76, 1 (1997), pp. 35–49. On Anatoly Chubais see Alla Startseva, "Divinely Inspired Chubais Plans Ascension," *Moscow Times*, December 5, 2003, reprinted in *Johnson's Russia List*, no. 7456, December 7, 2003. Marshall Goldman, *The Piratization of Russia: Russian Reform Goes Awry*, Routledge, London, 2003, p. 120.

11 Marshall Goldman reports that 620 mutual funds attracted 60 million vouchers by February 1994, but within a few months almost half collapsed. Sergei Mavrodi and his two brothers enticed five million people to invest in MMM promising high yields. He paid interest to initial investors with new money giving credence to his promises, and then absconded, avoiding prosecution by becoming a parliamentarian. See Marshall Goldman, *The Piratization of Russia*, p. 88.

12 Anders Aslund, "Russia's Business Tycoons after the Decline of Oligarchy," University of North Carolina, Chapel Hill, November 13–14, 2002 (lecture). United Nations, "RUSSIA: Land Ownership Redistribution Progresses," *Johnson's Russia List*, no. 8055, Article 5, February 9, 2004. The Russian Federation has made significant progress in redistributing land ownership since the 1990s, but government administration on the issue is plagued by conflicts of interest, according to a United Nations report released today in Moscow. Over 50 million people and legal entities acquired private ownership rights in the country, and by the end of the 1990s some 7.6 percent of the Russian Federation's territory was privately owned, the report states. This percentage represents 129 million hectares of land and is comparable to the area of continental western Europe. The report says the most controversial elements of Russia's land and property administration stem from the mixture of public-law and private-law functions within one state authority. "An obvious conflict of

interest arises when decisions on land and other real property are taken by the agency that also has the authority to represent the interests of the owner of the [federal] property," the Commission says, calling this situation a legacy of Soviet land law which put all holdings under state ownership.

13 Yelena Fedorova, RIA Novosti, "Many Russian Enterprises Will Go Broke if the State Duma (the Lower Chamber of Russian Parliament) Does Not Adopt Amendments in the Land Code by the End of 2003," *Johnson's Russia List*, no. 7370, Article 2, October 16, 2003. Oleg Kiselev, a member of the Russian Industrialists and Entrepreneurs Union, and chief of the RSPP working group on the reform of land relations proposed that the redemption price (one-quarter the market price) be set for the purchase of all "enterprise" land after January 1, 2004, when the "permanent free use of land occupied by enterprises" ends. He also proposed that land redemption be postponed until 2006, and limiting the lessor's rights for enterprises. An earlier program proposed granting the land to enterprises gratis.

14 Eugenia Belova, "Legal Contract Enforcement in the Soviet Economy," *Comparative Economic Studies*, 47, 2 (2005), pp. 387–401.

15 M. A. Shabanova, "Institutsional'nye izmereniia i nepravovye praktiki," Moskovskaia vyshiia shkola sotsial'nykh i ekonomicheskikh, Intertsentr, 2001, pp. 319–27.

16 "Fewer Russians Living Below Poverty Line at End of 2003," *Johnson's Russia List*, no. 8072, Article 9, February 18, 2004. Great strides were claimed for poverty reduction in 2003. The number of Russians living on a per capita income below the official subsistence level fell to 23.1 million people in October–December 2003 from 31.2m people in July–September, according to data released by the State Statistics Committee on Tuesday [17 February]. Of the total Russian population, 16.2 percent had per capita incomes below the subsistence level in the fourth quarter of the year, down from 21.9 percent in the third quarter. Russia's government set the average official subsistence level at R2,143, or 75 dollars per capita [per month] in the fourth quarter of 2003, up from R2,121 in the third quarter. But this is a misleading benchmark. People who are well above 900 dollars per year are still obviously impoverished. Also, it is becoming fashionable to blame the poor for their poverty instead of the system. "Russians Want to Be Poor," *Johnson's Russia List*, no. 8073, Article 3, February 19, 2004. According to the Institute for Social Studies of the Russian Academy of Sciences, a quarter of its population (about 35 million people) live below the poverty line. And a third of them are really poverty stricken people. Most poor Russians are pensioners, workers, and unemployed people. Half of them have monthly incomes of no more than RUR1,500. And the other half no more than RUR3,000. Most of them live in small towns and villages. In many regions of Russia, almost all people are poor. Their average age is 47 years. Only 7 percent of poor Russians have savings, and about 40 percent have debts, including for communal services. Prices for communal services doubled across the country over the past two years. One reason for poverty in Russia is the lack of social protection. But the main reason is that a great number of Russian people lack ambition, and they are satisfied with their poor living conditions. So, 40 percent of poor people think their job has no prospects. Meanwhile, about 5 percent of Russia's population (7 million people) are rich. They have monthly incomes of no less than RUR40,000, or 16,667 dollars per year.

17 "Capital Flight from Russia Declines," *Johnson's Russia List*, no. 8002, Article 2, January 6, 2004. Capital flight from Russia's private sector declined to 2.9 billion dollars in 2003, down from 8.1 billion in 2002, and 14.8 billion in 2001, according to the Russian Central Bank. Vladimir Tikhomirov, "Capital Flight: Causes, Consequences and Counter-measures," in Klaus Segbers, *Explaining Post-Soviet Patchworks, Pathways from the Past to the Global*, vol. 2, Ashgate, Aldershot, 2001, pp. 251–80.

18 According to Alexander Dynkin, first deputy director of the Global Economy and International Relations Institute (IMEMO)the ten largest integrated business groups (IBGs) accounted for 38.7 of industrial output, 21 percent of all capital investment, 31 percent of

exports, and 22 percent of all profit tax revenue collected by the state. Average labor productivity at these holding companies is 3.7 times higher than the industrial average. The concentration of the Russian economy is greater than the European level (the top ten IBGs in Germany account for only 15 percent of industrial output), and the United States (27 percent). See Boris Grozovsky, and Anna Nikolaeva, "Reformed" Oligarchs," *Johnson's Russia List*, no. 8014, January 14, 2004.

19 Anders Aslund, "Amnesty the Oligarchs," *Moscow Times*, March 14, 2003, reprinted in *Johnson's Russia List*, no. 7102, March 14, 2003.Cf. Joseph Stiglitz, "Tax Russia's Oligarchs," *The Straits Times*, December 11, 2003, reprinted in *Johnson's Russia List*, no. 7462, Article 6, December 11, 2003. Also see, Anders Aslund, "The Drama is Putin's, But so Are the Results," *Moscow Times*, June 25, 2003; "Russia's 'Curse'," *Moscow Times*, January 16, 2004, reprinted in *Johnson's Russia List*, no. 8018, January 16, 2004. Aslund argues here that great wealth in the west was acquired unethically (for example America's robber barons), and so there should be no problem granting amnesty to Russia's oligarchs. Jacques Sapir and Sergei Glazyev propose that the government use resources rental taxes instead of re-nationalization as the best way of remedying Yeltsin's oligarchic grants. See Sergei Glazyev, "The Bureaucracy Controls the Duma Now," *Vedomosti*, January 20, 2004, reprinted in *Johnson's Russian List*, no. 8024, Article 10, January 20, 2004. Jacques Sapir, "Taxing Resources and the Future of Russia," *Moscow Times*, January 20, 2004, reprinted in *Johnson's Russia List*, no. 8024, Article 6, January 20, 2004.

20 Rosefielde, *Russia in the 21st Century*. Olga Kryshtanovskaya and Stephen White, "Putin's Militocracy, *Post-Soviet Affairs*, 19, 4, (2003), pp. 289–306. Kryshtanovskaya and White think that the rise of the "neo-authoritarian Putin militocracy" is depriving Russia's democratic institutions of real substance and re-creating a "wholly formal" or "facade" democracy of the kind that existed in the Soviet period. See *Johnson's Russia List*, no. 8013, January 13, 2004. Cf. Albert Weeks who accuses Kryshtanovskaya and White of "sucking the figures out of their fingers," arguing that Russia isn't a militocracy because current defense spending is low. See Albert Weeks, "Silovki: Soviet and Post-Soviet," *Johnson's Russia List*, no. 8015, Article 8, January 15, 2004.

21 For an American professional legal opinion, see "Report on Criminal Case #1814-03," *Johnson's Russia List*, no. 7461, Article 9, December 10, 2003. Clateman concludes that the indictment is serious and cannot be "thrown out of court." Peter Clateman, "Yukos Affair VII: Review of Criminal Sentence and Appeal," *Johnson's Russia List*, no. 77, March 29, 2006.

22 Goldman, *The Privatization of Russia*, pp. 108–10. Cf. Gregory Yavlinsky, *Periphery Captialism*, Yabloko, 2003. Andrei Panov and Nikolay Borisov, "The State's Share in Capitalization is 30 percent and Growing Everywhere," *Johnson's Russia List*, no. 41, Article 7, February 13, 2006.

23 Many political analysts contend that Putin needs oligarchs to finance his re-election campaigns. This is implausible. Oligarchs are only one of many venues the Kremlin can use to launder money for the leader's personal use. And there are always non-pecuniary ways of achieving the same objective through the security services and the nomenclature. No one except the ruler is indispensable in the Muscovite system.

24 "Bruised Yukos Faces More Blows in Russia," *Johnson's Russia List*, no. 7426, Article 1, November 19, 2003, Dmitry Zhdannikov, "Russia threatens Yukos Again as Putin Tours West," *Johnson's Russia List*, no. 7402, Article 12, November 6, 2003.

25 Steven Rosefielde, "Illusion of Transition: Russia's Muscovite Future," *Eastern Economic Journal*, 31, 2, 2005.

26 Olga Kryshtanovskaya, "Dangerous People in Civilian Clothing: The Rise of the Security and Law Enforcement People," *Yezhenedelnyi Zhurnal*, no. 10, March 2004, reprinted in *Johnson's Russia List*, no. 8130, Article 13, March 22, 2004. Kryshtanovskays, Director of the Center for the Study of Elites at the Sociological Institute of the Russian Academy

of Sciences sees a burgeoning neo-authoritarianism limited by global processes. "Putin said once, 'There cannot be former KGB agents.' This is an acting brotherhood, a kind of 'group of mutual assistance.' It is stronger than the 'family' (Russian klans). They were taught to act illegally and to hide their real intentions. They studied the laws to manipulate them. They are a caste of untouchables because they are under the state protection . . . Are they a danger to society? In my opinion, yes."

27 *Reformirovanie i razvitie oboronno-promyshlennovo kompleksa 2002–2006 gody* (*The Reform and Development of the Defense Industrial Complex 2002–2006*), Moscow 2001. Vitaly Shlykov, "Russia's Defense Industrial Complex after 9–11," paper presented at the conference on Russian Security Policy and the War on Terrorism, US Naval Postgraduate School, Monterey, California, June 4–5, 2002. Cf. Alexei Izyumov, Leonid Kosals and Rosalina Ryvkina, "Privatization of the Russian Defence Indusry: Ownership and Control Issues," *Post-Communist Economies*, 12, 4, 2001, pp. 485–96. Izyumov, Kosals and Ryvkina, "Defense Industrial Transformation in Russia – Evidence From a Longitudinal Survey," *Post-Communist Economies*, 12, 2, pp. 215–27. Mikhail Yuriev, "Krepost' Rossiia: Kontseptsiia dlia presidenta" *Novayagazeta*, 17, March 15, 2004. Cf. Steven Rosefielde, "Russia 2084: The Treadmill of Muscovite Radical Reform," paper presented at the conference "Whither Russia?" May 6–7, 2004, FOI, Stockholm, Sweden.

28 Alec Nove recognized long ago that Soviet (Russian) leaders, planners, ministers, red directors and apparachniki didn't adhere to Bergson's rationalistic strictures, but abided instead by the traditional satisficing rules of Muscovy. Alec Nove, *The Soviet Economic System*, George Allen and Unwin, London, 1977. On contemporary prospects see Steven Rosefielde, and Masaaki Kuboniwa, "Russian Growth Retardation Then and Now," *Eurasian Geography and Economics*, 44, 2 (2003), pp. 87–101.

29 Rosefielde, *Prodigal Superpower*.

30 Ronald McKinnon, *The Order of Economic Liberalization: Financial Control in the Transition to a Market Economy*. McKinnon's monetarism exemplified one aspect of policy often called the Washington consensus which broadly advocates of democratic free enterprise. See John Williamson, "Democracy and the 'Washington Consensus,'" *World Development*, vol. 21, 1993. Williamson, "What Washington Means by Policy Reform," in Williamson (ed.), Latin *American Adjustment: How Much Has Happened*, Institute for International Economics, Washington, DC, 1989, pp. 5–38. Williamson, "Did the Washington Consensus Fail?" Outline of Remarks at the Center for Strategic and International Studies, 6 November 2003, www.iie.com/publications/papers/williamson1102.htm

31 Steven Rosefielde and Natalia Vennikova, "Fiscal Federalism in Russia: A Critique of the OECD Proposals," *Cambridge Journal of Economics*, 28, 2 (2004). Steven Rosefielde, "Russian Competitiveness," *Russian Economic Trends*, 1, 4 (2002).Anders Aslund and Andrew Warner, *The Enlargement of the European Union: Consequences for the CIS*, Russian Eurasian Program, Carnegie Endowment for International Peace, 36, April (2003). Aslund, *Building Capitalism: The Transformation of the Former Soviet Bloc*, Cambridge University Press, Cambridge, 2002.

32 Simon Ostrovsky, "UN Think Tank Rips 'Naive' Reforms," *Moscow Times*, December 18, 2003, reprinted in *Johnson's Russia List*, no. 7474, December 18, 2003. Commenting on Robert McIntyre's report for the Helsinki-based World Institute for Development Economic Research, Ostrovsky writes, "Policies advocated by the IMF and World Bank in the 1990s and pursued by early reformers such as Anatoly Chubais were destructive and naïve. Egged on by Western consultants, early reformers of Soviet bloc economies – especially Russians like Chubais and Yegor Gaidar – rushed too fast to dismantle the communist system, ignoring the long-term consequences of their actions, and more important issue of institution-building." "The World Bank acknowledges that things could have been done differently, but it downplayed its role in the way events panned out." "The transfer of existing assets over the creation of new ones was in theory the wrong priority. But the

most decisive privatizers were Russians," said Christof Ruehl, the Washington based institution's chief economist for Russia."

33 Joseph Stiglitz, "Rewriting History," *Moscow Times*, reproduced in *Johnson's Russia List*, no. 6575, Article 6, November 27, 2002. Stiglitz, "Whither Reform? Ten Years of Transition," Annual Bank Conference on Development Economics, ed. Boris Pleskovic and Joseph Stiglitz, World Bank, Washington, DC, 2000, pp. 27–56. Cf. Marek Dabrowski, Stanislaw Gomulka, and Jacek Rostowski, "Whence Reform" A Critique of the Stiglitz Perspective," *Policy Reform*, 2001, pp. 1–34. Stanislaw Gomulka and John Lane, "The Transformational Recession under a Resource Mobility Constraint," *Journal of Comparative Economics*, September 2001. Pekka Sutela, *The Russian Market Economy*, Kikomora, Helsinki, 2004.

34 Grigorii Khanin was a leading critic of Soviet statistics. See G. I. Khanin, *Dinamika ekonomicheskovo razvitiia*, Nauka, Novosibirsk, 1991. He contends that things haven't changed. See G. I. Khanin, "Ekonomicheskaia razvitiia Rossii 1999–2004 gody: predvaritel'naia alternativnaia otsenka sostoiania rossiiskoi ekonomiki i analiz," paper presented at the VI World Congress of the International Council for Central and East European Studies, Europe – Our Common Home?" Berlin, Germany, July 25–30, 2005.

35 Steven Rosefielde, "Russia's Physical and Social Infrastructure: Implications for Future Development," National Intelligence Council, CR 2000-06, December 2000; "Russia's Productive Capital Stock: Trends and Prospects," paper prepared for the National Intelligence Council, Workshop on Russia's Capital Structure, Rosslyn, VA, February 1, 2000.

36 Steven Rosefielde, "The Civilian Labor Force and Unemployment in the Russian Federation," *Europe–Asia Studies*, 52, 8 (2000), table 6, p. 1439.

37 Murray Feshbach, *Russia's Health and Demographic Crises: Policy Implications and Consequences*, Chemical and Biological Arms Control Institute, Washington, DC, 2003.

38 Steven Rosefielde, *Efficiency and Russia's Economic Recovery Potential to the Year 2000 and Beyond*, Ashgate, Aldershot, 2000, table S1, p. xxii. Also see UN, *International Comparison of Gross Domestic Product in Europe*, 1990, p. 71; OECD, *Purchasing Power Parities and Real Expenditures*, 1990 EKS Results, vol. 1, p. 49, and Goskomstat RF, *International Comparisons of Gross Domestic Product*, 1993, pp. 114–17, 123–6.

12 Prospects

1 Tim Daniel, *The Agony of the Russia Idea*, Princeton University Press, Princeton, New Jersey, 1996.

2 Washington Profile: "It All Boils Down to Plagiarism," an interview with Brookings Senior Fellow Clifford Gaddy (re Putin's Dissertation). *Johnson's Russia List*, no. 78, Article 3a, March 31, 2006. Putin cribbed 16 pages from the Russian language version of a book by David Cleland and William King, two American business school professors at the University of Pittsburgh for his dissertation (*Kandidat Ekonomicheskikh Nauk*). Purchased PhDs. were commonplace in the Soviet era.

3 Andrei Shleifer and Daniel Treisman, "A Normal Country," *Foreign Affairs*, 84, 2, (2004), pp. 20–38. Cf. Steven Rosefielde, "Russia: An Abnormal Country," *The European Journal of Comparative Economics*, 2, 1 (2005), pp. 3–16. See Janine Wedel, *Collision and Collision: The Strange Case of Aid to Eastern Europe 1989–1998*, St. Martin's Press, New York, 1998.

Glossary

Academy of the National Economy Soviet managerial training academy founded May 1978.

adjusted factor costing A technique for adjusting fiat unit production prices (fiat value added) to conform with Western price formation principles. Soviet ruble prices (fiat values) were factor cost adjusted by stripping nonwage components (retail turnover taxes and profits) and adding imputed interest charges. The resulting adjusted ruble prices had the form of properly constructed value-added prices but not the content because neither wages nor imputed interest charges were competitively determined.

administrative command planning A summary description of Soviet physical systems management emphasizing the key aspects of state economic management, command, and administration. *Khozraschyot* incentivization is subsumed under administration.

adverse selection A Pareto-inferior choice caused by moral hazards.

agent Independent for-profit, service provider hired to represent business principals. Agents typically have more autonomy than employees tasked to perform the same jobs.

anti-parasite laws Laws prohibiting able-bodied Soviet citizens being unemployed or malingering on their jobs. Such individuals were deemed parasites, free riding off the proletariat's labor.

apparachnik Professional functionary of the Soviet Communist Party and/or the government. A bureaucrat.

arenda Leasing of Soviet state property for private business purposes. During NEP most lessees were private individuals. Under Gorbachev, they were mostly cooperatives.

asset grabbing Insider appropriation or privatization of state assets in an unsettled legal environment. Assets are seized in their entirety.

asset stripping Selective seizure of valuable enterprise property like furniture and fixtures, or spinning off profitable activities to wholly owned firms at discount, leaving the state with the debt baby. Pieces are stripped, but some of the original asset is preserved.

ASUP Automatic system of management and planning. Soviet program for constructing a self-regulating computer-based national economic management and planning network.

autarky National economic self-sufficiency achieved by prohibiting foreign imports and living entirely on domestic resources. More loosely, any regime that severely restricts foreign trade.

authoritarian laissez-faire An economic system with an authoritarian government that encourages some aspects of free enterprise.

authoritarianism Political rule by an individual (autocracy) or coterie. More generally, any system where individual autonomy is subordinated, or tightly constrained by dictate, coercion, administration, rules, and management.

autocracy A political regime where the ruler's commands supersede others' authority, and the written law. A dictatorship, even if disguised by various consultative institutions.

bads Products that generate negative utility-like pollutants.

blat The use of network obligations, favors and bribes to acquire sinecures, privileged access or consummate business deals in the second economy. The root sense is criminal behavior.

Bolshevik coup d'etat The coup d'etat that brought Lenin's Bolshevik party to power in 1917.

Bolshevik market The morally hazardous market institutions of NEP which prohibited most private ownership, substituted leasing, restricted enterprise size, allowed officials in state industry not only to contract with nepmen, but to outsource to themselves or partners, all without the benefit of the rule of contract law.

Bolshevik Party The minority faction of the Marxist Russian Democratic–Labor Party that called itself the majority (*Bol'shintsvo*), and seized the Russian government in a coup d'etat November 7, 1917 under the leadership of Vladimir Lenin.

Bolshevik Revolution A misnomer erroneously suggesting that Lenin's coup d'etat was a legitimate mass popular uprising in the name of the proletariat of the future that was replacing Muscovite Czarist autocracy and/or capitalism with proletarian sovereign democratic socialism. The reality was the old Muscovite authoritarian martial police state in working-class garb.

capital deepening Improving the embodied technological content and hence the productivity of the capital stock.

capital widening Increasing the size of the capital stock with machines embodying standard technologies. Capital widening enhances combined factor productivity, but not the productivity of the capital stock itself.

capitalism A loose term for a market economy where owners of real and financial capital are sovereign. The concept is also indiscriminately applied to all market economies based on private ownership of the means of production. Critics portray capitalism as anarchic, internally contradictory, self-destructive, and exploitive. Advocates associate it with perfect competition, personal freedom, democracy and consumer sovereignty.

catastroika Catastrophic economic reform. The term refers to the hyper-depression caused by Mikhail Gorbachev's failed *perestroika* (radical economic reform).

centralization A term used to distinguish tightly disciplined state administrative control regimes where orders are centrally issued from decentralized regimes that allow regional and/or local entities a degree of autonomy. Many students of political economy seem to erroneously believe that the right administrative mix can produce Pareto-quality outcomes.

CES production function A linearly homogeneous production function with a constant elasticity of factor substitution, reflecting the ease with which one factor can be substituted for another.

chistka In Soviet parlance, a purge of undesirable elements from the Communist Party and state institutions.

chto delat' What is to be done? A classic Russian revolutionary battle cry used by Lenin in 1902, and traceable to Nikolai Chernyshevsky's 1862 novel of the same name.

class war Marxist concept that workers and capitalists were implacable enemies, engaged in a life and death struggle that would inevitably lead to the triumph of socialism.

Cobb–Douglas production function A linearly homogeneous production function with a unitary elasticity of factor substitution, meaning that capital and labor are perfect substitutes.

cold war Strategic, economic and ideological struggle between the USA and the Soviet Union and their allies which commenced in 1947 and terminated in 1991. The degree of military preparedness, the threat of armed conflict, tactical probes, and proxy combat short of open superpower conflagration distinguished this rivalrous relationship from ordinary great power engagement. The East–West struggle was partly concealed, and perhaps tempered by mutual endorsement of non-belligerency expressed in slogans like peaceful coexistence and detente.

collectivization A Soviet policy introduced in the late 1920s under Stalin's direction of consolidating land and labor into Communist Party controlled cooperatives designed to compel peasants to produce for the state, killing those who resisted and exiling agrarian "class enemies" or kulaks (fists) to farm the tundra.

Command Communism Autocratic, physically managed, state owned natural economy, criminalizing private business and entrepreneurship, and showcasing central planning and *khozraschyot* adopted by Stalin in 1929, and continuing until Khrushchev launched an epoch of reforms in 1955.

command economy Any economy planned or otherwise based on state dictate instead of markets.

commanding heights Key industries and economic activities singled out by the Bolsheviks for immediate nationalization on the premise that their control sufficed to establish socialist economic power. These activities included banking, insurance, petroleum, coal, iron, machinebuilding, and foreign trade.

commissar Official Soviet title for high ranking Bolshevik political, state, and military authorities.

communalism Social, economic, and political systems designed to promote group well-being by subordinating individual rights and freedom when they cause inequality and disharmony. Worker owned and managed enterprises, kibbutzim, and utopian communism are types of communalism.

communism An ideal, harmonious, egalitarian society that substitutes communal (community) ownership for private property, and eliminates the state. Karl Marx's utopia, elaborated in his *Communist Manifesto* advocates this romantic primitivism. But Lenin's Communist Party turned the concept on its head by adopting the Muscovite authoritarian martial police state as an interim device to "assure" a coercion free communitarian future.

Communist Party A Soviet political organization superseding the Bolshevik Party created by Lenin and assigned to exclusively oversee the state apparatus purportedly to realize Marx's pastoral communist dream.

comparative coefficient of factor productivity Formula used to compare factor productivities between and among countries assuming constant Cobb–Douglas elasticities of factor substitution, and constant returns to scale.

composite goods An aggregate of heterogeneous, but related, products used in compiling plans, and statistical reporting. Automotive output, encompassing cars, trucks and tanks, is a composite good, as are the familiar Keynesian categories of consumption, investment and government ($C + I + G = Y$).

computopia An ideal planned economy achieved through perfect computation. The term was coined by Egon Neuberger.

consumer choice In economic systems theory parlance, a state where private individual consumer preferences (demand) determine retail purchases, but not characteristics, assortments, and volumes of goods and services supplied. Consumer choices in the Soviet context was always associated with forced substitution, and consequently was Pareto inefficient.

consumer sovereignty A state where private individual consumer preferences (demand) determine the characteristics, assortments, and volumes of goods and services supplied. Ideal consumer sovereignty is Pareto efficient.

consumer utility standard A Pareto compatible welfare norm for appraising the merit of a nation's factor allocation, goods production, and distribution devised by Abram Bergson, making it possible to distinguish economic efficiency from production potential.

convergence In Sovietology, a hypothesis that capitalist and communist economic systems are destined to converge to a common mixed market and planned welfare state. The notion was fashionable during the 1970s. The post-Soviet variant predicts that economic systems and living standards of all nations will resemble each other; in particular in America the expectation that living standards of poor nations will rise to the level of rich countries due to technology transfer and superior profit opportunities. This assumes that the economic potential of all systems are the same, or that globalization will make them so.

cooperatives A business organization where labor hires capital, and compensation is tied to membership instead of capital shares. Cooperatives may or may not be egalitarian, and involve production, wholesale, and retail operations. They sacrifice some capital efficiency for egalitarianism and mutual support.

correlation of forces Soviet military strategic concept akin to "balance of power" (*sootnoshenie sil*), which takes account of military capabilities, readiness, as well as socio-political factors like the class struggle.

Council of Economic Ministers Soveta Ministrov SSSR (1946–91) Postwar successor to the Council of People's Commissars, composed of the heads of various national industries. Stalin was the first head of the Council of Economic Ministers.

Council of People's Commissars Soveta Narodnykh Komissarov SSSR (1923–46) Lenin's and Stalin's economic cabinet. Lenin was the Chairman 1923–4, but most important decisions were jointly passed with the Politburo of the CPSU. The chairman is the head of the government, even though he may or may not be the general secretary of the Communist Party.

creative destruction Term used by Joseph Schumpeter to convey the notion that entrepreneurial progress often entails rendering some productive activities obsolete.

Crimes of the Stalin Era Special Report to the Twentieth Congress of the Communist Party of the Soviet Union delivered by Nikita Khrushchev in closed session February 24–5, 1956, detailing the millions wrongfully imprisoned and killed by Stalin.

criminalization of private property, business, entrepreneurship Measures taken to achieve Soviet nationalization of the means of production and the establishment of an economy-wide state economic monopoly.

crony capitalism Strongly regulated capitalist economy operated for the benefit of the ruler's favorites.

culture Durable attitudes and patterns of behavior approved by communities which underlie, supplement, shape, and supersede transient public policies and edicts.

cybernetics The science of feedback mechanisms relevant to the study of economic interactions.

czar Russian title derived from the Latin Caesar meaning autocratic emperor or king. It was the primary title (1547–1721), before becoming subsidiary to Russian Autocrat until the end of the Romanov dynasty.

decentralization The devolution of decision-making authority in the Soviet economic control mechanism from the center to the periphery. See *centralization.*

dekulakization Stalin's policy of "liquidating" the kulaks as a class and destroying their agrarian power. Its main features were mass arrests, exile, and killings of Russia's marginally better off peasants. These actions were pendants to forced collectivization.

democracy Political device for achieving popular sovereignty over the provision of public goods via the ballot. The conceptual counterpart of Pareto optimal consumer sovereignty over private goods. Kenneth Arrow has shown the popular sovereignty in representative democracies cannot be made ideally efficient.

demokratizatsia Literally, democratization. Gorbachev era slogan for making Communist rule more responsive to popular preferences. Like Lenin's claim that Bolshevik democracy was a million times more democratic than parliamentary democracy in England, the assertion is an oxymoron because the dictatorship of the proletariat precludes popular sovereignty.

dictatorship of law Putin era slogan suggesting that the rule of law will replace the rule of men in Russia, tacitly acknowledging that laws will be imposed by the ruler, instead of reflecting popular preferences.

dictatorship of the proletariat Custodial Bolshevik dictatorship in the name of the proletariat of the future which Lenin claimed was an essential short-term expedient to forestall counter-revolution.

disembodied technological progress Improvements in productivity enhancing processes that do not require the acquisition of new capital durables.

disequilibrium economy An economy designed to prevent Walrasian price, and Marshallian quantity equilibration in order to achieve overfull employment and other political economic goals. Disequilibrium economies necessarily cause forced substitutions, and therefore are equated by some with "economies of consumer goods shortage," even though the system as a whole overfully employs its productive assets. Shortage on their reckoning depends primarily on consumers receiving goods with the right characteristics in the desired assortment, not on the absolute magnitude of consumer supplies.

duality theorem The mathematical demonstration that perfect plans and perfect markets yield identical outcomes if technology, factor endowments, wealth and income distributions, and tastes are the same.

economic system A set of motivations, mechanisms (markets, government, and obligation), institutions, and rules of conduct shaping demand and supply, and responding to disequilibrium under conditions of scarcity.

economies of scale Cost savings and productivity gains attainable by increasing the size of production units.

economies of scope Cost savings and productivity gains achievable by expanding input and output diversity.

economy of shortage An economy designed to be in disequilibrium that persistently generates consumer goods deficits because resources are diverted to priority activities like investment durables and defense. Shortage in such economies are compatible with steady GDP growth.

Edgeworth–Bowley box Diagramatic apparatus used to derive production possibility frontiers, and the efficient distribution of goods along contract curves.

embodied technological progress Productivity advances generated by new and improved machinery and equipment (investment durables) separate from other kinds of processing gains.

evil empire A term coined by the Reagan administration accusing the Soviet Union of imperialist despotism.

excess deaths The number of people dying above the actuarially predicted figure from all causes including disease, catastrophes, accidents and killings. The term is synonymous with premature deaths.

extensive growth Growth generated by capital widening.

fiat prices Prices arbitrarily fixed by state authorities.

500 days program *Programma "500 Dnei"* devised by Grigory Yavlinsky and Stanislav Shatalin in 1989 claiming that the Soviet administrative command planning systems could be transformed into a competitive market free enterprise regime in 500 days. The goal was aspirational, not scientific.

forced substitution Anti-competitive restrictions that compel people to consume goods they dis-prefer. In the Soviet case, forced substitution was considered an irremediable defect of its economy of shortage.

GEU Chief Economic Administration of the NEP directive apparatus.

glasnost Slogan used by Mikhail Gorbachev, borrowed from Czarism meaning openness, transparency, candor, and tolerance of free speech. It implied the rejection of the authoritarian culture of lies and deceit (Sovspeak).

glavk A main department of VSNKh, and later of Soviet ministries.

Golden Rule The Christian principle of doing unto others as you would have them do unto you (fair play), important for assuring the efficient operation of the rule of contract law.

Gosarbitrazh The Soviet state arbitrage agency which adjudicated inter-enterprise contractual disputes in the state sector. Soviet enterprises were legal entities permitted to contract with each other and sue.

Gosbank Soviet State Bank (Gosudarstvennyi Bank SSSR), the central bank tasked to monitor plan approved inter-enterprise transitions, clear accounts, and provide cash for wages and other authorized purposes. It provided little financial assistance, and unlike Western commercial banks didn't operate for profit. Gosbank was a monopoly from the 1930s to 1987 when Gorbachev created various specialized banks including Promstoibank (USSR Bank of Industrial Construction), Zhilstroibank (USSR Bank of Residential Construction), Agrobank (USSR Agricultural Bank), Vneshekonombank (USSR Foreign Trade Bank), and Sberbank (USSR Savings Bank).

Goskomstat Soviet and now Russian State Statistical Committee (Federal'naya Sluzhba Gosudarstvennoi Statistiki).

Goskomtsen State Committee for Prices (Goskomtsen) set and revised the majority of all Soviet prices, established regulations for "temporary" prices fixed by enterprise managers for new and improved goods, and negotiated prices for special order goods.

Gossnabsbyt' State Committee for Material-Technical Supply (Gossnab for short) was the wholesaling arm of the Soviet procurement system responsible for inter-enterprise supply and distributing final goods to state retail outlets.

Gosplan Soviet State Planning Agency (Gosudarstvennyi Komitet po Planirovaniyu) was created February 22, 1921, by decree of the Sovnarkhom of the RSFSR under the name "RSFSR State Planning Commission." It began compiling annual plans (*kontrol'nye tsifry*) in 1925, and five-year plans in 1928.

Gosstandart Soviet and now Russian state standards bureau.

GosTekhnika Soviet State Committee for New Technology.

Great Industrialization Debate 1924–8 Soviet political economic debate about the sustainability of NEP, and best strategy for socialist industrialization. Participants included Nikolai Bukharin, Evgeny Preobrazhensky, Leon Trotsky, and Josef Stalin.

gross domestic product (GDP) The aggregate value of all marketable goods and services computed at market or official state prices. This measure of aggregate activity excludes income derived from assets held abroad. The GDP is only economically meaningful when prices are competitive (or are shadow equivalents). Otherwise prices are weak indicators of utilities and opportunity costs.

gross national income The income paid to primary factors of production for their services computed at market or fiat prices. Gross national income is only economically meaningful when prices are competitive (or shadow equivalent).

growth retardation Term coined in the 1970s to describe the steady deceleration of Soviet economic growth, attributed to flagging technological progress and a low elasticity of capital labor substitution, both caused by the defects of the physical management system.

Gulag Glavnoe Upravlenie Ispravitel'no-Trudovykh Lagerei i Kolonii (Chief Directorate of Corrective Labor Camp Administration), a complex of World War I type concentration camps with Czarist antecedents for imprisoning and "rehabilitating" criminals and those deemed enemies of the people through forced labor. They served as killing fields during much of the Stalin period, and as a vast pool of cheap labor for state projects. The legal basis for the system was established June 27, 1929, with corrective labor camps (Ispravitel'no-trudovye Lageria) placed under the control of the OGPU (Soviet Secret Police). Gulag was officially liquidated by the MVD on January 25, 1960, but continues under other names.

harmonism A belief that there exists an ideal state where all human conflicts are reconcilable (like Marx's full communism). The insistence that if threats are placated they will be resolved by reason, or some higher "mystery."

Heckscher–Ohlin theory The hypothesis that comparative advantage in a competitive global economy is determined by differences in factor availabilities, implying that capital rich countries should export capital intensive and import labor intensive products, and vice versa for capital poor nations. The embodied factor content of Soviet international trade adhered to this efficiency norm, showing that administrative command planning wasn't entirely insensitive to factor scarcities.

hidden inflation Inflation concealed either by Goskomstat's misreporting, or by falsification from below. Many Sovietologists consider spurious innovation to have been the principal source of hidden inflation during the Command Communist period.

hyperinflation Extraordinarily rapid price inflation, the most drastic cases of which exceed 1,000 percent per annum. Post-Soviet inflation at its worst in the early 1990s was more than 2,500 percent per annum.

idea of the West The Enlightenment idea that democratic free enterprise, or social democracy is the most rational, and therefore the best way to organize society. Harmonists extend the concept by inferring that if the idea of the West is best, it is also ineluctable. Samuel Huntington has suggested an expanded list of characteristics including economic freedom, social justice, tolerance, diversity, and conflict avoidance. The interpretation of these ideals in practice is often contextual, subject to dispute, and qualified by subculture, shadow cultural, and counter-cultural values.

impoverished superpower A concept popularized by Charles Wolf, Jr. and Henry Rowan suggesting that the defining characteristic of the Soviet Union was the disparity between the nation's living standard and its military might. The concept implied that the USSR's threat potential was constrained by its impoverization.

index number relativity The effect of structural dissimilarity on size and growth estimates computed in alternative inter-temporal or international prices. Pronounced index number relativity in the Soviet case is usually interpreted as evidence of rapid structural transformation, and economic catch-up with the West.

input–output model An analytic model of a national economy, or activities that maps the flows of primary and intermediate inputs into final goods, assuming fixed coefficients (non-substitutability). The model is computable, and useful for national economic forecasting.

inspiration Paul Krugman's term for economic growth driven by technological progress and improved labor skills.

institutions Organizations which set the rules of various kinds of economic conduct.

intensive growth Growth generated by capital deepening.

invisible hand Unobserved actions of markets which allocate factors, produce, and distribute goods and services. The Walrasian automatic price, and Marshallian quantity adjustment mechanisms are the market's right and left hands.

J curve Economic recovery curve shaped like the letter J, marked by a brief sharp drop and leveling off, followed by a rapid ascent above the previously achieved GDP. The concept was used by transitologists who expected Russia's hyper-depression to be a fleeting prelude to rapid, sustained growth.

job rights Employment entitlements, benefits, and protections accorded by states or custom to labor. In the Soviet case, David Granick argued that job rights in the Reform Communist period significantly constrained managerial discretion.

Keynesian adjustment mechanism The use of monetary and fiscal policy to eradicate involuntary unemployment and underproduction by harnessing multiplier effects.

The multiplier, unlike Walrasian and Marshallian adjustment mechanisms, is semi automatic, often requiring government monetary and fiscal intervention.

khozraschyot Economic cost accounting. More specifically, the requirement that Soviet enterprises carry out their functions cost-effectively, without relying unduly on state subsidies, with considerable managerial discretion. The term is akin to *samofinansirovanie*.

kleptocracy An economic system run by corrupt state officials and their cronies in the private sector. It can be an aspect of a liberal Muscovite system.

kolkhoz Soviet collective farm where peasant income was a share of net sales (dividend), instead of a fixed wage. Common land was owned by the state. Peasants were permitted small private plots. The institution was imposed on the peasantry and managed by Communist Party appointees. Farmers preferred their traditional communal arrangements.

kolkhoznik A *kolkhoz* member.

Kremlin Moscow fortress that has been the seat of Russian government since the fifteenth century, and symbol of the Russian state.

krugovaya poruka Enterprise mutual support network known colloquially as a family circle.

kulak Literally, tight fisted, referring historically to moderately better off peasants. In Soviet times, a tiny segment of the peasantry classified as class enemies because they were suspected of aspiring to become large property owning capitalist farmers.

kustar An artisan, or craftsman.

Langean market socialism A socialist economy featuring state ownership of the means of production, a requirement that managers produce to the point where marginal cost equals price, and a price board instructed to continuously adjust prices until markets clear. Oscar Lange purported to prove that this type of market socialism was Pareto efficient, like Meadean social democracy with private ownership, but failed to consider the problem of moral hazard where red directors served their own interests first.

Laspeyres index Index devised by Etienne Laspeyres to measure economic growth using final year prices to weigh quantities. Laspeyres indices tend to yield lower growth estimates than indices computed in base year prices.

law of demand The principle that the desirability of goods and services are positive functions of utility and inversely dependent on prices.

law of supply The principle that the volumes of goods and services produced and distributed are positive functions of prices.

law of supply and demand equilibration Principle that supply and demand programs can be recomputed as prices are negotiated or varied until excess supplies or demands are eliminated and a stable equilibrium is established.

law of value Karl Marx's concept that manufactured goods are or should be exchanged in proportion with their embodied labor input. The hypothesis is an aspect of his labor exploitation theory.

leasing Rental of property without associated rights of ownership and capital gains.

leisure Non-work activities of any type including pleasure seeking and household maintenance excluded from GDP.

Liberman reform A proposal advocated by Evsei Liberman to base Soviet enterprise production programs on the maximization of "profitability" instead of the physical volume of output. The notion was vetted in 1962 and partially adopted in the Kosygin reforms of 1965.

linear programming Mathematical technique for formulating and solving complex factor allocation, production, and distribution problems where technology exhibits constant returns to scale (is linear).

liquidation (as a class) In Soviet Marxist parlance, the eradication of allegedly hostile groups like the kulaks as a social class through resettlement, exile and assimilation. Mass killings also were employed, but weren't a necessary ingredient of the process.

Lockean social contract Enlightenment notion that the harmony observed in human relations reflects the existence of an implicit social contract mandating that people refrain from preying on each other and act in accordance with ethical principles like the Golden Rule. The contract is the result of rational choice rather than a manifestation of genetically encoded behavior.

lump sum dividend Transfer payments paid without regard to work, based on a criterion like equal per capita social dividend distribution.

market Bolshevism The possibility of a Bolshevik economic system forged on the basis of NEP leasing markets, preserving state ownership of the means of production.

market communism A stateless economy with community ownership that creates asset usage rights permitting Paretian utility seeking factor allocation, production, and distribution. The concept was advocated by Mikhail Gorbachev, but considered an oxymoron by orthodox Marxian communists.

Marshallian quantity adjustment mechanism Cybernetic process where price disequilibria cause profit seeking production levels to rise or fall until a competitive profit maximizing equilibrium is attained.

material balances Rudimentary Soviet planning technique akin to imput–output programming, where a list of materials (factors, raw materials intermediate inputs) is compiled on a sector by sector basis, and then allocated to alternative use in a manner which tries to assure that estimated intermediate inputs can actually be produced. The technique is derived from War Communism requisitioning and rationing, and provides a formal method for developing alternative production programs.

Meadean social democracy A Pareto ideal form of EU social democracy with Arrow best social welfare programs.

mechanism A set of procedures and operations like markets, administration, and planning used to realize economic ends. The term can be a synonym for systems, but usually describes elements of the composite apparatus.

military-industrial complex (VPK) Voennyi-promyshlennyi kompleks, a formal institutional network encompassing the Soviet and Russian Genshtabs, Ministry of Defense, military enterprises, civilian firms, planners, civil defense organizations, military intelligence, and other security bodies. The scope and cohesiveness of the VPK are principal causes of structural militarization, a characteristic that distinguished them from America's loose military-industrial community of interest. The VPK has been renamed OPK, defense industrial complex.

mir Village authority overseeing peasant communities (*obshchina*) in Czarist Russia.

modernization Process through which less developed nations acquire the technological characteristics of advance countries. Since technology is separable from culture, societies can modernize without westernizing. The idea of the West implies that non-westernizing modernization will be less effective and provide lower welfare than Pareto efficient westernization.

Moorsteen effect The inference first drawn by Richard Moorsteen that Laspeyres Soviet GDP growth estimates during the 1930s more accurately reflected Stalin's preferred development path than slower growing Paasche estimates, deduced from the geometry of the production space.

moral hazard Danger that economic self-interest will impel people to place their own material considerations above their moral, professional, and legal obligations.

Muscovite model Authoritarian productive system based on what Stefan Hedlund calls mental frames dating to the post-Mongol rise of Muscovy stressing autocracy, "patrimonialism" (the view that all assets ultimately are the sovereign's), "pomestie" (tenure land grants to supporters, not unlike the revokable property rights of today's oligarchs), "kormlenie" (tax "farming" and rent-seeking) "krugovaya poruka" (network mutual support), "duvan" (plunder), "slavophilism" (nationalistic preferences), resulting in subjugation and extreme inequality. Liberal variants provide transactors with a significant degree of economic and political autonomy.

Muscovite authoritarian martial police state Muscovite economic system with a powerful military for imperializing neighboring states, and a formidable secret police for internal security control.

Muscovy The Great Princedom of Moscow, successor to Kievan Rus' northern lands, and foundation stone of Russian Czardom. The Kniazhestvo Moskovskoe started in the fourteenth century and persisted as the Grand Duchy of Muscovy (Velikoe Kniazhestvo Moskovskoe) until the late fourteenth century.

nationalization Transfer of property rights from private entities to the state, sometimes in the name of the people.

natural economy Economic activities calibrated and executed in physical terms without the intermediation of money including factor allocation, production and barter distribution.

NEP New Economic Policy (*Novaya Ekonomicheskaya Politika*). The state administrative and leasing strategies chosen by Lenin to replace War Communism, sometimes called market socialism because of negotiated business relations among various components of the economy including leased private business, state industry, and the agrarian sector. The policy began in 1921 and ended in 1929.

nepmen Tradesmen, peddlers, commercial and industrial lessees, and some private proprietors engaged in business activities among themselves and with the state sector.

NMP Net material product. Marxist national product concept, similar to GDP, but less comprehensive because it excludes "non-productive" personnel services like haircuts, leisure transportation, etc.

novoe myshlenie New thinking. Gorbachev era slogan for applying Enlightenment and humanitarian concepts to the formation of foreign and military policies, superseding cold war power politics.

obshchina Czarist era peasant communities based on collective responsibility and mutual support.

oligarchs Colloquial term for a small number of super rich dominating Russia's exclusionary markets, who acquired their wealth undeservingly through spontaneous privatization, other forms of asset seizing, asset stripping, presidential largesse, rent-seeking and a host of criminal activities. They tend to live non-productively off their assets, transferring their monies to safe havens abroad, under-producing, under-investing and suppressing competitive access to their preserves.

one-man-rule *Edinonachie*. Soviet management principle of undivided enterprise authority vested in red directors. Workers and worker councils could have voice, but had to obey managerial directives.

OPK Oboronnyi-promyshlennyi kompleks, or defense industrial complex. It is Russia's renamed military industrial complex.

order of financial liberalization Ronald McKinnon's concept that post-Soviet transition should begin with financial stabilization before proceeding with other aspects of privatization and liberalization.

Paasche index Index devised by Hermann Paasche weighing quantities with final year prices to compute GDP growth. Also, analogous price indices computed with late year quantity weights.

Pareto–Arrow Bergson welfare standard An ideal Pareto class set of consumer sovereign generally competitive economic outcomes, modified by popularly sovereign government programs and transfers (Bergson–Samuelson), subject to the intrinsic inefficiencies of democratic balloting (Arrow), which can serve as a standard of social merit in judging observed economic performance.

Pareto optimality Transactions carried to the point where no voluntary transactor can improve his/her utility without another losing. Achieving this condition means that all utilitarian possibilities have been realized. The concept encompasses every aspect of rational choicemaking for individuals, communities, nations, and the globe.

patrimonialism Principle of paternal rule. In the Russian historical case it extends to autocratic ownership of all national property, as well as the power to command and rent-grant.

peaceful coexistence *Mirovaya sosuchestvovannia*. Khrushchev era Soviet term for cold war adversaries respecting each other's territorial sovereignty and interests. The concept implied lower intensity engagement, and renunciation of military force as a means of resolving conflicts between ideological rivals.

perekhod Transition from Soviet administrative command planning to a market economy. This Yeltsin era term was close in meaning to Gorbachev's concept of *perestroika*, but implied a rejection of communism.

perestroika Radical economic reform.

perspiration Paul Krugman's term for economic growth generated by capital widening and increased factor input.

physical systems *Management* The administration, supervision, direction, management assignment, requisition, rationing, command, incentivization, regulation, and control of factor allocation, production, and distribution in physical terms (or in fiat prices), without the assistance of competitive market profit maximizing and laissez-faire utility seeking. Administrative command planning is a type of physical systems management.

piatiletka Soviet five-year plan first introduced by Stalin in 1928.

piratization Term coined by Marshall Goldman to describe the plunder of the "people's" property by Boris Yeltsin's and Vladimir Putin's oligarchs.

planned chaos Concept devised by Friedrich von Hayek stressing the detachment of optimal planning from individual utilities and real market values. Planners, he asserted, may have desired to simulate Pareto optimality, and often pretended that they maximized social welfare, but their efforts were chaotic and futile.

planning In Soviet context, the acquisition, and processing of information on input availability, production potential, and national priorities required to physically manage, regulate, administer, and govern national factor allocation, production, and distribution. The term also can be used broadly to include command, administration and incentivization.

Politburo Politicheskoe Biuro (Political Bureau). The central policy-making and governing body of the Communist Party of the Soviet Union. The party was superior to the state government.

Ponzi scheme Investment scam devised by the Italian swindler Charles Ponzi whereby high returns are paid to initial participants out of the funds of later investors until the pyramid ultimately collapses.

population deficit Shortfall between predicted and actual future populations attributable both to variations in natality and mortality. Where concern is for excess mortality alone, the appropriate measure is premature deaths.

post-Communism Period following the Soviet collapse, also called Market Muscovy. Contemporary Russia is an authoritarian martial police state with a mixed economy. It is comprised of two subperiods: Yeltsin's weak regime which indulged asset-seizing and revenue misappropriation (oligarchy), and Putin's which has strengthened central authority and restored social discipline.

post office socialism Notion that a marketless economy could outperform democratic free enterprise by having people mail supply requests to producers who would fill orders without concern for all the other complexities of factor allocation, production, and distribution. The catalog mail order scheme was first proposed by Friedrich Engels, and then showcased as the solution to War Communism by Vladimir Lenin in his tract on *State and Revolution.*

pre-cycling The recycling of new goods before they are used. A device used by some Soviet enterprises to exaggerate production and delivery of goods to final use without ever producing anything useful.

predpriyatie Enterprise.

premature deaths Deaths occurring before their actuarially expected date. The concept provides a benchmark for assessing whether discontinuities in mortality trends are attributable to natural or political causes. It is synonymous with excess deaths.

primitive socialist capital accumulation Concept advanced by Evgeny Preobrazhensky in 1920 suggesting that a Bolshevik socialist economy could not be constructed without creating an initial capital accumulation from the surplus value of the peasantry. The proposal was controversial because it implied violating Lenin's worker–peasant alliance. The notion of primitive (initial) capital accumulation was borrowed from the first volume of *Das Kapital* where Marx tries to explain the origins of capitalism in terms of pre-capitalist plunder. The term primitive socialist was coined by V. M. Smirnov.

privatization Transfer of people's (national), state, collective, or communal property to individuals, not necessarily prior owners, with associated rights of resale and use.

prodrazverstka Lenin's policy of forced requisitioning of foodstuffs from the peasantry adopted June 1918. It became a hallmark of War Communism and its abolition in March 1921 marks the beginning of NEP.

production feasibilities frontier Set of constrained efficient supplies generated from factors, only one point of which represents a constrained equilibrium of current supply and demand.

production possibilities frontier Set of efficient supplies generated from voluntary factors, only one point of which represents an equilibrium of current demand and supply, all other points being counterfactual. Best involuntary production frontiers are also conceivable, but another term should be used to indicate the suppression of labor and non-labor liberty.

production potential A term coined by Abram Bergson to distinguish economic from Soviet fiat cost-efficient production. Production potential is a supply side optimum disconnected from consumer utility and demand. Soviet supply efficiency is defined with respect to constrained physically managed production, and is not a counterfactual Pareto ideal.

production potential standard A supply side standard where the production frontier is generated by planning and false prices as in the Soviet Union. This is a pseudo-production possibility frontier, that provides measures of pseudo-supply efficiency.

proletariat Originally people with no wealth other than their human capital, transformed by Karl Marx into a synonym for the working class.

Promplan Industrial Planning Agency attached to the GEU.

purchasing power parity The valuation of a nation's GDP using the purchase prices of another country, bypassing the foreign exchange rate. The technique entails collecting export prices in two currencies, and matching characteristics of non-tradables so that prices correspond accurately with foreign and domestic values.

ratchet effect Principle of raising established norms to higher levels in response to the feats of pacesetters. A technique used by Soviet managers to set piecework norms. Hero pacesetters were called Stakhanovites after Aleksei Stakhanov's norm breaking achievements of 1935 that burgeoned into the Stakhanovite socialist competition movement. Ratcheting was borrowed from the industrial efficiency doctrine of the American Frederich Taylor (Taylorism).

rationing The allocation of goods on a quota basis, instead of through competitive sale in the market place.

red director The state appointed head of Soviet enterprises tasked to implement plans with no discretionary authority, as distinct from managers assigned to maximize goals like output volumes, or profitability.

Red Labor Army Term applied in 1920 to detachments of the Red Army assigned to production activities like logging and coal mining. The concept was borrowed and expanded by Leon Trotsky in his capacities as Commissar of the Army and Fleet Affairs, and Chairman of the Revolutionary Military Council into the notion that militarized labor was the best socialist form.

Reform Communism Period of post-Stalin economic reforms 1953–91.

regime change A change of government that doesn't infringe national sovereignty.

rent-granting Awarding the privilege of using state or autocrat rent-generating property to favorites for the grantor's and grantee's mutual benefit.

rent-seeking Aspiring to acquire the privilege of using state or autocrat rent-generating property for the grantor's and grantee's mutual benefit.

rentier An individual whose income is derived from economic rents, rather than his labor value added.

repressed inflation Price fixing that holds the price level down in the face of excess purchasing power.

requisitioning Commandeering supplies without compensation.

resource mobilization Activization of idle factors of production. In the Soviet case, the term implies mustering effort above the Paretian norm to a level consistent with a state of wartime emergency.

revolution A political regime change that ushers in a new economic and social order. The Bolshevik coup d'etat was a regime change with a fresh cast, not a revolution that eradicated the Muscovite socio-economic system.

rule of law In economics, the notion that a just society empowers individuals to Pareto maximize utility restricted only by voluntarily negotiated, and state enforced contracts instead of having outcomes dictated by non-democratic authorities (the rule of men). Courts under the rule of law must be impartial, not instruments of authoritarian administration.

rule of men In economics, the principle of dictate by the powerful, as distinct from voluntarily negotiated transactions enforced by the rule of law.

ruler sovereignty Principle of effective demand, where goods and services are supplied to satisfy some powerful entity, or ruler, rather than individual consumers.

samofinansirovanie Self-financing. The requirement that enterprises operate within their revenues, instead of expenses being covered out of the state budget.

samookupaemost' Self-repayment. The requirement that the costs of investments be fully recouped out of future profits.

satisficing Principle that the good obtained suffices so that there is no need to pursue the best even if search costs are low. Profit and utility equilibria consequently are found at multiple points in a fuzzy set.

Say's Law Hypothesis enunciated in the eighteenth century by Jean-Baptiste Say asserting that supply creates its own demand (if prices are flexible), from which it was deduced that gluts are self-correcting, and there is no need to expand the money supply to overcome depression and involuntary unemployment. Keynes challenged this hypothesis by counter-arguing that wages are sticky, managers often have unduly pessimistic expectations, and hold excessive idle cash balances.

second economy The informal, parallel Soviet economy where unauthorized goods were produced and traded in the state sector, as well as unreported private services in varying degrees of illegality, which Aron Katsenelinboigen called "colored markets."

science-production associations Associations of filial Soviet enterprises with shared scientific research and development facilities introduced in the 1970s as part of the Kosygin reforms to remedy the separation of technological development from enterprise requirements.

scissors crisis Name given to the precipitous rise in Soviet industrial terms of trade with the countryside during the early 1920s caused by relatively rapid agricultural rebound from the War Communist hyper-depression. The scissor is formed by plotting terms of trade and its reciprocal on the same graph. The event came to symbolize the danger of following a market path to Soviet industrial socialism.

sebestoimost' Prime cost; the labor, capital and rental cost of production before white collar overhead, profit mark ups and turnover taxes.

security services Common term for all branches of the Russian security community.

servitors Nobles required to provide state service in return for privileges and the retention of their estates. Contemporaries who provide Russia's presidents with services in return for granted rents.

shadow prices Estimated equilibrium prices computed from the dual of a linear or nonlinear production program. Shadow prices enabled Soviet planners to evaluate Goskomsten's fiat prices.

shock therapy Radical institutional or systems change undertaken to revitalize the economy. Often used as a term of derision for radical policies that have catastrophic consequences.

siloviki A shadowy power clique active in the early 2000s influencing Putin's personnel appointments.

smychka Literally marriage. Term used to convey the inviolability of Lenin's worker–peasant alliance.

social democracy A variant of the idea of the West in which a socially concerned state manages an otherwise free economy through democratic means to promote social justice. The model is often referred to as the welfare state.

social market economy Post-Soviet term mis-portraying Russia's Muscovite market as being responsive to popular needs, suggesting that good aspects of communism have been retained and the bad discarded.

socialism A loose concept encompassing a wide variety of political and mechanistic arrangements where the state claims to restrict free enterprise in society's interest, with special attention paid to the welfare of workers and the poor.

socialism with a human face A political program promulgated by Alexander Dubcek in 1968 calling for limited democracy, liberalization, and humanism while the Czech Communist Party retained real power.

socialist humanism A socialist variant of humanist ideal individual and societal conduct first advocated in Karl Marx's *Economic and Philosophical Manuscripts of 1844*, which contrasts sharply with Soviet authoritarianism, fashionable for several decades in Western intellectual circles after Stalin's death.

Sovereign democracy Euphemism for Puten-style authoritarianism, vetted in 2006 and claiming that facade democracy is an ingredient of the Russian idea.

Sovietology The discipline of Soviet studies. The term is broader than Kremlinology which focuses on domestic and international politics.

sovkhoz Soviet state farm where land is state owned and farmers are viewed as agrarian workers paid wages instead of sharing net income.

Sovnarkhoz Council of the National Economy, usually translated as Regional Economic Council (Sovet Narodnovo Khoziaistva). Introduced March 1957 by Nikita Khrushchev in an effort to decentralize planning from Moscow to the regions.

spontaneous privatization Unauthorized privatization of state enterprises by red directors to themselves under the Soviet regime 1987–91, and in Russia thereafter. This theft of the people's property was often construed by advocates of globalization as a progressive step in Russia's transition to democratic free enterprise.

spurious innovation Development of products and process that have new or altered characteristics and are assigned higher prices without commensurate increases in value. Spurious innovation is a source of hidden inflation because price increases have no utilitarian justification.

Stakhanovism An effort mobilization movement started by the "heroic" norm breaking example of Aleksei Stakhanov in 1935, applauded by Stalin. Stakhanovites were portrayed as shock pacesetters who roused ordinary workers to actualize their full potential.

STO Soviet Labor and Defense Council established by Lenin and his commissars for strategic economic intervention during War Communism.

Stolypin reforms Imperial Russian agrarian reform begun by Prime Minister Peter Stolypin November 1906 establishing the right of unconditional private ownership.

Some progress was made before 1917, but Czarist agriculture remained predominantly communal.

storming In Soviet economic parlance, frenzied effort to meet plan targets just before deadlines.

straitjacket authoritarianism A term conveying restrictedness of individual liberty in authoritarian societies which verge on, but do not achieve absolute totalitarian control.

strakh Russian word for fear that epitomizes the psychological impact of Stalin's terror.

structural militarization Term used to describe a productive system with a large embedded military-industrial sector capable of persuading government leaders to provide sufficient resources to deal with worst case security threats.

superpower Preeminent nuclear states. During the cold war America and the Soviet Union were considered superpowers because they possessed more than 90 percent of the planet's nuclear weapons, and were said to have rough strategic parity. Some analysts insist that America today is the only superpower because of its economic superiority.

systems directors Term coined by Abram Bergson to describe the high authorities directing the Soviet administrative command planning apparatus.

Team B A group of external experts approved by CIA Director George Bush to provide an alternative assessment of Soviet military capabilities, and be included in the yearly National Intelligence Estimates (NIEs). Prominent members included Richard Pipes, Paul Nitze, Paul Wolfowitz, I. Lewis Libby, William Casey, John Connolly, Zbigniew Brzezinski, John Foster, Clare Booth Luce, and Edward Teller.

technical efficiency Cost-efficiently produced goods, that nonetheless fail to maximize consumer utility. The concept applies to all counterfactual equilibria along the production possibility frontier.

technological diffusion The process by which new technologies are transferred from the laboratory into productive service.

tekhpromfinplany Technical, industrial, and financial plans compiled by the main departments of Soviet industrial ministries from aggregate Gosplans, assigned to enterprises for micro-implementation.

the thaw Title from a novel by Ilya Ehrenburg about the prospects for post-Stalin Soviet liberalization which symbolized the possibilities of peaceful coexistence during the Khrushchev era.

Third International Communist successor to the First and Second International Workingmen's Association (nineteenth entury), formally called the Comintern (Kommunisticheskii Internatsional), a purportedly "independent" communist organization founded March 4, 1919, by Vladimir Lenin, Leon Trotsky, and the Russian Communist Party to advance the cause of world revolution. A rival Fourth International was founded by Leon Trotsky after his exile in the 1930s.

tolkach Literally a "pusher," that is someone assigned by a Soviet enterprise to barter for inputs anywhere within the Soviet system. *Tolkachi* collectively functioned as an informal wholesale network parallel to Gossnab.

totalitarianism A typology used by political scientists to describe modern states that regulate (control) nearly every aspect of public and private behavior. The distinction between regulation and control is crucial. There are no examples of totalitarian nano-control, including Stalin's Russia, only societies that attempt to control nearly every aspect of individual activity.

transition Literally, a movement from one state or system to another. But the term is usually employed to suggest that former planned economies inevitably will be transformed into democratic free enterprise systems, or EU social democracies.

transitologist Experts who believe that all nations must transform into democratic free enterprise systems, or EU social democracies, and try to assist the process.

treadmill of reform A term used by Gertrude Schroeder to express the futility of Soviet administrative economic reforms.

trudovye kollektivy Worker collectives aiding Soviet enterprise managements.

trusts Industrial cartels established during NEP that had the effect of separating administrative from productive functions in the state industrial sector, while preserving a degree of inter-enterprise coordination.

Tsugprom Central Industrial Directorate of VSNKh.

uskorenie Accelerated GDP growth, a goal showcased in Gorbachev's initial 1985 economic reform package.

utility possibilities frontier A set of best utility outcomes derived from the supply alternatives provided by the economy's production possibility frontier.

Utopian Bolshevism The notion that Lenin's War Communist economic arrangements were ideal, allowing Russia to achieve the first stage of communism in 1918 as elaborated by Evgeny Preobrazhensky and Nikolai Bukharin in their *ABC's of Communism*.

value subtracted Processing that reduces the value of raw materials or intermediate inputs. Some erroneously define value subtracted more broadly to include the production of domestic goods from raw materials that have a higher value abroad. But this phenomenon is mis-trading. As long as the domestic value of the fabricate exceeds the domestic raw material cost, value is added, not subtracted.

vanguard of the proletariat Progressive elements self-tasked with leading the working class in its march to full communism. Lenin claimed that his Bolshevik Party was anointed by history to play this role in the Soviet Union.

visible hand State directive, administrative, and regulatory economic actions.

virgin lands program Nikita Khrushchev's campaign in 1954 to open up vast tracts of semi-arid land for agriculture which began with a bang but ended badly with diminished soil fertility and erosion. The strategy came to symbolize the shortsightedness and futility of Soviet resource mobilization tactics.

virtual economy Term coined by Clifford Gaddy and Barry Ickes to convey the idea that physical productive management remains the predominant principle governing Russian economic activity after the demise of planning, despite the emergence of subsistence and exclusionary markets.

voucher privatization A scheme advocate by Andrei Shleifer and others, adopted by Boris Yeltsin whereby vouchers for the acquisition of shares in denationalized enterprises were distributed to citizens in recognition of their ownership stake in the Soviet capital stock. The scheme degenerated into a scam when mutual funds acting as intermediaries declared bankruptcy, absconded with the vouchers, and used them as a basis for creating ill-gotten fortunes.

VPK Voennyi promyshlennyi kompleks (Soviet and Russian military industrial complexes).

vrag naroda Enemy of the people. A term used to stigmatize anyone, or group that disagreed with the Bolsheviks. Even the mere suspicion of being hostile made people vulnerable to persecution, judicial action, terror and extermination.

VSNKh Soviet All-Union Council of State Economy, or Council of the National Economy (Vysshii Sovet Narodnovo Khoziaistva), founded in 1917, dissolved in 1932. It controlled all nationalized industries.

Walrasian price adjustment mechanism Cybernetic process where quantity disequilibria, excess supplies or demands, are diminished by price decreases or increases until a stable market clearing equilibrium is achieved.

War Communism A period of Russian civil war between forces loyal to the Czar and the Bolsheviks, as well a series of utopian and expedient attempts to construct a communist society. It can also be construed as a period of Muscovite restoration in proletarian guise.

Washington Consensus A term coined by John Williamson to describe a set of micro- and macroeconomic principles that leading international institutions in Washington, DC, like the IMF, and World Bank, believe best serve the cause of economic development and global prosperity. The key elements are free enterprise, financial discipline, and democracy. The Washington Consensus champions liberal globalization, opposes systemic diversity, and believes that only liberal principles are universally applicable regardless of culture or systems.

westernization The adoption of the ideals of the West including economic liberty, democracy, social justice, tolerance, diversity, and conflict avoidance by developing and transitioning economies. Westernization is a more demanding concept than modernization which only entails adopting Western technologies.

work In national income accounting terms, any labor activity that generates marketable value added, as distinct from non-marketable activities for own consumption.

worker–peasant alliance Concept of a political alliance between working class and agrarian revolutionaries devised by Vladimir Lenin in the 1890s to draw supporters away from populism. The slogan also called *smychka* (marriage), was retained and incorporated into Bolshevism even after Stalin's forced collectivization in 1929.

Workers Opposition A faction of the Soviet Communist Party which emerged in the 1920s led by Alexander Shlyapnikov and Alexandra Kollontai championing a leading role for trade unions (syndicalism) in directing state industry until stigmatized as a deviant faction. The group was viewed by some Western analysts as a viable democratic proletarian alternative to Bolshevik bureaucratic industrial administration. Shlyapnikov was tried in secret as *vrag naroda* and executed September 2, 1937. Kollontai was one of the few Old Bolsheviks to avoid execution.

Yukos Affair A sequence of events triggered by the arrest of Russian oligarch Mikhail Khodorkovsky that culminated in his conviction and imprisonment in 2005 for various crimes, and the effective renationalization of his Yukos oil empire. These events are widely viewed as stepping-stones in suppressing the post-Soviet transition process and restoring a Muscovite authoritarian martial, police state.

zastoi Economic stagnation. Gorbachev's growth acceleration campaign was justified by the claim that Soviet GDP halted in 1980, despite Goskomstat statistics to the contrary.

Bibliography

Abouchar, Alan (ed.), 1977: *The Socialist Price Mechanism*, Duke University Press, Durham, North Carolina.

Aganbegyan, Abel, 1988: *The Economic Challenge of Perestroika*, Indiana University Press, Bloomington, p. 2.

Allen, Robert, 2003: *Farm to Factory: A* Reinterpretation *of the Soviet Industrial Revolution*, Princeton, NJ, Princeton University Press.

——, 2005: "A Reassessment of the Soviet Industrial Revolution," *Comparative Economic Studies*, 47, 2, pp. 315–32.

Anton-Ovseenko, 1980: *The Time of Stalin: Portrait of a Tyranny*, Harper and Row, New York.

Applebaum, Anne, 2003: *GULAG: A History*, Doubleday, New York.

Arrow, Kenneth, 1963: *Social Choice and Individual Values*, Wiley, New York, 2nd edn.

——, 1981: "Optimal and Voluntary Income Distribution," in Steven Rosefielde (ed.), *Economic Welfare and the Economics of Soviet Socialism*, Cambridge University Press, Cambridge, pp. 167–88.

Aslund, Anders, 2002: *Building Capitalism: The Transformation of the Former Soviet Bloc*, Cambridge University Press, Cambridge.

——, 2002: "Russia's Business Tycoons after the Decline of Oligarchy," University of North Carolina, Chapel Hill, November 13–14 (lecture).

Aslund, Anders and Andrew Warner, 2003: *The Enlargement of the European Union: Consequences for the CIS*, Russian Eurasian Program, Carnegie Endowment for International Peace, no. 36, April.

Aukutsionek, S., R. Kapliushnikov and V. Zhukov, 1998: "Dominant Shareholders and Performance in Industrial Enterprises," *The Russian Economic Barometer*, no. 1, pp. 8–41.

Avtorkhanov, Abdurakhman, 1976: *Zagadka Smerti Stalina*, Posev, Frankfurt/Main, Germany.

Bacon, Edwin, 1994: *The Gulag at War*, Macmillan, Birmingham.

Bagrinovsky, K. A. and V. S. Prokopova, 1989: *Imitatsionnye Sistemy Priniatia Ekonomicheskikh Reshennii*, Nauka, Moscow.

Becker, Abraham, 1969: *Soviet National Income, 1958–64*, University of California Press, Berkeley and Los Angeles.

Belova, Eugenia, 2005: "Legal Contract Enforcement in the Soviet Economy," *Comparative Economic Studies*, 47, 2, pp. 387–401.

Belova, Eugenia and Paul Gregory, 2002: "Dictator, Loyal, and Opportunist Agents: The Soviet Archives on Creating the Soviet Economic System," *The Public Choice*, 113, pp. 265–86.

Bergson, Abram, 1938: "A Reformulation of Certain Aspects of Welfare Economics," *Quarterly Journal of Economics*, 52, 1, pp. 210–34.

——, 1948: "Socialist Economics," in H. Ellis (ed.), *A Survey of Contemporary Economics*, Richard D. Irwin, Homewood, IL, pp. 412–48.

——, 1953: "The Reliability and Usability of Soviet Statistics: A Summary Appraisal," *American Statistician*, 7, 3, pp. 13–16.

——, 1954: "The Concept of Social Welfare," *Quarterly Journal of Economics*, 68, 2, pp. 233–53.

——, 1961: *The Real National Income of Soviet Russia Since 1928*, Harvard University Press, Cambridge, MA.

——, 1963: "National Income," in Bergson and Simon Kuznets (eds.), *Economic Trends in the Soviet Union*, Harvard University Press, Cambridge, MA, pp. 1–35.

——, 1964: *The Economics of Soviet Planning*, Yale University Press, New Haven.

——, 1965: "Socialist Economics," in Abram Bergson, *Essays in Normative Economics*, Belknap Press, Cambridge MA, pp. 234–6.

——, 1966: "Socialist Calculation: A Further Word," in Bergson, *Essays in Normative Economics*, Harvard University Press, Cambridge, MA, pp. 237–42.

——, 1967: "Market Socialism Revisited," *Journal of Political* Economy, 75, 4, pp. 655–73.

——, 1968: *Planning and Productivity under Soviet Socialism*, Columbia University Press, New York.

——, 1972: "Productivity Under Two Systems: The USSR versus the West," in Jan Tinbergen, Abram Bergson, Fritz Machlup, and Oskar Morgenstern (eds.), *Optimal Social Welfare and Productivity: Comparative View*, Barnes and Noble, New York.

——, 1976: "Social Choice and Welfare Economics under Representative Government," *Journal of Public Economics*, 6, 3, pp. 171–90.

——, 1978: *Productivity and the Social System: The USSR and the West*, Harvard University Press, Cambridge, MA.

——, 1978: "Managerial Risks and Rewards in Public Enterprise," *Journal of Comparative Economics*, 2, 3, pp. 211–25.

——, 1983: "Technological Progress," in Abram Bergson and Herbert Levine (eds.), *The Soviet Economy Toward the Year 2000*, George Allen and Unwin, London.

——, 1987: "Comparative Productivity: The USSR, Eastern Europe and the West," *American Economic Review*, 77, 3, pp. 342–57.

Berliner, Joseph, 1976: *The Innovation Decision in Soviet Industry*, MIT Press, Cambridge, MA.

——, 1983: "Planning and Management," in Abram Bergson and Herbert Levine (eds.), *The Soviet Economy: Toward the Year 2000*, George Allen and Unwin, London, pp. 350–90.

Billington, James, 1966: *The Icon and the Axe*, Vintage Books, New York.

Blank, Stephen, 2006: "The 18th Brumaire of Vladimir Putin," in Uri Ra'anan (ed.), *Flawed Succession: Russia's Power Transfer Crisis*, Lexington Books for Rowman and Littlefield, Lanham, MD, pp. 133–70.

Blasi, Joseph, Maya Kroumova, and Douglas Kruse, 1997: *Kremlin Capitalism: Privatizing the Russian Economy*, Cornell University Press, Ithaca, New York.

Blum, Jerome, 1969: *Lord and Peasant in Russia from the Ninth to the Nineteenth Century*, Atheneum, New York.

Bonin, John, 1976: "On the Design of Managerial Incentive Structures in a Decentralized Planning Environment," *American Economic Review*, 66, 4, pp. 682–7.

Bonin, John and Wataru Fukuda, 1987: "Controlling a Risk-averse, Effort-selecting Manager in the Soviet Incentive Model," *Journal of Comparative Economics*, 11, 2, pp. 221–34.

Borodkin, L., Paul Gregory, and Oleg Khleonyuk (eds.), 2005: *Gulag: Ekonomika prinuditel' novo truda, Rosspen*, Moscow.

Brada, Josef and Arthur King, 1992: "Is there a J-curve for Economic Transition from Socialism to Capitalism?" *Economics of Planning*, 25, 1, pp. 37–53.

Brainard, Elizabeth, 2005: "Reassessing the Standard of Living in the Soviet Union: An Analysis Using Archival and Anthropometric Data," *Comparative Economic Studies*, 47, 2, pp. 315–22.

Brown, J. David and John Earle, "Privatization, Competition, and Transition Policy Strategies: Theory and Evidence from Russian Enterprise Panel Data," paper presented at the American Economics meetings, New Orleans, January 5, 2001.

Buck, Trevor, Igor Filatotchev, Mike Wright, and Vladimir Zhukov, 1999: "Corporate Governance and Employee Ownership in an Economic Crisis: Enterprise Strategies in the Former USSR," *Journal of Comparative Economics*, 27, 3, pp. 459–74.

Bukharin, Nikolai, 1924: "Novoe otkrovenie o sovetskoi ekonomike ili kak mozhno pogubit' raboche-krest'yanskii blok" ("New Revelation of the Soviet Economy or How Can the Worker–Peasant Bloc Be Destroyed, Bolshevik"), December 10.

——, 1925: *K voprosu o trotskizme* (*On Trotskyism*), Moscow–Leningrad.

——, 1926: *Building Up Socialism*, London.

Bukharin, Nikolai and Evgeny Preobrazhensky, 1969: *The ABC's of Communism*, Penguin Books, Baltimore, MD.

Cave, Martin, 1980: *Computers and Economic Planning: The Soviet Experience*, Cambridge University Press, Cambridge.

Cave, Martin and Paul Hare, 1981: *Alternative Approaches to Economic Planning*, St. Martin's Press, New York.

Chapman, Janet, 1963: "Consumption," in Abram Bergson and Simon Kuznets (eds.), *Economic Trends in the Soviet Union*, Harvard University Press, Cambridge MA.

Chayanov, Alexander, 1996: *The Theory of Peasant Economy*, Richard Irwin, Homewood, IL.

Churchill, W. S., *The Second World War, Volume IV: The Hinge of Fate*, London 1951.

CIA, 1990: *Measures of Soviet Gross National Product in 1982*, Joint Economic Committee of Congress, Washington DC, November.

Collier, Irwin, 2003: "The 'Welfare Standard' and Soviet Consumers," *Comparative Economic Studies*, 47, 2, pp. 333–45.

Conn, David, 1979: "A Comparison of Alternative Incentive Structures for Centrally Planned Economic Systems," *Journal of Comparative Economics*, 3, 3, pp. 235–53.

——, 1982: "Effort, Efficiency and Incentives in Economic Organizations," *Journal of Comparative Economics*, 6, 3, pp. 223–4.

Conquest, Robert, 1980: *The Great Terror: Stalin's Purge of the Thirties*, Macmillan, New York.

——, 1989: *Stalin and the Kirov Murder*, Oxford University Press, London.

——, 1990: *The Great Terror: A Reassessment*, Oxford University Press, London.

——, 1994: "Communications to the Editor," *American Historical Review*, June, p. 1039.

——, 1999: *Reflections on a Ravaged Century*, Norton, New York.

Cooper, Julian, 1991: *The Soviet Defense Industry: Conversion and Reform*, Royal Institute of International Affairs, London.

Coutois, Stephane, Nicolas Worth, et al., 1999: *Black Book of Communism*, Harvard University Press, Cambridge, MA.

Dabrowski, Marek; Stanislaw Gomulka, and Jacek Rostowski, 2001: "Whence Reform A Critique of the Stiglitz Perspective," *Policy Reform*, pp. 1–34.

Dallin, David, 1964: *From Purge to Coexistence: Essays on Stalin's and Khrushchev's Russia*, Regnery, Chicago.

Daniel, Tim, 1996: *The Agony of the Russian Idea*, Princeton University Press, Princeton, NJ.

Daniels, Robert, V., 1965: *The Conscience of the Revolution*, Harvard University Press, Cambridge, MA.

Danilin, V., Knox Lovell, I. Materov, and S. Rosefielde, "Measuring and Improving Enterprise Efficiency in the Soviet Union," *Economica*, 52, 206, pp. 225–34.

Davies, R. W., 1994: "Changing Economic Systems: An Overview," in R. W. Davies, Mark Harrison, and Stephen Wheatcroft (eds.), *The Economic Transformation of the Soviet Union, 1913–1945*, Cambridge University Press, Cambridge.

——, 1994: "Industry," in R. W. Davies, Mark Harrison, and Stephen Wheatcroft (eds.), *The Economic Transformation of the Soviet Union, 1913–1945*, Cambridge University Press, Cambridge, pp. 135–6.

——, 2005: "Closing the Bergson Gap: New Data on a Problem in Soviet Statistics," *Comparative Economic Studies*, 47, 2, pp. 274–88.

Desai, Padma, 1989: *Perestroika in Perspective: The Design and Dilemmas of Soviet Reform*, Princeton University Press, Princeton, NJ.

Dmitriev, Vladimir, K., 1974: *Economic Essays on Value, Competition and Utility*, ed. D. M. Nuti, Cambridge University Press.

Dobb, Maurice, 1949: *Soviet Economic Development Since 1917*, International Publishers, New York.

Domar, Evsey, 1957: *Essays in the Theory of Economic Growth*, New York.

——, 1974: "On the Optimal Compensation of a Socialist Manager," *Quarterly Journal of Economics*, 88, 1, pp. 1–18.

Dorfman, Robert, Paul Samuelson, and Robert Solow, 1958: *Linear Programming and Economic Analysis*, McGraw-Hill, New York.

Dudkin, Lev and Anatol Vasilevsky, 1987: "The Soviet Military Burden: A Critical Analysis of Current Research," *Hitotsubashi Journal of Economics*, 28, 1.

Dunlop, John and Nikolay Fedorenko, 1969: *Planning and Markets: Modern Trends in Various Economic Systems*, McGraw Hill, New York.

Dyker, David, 1981: *The Process of Investment in the Soviet Union*, Cambridge University Press.

Eason, Warren, 1963: "Labor Force," in Abram Bergson and Simon Kuznets (eds.), *Economic Trends in the Soviet Union*, Harvard University Press, Cambridge, MA.

Economic Impact of Soviet Military Spending, 1974: (CIA), ER-IR-75-3, April.

Ehrenburg, Ilya, 1962: *The Thaw*, Alfred Knopf, New York.

Ellman, Michael, 1971: "Soviet Planning Today," *Proposals for an Optimally Functioning Economic System*, Cambridge University Press, Cambridge.

——, 1975: "Did the Agricultural Surplus Provide the Resources for the Increase in Investment During the First Five Year Plan?" *Economic Journal*, 85, 340, pp. 844–63.

——, 1979: *Socialist Planning*, Cambridge University Press, Cambridge, 1979.

Engerman, David, *Modernization from the Other Shore*, Harvard University Press, Cambridge, MA, 2003.

Epstein, David, 1990: "The Economic Cost of Soviet Security and Empire," in Charles Wolf, Jr. and Henry Rowan, (eds.), *The Impoverished Superpower: Perestroika and the Soviet Military Burden*, Institute of Contemporary Studies, San Francisco, CA, pp. 155–84.

Erlich, Alexander, 1960: *The Soviet Industrialization Debate, 1924–1928*, Harvard University Press, Cambridge, MA.

Ertz, Simon, 2005: "Trading Effort in Freedom: Workday Credits in the Stalinist Camp System," *Comparative Economic Studies*, 47, 2, pp. 476–91.

Ertz, Simon and Leonid Borodkin, 2005: "The Labor Economics of the Soviet Gulag: Forced Labor and Search for Incentives," *Comparative Economic Studies*, 47, 2, pp. 418–36.

Estrin, Saul and Mike Wright, 1999: "Corporate Governance in the Former Soviet Union: An Overview," *Journal of Comparative Economics*, 27, 3, pp. 398–421.

Fedorenko, Nikolay, 1974: *Optimal Functioning System for a Socialist Economy*, Progress, Moscow.

Feldman, G. A., 1928: "K teorii tempov narodnogo dokhoda," ("On the Theory of the Rate of Growth of the National Income"), *Planovoe khoziaistvo*, November and December.

Feshbach, Murray, 2003: *Russia's Health and Demographic Crises: Policy Implications and Consequences*, Chemical and Biological Arms Control Institute, Washington, DC.

Firth, Noel and James Noren, 1998: *Soviet Defense Spending: A History of CIA Estimates, 1950–1990*, Texas A&M University Press, College Station.

Fisher, Irving, 1970: *The Theory of Interest*, Augustus M. Kelley, New York.
Fitzpatrick, Shelia, 1994: *The Russian Revolution*, Oxford University Press, Oxford.
Garvey, George, 1977: *Money, Financial Plans and Credit in the Soviet Union*, Ballinger, New York.
Gerschenkron, Alexander, 1962: "Russia: Patterns and Problems of Economic Development, 1861–1958," in Gerschenkron, *Economic Backwardness in Historical Perspective*, Harvard University Press, Cambridge, MA, pp. 119–51.
Getty, J. A. and R. T. Manning (eds.), 1993: "Victims of the Soviet Penal System in the Pre-war Years: A First Approach on the Basis of Archival Evidence," *American Historical Review*, October, pp. 1017–49.
Ginzburg, Evgeniia, 1967: *Into the Whirlwind*, Harcourt Brace and World, New York.
Glazyev, Sergei, 1998: *Genotsid (October 1993–August 1998), Rossiya i novyi mirovoi poryadok, Strategiya ekonomicheskogo rosta na poroge XXI veka*, 2nd edn., TERRA, Moscow.
Goldman, Emma, 1970: *My Disillusionment in Russia*, Apollo, New York.
Goldman, Marshall, 2003: *The Piratization of Russia: Russian Reform Goes Awry*, Routledge, London.
Gomulka, Stanislaw and John Lane, 2001: "The Transformational Recession under a Resource Mobility Constraint," *Journal of Comparative Economics*, September.
Goskomstat, R. F., 1993: *International Comparisons of Gross Domestic Product*, pp. 114–17, 123–6.
Granick, David, 1962: "On Patterns of Technological Choice in Soviet Industry," *American Economic Review*, 52S, pp. 149–57.
——, 1980: "The Ministry as a Maximizing Unit in Soviet Industry," *Journal of Comparative Economics*, 4, 3, pp. 255–73.
Gregory, Paul, 1990: "National Income," in R. W. Davies (ed.), *From Tsarism to the New Economic Policy: Continuity and Change in the Economy of the USSR*, Macmillan, London, pp. 237–48, 332–7.
——, (ed.), 2002: *Behind the Facade of Stalin's Command Economy*, Princeton University Press, Princeton, NJ.
——, 2003: *The Political Economy of Stalinism: Evidence From the Soviet Secret Archives*, Cambridge University Press, London.
——, 2005: "Bergson's Basic Hypothesis and the Soviet Archives: Insights from the Political Economy of Socialism," *Comparative Economic Studies*, 47, 2, pp. 402–17.
——, 2006: *Russian National Income 1885–1893*, Cambridge University Press, Cambridge.
Gregory, Paul and Valery Lazarev (eds.), 2003: *The Economics of Forced Labor: The Soviet Gulag*, Hoover Institution Press, Stanford.
Gregory, Paul and Wolfram Schrettl, 2001: "Administration and Reform of the Russian Economy," in *Russia's Uncertain Future*, Joint Economic Committee of Congress, Washington, DC, December, pp. 81–96.
Guttemplan, D. D., 2001: "The Holocaust on Trial," *Atlantic Monthly*, 285, 2, pp. 45–66.
Hansen, George, 1987: *Correlation of Forces: Four Decades of Soviet Military Development*, Praeger, New York.
Hardt, John, Marvin Hoffenberg, Norman Kaplan, and Herbert Levine, 1967: *Mathematics and Computers in Soviet Economic Planning*, Yale University Press, New Haven, CT.
Harrison, Mark, 2005: "Command and Collapse: The Fundamental Problem of Command in a Partially Centralized Economy," *Comparative Economic Studies*, 47, 2, pp. 296–314.
Hayek, Friedrich von, 1935: *Collectivist Economic Planning*, London.
——, 1940: "Socialist Calculation: The Competitive Solution," *Economica*, May.
——, 1945: "The Use of Knowledge in Society," *American Economic Review*, September.
Hedlund, Stefan, 2005: *Russian Path Dependence*, Routledge, London.
Herman, Victor, 1979: *Coming Out of the Ice*, Harcourt Brace Jovanovich, New York.

Holmstrom, Bengt, 1982: "Design of Incentive Schemes and the New Soviet Incentive Model," *European Economic Review*, 17, 2, pp. 128–48.

Holzman, Franklyn, 1963: "Foreign Trade," in Abram Bergson and Simon Kuznets (eds.), *Economic Trends in the Soviet Union*, Harvard University Press, Cambridge, MA.

——, 1975: *Financial Checks on Soviet Defense Expenditures*, Lexington Books, Lexington, MA.

——, 1980: "Are the Soviets Really Outspending the U.S. on Defense?" *International Security*, 4, 4, pp. 86–104.

——, 1982: "Soviet Military Spending: Assessing the Numbers Game," *International Security*, 6, 4, pp. 78–101.

——, 1989: "Politics and Guesswork: CIA and DIA Estimates of Soviet Military Spending," *International Security*, 14, 2, pp. 101–31.

——, 1994: "Politics, Military Spending, and the National Welfare," *Comparative Economic Studies*, 36, 3, pp. 1–4.

Hosking, Geoffrey, 2001: *Russia and the Russians*, Harvard Univeristy Press, Cambridge, MA.

Hotelling, Harold, 1932: "Edgeworth's Taxation Paradox and the Nature of Demand and Supply," *Journal of Political Economy*, 40, pp. 577–616.

——, 1935: "Demand Functions with Limited Budgets," *Econometrica*, 3, pp. 67–78.

Hough, Jerry and Merle Fainsod, 1979: *How the Soviet Union is Governed*, Harvard University Press, Cambridge, MA, p. 152.

Huntington, Samuel, 1996: "The West: Unique, Not Universal," *Foreign Affairs*, 75, 6, pp. 28–46.

Ireland, N. and Peter Law, 1980: "Incentive and Efficiency in the Kosygin Reforms," *Journal of Comparative Economics*, 4, 1, pp. 33–9.

Ivanova, Galina, 2000: *Labor Camp Socialism: The Gulag in the Soviet Totalitarian System*, M. E. Sharpe, Armonk, NY.

Izyumov, Alexei, Leonid Kosals, and Rosalina Ryvkina, 2001: "Privatization of the Russian Defence Industry: Ownership and Control Issues," *Post-Communist Economies*, 12, 4, pp. 485–96.

Izyumov, Kosals and Rosalina Ryvkina, 2001: "Defense Industrial Transformation in Russia – Evidence From a Longitudinal Survey," *Post-Communist Economies*, 12, 2, pp. 215–27.

Johnson, Gale, 1963: "Agriculture," in Abram Bergson and Simon Kuznets, *Economic Trends in the Soviet Union*, Harvard University Press, Cambridge, MA.

Judy, Richard, 1967: "Information, Control, and Soviet Economic Management," in John Hardt et al. (eds.), *Mathematics and Computers in Soviet Economic Planning*, Yale University Press, New Haven, CT.

Kantorovich, L. V., 1965: *The Best Use of Economic Resources*, Harvard University Press, Cambridge, MA.

Kennan, George, F., 1951: "The Sources of Soviet Conduct," *Foreign Affairs*, 29, 3, pp. 351–70.

Keren, Michael, I. Miller, and J. Thornton, 1983: "The Rachet Effect: A Dynamic Managerial Incentive Model of the Soviet Enterprise, *Journal of Comparative Economics*, 7, 4, pp. 347–67.

Khachaturov, T. S., 1958: "Capital Investment Decisions in the USSR," *American Economic Review*, 48S, pp. 368–84.

Khanin, G. L., 1991: *Dinamika ekonomicheskovo razvitiya*, Nauka, Novosibersk.

——, 2005: "Ekonomicheskoe razvitie Rossii za 1999–2004 gody: predvaritel'naia alternativnaia otsenka sostoiania rossiiskoi ekonomiki i ee analiz," paper presented at the VI World Congress of the International Council for Central and East European Studies, "Europe-Our Common Home?" Berlin, Germany, July 25–30.

Khlevnyuk, O., 2003: "Why Did the Terror Take Place? The Objectives of the 'Great Terror,'" in Christopher Read (ed.), *The Stalin Years*, Palgrave, New York.

Khrushchev, N. S., 1956: *Crimes of the Stalin Era, Special Report to the 20th Congress of the Communist Party of the Soviet Union*, annotated by Boris Nicolaevsky, New Leader, New York.

——, 1974: *Khrushchev Remembers: The Test Testament*, Little Brown, Boston, 1974.

Kleiner, George, 2001: *Mezoekonomika perekhodnovo perioda: Rynki, otrasli, predpriiatia*, Nauka, Moscow.

——, 2004: *Evoliutsiia institutsional'nykh sistem*, Nauka, Moscow.

Kopelev, Lev, 1977: *To Be Preserved Forever*, J .B. Lippincott Co., Philadelphia.

Kornai, Janos, 1967: *Mathematical Planning of Structural Decisions*, Amsterdam: North-Holland Publishing Company.

Kosgyin, A., 1965: "Ob uluchshenii upravleniia promyshlennostiu sovershenstvovanii planirovania i usileniia ekonomicheskovo stimulirovanii promyshlennovo proizvodstva" ("On Improving Industrial Management, Perfecting Planning, and Increasing Economic Incentives for Industrial Production"), *Pravda*, September 28.

Kroll, Heidi, 1986: "Decentralization and the Pre-contract Dispute in the Soviet Industry," *Soviet Economy*, 2, January–March, pp. 51–71.

Krugman, Paul, 1994: "The Myth of Asia's Miracle," *Foreign Affairs*, 73, 6, pp. 62–79.

Kryshtanovskaya, Olga and Stephen White, 2003: "Putin's Militocracy, *Post-Soviet Affairs*, 19, 4, pp. 289–306.

Kuhn, H. and A. Tucker, 1951: "Nonlinear Programming," in J. Neyman (ed.), *Proceedings of the Second Berkeley Symposium on Mathematical Statistics and Probability*, University of California Press, Berkeley and Los Angeles, CA, pp. 481–92.

Kuznets, S. A., 1963: "A Comparative Appraisal," in Bergson and Kuznets (eds.), *Economic Trends in the Soviet Union*, Harvard University Press, Cambridge, MA, pp. 333–82.

Kuznetsov, S. A., V. L. Makarov, and V. D. Marshak, 1982: Informatsionnaia *Baza, Perspektivnovo Planirovaniia v OASU*, Ekonomika, Moscow.

Lange, Oscar and Fred M. Taylor, 1938: *On the Economic Theory of Socialism*, University of Michigan Press.

Laqueur Walter, 1994: *The Dream that Failed: Reflections on the Soviet Union*, Oxford University Press, New York.

Lee, William, 1955–75: *The Estimation of Soviet Defense Expenditure*, Praeger, New York.

——, 1995: *CIA Estimates of Soviet Military Expenditures: Errors and Waste*, American Enterprise Institute, Washington, DC.

Lenin, Vladimir Ilyich, 1917: *State and Revolution*, International Publishers.

——, *Modern History Sourcebook: State and Revolution, 1918*, www.fordham.edu/halsall/mod/lenin-statere v.html.

Leontief, Wassily, 1936: "Quantitative Input–Output Relations in the Economic System of the United States," *Review of Economic Statistics*, 18, 3.

——, 1941: *The Structure of the American Economy*, Oxford University Press, Oxford.

——, 1966: *Input–Output Economics*, Oxford University Press, New York.

Levkova-Lamm, Innessa, 2004: *Face of Square: Mysteries of Kazimir Malevich*, Pinakotheke, Moscow.

Levy, Robert, 1984: *Mesocosim: Hinduism and Organization of a Traditional Newar City in Nepal*, University of California Press, Berkeley, CA.

Lewin, Moshe, 1968: *Russian Peasants and Soviet Power*, Northwestern University Press, Evanston, IL.

Liberman, Evsei, 1970: *Ekonomicheskie methody povysheniya effektivnosti* proizvodstva; English *translation, Economic Methods and the Effectiveness of Production*, New York, 1972.

Lodder, Christina, 1983: *Russian Constructivism*, Yale University Press, New Haven, CT.

Loeb, M. and W. Magat, 1978: "Success Indicators in the Soviet Union: The Problem of Incentives and Efficient Allocations, *American Economic Review*, 68, 1, pp. 173–81.

Maddison, Angus, 2003: *The World Economy: Historical Statistics*, OECD, Paris.

Malle, Silvana, 2002: *The Economic Organization of War Communism 1918–1921*, Cambridge University Press, Cambridge.

Malia, Martin, 1994: *The Soviet Tragedy: A History of Socialism in Russia, 1917–1991*, Simon and Schuster, New York.

Mandelstam, Nadezhda, 1974: *Hope Abandoned*, Random House, New York, 1974.
Markevich, Andrei, 2005: "Soviet Planning Archives: The Files That Bergson Could Not See," *Comparative Economic Studies*, 47, 2, pp. 364–86.
McKinnon, Ronald, 1991: *The Order of Economic Liberalization: Financial Control in the Transition to a Market Economy*, Johns Hopkins, Baltimore.
McLoughlin, Barry and Kevin McDemott (eds.), 2003: *Stalin's Terror*, Palgrave, New York.
Meade, James, 1978: *The Just Economy*, George Allen and Unwin, London.
Measures of Soviet Gross National Product in 1982 Prices, 1990: Joint Economic Committee of Congress, Washington, DC, November.
Medvedev, Roy, 1972: *Let History Judge*, Alfred Knopf, New York.
Meek, James, 2005: *The People's Act of Love*, Canongate, Edinburgh.
Millar, James, 1970: "Soviet Agricultural Development and the Agricultural Surplus Hypothesis," *Soviet Studies*, 22, 1, pp. 77–93.
——, 1974: "Mass Collectivization and the Contribution of Soviet Agriculture to the First Five-Year Plan: A Review Article," *Slavic Review*, 33, 4, pp. 750–66.
Millar, James and Alec Nove, 1976: "A Debate on Collectivization: Was Stalin Really Necessary?" *Problems of Communism*, 25, 4, pp. 56–7.
Milner, John, 1983: *Vladimir Tatlin's and the Russian Avant-Garde*, Yale University Press, New Haven, CT.
Mises, Ludwig von, 1936: *Socialism*, London.
Modin, A., N. V. Makhrov, and V. I. Danilin, 1984: *Dinamika Proizvodstvennykh Ob"edinii i Modeli Planirovaniia Ikh Deiatel'nosti*, Nauka.
Nachno-Tekhnicheskii Progress v SSSR, Statisticheskii Sbornik, Goskomstat SSSR, 1990: Moscow, p. 14.
Narodnoe Khoziaistvo SSSR 1990, 1991: Moscow, Goskomizat.
Narodnoe Khoziaistvo SSSR za 70 Let, 1987: Finansy i Statistika, Moscow.
Noren, James and Laurie Kurtzweg, 1993: "The Soviet Economy Unravels: 1985–91," in *The Former Soviet Union in Transition*, Joint Economic Committee, Washington, DC, February.
Nove, Alec, 1964: *Economic Rationality and Soviet Politics, or Was Stalin Really Necessary?* Praeger, New York.
——, 1972: *An Economic History of the USSR*, Pelican, London.
——, 1975: *Stalinism and After*, George Allen and Unwin, London.
——, 1977: *The Soviet Economic System*, George Allen and Unwin, London.
OECD, 1992: *Purchasing Power Parities and Real Expenditures*, 1990 EKS Results, vol. 1, Paris.
Orlov, Alexander, 1953: *The Secret History of Stalin's Crimes*, Random House, New York.
Pareto, Vilfredo, 1896–7: *Cours d'economie politique professe a l'Universite de Lausanne*, 3 vols.
——, 1906: *Manuel of Political Economy*.
Perevalov, Y., I. Gimadi, and V. Dobradei, 1999: "Vliiaet li privatizatsiia na deiatel'nost'pred-priitatii," ("Has Privatization Influenced Enterprise Performance?") *Voprosy ekonomiki*, pp. 76–89.
Pipes, Richard, 1996: *A Concise History of the Russian Revolution*, Vintage Books, New York.
Poe, Marshall, 2003: *The Russian Moment in World History*, Princeton University Press, Princeton, NJ.
Popov, G., 1963: *Elektronnye mashiny i upravlenie ekonomikoi*, Moscow.
Popov, Vladimir and Nikolai Shmelev, 1989: *The Turning Point: Revitalizing the Soviet Economy*, Doubleday, New York.
Powell, Raymond, 1963: "Industrial Production," in Abram Bergson and Simon Kuznets (eds.), *Economic Trends in the Soviet Union*, Harvard University Press, Cambridge, MA.
Preobarzhensky, Evgeny, 1926: *Novaya ekonomika* (*New Economy*), Moscow; available in English, Oxford University Press, London, 1965.
Pugachev, V. F., 1964: "Voprosy optimal'novo planerovaniia narodnovo khoziaistvo s pomoshch' iu edinoi gosudarstvennoi seti vychislitelnykh isentrov," *Voprosy ekonomiki*, no. 7.

Radygin, A., 1999: "Pereraspredelennie prav sobstvennosti v postprivatizasionnoi Rossii" ("The Redistribution of Property Rights in Post-privatized Russia"), *Voprosy ekonomiki*, June, pp. 54–75.

Rayfield, Donald, 2004: *Stalin and his Hangmen: An Authoritative Portrait of a Tyrant and Those Who Served Him*, Viking, New York.

Reddaway, Peter and Dmitri Glinski, 2001: *The Tragedy of Russia's Reforms: Market Bolshevism Against Democracy*, US Institute of Peace Press, Washington, DC.

Rees, E. A., 2003: *The Nature of Stalin's Dictatorship*, Palgrave, New York.

Reformirovanie i razvitie oboronno-promyshlennovo kompleksa 2002–2006 gody, 2001: (*The Reform and Development of the Defense Industrial Complex 2002–2006*) Moscow.

Remnick, David, 1997: "Can Russia Change?" *Foreign Affairs*, 76, 1, pp. 35–49.

Robbins, Lionel, 1935: *Nature and Significance of Economic Science*, London.

Rosefielde, Steven, 1973: *Soviet International Trade in Heckscher–Ohlin Perspective*, Heath Lexington, Lexington, MA.

——, 1974: *The Complete Soviet Producers' Price Soviet Input–Output Table for 1966*, 1974: Duke–UNC Occasional Papers on Soviet Input-Output Analysis, Durham, Chapel Hill, June.

——, 1975: *The Transformation of the 1966 Soviet Input-Output Table from Producers to Adjusted Factor Cost Values*, G. E. Tempo, Washington, DC.

——, 1980: "The First 'Great Leap Forward' Reconsidered: Lessons of Solzhenitsyn's Gulag Archipelago," *Slavic Review*, 39, 4, pp. 559–87.

——, 1981: "An Assessment of the Sources and Uses of Gulag Forced Labour 1929–56," *Soviet Studies*, 32, 1, p. 65.

——, 1981: *Economic Welfare and the Economics of Soviet Socialism*, Cambridge University Press, Cambridge.

——, 1983: "Excess Mortality in the Soviet Union: A Reconsideration of the Demographic Consequences of Forced Industrialisation, 1929–1949," *Soviet Studies*, 35, 3.

——, 1986: "Competitive Market Socialism Revisited: Impediments to Efficient Price-Fixing," *Comparative Economic Studies*, 27, 3, pp. 17–23.

——, 1987: *False Science: Underestimating the Soviet Arms Buildup*, Transaction Press, Rutger NJ.

——, 1990: "Soviet Defense Spending: The Contribution of the New Accountancy," *Soviet Studies*, 42, 1, pp. 59–80.

——, 1995: "Neoclassical Norms and the Valuation of National Product in the Soviet Union and Its Postcommunist Successor States," *Journal of Comparative Economics*, December, pp. 375–89.

——, 1996: "Stalinism in Post-Communist Perspective: New Evidence on Killings, Forced Labour and Economic Growth in the 1930s," *Europe–Asia Studies*, 48, 8, pp. 959–87.

——, 1996b: "Systemzerruttung und Stalinismus: Die okonomischen Grundlagen und Funktionen von Terror, Gulag, Zwangsarbeit, Massenvernichtung und Militarismus in postkommunistischer Perspektive" ("Systemic Disorder and Stalinism: The Economic Foundations and Functions of Terror, Gulag, Forced Labor, Mass Homicide and Militarism in Postcommunist Perspective," in Dittmar Dahlmann and Gerhard Hirschfeld (eds.), *Lager, Zwangsarbeit, Vertreibung und Deportation: Dimensionen der Massenvernichtung in der Sowjetunion und Deutschland 1933 bis 1945*, Klartext Verlag, Essen, pp. 223–4.

——, 1997: "Documented Homicides and Excess Deaths: New Insights into the Scale of Killing in the USSR During the 1930s," *Communist and Post-Communist Studies*, 30, 3, pp. 321–31.

——, 1998: "Comparative Production Potential in the USSR and the West: Pre-transition Assessments," in Rosefielde (ed.), *Efficiency and Russia's Economic Recovery Potential to the Year 2000 and Beyond*, Ashgate, Aldershot, pp. 101–35.

——, 1998: "The Misspecification of Soviet Production Potential: Adjusted Factor Costing and Bergson's Efficiency Standard, in Rosefielde (ed.), *Efficiency and Russia's Economic Recovery Potential to the Year 2000 and Beyond*, Ashgate, Aldershot, London, pp. 11–31.

——, 2000: "The Civilian Labour Force and Unemployment in the Russian Federation," *Europe Asia Studies*, 52, 8, pp. 1433–47
——, 2000: *Efficiency and Russia's Economic Recovery Potential to the Year 2000 and Beyond*, Ashgate, Aldershot.
——, 2000: "Russia's Physical and Social Infrastructure: Implications for Future Development," National Intelligence Council, CR 2000-06, December.
——, 2000: "Russia's Productive Capital Stock: Trends and Prospects," paper prepared for the National Intelligence Council, Workshop on Russia's Capital Structure, Rosslyn, VA, February 1.
——, 2001: "Premature Deaths: Russia's Radical Economic Transition in Soviet Perspective," *Europe–Asia Studies*, 53, 8, pp. 1159–76.
——, 2002: *Comparative Economic Systems: Culture, Wealth and Power in the 21st Century*, Blackwell, Oxford.
——, 2002: "Klepto-Banking: Systemic Sources of Russia's Failed Industrial Recovery," in Howard Stein, Olu Ajakaiye, and Peter Lewis (eds.), *Deregulation and the Banking Crisis in Nigeria: A Comparative Study*, Palgrave, Houndmill, Basingstoke, pp. 193–210;
——, 2002: "Russian Competitiveness," *Russian Economic Trends*, 1, 4.
——, 2003: "The Riddle of Postwar Russian Economic Growth: Statistics Lied and Were Misconstrued," *Europe–Asia Studies*, 55, 3, pp. 469–81.
——, 2004: "Russia 2084: The Treadmill of Muscovite Radical Reform," paper presented at the conference "Whither Russia?" May 6–7, FOI, Stockholm.
——, 2005: "Illusion of Transition: Russia's Muscovite Future," *Eastern Economic Journal*, 31, 2, pp. 283–96.
——, 2005: "Russia: An Abnormal Country," *European Journal of Comparative Economics*, 2, 1, pp. 3–16.
——, 2005: *Russia in the 21st Century: The Prodigal Superpower*, Cambridge University Press, London.
——, 2005: "Tea Leaves and Productivity," *Comparative Economic Studies*, 47, 2, pp. 259–73.
Rosefielde, Steven, and Stefan Hedlund, 2007: *Russia After 1984: Wrestling with Westernization*, Cambridge University Press, London.
Rosefielde, Steven and Masaaki Kuboniwa, 2003: "Russian Growth Retardation Then and Now," *Eurasian Geography and Economics*, 44, 2, pp. 87–101.
Rosefielde, Steven and Quinn Mills, 2006: *Masters of Illusion: American Leadership in the Media Age*, Cambridge University Press, London.
Rosefielde, Steven and R. W. Pfouts, 1998: "The Mis-specification of Soviet Production Potential: Adjusted Factor Costing and Bergson's Efficiency Standard," in Rosefielde (ed.), *Efficiency and Russia's Economic Recovery Potential to the Year 2000 and Beyond*, Ashgate, Aldershot, pp. 11–31.
Rosefielde, Steven and Natalia Vennikova, 2004: "Fiscal Federalism in Russia: A Critique of the OECD Proposals," *Cambridge Journal of Economics*, 28, 2.
Rossiskii statisticheskii ezhegodnik, statisticheskii sbornik, 1997: Moscow.
Samuelson, Paul, 1951: "Abstract of a Theorem Concerning Substitutability in Open Leontief Models," in T. C. Koopmans (ed.), *Activity Analysis of Production and Allocation*, Wiley, New York.
——, 1977: "Reaffirming the Existence of a 'Reasonable' Bergson Samuelson Social Welfare Function," *Economica*, 44, pp. 81–8.
——, 1981: "Bergsonian Welfare Economics," in Steven Rosefielde (ed.), *Economic Welfare and the Economics of Soviet Socialism*, Cambridge University Press, Cambridge, pp. 223–66.
Schapiro, Leonard, 1956: "The Great Purge," in B. H. Liddell Hart (ed.), *The Soviet Army*, Weidenfeld and Nicolson, London, pp. 65–72.
——, 1959: *The Communist Party of the Soviet Union*, New York, Random House.

Schroeder, Gertrude, 1979: "The Soviet Economy on a Treadmill of Reforms," in *Soviet Economy in a Time of Change*, Joint Economic Committee of Congress, Washington, D.C., October 10, pp. 312–66.

——, 1982: "Soviet Economic 'Reform' Decrees: More Steps on the Treadmill," *Soviet Economy in the 1980s: Problems and Prospects*, vol. 1, Joint Economic Committee of Congress, Washington, DC, pp. 79–84.

——, 1987: "Organizations and Hierarchies: The Perennial Search for Solution," *Comparative Economic Studies*, winter, pp. 7–28.

——, 1993: "Post-Soviet Economic Reforms in Perspective," in *The Former Soviet Union in Transition*, vol. 1, Joint Economic Committee of the United States, February, pp. 57–80.

Schroeder, Gertrude and Elizabeth Denton, 1982: *"An Index of Consumption in the USSR," in USSR: Measures of Economic Growth and Development*, Joint Economic Committee of Congress, Washington, DC, December 8, pp. 317–401.

Segbers, Klaus (ed.), 2001: *Explaining Post-Soviet Patchworks: Pathways from the Past to the Global*, vol. 2, Ashgate, Aldershot.

Sen, Amartya, 1971: *Collective Choice and Social Welfare*, Holden-Day, San Francisco.

Sergei, Roy, 2004: "Brezhnev Era Economy," in *Moscow News*, February 11–17.

Shabanova, M. A., 2001: "Institutsional'nye izmereniia i nepravovye praktiki," Moskovskaia vyshiia shkola sotsial'nykh i ekonomicheskikh Intertsentr, pp. 319–27.

Shanin, Lev M., 1925: "Ekonomicheskaya priroda nashevo beztovariya," ("The Economic Essence of Our Commodity Shortage"), *Ekonomicheskoe obozrenie*, November.

Shatalin, Stanislav, et al., 1991: *Transition to the Market: 500 Days*, part I (English edition), St. Martin's Press, New York.

Sheviakov, A. Iu. and A. Ia. Kiruta, 1986: *Modelirovanie Sbalansirovannosti i Soglasovaniia Planovykh Reshenii v Sfere Narodnovo Blagosostoianiia*, Nauka.

Shifman, Avraam, 1973: *Chetvertoe izmerenie*, Posev, Frankfurt/Main, Germany.

Shleifer, Andrei, 2005: *A Normal Country: Russia After Communism*, Harvard University Press, Cambridge, MA.

Shleifer, Andrei, and Daniel Treisman, 2004: "A Normal Country:" *Foreign Affairs*, 84, 2, pp. 20–38.

Shlykov, Vitaly, 2001: *Chto Pogubilo Sovetskii Soiuz? Amerikanskaia Razvedka o Sovetskikh Voennykh Raskodakh* (*Who Destroyed the Soviet Union? American Intelligence Estimates of Soviet Military Expenditures*), Voennyi Vestnik, no. 8, Moscow, April.

——, 2002: *Chto Pogubilo Sovetskii Soiuz? Genshtab i Ekonomika*, Voennyi Vestnik, no. 9, Moscow, September.

——, 2002: "Russia's Defense Industrial Complex after 9–11," paper presented at the conference on Russian Security Policy and the War on Terrorism, US Naval Postgraduate School, Monterey, California, June 4–5.

Solow, Robert, 1956: "A Contribution to the Theory of Economic Growth," *Quarterly Journal of Economics*, 70, February, pp. 65–94.

Solzhenitsyn, Alexander, 1973–5: *Arkhipelag Gulag 1918–1956*: Opyt khudozhestvennogo issledovaniia, I–VII, 3 vols., YMCA, Paris.

——, 1974: *Gulag Archipelago 1918–56*, vol. 2, Harper and Row, New York, pp. 591–3.

Spulber, Nicolas, 2003: *Russia's Economic Transitions: From Late Tsarism to the New Millennium*, Cambridge University Press, Cambridge.

Stalin, Joseph, 1930: "Dizzy With Success: Concerning Questions of the Collective Farm Movement," *Pravda*, no. 60, March 2.

Steinberg, Dmitri, 1986: *Reconstructing the Soviet National Economic Balance, 1965–1984: An Alternative Approach to Estimating Soviet Military Expenditures, Vol. 1: Technical Discussion*, Decision-Sciences Applications, DSA Report no. 692, March 11; *Vol. 2: Compilation of Working Tables*, March 21.

——, 1987: "Estimating Total Soviet Military Expenditures: An Alternative Approach Based on Reconstructed Soviet National Accounts," in Carl Jacobsen, ed., *The Soviet Defense Enigma*, SIPRI, New York, pp. 27–58.

——, 1990: "Trends in Soviet Military Expenditures, *Soviet Studies*, 42, 4.

Stiglitz, Joseph, 2000: "Whither Reform? Ten Years of Transition," Annual Bank Conference on Development Economics, ed. Boris Pleskovic and Joseph Stiglitz, World Bank, Washington, DC, pp. 27–56.

Sutela, Pekka, 2004: *The Russian Market Economy*, Kikomora, Helsinki.

The Case of the Trotskyite–Zinovievite Terrorist Centre, 1936: Report of Court Proceedings Heard before the Military Collegium of the Supreme Court of the USSR, August 1924, People's Commissariat of Justice of the USSR, Moscow.

The Case of the Anti-Soviet Trotskyite Centre, 1937: Report of Court Proceedings Heard before the Military Collegium of the Supreme Court of the USSR, Moscow January 23–30, People's Commissariat of Justice of the USSR, Moscow.

Tikhomirov, Vladimir, 2001: "Capital Flight: Causes, Consequences and Counter-measures," in Klaus Segbers (ed.), *Explaining Post-Soviet Patchworks, Pathways from the Past to the Global*, vol. 2, Ashgate, Aldershot, pp. 251–80.

Tolts, Mark, 1995: "The Soviet Census of 1937 and 1939: Some Problems with Data Evaluation," paper presented at the Conference on Soviet Population in the 1920s and 1930s, Toronto, January 27–9.

Treml, Vladimir (ed.), 1977: *Studies in Soviet Input-Output Economics*, Praeger, New York.

Treml, Vladimir, Dimitri Gallik, Barry Kostinsky, and Kurt Kruger, 1972: *The Structure of the Soviet Economy: Analysis and Reconstruction of the 1966 Soviet Input–Output Table*, Praeger, New York.

Tucker, Robert and Stephen Cohen (eds.), 1965: *The Great Purge Trial*, Grosset and Dunlap, New York.

Tugan-Baranovsky, Mikhail, 1970: *The Russian Factory in the 19th Century*, Richard Irwin, Homewood, IL, p. 270.

United Nations, 1990: *International Comparison of Gross Domestic Product in Europe*.

——, 1999: *Economic Survey of Europe*, United Nations, no. 2.

——, 2000: *Economic Survey of Europe*, United Nations, nos. 2–3.

United Nations, 2003: *Economic Survey of Europe*, United Nations, no. 1.

Uralov, Alexander (Abdurakhman Avtorkhanov), 1953: *The Reign of Stalin*, Bodley Head, London.

Van de Graaf, Jan, 1957: *Theoretical Welfare Economics*, Cambridge University Press, Cambridge.

Wedel, Janine, 1998: *Collision and Collusion: The Strange Case of Aid to Eastern Europe 1989–1998*, St. Martin's Press, New York.

Weeks, Albert, 2003: *Stalin's Other War: Soviet Grand Strategy 1939–1941*, Rowman and Littlefield, Lanham, MD.

Weitzman, Martin, 1970: "Soviet Postwar Economic Growth and Capital–Labor Substitution," *American Economic Review*, 60, 4, pp. 676–92.

——, 1970: "Iterative Multi-Level Planning with Production Targets," *Econometrica*, pp. 50–65.

——, 1974: "Prices versus Quantities," *Review of Economic Studies*, 41, pp. 477–91.

——, 1976: "The New Soviet Incentive Model," *Bell Journal of Economics*, 7, pp. 251–7.

Wheatcroft, Stephen, 1990: "More Light on the Scale of Repression and Excess Mortality in the Soviet Union in the 1930s," *Soviet Studies*, 42, 2.

——, 1996: "The Scale and Nature of Soviet Repression and Mass Killings, 1930–45," *Europe–Asia Studies*, 48, 8, pp. 1319–54.

——, 1999: "Assessing the Victims of Repression, 1930–1945: Their Condition with Particular Reference to Soviet Victims in the Famine of 1932/33," in Dittmar Dahlmann and Gerhard Hirschfeld (eds.), *Lager, Zwangsarbeit, Vertreibung un Deportation: Dimensionen de*

Massenvernichtung in der Sowjetunion und in Deutschland 1933 bis 1945, Klartext Verlag, Essen.

Williamson, John, 1989: "What Washington Means by Policy Reform," in Williamson, (ed.), *Latin American Adjustment: How Much Has Happened*, Institute for International Economics, Washington, DC, pp. 5–38.

——, 1993: "Democracy and the 'Washington Consensus,'" *World Development*, vol. 21.

——, 2003: "Did the Washington Consensus Fail?" Outline of Remarks at the Center for Strategic and International Studies, 6 November. Available at www.iie.com/publications/papers/williamson1102.htm

Winiecki, Jan, 1988: *The Distorted World of Soviet-Type Economies*, University of Pittsburgh Press, Pittsburgh.

Yakovlev, Alexander, 2002: *A Century of Violence in Soviet Russia*, Yale University Press, New Haven.

Yavlinski, Gregory, 2003: *Periphery Capitalism*, Moscow: Yabloko.

Zaleski, Eugene, 1967: *Planning Reforms in the Soviet Union, 1962–1966*, University of North Carolina Press, Chapel Hill.

——, 1980: *Stalinist Planning for Economic Growth, 1933–1952*, University of North Carolina Press, Chapel Hill.

Index